FIFTY STATES

Every Question Answered

FIFTY STATES
Every Question Answered

Lori Baird • Marcel Brousseau • Amber Rose

THUNDER BAY
P·R·E·S·S

San Diego, California

Thunder Bay Press

An imprint of Printers Row Publishing Group
10350 Barnes Canyon Road, Suite 100, San Diego, CA 92121
www.thunderbaybooks.com

This 2017 edition is published by Thunder Bay Press by arrangement with Moseley Road, Inc.

Printers Row Publishing Group is a division of Readerlink Distribution Services, LLC.
Thunder Bay Press is a registered trademark of Readerlink Distribution Services, LLC.

All notations of errors or omissions should be addressed to Thunder Bay Press, Editorial Department, at the above address. All other correspondence (author inquiries, permissions) concerning the content of this book should be addressed to Moseley Road Inc.,123 Main St., Irvington, NY 10533.

Thunder Bay Press
Publisher: Peter Norton
Associate Publisher: Ana Parker
Publishing Team: April Farr, Kelly Larsen, Kathryn C. Dalby
Editorial Team: JoAnn Padgett, Melinda Allman, Traci Douglas
Production Team: Jonathan Lopes, Rusty von Dyl

Moseley Road Inc. www.moseleyroad.com
Art Director: Brian MacMullen
Senior Editor: Ward Calhoun
Desginers: Eunho Lee, Hwaim Lee
Photo Research: Benjamin DeWalt
Production: Eunho Lee

Photo credit: John Shultz House, page 79, attributed to Ron Shawley via Wikimedia Commons

ISBN: 978-1-68412-026-0

The Library of Congress has cataloged the original Thunder Bay edition as follows:

Baird, Lori.
  Fifty states: every question answered / Lori Baird, Marcel Brousseau, Amber Rose.
    pages cm
  Summary: "50 States, Every Question Answered offers readers an in-depth look at the individual states that together make up this fascinating nation. From the skyscrapers of New York to the mountains of Colorado to the beaches of California, just about every interesting corner of America is explored in this informative guide"-- Provided by publisher.
  Includes bibliographical references and index.
  ISBN 978-1-62686-233-3 (hbk.) -- ISBN 1-62686-233-8 (hbk.)
1. U.S. states--Miscellanea. 2. United States--Miscellanea. I. Brousseau, Marcel. II. Rose, Amber. III. Title.
  E180.B34 2014
  973--dc23
                            2014003721

23 22 21 20 19 4 5 6 7 8

Printed in China.

FIFTY STATES
TABLE OF CONTENTS

John Trumbull's Declaration of Independence (1817) depicts the founding fathers' 1776 presentation of the draft of the Declaration of Independence, which asserted American sovereignty, at Philadelphia's Independence Hall.

The Lincoln Memorial and Washington Monument dominate the National Mall in Washington, D.C. At the east end of the Mall sits the United States Capitol, home to the United States Congress, where senators and representatives from all 50 states convene.

THE PACIFIC STATES 314

Top right: Morning mist cloaks the Chattahoochee River in northern Georgia. Right: The San Diego skyline turns fluorescent as night falls on California's southernmost metropolis. Below: Nature reclaims a dilapidated cabin in the shadow of Colorado's towering Sangre de Cristo Range. Opposite page: The midwestern United States produce nearly half of the world's corn harvest.

Out of Many, One

In the beginning, they came from . . . well, nobody's quite sure about that anymore. For many years, anthropologists believed that the earliest Americans migrated from Asia across the Bering Land Bridge, which linked what is now Alaska and Siberia. Once across, these Paleolithic pioneers, known as the Clovis culture, moved south and east, populating both North and South America. But this history has recently been disputed due to archaeological and genetic discoveries, and now the earliest Americans seem less unified in their ancestry than previously thought. Some say that a seafaring culture may have settled western North America before the Clovis culture pushed south from Alaska. Others speculate that Paleolithic Europeans walked a coast of North Atlantic ice to occupy the northeastern United States. Consensus will take some time to form. The Clovis culture may have populated the entirety of the Americas, after all. But perhaps, as the last ice age receded, America was a prehistoric melting pot.

Multicultural origins would be appropriate for the entity now called the United States of America. Millennia after those Paleolithic migrations, myriad Indian nations populated the entirety of this land, speaking varied languages, worshipping a range of deities, and following numerous paths of cultural expression. They farmed and hunted the flora and fauna of multiple ecosystems, from the wooded river valleys of the Northeast, to the sticky swamplands of the South, to the harsh desert country of the Southwest. Today, America's indigenous people are collectively called American Indians, but it was not long ago that they existed apart—united through trade and mutual interest, and divided in battle for land and resources. It was cultural calamity that drove America's diverse Indian nations to ally as one unified culture—calamity resulting from droves of European immigration to the Americas, and the devastating disease and warfare that accompanied the settlers. Such gatherings of disparate groups into a unified whole occur time and again in the narrative of the United States.

Left: An 1876 French gift to the United States, the Statue of Liberty has become a symbol of the American ideals of democracy and freedom.
Above: Colonization brought Plains Indians the horse but also brought conflict with American settlers, who had spread over the West by 1900.

Founding a Diverse Republic

The immigrants sailed from Spain first, then England, Holland, and France. They came from Germany, Scotland, and Ireland. They staked separate claims and settled what seemed a virgin land. The Spanish colonized what is now the southern United States, from Florida west to California. The English colonized the Atlantic coast, from Georgia to Maine. The Dutch occupied the Hudson Valley of New York, and the French colonized the Midwest, from the Great Lakes along the Mississippi River all the way south to Louisiana. The Germans pushed inland through Pennsylvania, and the Scots-Irish rooted in Appalachia. African slaves, imported by the millions, were held in bondage across the eastern seaboard, in particularly large numbers on the tobacco plantations of the southern colonies.

After years of colonial warfare, these divided territories overcame the religious and nationalistic strife that rent their European ancestors and unified to revolt against British rule. The British expelled, the colonies became states of a new republic, and from many strands, a new nationality—American—was woven. But the diverse fabric of the United States portended an uneasy unity. On numerous occasions, states have resisted the dominion of the Union, most destructively during the Civil War, from 1861–65, when southern states, asserting their right to own slaves, fought to sever themselves from the United States. The impulse for self-determination is never far from public sentiment—though united, the 50 states are also undeniably divided, by geography and economy, by politics and ancestry. Each state possesses its own history, character, and priorities, which sometimes find friction with those of its neighbors. The achievement of

Crowded Manhattan in 1900. From 1892 to 1954 more than 12 million immigrants were naturalized at New York City's Ellis Island.

the American experiment is that numerous unique principalities have, with occasional exceptions, been able to stay peacefully conjoined through the system of liberal democracy for more than two centuries.

Boundaries Braved and Made

Flying high above America, one cannot see the borders that define each state. One cannot trace the obtuse angle of Nevada, or distinguish the panhandle of Oklahoma. America is, it seems, undivided country. Yet, for much of American history, it was the landscape that determined the borders of colonial settlement and westward expansion. Settling the land meant braving the hazards of the country—fording and following rivers, crossing mountains and deserts. In this context, many borders were formed by prominent landforms. The Mississippi River, bisecting the nation, was once the dividing line between British territory in the east and Spanish territory in the west. Similarly, the Louisiana Purchase of 1803 gave the United States hundreds of thousands of square miles of new land and extended the nation's western boundary to the Rocky Mountains. Today, though many state borders are drawn along lines of longitude and latitude, many are also formed by natural features—the Bitterroot Mountains separate Idaho and Montana, the Mississippi, Ohio, and Wabash rivers flank Illinois, and the meandering Rio Grande forms the southern border of Texas.

Before European migrants transformed the land into separate colonies, it was natural boundaries that determined the territories of the American Indian nations. Indian customs of land ownership contrasted sharply with

The Old Plantation (c. 1790, artist unknown) depicts southern slaves performing a dance. One musician plays an early type of banjo.

European modes. Territory was contested, but land was not bought and sold and demarcated according to private boundaries. Rather, land that was being farmed belonged to the farmer, and land that was uncultivated belonged to the entire village. More profoundly, the cultivators were merely trustees of their children—the land truly belonged to the future generations. This ethic of communal land, tended with an eye toward the future, has found an analogue in the National Park Service, active in nearly every state in the Union, which preserves the great wilderness zones of the United States so that future generations may experience the majesty of the American land.

The American Collage

It is not certain who the first Americans were, or when they came, but today Americans hail from all over the globe. The founding waves of European migrants were followed, over centuries, by numerous nationalities. In the second half of the 19th century, hundreds of thousands of Chinese escaped economic crises and warfare by migrating to the United States. Starting in the mid-1800s scores of Irish immigrated to America, as did millions of Germans, Swedes, Norwegians, and Eastern Europeans, particularly Polish, well into the 20th century. The early 1900s saw millions of Italian immigrants, as well as waves of Syrians and Lebanese. In recent years immigration from Latin America has increased, and Asians, particularly Indians, Koreans, and Vietnamese, have also migrated in droves.

As a nation of diverse states coexisting by participating in a vigorous and sometimes acrimonious political discussion, America has become a place where numerous cultural influences gather under one national tradition. Foods, music, accents, dialects, religions, and landforms all vary as one travels the nation. For a Vermonter, the stark Utah desert may seem another nation; for a Floridian, the mossy rain forests of Washington are decidedly foreign. Likewise, the ubiquitous tacos of Los Angeles are curious to a hot dog–prone New Yorker, as is the rich harvest of New England seafood to a corn-fed midwesterner.

This book offers a voyage across America's diverse regions and through this nation's varied history, by focusing on the pieces that form the American puzzle—the 50 states. From the wooded, rocky shores of Maine to the distant green isolation of Hawaii, from paleo-Indians to gold prospectors, trace the separate histories and experience the unique ecology of each state. Learn the issues that face the states today, and by extension, gauge the progress of the entire nation. Each state, and every region, is the product of a unique narrative—of the indigenous peoples that occupied them and still do, of the European, African, and Asian migrants that adopted them, and of the continual immigrations and emigrations that are changing the face of the United States in our time. Each state tells its own tale of settlement and strife, of culture and invention, of water, earth, and sky; this book unites them in a collage of landscape and lore.

Gentle green hills in the East, collossal, cragged peaks in the West: The lushly forested Appalachian Mountains, which extend from Canada to Alabama, can rise to more than 6,000 feet, while the Rocky Mountains, ranging from Canada to New Mexico, soar to more than double that height.

PACIFIC

OCEAN

WASHINGTON

Seattle

Olympia

Salem

OREGON

MONTANA

Helena

NORTH
DAKOT

Bisma

Boise

IDAHO

WYOMING

SOUTH DA

Pier

NEVADA

Sacramento

Carson City

Salt Lake City

Cheyenne

NEBRAS

San Francisco

UTAH

Denver

COLORADO

KA

CALIFORNIA

Las Vegas

Los Angeles

San Diego

ARIZONA

Phoenix

Santa Fe

NEW
MEXICO

Okla

El Paso

TEX

Gulf of California

MEXICO

KAUAI

Lihue

OAHU

Wahiawa

Honolulu

MAUI

PACIFIC

OCEAN

Kailua

Hilo

HAWAII

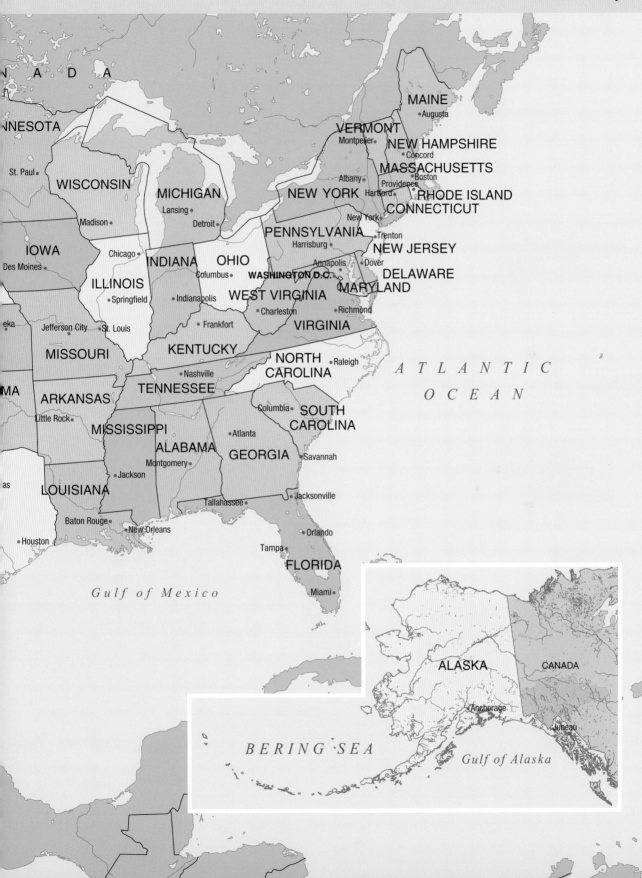

CANADA

MINNESOTA

St. Paul •

WISCONSIN

Madison •

IOWA

Des Moines •

eka •

MISSOURI

Jefferson City •   • St. Louis

MA

ARKANSAS

Little Rock •

MISSISSIPPI

LOUISIANA

Baton Rouge •   • New Orleans

• Houston

as

MICHIGAN

Lansing •

• Detroit

Chicago •

INDIANA

ILLINOIS

• Springfield

• Indianapolis

OHIO

Columbus •

WASHINGTON D.C.

WEST VIRGINIA

• Charleston

• Frankfort

KENTUCKY

• Nashville

TENNESSEE

ALABAMA

Montgomery •

• Jackson

• Atlanta

GEORGIA

Tallahassee •

FLORIDA

Miami •

• Orlando

Tampa •

Gulf of Mexico

MAINE

• Augusta

VERMONT

Montpelier •

NEW HAMPSHIRE

• Concord

MASSACHUSETTS

Albany •   • Boston

NEW YORK

Providence •

Hartford •

RHODE ISLAND

CONNECTICUT

New York •

PENNSYLVANIA

Harrisburg •

• Trenton

NEW JERSEY

Annapolis •   • Dover

DELAWARE

MARYLAND

• Richmond

VIRGINIA

NORTH
CAROLINA

• Raleigh

Columbia •

SOUTH
CAROLINA

• Savannah

• Jacksonville

A T L A N T I C

O C E A N

ALASKA

CANADA

• Anchorage

• Juneau

B E R I N G   S E A

Gulf of Alaska

WASHINGTON

Cascade Range

Bitterroot Range

OREGON

Goose Lake

IDAHO

Coast Range

Sierra Nevada

Lake Tahoe

NEVADA

Wasatch Range

Great Salt Lake

UTAH

Lake Mead

CALIFORNIA

Salton Sea

ARIZONA

Gila

Colorado

PACIFIC OCEAN

Gulf of California

Rocky Mountains

MONTANA

Missouri

C A

Great Plains

NORTH DAKOTA

SOUTH DA

WYOMING

NEBRAS

Platte

COLORADO

Arkansas

NEW MEXICO

Canadian

MEXICO

Rio Gran

Kauai

Honolulu

Maui

PACIFIC OCEAN

Hawaii

D A

Lake of the Woods

Red Lakes

Lake Superior

MINNESOTA

MAINE

Gulf of Maine

VERMONT

NEW HAMPSHIRE

WISCONSIN

Lake Huron

Lake Ontario

NEW YORK

MASSACHUSETTS

RHODE ISLAND

CONNECTICUT

Lake Erie

Lake Michigan

MICHIGAN

Mississippi

IOWA

PENNSYLVANIA

NEW JERSEY

OHIO

DELAWARE

INDIANA

WASHINGTON D.C.

WEST VIRGINIA

MARYLAND

ILLINOIS

Appalachian Mountains

VIRGINIA

MISSOURI

KENTUCKY

Roanoke

ATLANTIC OCEAN

TENNESSEE

Mississippi

NORTH CAROLINA

Coastal Plains

MA

ARKANSAS

SOUTH CAROLINA

Lake Marion

Red

Alabama

GEORGIA

MISSISSIPPI

ALABAMA

LOUISIANA

FLORIDA

Mississippi Delta

Lake Okeechobee

Gulf of Mexico

Brooks Range

ALASKA

Yukon

Alaska Range

CANADA

BERING SEA

Gulf of Alaska

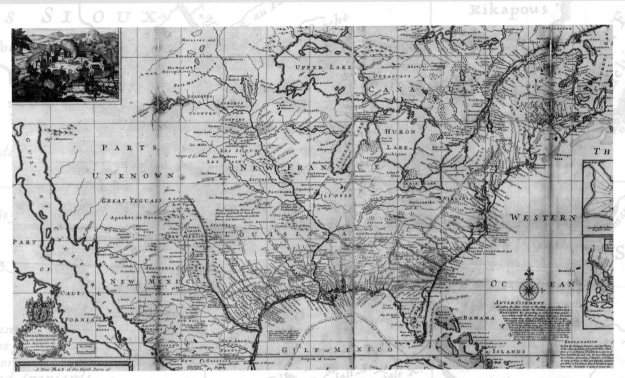

A 1720 map of the future United States of America, claimed by Britain, France, and Spain and occupied by myriad Indian nations. Europeans had sailed to the Pacific coast, but most western lands from the ocean to the Great Plains were unexplored and thus labeled "Parts Unknown."

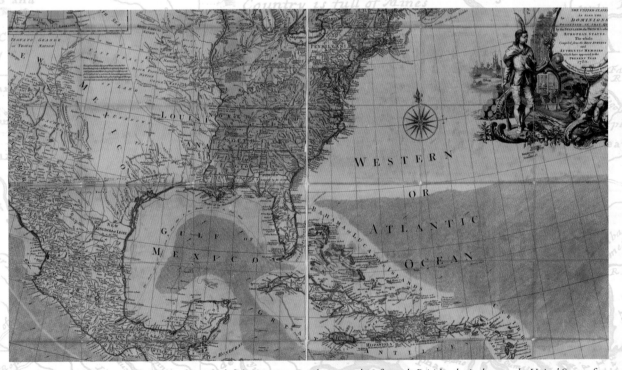

In 1783, the year of this map, the Treaty of Paris ended the American Revolution, and 13 formerly British colonies became the United States of America. The borders of southern states extended west to the Mississippi River. Spain controlled Florida and the land beyond the Mississippi River.

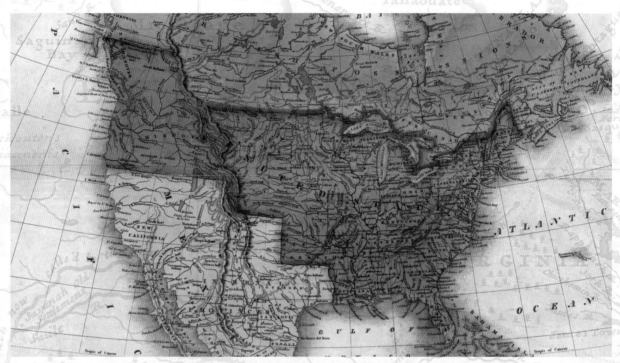

By 1826 the Louisiana Purchase had given the United States a huge swath of territory extending west to the Rocky Mountains. Also, the Anglo-American Convention of 1818 had declared joint British and American control of the Oregon Country, northwest of newly independent Mexico.

By 1890 the contiguous United States was essentially in shape. The Mexican-American War gained the nation land from Texas to California. This population map shows that the East remained densely populated, while the West was sparsely settled but for coastal areas and boomtowns.

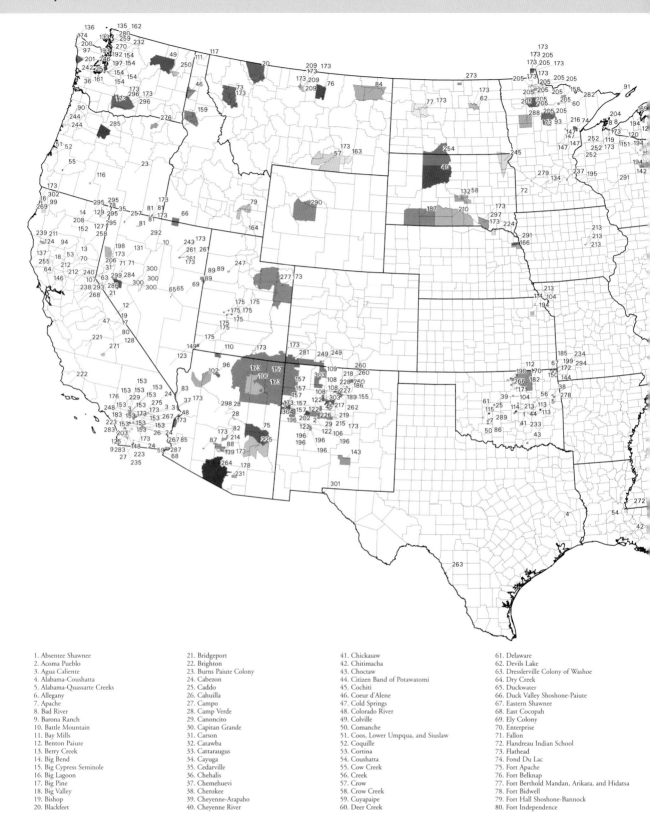

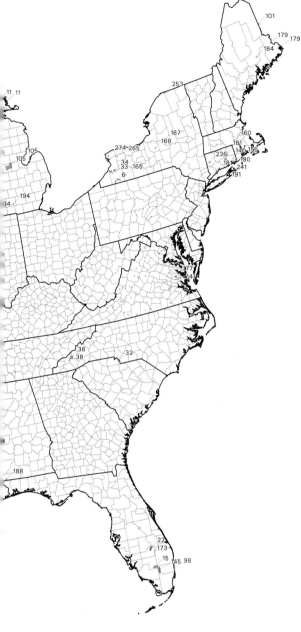

119. Lac Courte Oreilles
120. Lac Du Flambeau
121. Lac Vieux Desert
122. Laguna
123. Las Vegas
124. Laytonville
125. La Jolla
126. La Posta
127. Likely
128. Lone Pine
129. Lookout
130. Los Coyotes
131. Lovelock Colony
132. Lower Brule
133. Lower Elwah
134. Lower Sioux
135. Lummi
136. Makah
137. Manchester
138. Manzanita
139. Maricopa
140. Mashantucket Pequot
141. Mattaponi
142. Menominee
143. Mescalero
144. Miami
145. Miccosukee
146. Middletown
147. Mille Lacs
148. Mission
149. Moapa
150. Modoc
151. Mole Lake
152. Montgomery Creek
153. Morongo
154. Muckleshoot
155. Nambe
156. Narragansett
157. Navajo
158. Nett Lake
159. Nez Perce
160. Nipmuc-Hassanamisco
161. Nisqually
162. Nooksack
163. Northern Cheyenne
164. Northwestern Shoshone
165. Oil Springs
166. Omaha
167. Oneida
168. Onondaga
169. Ontonagon
170. Osage
171. Otoe-Missouri
172. Ottawa
173. Out
174. Ozette
175. Paiute
176. Pala
177. Pamunkey
178. Pascua Yaqui
179. Passamaquoddy
180. Pawcatuck Pequot
181. Paugusett
182. Pawnee
183. Pechanga
184. Penobscot
185. Peoria
186. Picuris
187. Pine Ridge Sioux
188. Poarch Creek
189. Pojoaque
190. Ponca
191. Poosepatuck
192. Port Gamble
193. Port Madison
194. Potawatomi
195. Prairie Isle
196. Puertocito
197. Puyallup
198. Pyramid Lake Paiute
199. Quapaw
200. Quileute
201. Quinault
202. Ramah
203. Ramona
204. Red Cliff
205. Red Lake
206. Reno-Sparks
207. Rincon
208. Roaring Creek
209. Rocky Boys
210. Rosebud
211. Round Valley
212. Rumsey
213. Sac and Fox
214. Salt River
215. Sandia
216. Sandy Lake

217. Santa Ana
218. Santa Clara
219. Santa Domingo
220. Santa Rosa
221. Santa Rosa (North)
222. Santa Ynez
223. Santa Ysabel
224. Santee
225. San Carlos
226. San Felipe
227. San Ildefonso
228. San Juan
229. San Manual
230. San Pasqual
231. San Xavier
232. Sauk Suiattle
233. Seminole
234. Seneca-Cayuga
235. Sequan
236. Shagticoke
237. Shakopee
238. Sheep Ranch
239. Sherwood Valley
240. Shingle Spring
241. Shinnecock
242. Shoalwater
243. Shoshone
244. Siletz
245. Sisseton
246. Skokomish
247. Skull Valley
248. Soboba
249. Southern Ute
250. Spokane
251. Squaxon Island
252. St. Croix
253. St. Regis
254. Standing Rock Sioux
255. Stewarts Point
256. Stockbridge Munsee
257. Summit Lake
258. Susanville
259. Swinomish
260. Taos Pueblo
261. Te-Moak
262. Tesuque
263. Texas Kickapoo
264. Tohono O'odham
265. Tonawanda
266. Tonikawa
267. Torres Martinez
268. Toulumne
269. Trindad
270. Tulalip
271. Tule River
272. Tunica-Biloxi
273. Turtle Mountains
274. Tuscarora
275. Twentynine Palms
276. Umatilla
277. Uintah and Ouray
278. United Keetoowah Band of Cherokee
279. Upper Sioux
280. Upper Skagit
281. Ute Mountain
282. Vermilion Lake
283. Viejas
284. Walker River
285. Warm Springs
286. Washoe
287. West Cocopah
288. White Earth
289. Wichita
290. Wind River
291. Winnebago
292. Winnemucca
293. Woodford Indian Community
294. Wyandotte
295. Xl Ranch
296. Yakama
297. Yankton
298. Yavapai
299. Yerington
300. Yomba
301. Ysleta del Sur Pueblo
302. Yurok
303. Zia
304. Zuni

81. Fort McDermitt Paiute and Shoshone
82. Fort McDowell Yavapai
83. Fort Mohave
84. Fort Peck Assiniboine and Sioux
85. Fort Yuma
86. Fort Sill Apache
87. Gila Bend
88. Gila River Pima and Maricopa
89. Goshute
90. Grande Ronde
91. Grand Portage
92. Grand Traverse
93. Greater Leech Lake
94. Grindstone
95. Hannahville
96. Havasupai
97. Hoh
98. Hollywood
99. Hoopa Valley

100. Hopi
101. Houlton Maliseets
102. Hualapai
103. Inaja
104. Iowa
105. Isabella
106. Isleta
107. Jackson
108. Jemez
109. Jicarilla
110. Kaibab
111. Kalispel
112. Kaw
113. Kialegee Creek
114. Kickapoo
115. Kiowa
116. Klamath
117. Kootenai
118. L'Anse Ojibwa

Olympic
North Cascades
WASHINGTON
Glacier
Mount Rainier
MONTANA
NORTH DAKOTA
Theodore Roose
OREGON
Crater Lake
IDAHO
Yellowstone
Grand Teton
SOUTH DAKO
Redwood
Wind Cave
Badlands
Lassen Volcanic
WYOMING
NEVADA
NEBRASK
Rocky Mountain
CALIFORNIA
UTAH
Yosemite
Capitol Reef
Arches
COLORADO
Kings Canyon
Bryce Canyon
Black Canyon Of The Gunnison
Death Valley Zion
Canyonlands
KAN
Sequoia
Mesa Verde
Great Sand Dunes
Channel Islands
Grand Canyon
PACIFIC OCEAN
ARIZONA
NEW MEXICO
Joshua Tree
Petrified Forest
Saguaro
Carlsbad Caverns
Guadalupe Mountains
TE
Big Bend
MEXICO

C A N

Kauai
Honolulu
Maui
Haleakala
PACIFIC OCEAN
Hawaii
Hawaii Volcanoes

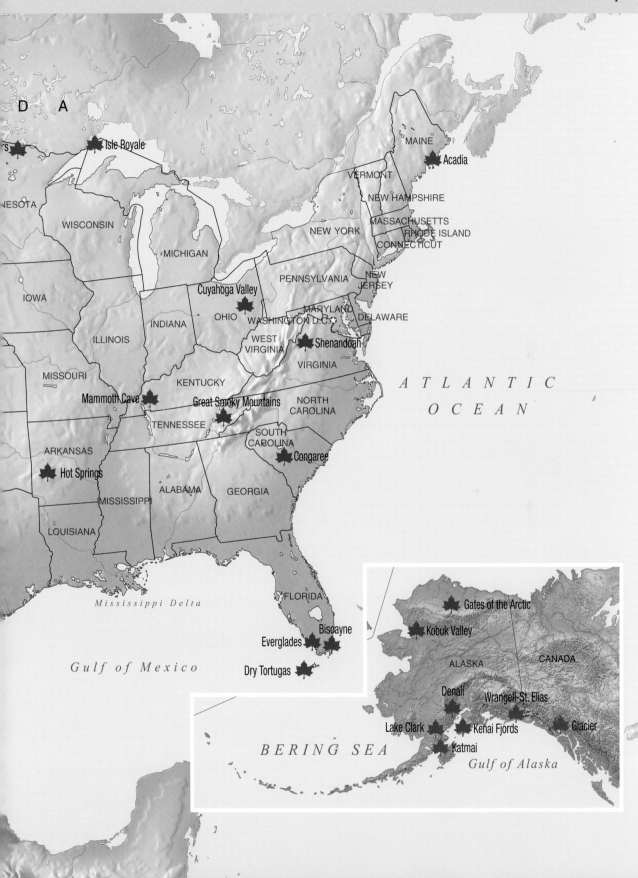

D A

Isle Royale

NESOTA

WISCONSIN

MICHIGAN

IOWA

INDIANA

ILLINOIS

OHIO

Cuyahoga Valley

PENNSYLVANIA

MARYLAND

WASHINGTON D.C.

DELAWARE

NEW JERSEY

NEW YORK

MASSACHUSETTS

RHODE ISLAND

CONNECTICUT

VERMONT

NEW HAMPSHIRE

MAINE

Acadia

MISSOURI

KENTUCKY

WEST VIRGINIA

Shenandoah

VIRGINIA

Mammoth Cave

Great Smoky Mountains

NORTH CAROLINA

TENNESSEE

ARKANSAS

SOUTH CAROLINA

Congaree

Hot Springs

ALABAMA

GEORGIA

MISSISSIPPI

LOUISIANA

Mississippi Delta

FLORIDA

Biscayne

Everglades

Dry Tortugas

Gulf of Mexico

A T L A N T I C

O C E A N

Gates of the Arctic

Kobuk Valley

ALASKA

CANADA

Denali

Wrangell-St. Elias

Glacier

Lake Clark

Kenai Fjords

Katmai

B E R I N G   S E A

Gulf of Alaska

Washington, D.C.

The District

Justitia Omnibus (Justice for all)

Called upon to plan a city worthy of the new American republic, French architect Pierre-Charles L'Enfant produced a masterpiece. His scheme was sweeping and majestic, and reflected American ideals, as L'Enfant placed the Capitol Building on Jenkins Hill and intended its Rotunda to be centered precisely on the center of the city. Thus the Capitol—from whence the people reigned—occupied the most visually impressive, and symbolically significant, point in the city.

Washington, the capital of the United States of America, was born. Named for its first president (who himself called it the Federal City out of modesty), Washington emerged slowly over the centuries. Today, it is a truly impressive city, not without its flaws (some of which, such as its hot, stuffy climate, were foreseen in the beginning), but certainly a positive assessment of American ideals. Once derided as a muddy swamp, Washington—coextensive with the District of Columbia—now attracts millions of visitors, eager to attend tours of the White House, view the many monuments, or experience culture, history, and science in the largest museum complex in the world, established by the Smithsonian Institution.

As one might expect in a city designed for and dedicated to the government of the country, most of the city's economy relies on the government in one way or another. This has spurred economic issues, however, since many of these industries cannot be taxed by the city. Congress has ultimate jurisdiction over the city, as well; citizens must be content with less standing in the federal government than their state-dwelling neighbors. Not until 1961 did residents receive the right to vote for the president, and in recent years many have taken to wryly displaying an old battle cry of the Revolutionary War, "No taxation without representation," to protest their lack of representation in Congress. Their sole delegate attends the House of Representatives, but cannot vote.

At one point the Potomac River became so heavily polluted that President Lyndon B. Johnson described it as a "national disgrace." Today, it is clean and vibrant, thanks to the concerted efforts of concerned citizens. In fact, Washington, D.C., despite its overwhelmingly urban character, protects an array of wild areas—yet another tourist attraction in a city famed for its monuments and museums. An architectural ode to the political ideals of America, Washington is fittingly complex and striking, a capstone of the United States of America.

The United States Capitol houses both chambers of the legislative branch. The Statue of Freedom tops the dome at 288 feet.

Washington, D.C. Facts

Full Name: Washington, District of Columbia
Meaning of Name: From George Washington, the first president
Established: July 16, 1790

Flower: American Beauty rose
Tree: Scarlet oak
Bird: Wood thrush

The District

At the end of the Revolutionary War, the new states found themselves struggling over wartime debts. Most southern states had already paid theirs; most northern states had not. Consequently, the North favored allowing the federal government to assume these debts. The South, annoyed by the prospect of increased federal taxes, objected. Resolution came, as it often does, with a compromise: the federal government would take over the debts, but the capital of the new nation would be based in the South.

So, at a dinner hosted by Thomas Jefferson, the two early statesmen Alexander Hamilton and James Madison hammered out the deal, and in 1790 Congress appointed George Washington to choose a location. Hoping to one day build a canal linking the Tidewater to the Ohio River, Washington chose a site at the confluence of the Potomac and Anacostia rivers.

European Design

The great genius behind the city's design came from France, an architect and engineer named Pierre-Charles L'Enfant. Taking his cue from the baroque style of European cities then in vogue, L'Enfant called for grand avenues, open circles at cross-streets, and views orchestrated by running long, straight streets from hills and high points.

L'Enfant's expansive designs were realized slowly. Before President Washington marked out the 100-square-mile capital (carved out of Maryland and Virginia land), only the little town of Georgetown had existed nearby; otherwise, no one had attempted to settle the swampy land once inhabited by the Piscataway Indians. With no established commerce and few inhabitants besides federal government employees, for the first years of its life the capital resembled nothing so much as a muddy ruin.

The United States Capitol as it appeared in 1846. The building has been restored and renovated several times since its construction in 1811.

Congress moved into the Capitol and President John Adams into the White House (then called the President's House) in 1800, but the buildings were unfinished and the National Mall an impassable swamp. Indeed, when the British burned the capital during the War of 1812, it barely affected the city's construction.

Lincoln's Legacy

The capital did not truly begin to emerge until the Civil War, when the population exploded. The District was smaller now, having returned land given to the government by Virginia in 1846, but the war forced new industries to develop almost overnight. In 1864, Abraham Lincoln became the only sitting president to be present during a battle, and later became the first presidential assassination victim, in Ford's Theater on Tenth Street. Almost immediately the city became a staging ground for the nation's troubled race relations. Most impressively of this history, perhaps, Martin Luther King Jr. gave his most famous speech, "I Have a Dream," from the steps of the Lincoln Memorial.

Capital Improvements

Today, although the city struggles with a severe economic gap between its affluent and impoverished citizens, the capital has become what Thomas Jefferson, George Washington, and Pierre-Charles L'Enfant had always intended it to be, a beacon of American republicanism and a true cosmopolitan arena. As a city, Washington, D.C., still has work to do addressing poverty, corruption, and a burdened educational system, but as a symbol, nothing better represents the promise of America than its monuments, museums, and dignified facades.

The celebration of Independence Day is an elaborate affair, with fireworks lighting the city's monuments and buildings.

All United States presidents since John Adams have lived in the White House, one of the world's most recognizable homes.

The Jefferson Memorial commemorates America's third president and the architect of the Declaration of Independence.

Maine

The Pine Tree State

Dirigo (I lead)

The northernmost state in New England and the easternmost state in the United States, Maine is perhaps best known for its natural features and exports: a rugged 3,500-mile coastline dotted by hundreds of islands; fresh-caught local lobster and clams; lumbering moose that wander its wilderness; bountiful blueberry and potato harvests; and the vast Great North Woods.

Historically, Maine has been important as a center of fishing, timber, and shipbuilding. Today, those industries remain important, although to different extents. Commercial fishing has experienced a decline, but Maine continues to be the largest source of lobster in the United States. And although wooden shipbuilding has been replaced by naval shipbuilding and construction, lumber is now the largest industry in the state, nearly 90 percent of which is forested. Paper, pulp, cardboard, and toothpicks are dominant products.

Maine's reputation as a tourist destination began to grow in the late 1800s, and today tourism provides a vital source of revenue in the state. Each summer, millions of visitors flock to the seaside towns on the state's rocky coast, and to its interior, abounding with lakes and mountains. Maine's winters are long and harsh but provide ample opportunities for those who enjoy skiing, snowboarding, ice fishing, and even dogsledding.

While Maine isn't often thought of as a farming state, it leads the world in the production of wild blueberries. Other important agricultural products include potatoes, eggs, and dairy products. It is also the country's second-leading producer of maple syrup.

Most of Maine's population of 1.33 million live in and around the state's largest cities: Portland, Lewiston, and Bangor. Its capitol, Augusta, with fewer than 20,000 residents, might seem almost rural compared with Boston and Hartford. A slightly left-leaning state, Maine has voted Democratic in the past several presidential elections. Perhaps more telling is the fact that Independent voters outnumber both Democrats and Republicans in the state.

Maine enjoys its fair share of firsts: Acadia National Park, located on Mount Desert Island on the state's northern coast, was the first national park established east of the Mississippi. Cadillac Mountain (1,532 ft.), on the eastern side of the island, is the first spot in the U.S. to receive the morning sun (and thus is a favorite spot for watching sunrise). The Revolutionary War's first naval battle was fought off Machias in 1775. And Mainer Margaret Chase Smith (1897–1995) was the first American woman to serve in both houses of Congress.

Portland Head Lighthouse is but one iconic Maine structure.

Maine State Facts

Full Name: State of Maine
Meaning of Name: Probably comes from *mainland*, used by early fishermen to differentiate between mainland and the islands.
Admitted to the Union: March 15, 1820 (23rd state)

Inhabitant: Mainer
Capital City: Augusta
Flower: White pine cone
Tree: White pine
Bird: Chickadee

Geography and Ecology

Maine is generally recognized as having three primary land regions. The White Mountains region of the northwest is part of the Appalachian Mountain system. The state's highest peak and the northern terminus of the Appalachian Trail, Mt. Katahdin (5,267 ft.) is in this region, as are eight other peaks over 4,000 feet. This rugged area, about 50 miles wide and 150 miles long, is heavily forested and includes thousands of streams and lakes, including Moosehead Lake, at 117 square miles, the largest in the state. Within this region lies the 209,501-acre Baxter State Park. This enormous wilderness park attracts visitors year-round for its hunting, fishing, photography, camping, hiking, and backpacking opportunities. Wildlife abounds in the White Mountains region, from moose and black bear to bobcats, fishers, and coyote.

Rolling Plateau

The Eastern New England Upland region is the largest land region in the state. Covering the northern, eastern, and central part of the state, this rolling plateau contains hundreds of lakes and rivers. Farmers in this area grow most of Maine's substantial potato crop.

The Coastline

The Coastal Lowlands region runs along the entire New England coast. In Maine the lowlands, which lie near or at sea level, extend to between 10 and 40 miles inland from the Atlantic Ocean. In the south, sandy beaches are the predominant feature; farther north, the sandy beaches give way to a rocky coast. It's here that tourists flock each summer, for the coastal scenery, idyllic New England villages, and historic and cultural attractions.

LOBSTER

Few other foods are as closely identified with Maine as the lobster. These cold-water-loving crustaceans form the backbone of the state's commercial fishing industry—and provide seafood lovers across the country with their rich meat. More lobsters are caught in Maine than anywhere else in the United States—the 2015 catch exceeded 121 million pounds.

Most lobsters are caught within 12 miles of shore, where boat captains set traps and mark them with colorful buoys. The markings on the buoys are registered trademarks that identify each captain's traps or pots, as they are also known.

Lobster fishing is serious business in Maine, and captains trademark their "colors" to protect their traps.

Maine's coast offers ample opportunity for those in search of wildlife viewing. Dolphins and porpoises, seals, humpback, finback, and minke whales, and birds including the North Atlantic puffin and bald eagle can

At 5,267 feet, Mt. Katahdin is Maine's highest peak, and the northern terminus of the Appalachian Trail. The mountain lies within the borders of Baxter State Park, a 200,000-acre wilderness area. The park is home to 46 peaks, 18 of which exceed 3,000 feet.

be seen from shore or the whale-watching tours that frequent the waters.

Weather and Climate

As would be expected, Maine's weather is generally cooler than more southern states. Summer temperatures range in the 70s; the average July temperature is 67° F. Winter temperatures range in the 20s; the average January temperature is 15° F.

Maine can receive substantial snowfall. Many areas in the north average more than 100 inches each season; nearer the coast, the average is less than 80 inches.

The Pine Tree State

The earliest known inhabitants of what is now Maine were members of a dozen Indian nations, including the Abnakis, the Micmacs, the Passamaquoddies, and the Penobscots.

Following explorations by Leif Eriksson (c. 1000) and Florentine navigator Giovanni da Verrazano (1524), most early colonies failed, owing to the brutal winter conditions and Indian attacks. But by the 1620s a few British settlements had taken root in the south. In 1622 the area was given its modern name by British entrepreneur Sir Ferdinando Gorges.

Tensions between the English and French led Massachusetts to annex Maine in 1652 as a defensive position against potential French and Indian attack. By now, a nascent Maine economy had begun to blossom, with trading posts, sawmills, and local government coming into being. But by the early 18th century, only a few British settlements had survived King Philip's War and the early French wars. Fighting and border disputes continued until 1763, when France surrendered its New World lands to the British.

Statehood

In the lead-up to the Revolution, Maine, at the time still part of Massachusetts, staged its own version of the Boston Tea Party: in 1774 a mob burned a shipment of tea in York. And when war did break out, the province played a major role, but received little support from its faraway capital city. Following the Revolution, some began to bristle at Massachusetts rule; that resentment came to a head during the War of 1812. The British seizure of the coast of Penobscot Bay all but crippled the state's economy. Massachusetts's refusal to take action helped turn popular opinion in favor of independence from the Bay State. Maine did achieve independence in 1820, joining the Union as a free state as part of the Missouri compromise.

Economic Boom and Bust

Between 1800 and 1860 Maine experienced tremendous growth. The lumber industry, as well as paper manufacturing, fishing, shipbuilding, mining, and textile production, all thrived leading up to the Civil War. The Portsmouth Naval Shipyard—still in operation today—opened; numerous schools and colleges—Bangor Theological Seminary, Colby College, and Bates College

Augusta became Maine's capital in 1827. The state's Capitol Building was designed by Charles Bulfinch, who also designed the Massachusetts State House and parts of the U.S. Capitol.

among them—were established, and culture blossomed.

But the Civil War took its toll. Nearly 75,000 men lost their lives. The nation began to rely less on wood products both for shipbuilding and fuel. And the fishing industry took a downturn. Maine's economy would have to adapt.

An Evolving Maine

The economy did adapt, but not without struggle. Two World Wars and the intervening Depression continually changed the face of Maine's economy. Textile mills flourished and then closed, but the paper and pulp industry expanded; wooden ships all but disappeared, but shipyards were built to take over construction of iron and steel vessels; small family farms died off, but larger-scale potato production was born. And tourism became a major source of jobs. Today, Maine, like the rest of the nation, is transitioning from manufacturing toward a service-based economy.

The map at right shows the extent of Maine's railroad system in 1899. Today, passenger railroad travel is restricted to the southern coast.

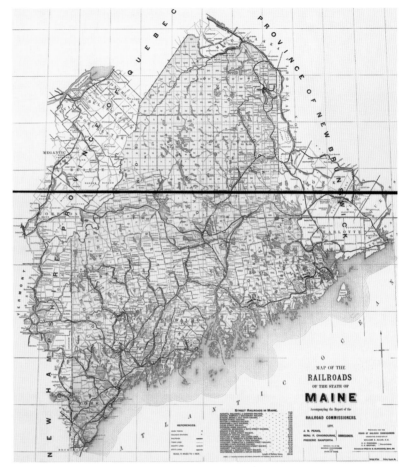

The resort town of Old Orchard Beach is a favorite destination for families in the summer. Maine's 3,478-mile coastline—which, straightend out, would be longer than California's—is lined by rocky beaches, iconic lighthouses, and picture-perfect small towns.

New Hampshire

The Granite State

Live Free or Die

This northern New England state has played an important role throughout U.S. history. New Hampshire was the first of the 13 original colonies to adopt its own state constitution. The U.S. Navy's first shipyard opened in Portsmouth in 1800. In 1822 the nation's first free public library was established in Dublin; that town is also home to the country's oldest continuously published periodical—*The Old Farmer's Almanac*, which debuted in 1792. The MacDowell Colony in Peterborough is the largest and oldest artists' colony in the country. And both the International Monetary Fund and the World Bank were planned during the 1944 Bretton Woods Conference, when representatives of all 44 allied countries met to discuss the stabilization of the world financial system after World War II.

But New Hampshire is also known for more than its historical importance. Today, the state has many faces. From hiking and skiing in the White Mountains of the north to boating and fishing on Lake Winnipesaukee to the world-class music of the Monadnock Music series, the state is well-known for the wide array of recreational opportunities it offers.

New Hampshire is also known as a leading producer of electronics and computer equipment. In fact, the manufacture of those products employs more people than any other industry in the state.

Most of New Hampshire's residents live in one of the state's two metropolitan areas, one being part of the Boston, Massachusetts, metro region, and the other in the Manchester–Nashua area. Manchester, the state's largest city, is also its cultural center; Opera New Hampshire, the New Hampshire Philharmonic, and the New Hampshire Symphony Orchestra are all based in the city. Concord is the state capital and is home to the New Hampshire Historical Society and the Christa McAuliffe Planetarium, which was named for the local schoolteacher who perished aboard the Space Shuttle *Challenger* in 1986.

New Hampshire takes its nickname, the Granite State, from the fact that much of the state's bedrock is composed of that stone. Granite from New Hampshire has been used in construction at Arlington National Cemetery, the Library of Congress, New York's Brooklyn Bridge, and Civil War monuments throughout the country. Like the stone at its core, the state of New Hampshire is both durable and beautiful.

The Flume, a granite gorge in Franconia Notch, is a stunning natural wonder and one of America's most beautiful state parks.

New Hampshire State Facts

Full Name: State of New Hampshire
Meaning of Name: From the English county of Hampshire
Admitted to the Union: June 21, 1788 (9th state)
Inhabitant: New Hampshirite
Capital City: Concord

Flower: Purple lilac
Tree: White birch
Bird: Purple finch

Geography and Ecology

New Hampshire comprises three major landforms: the Coastal Lowlands in the southeastern part of the state, the New England Uplands, which cover most of the southern and western parts of the state, and the White Mountains in the north.

The Coastal Lowlands

This region is found along New Hampshire's 13-mile coastline along the Atlantic and from 15 to 20 miles inland. It is generally characterized by sandy beaches and tidal wetlands.

The Eastern New England Uplands

This large region is made up of three smaller areas: the Merrimack Valley, the Hills and Lakes, and the Connecticut River valley. The landscape in these areas varies, from hilly and fertile to heavily forested.

The White Mountains

Part of the Appalachian Mountain system, the White Mountains cover approximately 1,000 square miles. Of the several ranges within the Whites, the Presidential Range is the best known; it includes the highest peak in the Northeast, Mt. Washington, at 6,288 feet. Profile Mountain was once the site of the iconic natural formation known as the Old Man of the Mountain, which appears on the state quarter. In May 2003 the formation collapsed after years of erosion.

Notable Natural Features

New Hampshire is home to approximately 1,300 lakes and ponds; the largest is Lake Winnipesaukee, which covers about 70 square miles. The Connecticut River, the longest in the state, is also the largest in New England. It flows from the town of Fourth Connecticut Lake, New Hampshire, to Long Island Sound, and forms New Hampshire's border with Vermont.

About 10 miles off the New Hampshire coast are nine small islands called the Isles of Shoals. Four of these islands are in New Hampshire; the other five are in Maine. The islands are a favorite day-trip destination for locals and tourists alike during the summer season.

In addition to Mt. Washington, New Hampshire is home to the nation's most-climbed mountain: Mt.

Monadnock, in southern New Hampshire. This beautiful, isolated mountain offers unobstructed views of the surrounding countryside.

Climate

Summers in New Hampshire are short and cool, with low humidity; July temperatures range from around 66° F to 70° F. Winters are long and cold, with heavy snow falling in much of the state. January temperatures range from 16° F to 22° F.

THE WORLD'S MOST DANGEROUS SMALL MOUNTAIN

At only 6,288 feet, Mt. Washington is dwarfed by dozens of other mountains in the United States—but more people have died climbing this peak than any other mountain in the country. Climbers preparing for some of the world's most challenging ascents, including Everest, have been known to climb the mountain in winter as part of their training.

The highest surface wind speed ever measured on earth—231 miles per hour—was recorded by the weather observatory atop Mt. Washington in April 1934. And with the exception of some areas of the Arctic and Antarctica, Mt. Washington experiences the most severe weather on earth. But why?

According to the observatory, the mountain lies at the juncture of three major storm tracks. And as the highest point in the region, Mt. Washington receives the brunt of passing storms.

Windchills atop Mt. Washington have dipped to -120° F in the winter. Snowfall averages around 250 inches a winter.

CANADA

Second Lake

First Connecticut Lake

Lake Francis

Swift Diamond River

Coos

Umbagog Lake

Groveton

Lancaster

Berlin

Whitefield

Israel River

Gorham

Moore Res.

Littleton

Ammonoosuc River

White Mountains

Lisbon

Woodsville

93

North Conway

Conway

Swift River

Conway Lake

Carroll

Grafton

Silver Lake

Beavamp River

Ossipee Lake

Plymouth

Squam Lake

Newfound Lake

NEW HAMPSHIRE

MAINE

VERMONT

Hanover

Lebanon

Enfield

Mascoma Lake

Bristol

Winnisquam Lake

Lake Winnipesaukee

Wolfeboro

Franklin Falls Res.

Laconia

Claremont

Newport

Sunapee Lake

Franklin

Belknap

Sullivan

Charlestown

89

Merrimack

93

Pittsfield

Rochester

Salmon Falls River

Somersworth

Henniker

Concord

393

Strafford

Highland Lake

Hillsboro

Suncook

Newmarket

Connecticut River

Ashuelot River

Cheshire

Keene

Marlborough

Contoocook River

Hillsborough

293

Manchester

Raymond

Epping

Exeter

Portsmouth

Great Bay

Piscataqua River

Rockingham

Hampton

95

Hinsdale

Winchester

Jaffrey

Wilton

Milford

Greenville

Nashua

Hudson

Atlantic Ocean

MASSACHUSETTS

The Granite State

Prior to the arrival of European settlers, several Algonquian Indian tribes roamed the area that is now New Hampshire. During the 1500s navigators from the Netherlands, England, and France explored the region. In 1623 the first English settlement was established along the Piscataqua River, which runs along the modern border between New Hampshire and Maine. From the mid to the late 1600s, the New Hampshire economy was based around fishing, farming, lumber cutting and sawing, shipbuilding, and overseas trade.

Independence and Immigration
New Hampshire was the first of the original 13 colonies to establish its own

Franklin Pierce (1804–69)—the nation's 14th president—was born and raised in New Hampshire.

government, six months before the signing of the Declaration of Independence. Though the Revolutionary War brought very little fighting to New Hampshire, many men from the state, including General John Stark, fought valiantly for the American cause. In fact it was Stark who supplied the state with the words that would later become its motto: Live free or die.

Over the course of the 1800s, textile manufacturing became more important to the economy than overseas trade. Mills sprung up, especially in the Merrimack River valley. And as that industry began to thrive, immigrants from Europe, and then Quebec, came to the region in great numbers.

Concord, New Hampshire, 1899. In the 19th century, New Hampshire's capital city was a hub for furniture making, quarrying, and textiles. One of the city's best-known industries was carriage manufacturing. Concord coaches, known worldwide, were built throughout the 1800s.

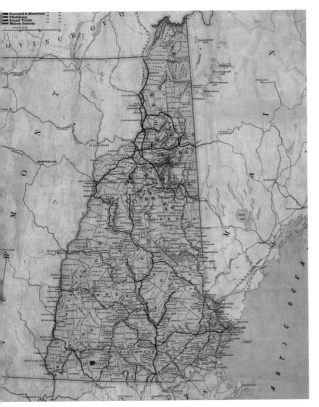

In the 19th century, Concord became a hub for the railroad. This map, from 1894, shows the lines running through the state.

THE MACDOWELL COLONY

Leonard Bernstein

In 1907 composer Edward MacDowell and his wife, Marian, founded the MacDowell Colony as a community where artists from all media could work. It was the first such retreat in the nation.

Today, more than 250 artists in varied disciplines—architecture, composing, film, photography, printmaking, and writing—visit the colony each year. Residents of the colony receive room, board, and separate studio space in which to work.

The list of MacDowell alumni is long and impressive. It includes such notable artists as Aaron Copland, James Baldwin, Leonard Bernstein, Willa Cather, Spalding Gray, Alice Walker, and Thornton Wilder—just to name a few.

Economic Woes

After the First World War and through the 1960s, the New Hampshire economy entered a slump. Textile jobs were moving to the South, where factories were newer and labor cheaper. Towns in northern New Hampshire, which relied on logging and paper manufacturing, fared better than those in the south. But the economy took a further dive when the state's railroad system collapsed during the Great Depression.

Recovery

In the 1970s and 1980s, several favorable factors—its proximity to Boston, interstate highway construction, and New Hampshire's lack of a personal income tax—helped attract people and businesses to the state. High-tech companies, in particular, came to the area. This influx helped reverse the economic decline and double the state's population between 1960 and 1988. Most

Four-time Pulitzer Prize winning poet Robert Frost (1874-1963) lived and worked in Franconia, New Hampshire.

of the newcomers were young and affluent, with more liberal social and political views than those of longtime New Hampshirites.

New Hampshire elected its first woman governor—Democrat Jeanne Shaheen—in 1996. Shaheen, also the first Democrat to hold that office since 1982, was reelected twice, holding office until 2003.

Taxing Issues

As did most of the New England states, New Hampshire suffered during the national recession of the late 1980s and early 1990s, but the economy did rebound in the mid-1990s. Today, New Hampshire remains one of the few states that collect neither a traditional income tax nor a general sales tax. This low-tax policy has been a double-edged sword for the state: although it does attract industry and residents, it has also caused fiscal difficulties for state- and community-funded services. It seems even living free has its price.

Vermont

The Green Mountain State

Vermont, Freedom, and Unity

The New England state of Vermont is known for its ski resorts and the Green Mountains, Ben & Jerry's ice cream, maple syrup, the Morgan horse, and the Trapp Family Lodge—owned by the von Trapps of *The Sound of Music* fame.

The Green Mountain State is also one of small towns, making it one of the most rural and sparsely populated states in the country. In fact, only Wyoming has fewer residents. The capital, Montpelier, is home to just over 8,000, making it the smallest capital in the nation. Burlington, Rutland, and South Burlington are the largest cities in Vermont.

Burlington lies on the eastern shore of Lake Champlain in the northern part of the state. With a population of around 40,000, it is the largest city in Vermont and home to the University of Vermont. Burlington also boasts a monument to one of the Revolutionary War's most famous figures and Vermont's most famous patriot, Ethan Allen. Allen organized a volunteer militia called the Green Mountain Boys, which played a key role in the capture in 1775 of Fort Ticonderoga, which held a cache of British weapons.

Vermont's political history is somewhat unusual. Until the 1992 presidential election, Vermonters supported a Democratic candidate only once since 1854—that was Lyndon B. Johnson in his victory over Barry Goldwater in 1964. But since 1992 the state has supported Democratic candidates in presidential elections and now has a reputation for its liberal leanings. In 2000 Vermont passed a Civil Union law, which granted the benefits of marriage to same-sex couples. And in 2007, state senators voted to call for the impeachment of President George W. Bush and Vice President Dick Cheney, saying that their actions with regard to the Iraqi war raised "serious questions of constitutionality." The state is no stranger to the executive office, as two U.S. presidents—Chester A. Arthur and Calvin Coolidge—were born in Vermont.

Tourism plays an important role in the state's economy, employing up to a quarter of Vermont's workers. Tourists come to Vermont year-round, but especially in winter, when skiers and snowboarders arrive in droves to test the numerous mountains and trails. Autumn is also a favorite time in the Green Mountain State, when the hills are alive, so to speak, with the colors of fall.

Vermont's Quechee Gorge, a mile-long gorge on the Ottauquechee River in southern Vermont. It is now a state park.

Vermont State Facts

Full Name: Vermont
Meaning of Name: From French *vert*, meaning green, and *mont*, meaning mountain
Admitted to the Union: March 4, 1791 (14th state)
Inhabitant: Vermonter

Capital City: Montpelier
Flower: Red clover
Tree: Sugar maple
Bird: Hermit thrush

Geography and Ecology

Vermont's landscape comprises six primary land regions: the Northeast Highlands, the Western New England Upland, the Green Mountains, the Vermont Valley, the Taconic Mountains, and the Champlain Valley.

Regional Characteristics

The Northeast Highlands region of Vermont is characterized by an array of granite mountains, streams, and rivers. In the eastern part of the state (but the western portion of New England) the Western New England Upland is filled with granite hills and fertile lowlands, where many farms are found. The Green Mountains, in central Vermont, are abuzz with all types of tourist activity. Summer hiking and winter skiing are just two of the pursuits that draw both American and international visitors to this area.

Vermont's Green Mountains attract hikers in summer and winter.

Mt. Mansfield (4,393 ft.), Vermont's highest peak, is in this region; granite, marble, and slate deposits make the area Vermont's most important mining belt. The Vermont Valley, located halfway up the western part of the state, is etched by several small river valleys. In southwestern Vermont, the Taconic Mountains area includes many peaks—including Equinox Mountain (3,816 ft.) and Dorset Peak (3,770 ft.)—as well as lakes and streams. Finally, the Champlain Valley is found around Lake Champlain, the largest lake in New England. The land here is fertile, and the area supports many dairy farms and orchards.

Lake Champlain

New England's largest lake lies between the Green Mountains and New York's Adirondack Mountains.

MAPLE SUGARING IN VERMONT

Vermont is the nation's largest producer of maple syrup—the thick, sweet liquid that many of us love to enjoy drizzled on pancakes and waffles and into yogurt and baked beans.

Maple syrup is made by concentrating the sap of the sugar maple—the most common tree in Vermont. In the early spring, syrup producers bore holes in the trees. Taps are placed into the holes, and then buckets are hung below the taps to catch the sap. Each tree can produce about 15 gallons of sap, and each gallon of finished maple syrup requires around 40 gallons of sap. The sap is collected, and then boiled and filtered to make the finished syrup.

Large buckets hung on sugar maple trees are a common sight in many parts of Vermont in the springtime.

Lake Champlain is New England's largest lake. Its borders are shared by Vermont, New York, and Canada.

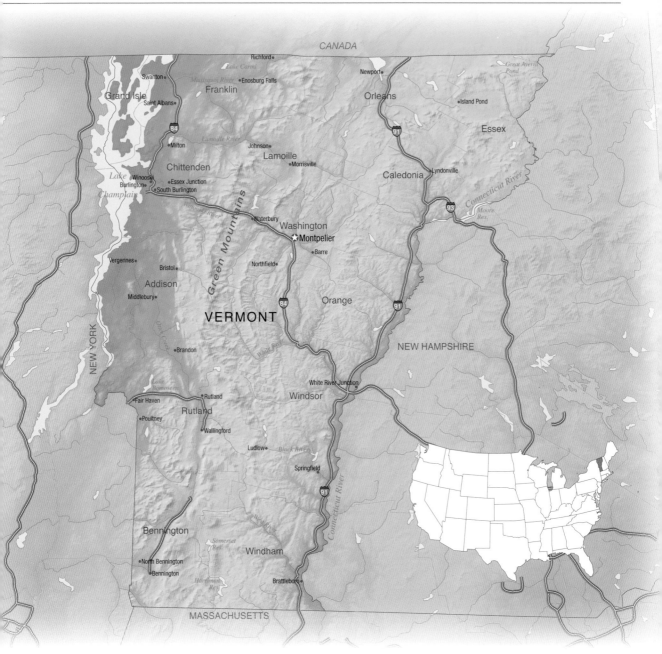

About two-thirds of this 490-square-mile lake lies in Vermont; the remainder is part of New York or Canada. Lake Champlain is dotted with islands; in fact, an entire county of the state, Grand Isle, is made up of islands. Parks and beaches surround the lake and make it a favorite destination for tourists in summer. In winter, when the lake freezes, anglers fish for lake sturgeon, pike, bass, and other fish. Lake Champlain is also rumored to be the home of Champ, an amphibious sea creature akin to the Loch Ness monster. In the late 1880s P. T. Barnum offered a reward of $20,000 to anyone who could produce the monster dead or alive, but the prize was never claimed.

White Gold

Vermont summers are short and cool; very hot days are rare. July temperatures average 68° F. Winters in the state are long and cold. The average temperature in January is 17° F, and depending on location, as much as 120 inches of snow can fall during a single winter season—music to the ears of ski resorts throughout the state.

The Green Mountain State

The Abenaki tribe of the Algonquian Indians were some of the earliest residents of Vermont. In 1609 Samuel de Champlain was probably the first European to explore the heavily wooded region. Traveling with a group of Algonquians, in July he arrived at the lake that would later bear his name—Lake Champlain—and claimed the area for France. After the French and Indian Wars, control of the land went to England.

The Green Mountain Boys

During the American Revolution, a military force called the Green Mountain Boys—which had been organized by patriot Ethan Allen during an earlier skirmish against New York over lands—captured Fort Ticonderoga from the British, sealing their place in Vermont, and American, history. On March 4, 1791, Vermont became the 14th state, thereby having the honor of being the first state admitted outside the original 13.

Ethan Allen founded the Green Mountain Boys—a citizens' militia—in Fay's Tavern in Bennington, Vermont, in 1770.

The 1800s

As lands in the Midwest opened for settlement, people began to leave Vermont to move west, where farmland was better and the winters more agreeable. Sheep farming thrived after the 1823 opening of the Champlain Canal, which allowed farmers to ship wool to New York City. But they too soon experienced hardship, as wool from the Midwest caused prices to drop. In the early and mid 1800s, the state's agricultural base shifted from sheep to dairy farming.

Vermont was active in the early anti-slavery movement. In 1834 the state formed the Vermont Anti-Slavery Society, which sought to "abolish slavery in the United States and to improve the mental, moral, and political condition of the colored population." And many slaves escaped to Canada through Vermont.

As it did in many parts of the country, the economy began to shift in Vermont after the Civil War. Farming decreased and manufacturing increased, as immigrants moved to cities to pursue factory work. The late 1800s brought prosperity to the lumber, dairy, and granite industries.

The gold-domed State House in Montpelier, Vermont. In terms of population, Montpelier is the smallest state capital in the country.

Changes in the 20th Century

By 1920 manufacturing had overtaken agriculture as Vermont's most important economic activity. The tourism industry was also born during this time, as city dwellers sought the respite of the state's bucolic setting. But the Great Depression brought difficult times; lumber mills and small factories shuttered their doors, and many were left unemployed.

World War II benefited the state's economy as factories began to produce war materials. After the war, the state worked hard to attract new industry. The manufacturing sector grew, and the population gradually became more urban. By the 1970s tourism was a major source of income for the state. It was also during this time that a movement began to protect the state's environment from damage caused by tourism and manufacturing—and to maintain the state's rural character. The Environmental Control Law, passed in 1970, was (and is) a fundamental tool used by the state to achieve those goals. Today, the push and pull between growth and development and protecting the environment remains Vermont's biggest challenge.

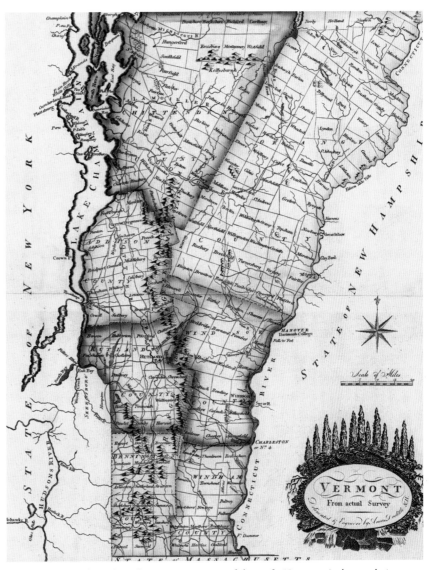

Vermont, 1817. The early 19th century was a time of change for Vermont. As the population grew, commercial farming began to grow as an industry, crowding out smaller subsistance farms.

"*We very cordially invite every Fugitive Slave in the United States to take VERMONT on his way towards FREEDOM in Canada. We are willing to guaranty that he can get a night's lodging and a free pass over the Lines, without any particular danger from that elevated species of the human race known as 'Slave catchers.'*"

—*Burlington Daily Free Press,* October 7, 1850

Massachusetts

The Bay State

Ense Petit Placidam Sub Libertate Quietem (By the sword we seek peace, but peace only under liberty)

Sharing a border with four of the remaining five New England states, Massachusetts highlights New England culture and history. Its capital city, Boston, is the largest city in the entire region. Thanks to Boston and its extensive suburbs, Massachusetts is the most populous New England state, counting 6.4 million inside its borders. Nationwide the state ranks third in population density, with 816.2 people per square mile. It is bested only by Rhode Island and New Jersey.

Historically, the state has been a center of politics, various religious movements, and social progressivism; in the 20th century it produced the nation's first Catholic president, John F. Kennedy. Today, Massachusetts remains a hotbed of political activity and a solid "blue" (Democratic) state in national elections. For many years, the state's entire congressional delegation has been Democratic.

The old economic mainstays of commercial fishing, shipping, and manufacturing have declined, replaced by higher education, health care, and high-technology industries. The state, and Boston in particular, is a national leader in all three areas. The second-most lucrative industry is tourism, which attracts visitors not only to the historic city of Boston but also to the lovely Berkshires in the west, with their multiple parks and artistic venues, and to Cape Cod and other coastal areas. Boston remains, however, the principal draw, with a history stretching to the earliest colonial era and landmarks famous in the early stages of American rebellion against Great Britain.

Nearby Boston lie tourist attractions for visitors interested in the state's colonial history, including Plymouth, where the country's second permanent European colony settled in 1620. Just across the Charles River is Cambridge, home to Harvard University, the nation's oldest institution of higher learning, founded in 1636. To the north is the town of Salem, whose tourist industry is almost entirely dedicated to the eponymous witch trials of 1692–93. The trials themselves actually occurred in neighboring Danvers, where certain sites related to the events can still be seen.

Though steeped in colonial history, Massachusetts is by no means defined by this one era. The state continues to be a fertile ground for music, art, and various other facets of metropolitan culture. Home to professional franchises in football, baseball, basketball, hockey, and soccer, it is also a focal point for New England's rabid sports fans. While Massachusetts, like much of the Northeast, has lost some of its most impressive animals, including the gray wolf and wolverine, black bears and moose are returning to the central and western parts of the state, and its shores are beginning to teem again with marine wildlife, including whales and the popular gray seal.

Nicknamed "Old Ironsides" and built from 1794 to 1797, the USS Constitution *was one of the first ships of the U.S. Navy.*

Massachusetts State Facts

Full Name: Commonwealth of Massachusetts
Meaning of Name: From Native American tribe name meaning, roughly, "by the Great Hill."
Admitted to the Union: February 6, 1788 (6th state)

Inhabitant: Bay Stater
Capital City: Boston
Flower: Mayflower
Tree: American elm
Bird: Black-capped chickadee

Geography and Ecology

The gentle beauty of the Berkshires, the southernmost portion of the Green Mountains, dominates the western third of Massachusetts, from the New York border to the Connecticut River. The area relies heavily on tourism and contains several attractions, including historic sites like Hancock Shaker Village and the homes of authors Edith Wharton and Herman Melville. The Berkshires also host a number of artistic and educational events and attractions, including Jacob's Pillow Dance Festival (an annual dance festival at a historic farm), the Tanglewood Music Festival, and the Norman Rockwell Museum, which boasts the world's largest collection of the artist's work. Arguably, however, the Berkshires' greatest appeal derives from the region's natural beauty, protected by numerous parks, wilderness preserves, and a portion of the Appalachian Trail.

Topography and Population

The highlands region stretching westward from the Connecticut River valley to Worcester and Fitchburg is

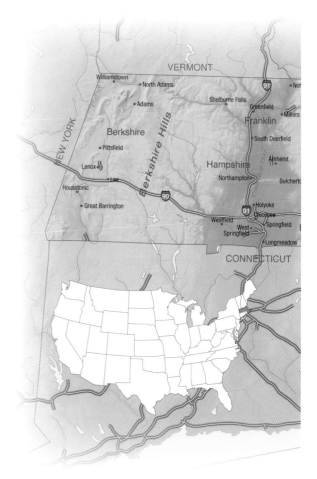

SEA CREATURES

Every year thousands of dedicated visitors stream to the popular whale-watching ships along the Massachusetts coast. Just north of the Cape lies an 842-square-mile federal marine sanctuary called Stellwagen Bank. Here hopeful whale-watchers can catch close-up views of humpback, minke, and endangered fin whales. Once threatened with extinction from whaling ships, whales are now making a comeback in Massachusetts waters, and towns once dominated by the whaling industry are capitalizing once again on their impressive natural resource.

A humpback whale breaches off the coast of Cape Cod, allowing observers to catch a quick glimpse of this enormous rarity.

rocky, dotted with forests and pastures. The Quabbin Reservoir, the state's largest body of water, lies in the western portion of the region. Built in the 1930s, the reservoir, together with the Wachusett Reservoir farther east, provides Boston and much of the metropolitan area with the majority of its water. The reservoir is a popular recreational destination.

The densely populated eastern third of the state is flat, sandy, and poorly suited for most types of agriculture. Today, the area is almost entirely suburban, with industries in Boston providing the surrounding areas with jobs and services. In the past the area subsisted on commercial fishing, shipping, and manufacturing. While prone to difficult currents, storms, and foggy conditions, the ocean provided Massachusetts with seemingly inexhaustible supplies. Although these traditional nautical enterprises have declined, the coast—made sandy by retreating glaciers some 18,000 years ago—is still popular for beachgoers, amateur fishermen, and whale- and seal-watchers.

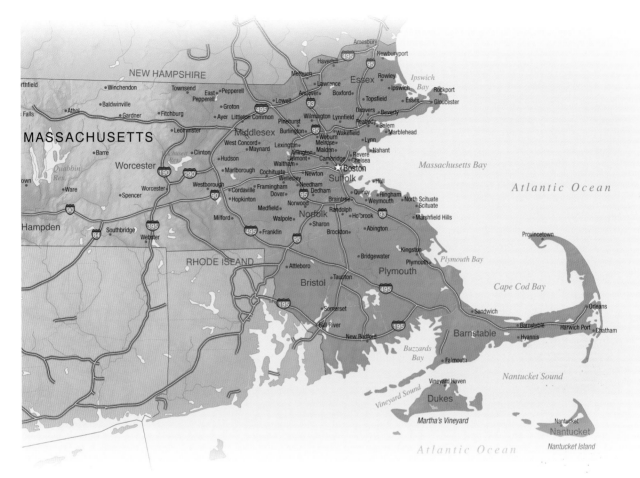

The Cape

This is particularly true for Cape Cod, known to locals simply as "the Cape." The Cape, a hook-shaped extension into the Atlantic off the southeast corner of the state, was formed during the Ice Age, about 23,000 years ago. Exposure to the Atlantic and rising sea levels have left the region vulnerable to erosion, although sediment removed in one place on the Cape is typically deposited elsewhere. Thus, while the Cape's mainland is eroded, the northern tip of the Cape—Provincetown Spit—and the southern Monomoy Islands continue to grow. Despite this ecological concern, the Cape is an extremely popular vacation spot.

Seasonal Changes

As with most of the Northeast, Massachusetts is subject to long summers and winters, with brief but intense autumns and springs. Summer is typically warm, with July averages around 80° F, but winter is cold, with January averages at or below freezing. Boston and the coast, moderated by the nearby ocean, experience slightly warmer winters but very humid summers. However, extreme temperatures are not uncommon; Boston's record high reached 104° F (July 4, 1911), while its record low, on February 9, 1934, was only -18° F. Statewide, the highest temperature ever recorded was 107° F, on August 2, 1975. The lowest temperature was -35° F, on January 12, 1981.

Massachusetts receives a fair amount of precipitation throughout the year. Generally, inland regions receive the most rain and significantly more snow, particularly in the western Berkshires, where precipitation averages top 56 inches per year. The state can also expect to receive a number of severe storms, both thunderstorms in summer—about 30 days per year experience thunderstorms—and nor'easters and blizzards in winter. Because of its coastal exposure, the state is also occasionally hit by hurricanes, although these have usually weakened from their tropical strength by the time they reach New England.

The Bay State

Some 10,000 years before Europeans dipped their oars into Cape Cod Bay, paleo-indians inhabited what is now the state of Massachusetts. These early Americans lived in migratory bands, supporting themselves by hunting, gathering, and fishing. In the following millennia, diverse tribal societies emerged, governed by religious and political laws, cultivating vegetables and grains, hunting deer and gamebird, and fishing the teeming waters. The Wampanoag—the "People of the East"—inhabited the state's south shore, the peninsula of Cape Cod, and the islands of Martha's Vineyard and Nantucket. The Massachusett tribe occupied the central shore, and the Pennacook lived along what are now the state's northeastern edges, in the Merrimack River valley. Inland, the fertile Connecticut River valley was home to the Nipmuc, and the rolling Berkshire hills were the territory of the Pocomtuc and Mahican tribes.

Early Exploration

Though legend persists that Leif Eriksson visited the shores of Massachusetts in the 11th century, John Cabot is presumed to be the first European to sail within sight of Cape Cod, in the late 1490s. During the 1500s fishermen sailed past en route to the Grand Banks off Canada. Around roughly 1616, European diseases began to plague the

The heavily trafficked Boston Harbor saw ships from all over the British Empire—and some from farther afield—in the 18th century.

American Indians of coastal Massachusetts, contributing to the death of nearly 90 percent of the population. Thus, in the winter of 1620–21, it was as a diminished and convalescent people that the Wampanoag Indians encountered a beleaguered group of English separatists encamped on the site of the old plague-decimated Patuxet village.

Settlement Hardships

These were the Pilgrims, religious exiles attempting to establish their own colony in the Americas. Arriving in late autumn, after a difficult voyage from England aboard the *Mayflower*, the Pilgrims found themselves unprepared for the ensuing winter—by December, sickness and malnutrition consumed the group. After foraging for a better campsite, they finally settled on the abandoned Patuxet village, which became the site of Plymouth Plantation, the earliest colonial town in Massachusetts. In March of 1621, as the season thawed, the Pilgrim encampment was surprised by the gregarious Samoset, an Abenaki Indian who, having learned some English from fishermen farther north, inquired of the Pilgrims' origins. He returned two days later, with Tisquantum (Squanto), a Patuxet fluent in English. In the coming months, with Squanto's help, the Pilgrims settled their village. Squanto also arranged the Pilgrims' priority over the former Patuxet land; here, however, were the seeds of dispute—the Pilgrims believed the land was theirs to own, a concept not embraced by the Wampanoag. In 1629 the first representatives of the Massachusetts Bay Colony crossed the Atlantic under the auspices of a prized royal charter granting them the right to settle Massachusetts "from sea to sea." The Great Migration, the exodus of tens of thousands of English Puritans to America, had begun.

TISQUANTUM (SQUANTO)

Most schoolchildren have heard the story of Squanto, the Patuxet Indian who introduced the Pilgrims to the Massachusetts wilderness and taught them to use fish to fertilize their cornfields. Less told, however, is Squanto's story before and after the arrival of the *Mayflower*. In 1614 an English fishing boat kidnapped Squanto and roughly 20 other Wampanoag Indians, intending to sell them as slaves. Saved from bondage by a group of Spanish priests who hoped to convert the Indians to Christianity, Squanto vanished from historical record. In 1617, however, he turned up in London, where he learned English; by 1619 he was headed home to Cape Cod, where he found his village and people obliterated by plague. When the Pilgrims arrived in 1620, Squanto's ability to speak English made him their guide and diplomat with the Wampanoag, but tying his fortunes to the Pilgrims isolated him from his fellow Indians. After unsuccessfully attempting to usurp the Wampanoag sachem (chief) Massasoit, Squanto retreated to the protection of the Pilgrims, where he died of a fever in 1622.

Expansion and Conflict

As English settlement expanded inland, the 17th century in Massachusetts became a fervent and bloody affair. Now established, the Massachusetts Puritans believed it their divine right to occupy the land and convert the American Indians to Christianity. By the 1660s the Wampanoag—the former allies of the Pilgrims—had decisively soured on the Puritan presence. Metacomet, the sachem of the Wampanoag, traveled throughout the countryside and arranged an alliance of tribes to expel the Puritans. In 1675 raids began on colonial villages, and the fighting progressed into some of the bloodiest and costliest combat ever waged on American soil. In August 1676 Metacomet—or King Philip, as the English knew him—was killed, and King Philip's War had effectively finished, having resulted in thousands of Puritan deaths, a swath of colonial villages destroyed, and a complete crippling of American Indian influence on the region. The remaining Indians were persecuted by the Puritans or fled to outlying tribal lands.

The 18th century saw Massachusetts firmly under British control as part of the British province of

Situated between the Massachusetts Bay and the Charles River, Boston boomed during the Industrial Revolution, although by 1873, when this map was published, other ports like New York City had overtaken its harbor in economic importance.

Massachusetts Bay, which also included portions of what are now New Hampshire, Maine, and Nova Scotia. The relationship between Puritan Massachusetts and the British Crown had always been uneasy, however, and though Puritan politics in Massachusetts had dissipated, rebellious sentiment lingered. A number of parliamentary acts restricting and taxing American commerce aroused indignation throughout the 13 American colonies, but in Boston—at this time one of the busiest ports in the

THE SALEM WITCH TRIALS

One of the darkest chapters of the Puritan story in Massachusetts was the Salem Witch Trials, a frenzy of superstition and murder played out beneath the banner of religious ethics and patriarchal law. In 1692, in Salem Village, a group of girls had a series of unexplainable fits, characterized by uncontrollable screaming, throwing objects, and bizarre physical contortions. Consensus emerged that the girls were afflicted by witchcraft, and accusations surged forth, one paranoid citizen implicating another. The poor and less-influential women of the community topped the list of suspects, and anyone questioning the proceedings became a suspect as well. In 1693, after interrogations, incarcerations, and affirmations from local religious leaders, the courts of Essex, Suffolk, and Middlesex counties executed 14 women and 6 men and imprisoned 9 others, 5 of whom died behind bars. In 2001, more than 300 years later, the Commonwealth of Massachusetts retroactively pardoned the convicted citizens.

A late example of the witchcraft panic that afflicted much of early modern European society, the strange and tragic events known as the Salem Witch Trials are still hotly debated by scholars.

world—Parliament's actions inspired particular outrage. British responses to Boston's libertarian fervor led to the infamous Boston Massacre and the Boston Tea Party, and on April 19, 1775, while British hunted agitators Samuel Adams and John Hancock, colonial "minutemen" and British regulars exchanged gunfire on the village green in Lexington, Massachusetts. The American Revolution had begun.

Driving the British Out

The war did not stay long in Massachusetts. The early skirmishes progressed into the colonists' siege of Boston, highlighted by the bloody Battle of Bunker Hill. During the months-long siege, the Continental Congress established the Continental Army, absorbing the Massachusetts minutemen into their fold. In July of 1775 George Washington arrived in Boston to lead the new army, and after a period of stalemate, in January of 1776 the Continental Army fortified their position with 60 tons of artillery. In March of 1776 the British vacated the city. Though the war would last another seven years, fighting would not occur in Massachusetts thereafter.

Dawn of a New Age

As the 19th century opened, Massachusetts was the sixth state of a fledgling nation, and as changes in the United States influenced the world, so too did a shifting world

Introduced to settlers by Native Americans, cranberries are still a major Massachusetts crop. Although now better known as a vacation destination, the island of Nantucket—shown here during harvest in 1880—still hosts an annual Cranberry Harvest Festival.

affect the United States. Massachusetts became a hive of industrial activity. The textile mills in Lowell and Lawrence were among the most efficient and productive in the world, though the mill workers were generally scantly paid women, children, or immigrants. Boston, the primary city of New England, became a national center of finance and learning, and the ports of southeastern Massachusetts, especially the islands of Nantucket and Martha's Vineyard, became hubs for the whaling industry, as immortalized in Herman Melville's novel *Moby Dick*. Progressive political and literary thought bloomed. In 1825 John Quincy Adams became the second Adams, after his father, John Adams, to serve as president of the United States. Daniel

MASSACHUSETTS SPORTS

With its hot summers, crisp autumns, and frigid winters, Massachusetts is home to a range of sports. It is the birthplace of basketball, a game devised by physical education teacher James A. Naismith in the city of Springfield, and every year Springfield's Basketball Hall of Fame inducts new members into its hallowed ranks. The Bay State's local team, the Boston Celtics, is the most successful team in the history of the National Basketball Association. Ice hockey is a popular winter pastime among children and adults, played in rinks and on frozen ponds statewide. As winter turns to spring, Massachusetts's baseball fans set their hearts on the fortunes of the Boston Red Sox, who after having not won a World Series since 1918, finally became baseball's best in 2004, and repeated the feat in 2007. Autumn, of course, brings football, another sport Massachusetts has excelled at in recent years. The New England Patriots, long an unspectacular franchise, are now one of the dominant teams in the National Football League.

Home to the Boston Red Sox, Fenway Park boasts a left field wall known as the "Green Monster," the highest in Major League Baseball.

Webster and Charles Sumner were powerful presences in the U.S. Senate; Sumner's calls for the abolition of slavery echoed the progressive stance among Massachusetts thinkers like William Lloyd Garrison. Meanwhile, Ralph Waldo Emerson philosophized Transcendentalism, emphasizing self-reliance and close adherence to nature; his protégé Henry David Thoreau became famous for *Walden*, his account of living simply within nature. Henry Wadsworth Longfellow became the most popular poet of his day, and in Amherst, in relative obscurity, Emily Dickinson composed unprecedented verse about death, love, loneliness, and God. As the American Civil War tore the country in half, Massachusetts made another progressive mark—the 54th Massachusetts Volunteer Infantry became the first all-black regiment to serve in the U.S. Army.

Issues of Industry

In the early 1900s, embroiled in bitter conflict over unionization and workers' rights and supplanted by commercial rivals elsewhere in the nation, Massachusetts's industry declined. The Great Depression exacerbated the state's simmering economic and societal problems. The lack of jobs caused higher migration into urban centers, increasing racial tensions among the working classes. After World War II, Massachusetts reckoned with a different world; the industry of old was not going to return, and the Civil Rights Movement and generational and cultural divide were sweeping the nation. In the 1960s Boston's wealthy Kennedy family became a progressive political force. In 1961 John F. Kennedy became the 35th president of the United States. His handsomeness, eloquence, and youthful character redefined the office, and his assassination in 1963 made him the symbol of a turbulent age. Robert F. Kennedy served as the attorney general of the United States and as a U.S. senator from New York. He was in the midst of his own presidential run, in 1968, when he too was assassinated. Edward "Ted" Kennedy became a U.S. senator in 1962 and was a leader in the Democratic Party. He was the second-longest serving U.S. senator in office when he died in 2009.

Originally designed to feed residents' cattle, Boston Common is the nation's oldest city park. Centrally located in the city, its 50 acres of ponds, fields, and trees are enjoyed by residents and visitors alike.

Massachusetts Today

The 21st century finds Massachusetts at a relatively stable point in its history. Its blighted industrial centers have started the transition to new economic activity. In an age of widespread college attendance, Massachusetts's prestigious universities—Harvard, Boston University, Boston College, MIT, Smith, Mount Holyoke, Amherst, and the University of Massachusetts, among others—have become economic stimulants, and sustain communities both east and west. Suburbanization continues, but much wilderness still exists in western Massachusetts and, with effective environmental protection, should exist for some time. The religiously fervent and culturally conflagrant Massachusetts Bay Colony has become one of the liberal and progressive bedrocks of the East Coast. If its history represents the conflicted beginnings of the United States, then perhaps its present symbolizes the complex choices all states face in an age of global economy and environmental unease.

"East of America, there stands in the open Atlantic the last fragment of an ancient and vanished land. Worn by the breakers and the rains, and disintegrated by the wind, it still stands bold."

—Henry Beston, referring to Cape Cod

Rhode Island

The Ocean State

Hope

One of the 13 original colonies and the smallest of the 50 states, Rhode Island has a rich history and cultural heritage. The state was founded in 1636 by Roger Williams, a colonial leader who challenged the religious intolerance of the Massachusetts Bay Colony leadership—and who was subsequently exiled by it. Rhode Island established the first law in North America outlawing slavery, in 1652. It is the birthplace of the American Industrial Revolution and a showcase of the Gilded Age: a time in the late 1800s marked by extravagant earnings and spending among the nation's richest families. The mansions of Newport are testament to their extravagant lifestyles.

Tourism is important to the Rhode Island economy. Visitors come for the Gilded Age mansions and music festivals of Newport and to sail the waters and enjoy the beaches of Block Island. Historic sites in the state abound. The nation's first synagogue—Touro Synagogue, built in 1759—is in Rhode Island, as are many buildings and sites important to the founding of the nation.

Providence is Rhode Island's capital and largest city, with a population of 183,730. Located at the head of Narragansett Bay, the city is also the cultural and educational center of the state. Brown University—an Ivy League institution and one of the country's oldest colleges—and the nationally known Rhode Island School of Design are both in Providence.

The city is also home to several important historic sites, including the house of Stephen Hopkins—signer of the Declaration of Independence—located near Brown University. Another Providence attraction, the Governor Henry Lippitt House Museum, was built in 1865 and was home to two Rhode Island governors.

Because the state is small and has few natural resources—aside from the waters of Narragansett Bay—Rhode Island's economy has historically been based on manufacturing. Today the service sector employs 78 percent of working Rhode Islanders.

Rhode Island is the most Roman Catholic state in the nation, but its voters also are primarily pro-choice. In recent national elections the state has been a Democratic stronghold; in the 1980 presidential elections Rhode Island was one of only six states to vote against Ronald Reagan.

Religion and politics aside, people are drawn to Rhode Island's quaint northeastern charm. From its lively ports to its beautiful beaches to its historical houses, the nation's smallest state has won a big place in America's heart.

Castle Hill Light on Narragansett Bay in Newport.

Rhode Island State Facts

Full Name: State of Rhode Island and Providence Plantations

Meaning of Name: Named by Dutch explorer Adriaen Block. He named it "Roodt Eylandt" meaning "red island," in reference to the red clay that lined the shore.

Admitted to the Union: May 29, 1790 (13th state)

Inhabitant: Rhode Islander
Capital City: Providence
Flower: Violet
Tree: Red maple
Bird: Rhode Island Red chicken

Geography and Ecology

Rhode Island's total land area is approximately 1,212 square miles—it could fit inside Alaska more than 485 times. The state is mostly flat; its highest point—Jerimoth Hill—is only 812 feet high. Rhode Island is bordered on the north and east by Massachusetts, on the west by Connecticut, and its most outstanding natural feature is Narragansett Bay, which opens to the Atlantic Ocean.

The bay and the adjoining sounds are home to 38 small islands. The largest of these, Block Island, is 9 miles southwest of Point Judith. The three largest islands within the bay are Prudence, Aquidneck (whose official name is Rhode Island), and Conanicut.

Topography

Rhode Island comprises two primary land regions: the New England Upland region and the Coastal Lowland.

Rhode Island vineyards produce some of New England's finest wines. Many are open to the public for tours and tastings.

The New England Upland covers the western two-thirds of the state. The terrain in this area is rocky and the soil unsuitable for farming. The landscape is forested and dotted by lakes.

The eastern third of the state constitutes the Coastal Lowlands. Here, sandy beaches and salt marshes are common. This area is home to several vineyards; the soil here, combined with the relatively moderate climate, has made this small area of the state well-known for wines.

Waterways and Lakes

Rhode Island's primary river is the Blackstone. It flows southward from Worcester, Massachusetts, entering Rhode Island at Woonsocket. From there it flows into Narragansett Bay.

Despite the state's location on the Atlantic, commercial fishing makes only a relatively small impact on the economy. In the 1970s and 1980s, many species—cod, flounder, and mackerel among them—were severely over-fished throughout New England; strict legal limits were imposed that caused the decline of commercial fishing in the entire region.

Weather and Climate

Rhode Island summers are short and warm; winters are cold. Average summer temperature is 73° F; in winter the average is 29° F. Average snowfall in winter is approximately 37 inches per year, although blizzards do occur. A blizzard in 1978 dumped a record 28.6 inches of snow on the state.

THE RHODE ISLAND RED

Rhode Island's state bird is the Rhode Island Red chicken. This domestic bird, America's best-known breed, was developed in the village of Little Compton around 1854.

Today, the birds are popular with poultry farmers because, as dual-purpose chickens, they provide eggs and meat. A monument to the bird was erected in 1925 in Little Compton.

Rhode Island Red chickens are popular dual-purpose birds. They are even known to make good pets.

Hurricanes are also an occasional threat in the state. The largest storm to hit the area in the 20th century was the Great Hurricane of 1938, which left 262 people dead and completely wiped out some coastal communities.

Flora and Fauna

Rhode Island's plant life is varied for such a small state. In marshy areas cattails are common, and the state is home to 30 species of indigenous orchid. The most common trees in the state include pin and post oak, tulip trees, and red cedar. The state's most notable wildlife is found in its waters: swordfish, tuna, and marlin are common, as is the quahog, a kind of clam.

Point Judith Light, in the distance, marks the entrance to Narragansett Bay to the north and Block Island Sound to the south.

The Ocean State

Two Indian groups lived in the area that is now Rhode Island prior to the arrival of Europeans: the Narragansett and the Wampanoag.

France explored the region in 1624, but the first permanent settlement in the area was not established until 1636, when Englishman Roger Williams and a group of followers from the Massachusetts Bay Colony founded Providence. Later settlements followed, and in 1663 a charter was granted by Charles II for Rhode Island and the Providence Plantations.

Rhode Island was the first colony to renounce English rule and the last of the original 13 colonies to join the union after the Revolutionary War.

The Industrial Revolution

The American Industrial Revolution began in Pawtucket, when Samuel Slater built the first water-powered cotton spinning mills, in 1791. The production of textiles quickly

After leaving the Massachusetts Bay Colony in 1636, Roger Williams was befriended by local Indians. Not long after, he and some followers settled at the headwaters of Narragansett Bay.

Providence, Rhode Island, 1896. The late 19th century was known as Providence's golden age. The city tripled in size by annexing several surrounding cities, and an influx of immigrants boosted its population and the strength of its economy.

became the backbone of the state's economy—by 1815, 100 mills were operating in the state, producing cotton, lace, and wool.

New industries developed in the 19th century as well, including the production of machinery and jewelry (Rhode Island was once known as the jewelry capital of the world). During the Civil War, Rhode Island was an important source of weaponry and other war supplies; and by century's end the state manufactured products as diverse as metal files, buttons, and hats.

Slater Mill, in Pawtucket, Rhode Island, is generally recognized as the birthplace of the Industrial Revolution in America. The mill produced cotton thread until 1829.

A Shifting Economy

In the 1920s textile jobs began to shift to the South, where costs were lower. Rhode Island's economy suffered and was further damaged by the Great Depression. Throughout the 1900s many of the state's factories went under, although World War II brought a brief revival of manufacturing.

Starting in the 1960s, tourism began to play an increasing role in the state's economy. By the end of the 20th century, service sectors, including those in government and health care, dominated.

Rhode Island Politics

Before the 1930s the Republican Party dominated in the state. The Democrats gained control during the Great Depression and have dominated local politics ever since. Recently elected Republicans have run and won by positioning themselves as "Republican reform" candidates. Clearly, politicians in the Ocean State know better than to swim against the prevailing tide.

The Breakers—Newport's grandest "cottage."

THE SUMMER COTTAGES OF NEWPORT

After the Civil War, industries such as shipping, railroads, and mining catapulted some to extraordinary wealth. Some of their names—Vanderbilt and Carnegie—are still familiar today.

Newport became the summer playground for many of these wealthy industrialists, dubbed "robber barons" by some. Starting in the late 1880s, some of these families built summer "cottages"—enormous mansions with names such as The Breakers, Chateau-sur-Mer, and Rosecliff—in Newport. Some employed world-class architects such as McKim, Mead, and White, and used extravagant building material. One mansion, Marble House, was constructed with $7 million worth of marble.

By 1920 the rise of labor unions, the establishment of an income tax, and the passage of the Sherman Anti-Trust Act all helped to bring to a close this Gilded Age, as it was known. Many of the mansions in Newport fell into disrepair in the ensuing years. Beginning in the late 1960s, some of the mansions were saved and restored by private and public funds and are today open to the public.

Connecticut

Qui Transtulit Sustinet (He who transplanted still sustains)

This New England state is known as a popular vacation destination. But it is also a center of industry—including many insurance companies—and an important player in the history of the United States. That's a big reputation for such a small state—but Connecticut pulls it off.

The state's shoreline on Long Island Sound is popular for the sailing, fishing, swimming, and boating opportunities it provides. Towns such as Litchfield, Essex, and Chester attract antiques collectors from near and far. And world-class museums, including Mystic Seaport and the Yale Center for British Art, display artifacts and works of art from America and beyond.

Connecticut can claim many firsts in U.S. history. In 1792 Yale University granted the nation's first medical diploma. What many claim to be the first newspaper in the nation, *The Hartford Courant*, published its first edition in 1764. In 1842 Hartford's Wadsworth Atheneum Museum opened, making it the country's first public art museum. The historic *Amistad* case, in which a group of illegally taken African slaves were tried for the murder of the ship's captain, was tried in Hartford.

Connecticut's economy is driven primarily by service industries. Hartford—the state capital and Connecticut's third-largest city—is known as a center of the insurance industry (the country's first insurance company, ITT Hartford Group, was established there in 1810), but finance and real estate are also important. Tourism, too, is a major contributor to the economy. Manufacturing in Connecticut has traditionally centered on military equipment: submarines, helicopters, guns and ammunition, and the like.

Bridgeport is Connecticut's largest city. Located on the southwest coast of the state, this gritty industrial city was home to P. T. Barnum, master showman who introduced "Siamese" twins Chang and Eng, General Tom Thumb, and Swedish soprano Jenny Lind to the U.S. public. Barnum also developed the Barnum and Bailey Circus—the Greatest Show on Earth. Today, the P. T. Barnum Museum attracts visitors for its exhibits about Barnum's life and career.

Outside of the state's urban centers, Connecticut's small towns reflect New England's picturesque reputation: villages with white-steepled churches and town greens framed by streets of small shops are common. Of course, some of Connecticut's most interesting history can be found in these small towns, belying their size—much like the state itself.

East Haddam—home of the Goodspeed Opera House—is just one of Connecticut's historic and picture-perfect towns.

Connecticut State Facts

Full Name: State of Connecticut
Meaning of Name: From Mohegan and other Algonquian words meaning "long river place"
Admitted to the Union: January 9, 1788 (5th state)
Inhabitant: Connecticuter

Capital City: Hartford
Flower: Mountain laurel
Tree: Charter oak
Bird: American robin

Geography and Ecology

Connecticut's landscape comprises five primary landforms. The Coastal Lowlands region is the state's shoreline along the Atlantic Ocean. This area runs inland for 6 to 16 miles. The Connecticut Valley Lowland is a 20-mile-wide swath of land that runs along the Connecticut River, which roughly bisects the state from north to south. The eastern part of Connecticut is made up of the Eastern New England Upland. The state's lowest point—where Connecticut meets Long Island Sound—is found in this heavily forested area. The Western New England Upland, an area of rivers and hills, is found in the western portion of Connecticut.

Mt. Frissell (2,380 ft.), the highest point in Connecticut, is found in the Taconic section of Connecticut, as are the state's other high peaks, including Bear Mountain (2,355 ft.), Mt. Gridley (2,200 ft.), and Mt. Riga (2,000 ft.).

The Thimble Islands

One of the most notable features of the Connecticut coastline is a group of small islands known as the Thimbles. This archipelago of 365 tiny islands (the largest is 17 acres) near New Haven was probably named for the thimbleberry, a kind of blackberry that used to grow in the area. Some of the islands are privately owned and are occupied by one to four homes. The 12-acre Money Island is home to an entire village, including a post office. The island was named Money because of a legend claiming that privateer William "Captain" Kidd buried a treasure there in the 17th century. Today, the best way to see the islands is by taking one of the Thimble Islands cruises available in the area.

Plants and Animals

More than 60 percent of Connecticut's land is forested: trees that grow within its borders include ash, birch, and maple. The mountain laurel, an evergreen flowering shrub, is found throughout the state; in fact, it is the state flower.

ON THE TRAIL OF DINOSAURS

Two hundred million years ago, dinosaurs made their way across central Connecticut through the Connecticut Valley. As these beasts lumbered across the landscape, they left behind enormous tracks.

In 1966, during excavation for the construction of a new state building, nearly 2,000 of these dinosaur tracks from the late Triassic period were discovered in Rocky Point, near the center of the state. Two years later Dinosaur State Park was established to protect and exhibit these tracks. Paleontologists believe the fossil tracks—called *Eubrontes*, which means "true thunder"—were made by a large carnivore similar to Dilophosaurus. To protect the tracks from erosion, the park constructed a dome over them. Today, the park offers visitors the opportunity to see and learn about these tracks, and even to make a cast of a footprint to take home.

Visitors at Dinosaur State Park can get a close-up look at 200-million-year-old dinosaur tracks.

Connecticut's coast borders Long Island Sound, which stretches from New York City to the Rhode Island border.

White-tailed deer are the largest mammals in Connecticut. Some other animals that make their homes within the state include foxes, hares, rabbits, and muskrats. Common birds include orioles, sparrows, and warblers.

Lobsters, oysters, and clams are all found in the waters of Long Island Sound; inland waters are home to fish including trout and shad. Commercial fishing is important to the state's economy, but much of the fish and shellfish taken are farmed.

Climate and Weather

Connecticut's weather is generally temperate; extremes of either hot or cold are uncommon. January temperature averages around 26° F, while temperatures in July average around 71° F. Annual snowfall averages from 25 to 35 inches.

An aerial view of Stamford, Connecticut. In the 19th century the town was a favorite summer community for New Yorkers.

The Constitution State

The Dutch were the first to explore the area that is now Connecticut; however, they were driven out by the English in 1654. The first permanent settlements in the area were established by English colonists who came from Massachusetts in search of religious and political freedoms.

Subsistence farming was the chief occupation of these early colonists, but by the early 18th century, the seed of manufacturing was planted and began to take root. In the 1800s clock making, shipbuilding, and silversmithing were the most important industries, although agriculture was still a mainstay.

The Industrial and Invention Boom

Between 1850 and 1900 that began to change, as more and more of the population were being employed in industry. By the dawn of the 20th

Former President John Q. Adams defended the abducted African men in the case of the Amistad *(above). The trial took place in Connecticut.*

Fishing and whaling were important industries in 19th-century Connecticut. Mystic, shown above in 1879, was one center of the whaling industry. Although whaling reached its peak in the 1840s in Connecticut, it continued into the 20th century.

century, the state's economy was overwhelmingly based on manufacturing. Many inventors who were either born in Connecticut, or spent their formative years there, helped this shift take place. After graduating from Yale College, Eli Whitney invented the cotton gin, which forever changed the way cotton was harvested and processed. In 1797 he also developed the concept of mass production and interchangeable parts, which revolutionized the manufacturing of rifles. Samuel Colt of Hartford patented the first workable repeating pistol in 1836. Three years later New Haven's own Charles Goodyear discovered a way to strengthen (or vulcanize) rubber. These inventions and innovations not only helped develop the Connecticut economy, but they also helped drive the entire Industrial Revolution.

The 20th Century

Connecticut's industry gained strength through the 1920s, until the Great Depression. It was during this time that many in the state, which had been traditionally a Republican stronghold, began to change their allegiances to the Democratic Party.

As it did for many manufacturing states, World War II buoyed Connecticut's economy, as the state's factories supplied airplanes, airplane engines, and submarines to the war effort. In 1954 Connecticut produced the world's first nuclear-powered submarine, the *Nautilus*. Later, the state began to produce materials for space exploration, including reentry vehicles. In the 1980s Connecticut was the

---

THE GREAT COMPROMISE

Connecticut's long coastline and geographic location—across Long Island Sound from British-controlled Long Island—made it vulnerable to attack during the American Revolution. Despite the fact that Connecticut was unable to adequately defend itself, it was pressed to supply large forces to defend the Hudson River. This difficulty led Connecticut's delegates at the 1787 Constitutional Convention to support a strong national government (and therefore defense). The ensuing debate resulted in the "Great Compromise" (sometimes known as the "Connecticut Compromise"), which created our current system of representation in proportion to population in the House of Representatives and equal representation in the Senate. This compromise encouraged both large and small states to support the concept of a national government.

---

wealthiest state in the nation, due in large part to military contracts. During this time, up to 70 percent of the state's manufacturing income came from defense contracts. The end of the Cold War hurt the state's economy, but by the mid-1990s it was on the upswing.

Today, Connecticut is among the most industrialized states in the union. Aerospace, financial services, health and biochemical businesses, and tourism are among the most economically important industries in the Constitution State.

The world's first nuclear-powered submarine, the USS Nautilus, *was built at the Electric Boat Shipyard in Groton in 1952.*

An insurance and financial center, Hartford—Connecticut's capital—is also home to major high-tech manufacturing firms.

New York

The Empire State

Excelsior (Ever upward)

When one hears the name "New York," the image that may come to mind is of New York City. But New York State is so much more than its best-known city. New York has been the site of some of the most significant events in our nation's history.

Nearly a third of all the battles that were fought in the Revolutionary War took place in New York. In fact the Battle of Saratoga—deemed by many the turning point of the war—was fought on New York soil. The resulting surrender of 9,000 British troops led to the rebel alliance with France and the eventual American victory.

Some of the country's most notable men and women were born in New York, including four U.S. presidents—Martin Van Buren, Franklin D. Roosevelt, Theodore Roosevelt, and Millard Fillmore—polio researcher Jonas Salk, and First Lady and humanitarian Eleanor Roosevelt. And Ellis Island was the first stop for more than 20 million immigrants who came to America in the late 19th and early 20th century in search of a better life.

New York's contributions to the cultural life of the nation are undeniable. It is home to the Chautauqua Institution. Founded in 1874, this landmark organization provided women access to cultural and educational opportunities not available to them elsewhere. Today, it remains a center of cultural life in the state. The internationally renowned Glimmerglass Opera in Otsego County is well known for introducing and training new opera artists.

Of course, the prominence of New York City's thousands of cultural institutions—museums, libraries, theaters, concert and performance halls, and historical societies—can't be overstated. Some of the city's neighborhoods, including Harlem and Greenwich Village, have rich histories themselves that have affected the nation's cultural history.

Visitors to New York can be overwhelmed by the breadth of recreational opportunities it presents. In the north, the Adirondacks offer rock climbing, skiing, and hiking. Professional sports fans have many teams from which to choose: football's Buffalo Bills play here, as do the New York Mets and Yankees of Major League Baseball. Hockey fans can watch the Buffalo Sabres, the New York Islanders, or the New York Rangers. Aficionados of horse racing can enjoy their sport at Belmont (home of the Triple Crown's Belmont Stakes) or take in a race in high style at Saratoga. The Finger Lakes region of west-central New York offers vineyard tours and wine tastings. And the beaches of eastern Long Island are ripe for those who wish to do nothing more than relax. New York really does offer a little bit of something for everyone.

New York City was our nation's capital for a brief time. Today, the metropolis is known as the city that never sleeps.

New York State Facts

Full Name: New York
Meaning of Name: Named in honor of the Duke of York
Admitted to the Union: July 26, 1788 (11th state)
Inhabitant: New Yorker
Capital City: Albany

Flower: Rose
Tree: Sugar maple
Bird: Bluebird

Geography and Ecology

Most of New York State falls into one of two regions, the Adirondack Mountains and the Appalachian Highlands.

The Adirondack Mountains

These mountains are located in the northeastern part of New York and cover about a quarter of the state's area. This heavily forested area, crisscrossed with trails and dotted with lakes, is popular with outdoor enthusiasts.

More than 40 mountains in the Adirondacks are higher than 4,000 feet, including the state's highest peak, Mt. Marcy (5,344 ft.). Adirondack Park, a 6-million-acre wilderness area and parkland in the Adirondack Mountains, is larger than Yellowstone, Yosemite, Grand Canyon, Glacier, and Olympic national parks combined.

The Appalachian Highlands

This region stretches across the southern half of New York State from the Hudson River Valley to the Lake Erie basin and includes the Catskill Mountains and the Shawangunk Mountains. The Catskills are popular for outdoor activities such as skiing and hiking; the Shawangunks area is known around the world for the rock-climbing opportunities it offers. In 1994 The Nature Conservancy designated the area as one the world's "Last Great Places."

Lakes and Waterways

New York borders Lake Erie and Lake Ontario for a combined 300 miles. The St. Lawrence River forms part of the state's border with Canada. Lake Champlain straddles the state's northeastern border with Vermont.

The Finger Lakes, a group of 11 long, narrow lakes in west-central New York, were created by glacial activity during the Ice Age. The terrain of the region is rolling and fertile; wooded areas, dairy farms, and vineyards dot the landscape today.

The Hudson River is New York's largest river. Running from the Adirondacks to New York Bay for 306 miles, it even-

Niagara Falls is not only an important tourist destination in New York, but it also supplies thousands with electricity.

NIAGARA FALLS

Niagara Falls is one of the world's natural wonders. Located on the U.S.–Canadian border near Buffalo, the falls were first seen by a European in 1678, when French priest Father Louis Hennepin traveled in the area. In his book *A New Discovery*, Hennepin wrote that the falls were "a vast and prodigious Cadence of Water which falls down after a surprising and astonishing manner, insomuch that the Universe does not afford its Parallel." This description inspired further exploration of the area, and today millions visit the falls each year.

Two sets of waterfalls—Horseshoe Falls (which lie in Canada) and the American Falls—make up Niagara Falls. There, the Niagara River flows over the falls and into a 200-foot-deep, 7-mile-long gorge below at an average rate of 100,000 cubic feet of water per second.

Since the discovery of the falls by Hennepin in 1678, the rock ledge below the falls has eroded roughly 1/4 mile. Today, the falls erode at a rate of about 1 foot per year.

tually feeds into the Atlantic Ocean. The river was an important waterway during the Revolutionary War, and after the completion of the Erie Canal it became a vital connection between the Port of New York and the Great Lakes. New York City lies at the mouth of the Hudson, which helped make it a popular starting place for newly arriving immigrants.

Climate

New York's climate and weather vary widely from region to region. Generally, winters are cold and summers are warm and humid. January average temperatures range from New York City's 32° F to 22° F in Albany. July averages range from 77° F in New York City to 72° F in Albany.

With more than 3,000 lakes, 30,000 miles of rivers and streams, and the largest system of hiking trails in the nation, Adirondack Park is a true New York treasure.

The Empire State

European settlement of the area that is now New York began when the Dutch East India Company established its first permanent trade settlement in Albany in 1624 (although the area had been explored earlier). Two years later New Amsterdam was founded when Peter Minuit allegedly purchased Manhattan Island from the local Indians for the equivalent of $24.

The following decades saw disputes over the land among the Dutch, the English, the French, and the local Indian populations. It was not until 1763, at the close of the French and Indian War, that all lands east of the Mississippi (including New York) were ceded to the British. The British immediately sought to tighten control over the colonies, which bristled under regulations such as the Sugar and Stamp acts. In 1774, when news of the Boston Tea Party reached New York, colonists there also dumped tea.

The Revolution

Nearly a third of all Revolutionary War battles were fought in New York. The first took place when Ethan Allen and his Green Mountain Boys captured Fort Ticonderoga in May 1775. The Battle of Saratoga, considered by many to be the war's turning point because it encouraged the French to enter the war in aid of the colonies, took place two years later. After the war George Washington bid farewell to his troops from lower Manhattan, at Fraunces Tavern, which still stands today. In July 1788 New York became the 11th state.

Railroads provided rapid economic growth in the decade prior to 1857, when this map was produced. However, the economy soon became turbulent when, on August 24, 1857, the New York branch of the Ohio Life Insurance and Trust Company failed, setting off a panic and deepening a national recession that lasted until the Civil War.

Fort Ticonderoga was built in 1755 by the French to prevent the British from gaining control of Lake Champlain from the east.

On December 4, 1783, after the Revolution, George Washington bade farewell to his troops at Fraunces Tavern in Manhattan.

Early Statehood

For five years, from 1785 to 1790, New York served as the American capital city. Lands in western New York were opened to settlement, and by 1820 the state was the most populous in the new country. A confluence of events and inventions in the early 1800s led to a boom of industry and commerce in the state: the first was the introduction of the first successful commercial steamship by Robert Fulton in 1807. This advance increased the speed and efficiency of transporting goods. The opening of the Erie Canal in 1825 caused an explosion of growth in the state and the entire country, opening western New York and the Great Lakes to commerce and travel.

Even in its earliest days, New York was a progressive cultural center; by the 1840s the city was known as a mecca of theater and literature. And before the Civil War broke out, New York had already long supported the antislavery movement. Adding to its progressive résumé, the state hosted the nation's first women's rights gathering in 1848.

The Civil War

The Civil War brought both turmoil and growth to New York. The largest civil insurrection in the nation's history occurred in New York City. Draft riots broke out, primarily

Franklin Roosevelt

due to a provision in the conscription law that allowed men to buy their way out of the draft for $300.

But the war also fueled prosperity in the state, as the manufacture of war supplies boosted the economy. The economy continued to grow after the war. Banking, commerce, and transportation all became important elements in New York's fiscal well-being.

Economic Ups and Downs

Two world wars helped further stimulate New York's economy. The years after World War II saw New York grow in peacetime. The United Nations established its headquarters in New York City in 1952. And the opening of the St. Lawrence Seaway in 1959 helped boost the economy of northern New York.

The 1970s were a difficult period for New York State, and New York City in particular. The manufacturing sector shrank, eliminating many jobs. New York City faced bankruptcy, with no bailout forthcoming from the federal government. In fact, when President Gerald Ford promised to veto any bill granting financial assistance to the Big Apple, it prompted the famous headline, "Ford to City: Drop Dead." However, the late 20th century brought a renewed prosperity to New York, which today boasts the largest economy in the country, with the exception of California's.

Terrorist Attacks

Perhaps the most notable event to occur in New York since its founding was the physical and emotional devastation wrought by the terrorist attacks of September 11, 2001. On that day, two commercial airlines piloted by al-Qaeda hijackers flew into the North and South Towers of the World Trade Center, destroying both buildings and killing 3,000 people. The event deeply scarred the city, and indeed the entire nation. But today the state remains unbowed. New construction of One World Trade Center was completed in 2014, and New York is still successfully moving forward.

> *"New York is to the nation what the white spire is to the village— the visible symbol of aspiration and faith, the white plume saying the way is up!"*
>
> —E. B. White

CENTRAL PARK

An 843-acre oasis in the center of Manhattan, Central Park is visited by 25 million people each year, making it the most visited city park in the United States. But its sweeping lawns, wooded trails, and peaceful ponds are not part of the site's original landscape—in fact, the entire park is manmade.

In the early 1800s New York City was home to 60,000 people. Most of them lived in lower Manhattan. Immigrants began pouring into the city in the 1830s, and by the 1850s the population swelled to more than half a million. Still, most people lived below 38th Street, in cramped, noisy conditions. To escape the noise and crowds, some residents began visiting the only peaceful green spaces close by: local cemeteries.

Public figures began calling for the creation of a large public park to which residents could escape the frenzied pace of the city; and beginning in 1853 the city purchased lands bound by 59th and 106th streets on the north and south, and Fifth and Eighth avenues on the east and west. The contract to design the park was awarded to Frederick Law Olmstead and Calvert Vaux.

The land purchased for the park was not ideally suited to use as a park; the soil was poor and the landscape rocky, muddy, and wet. By the park's grand opening in 1873, 500,000 cubic feet of topsoil had been carted in from neighboring New Jersey. Boulders were blasted out, and plants were brought in. According to the Central Park Conservancy, they included 4 million trees, shrubs, and plants. Other structures, including 36 bridges and archways, as well as four man-made ponds, were added to the park. Today it all seems a natural part of the landscape.

Central Park offers locals and tourists alike a place to play softball or soccer, have a picnic, or enjoy bird-watching. The park hosts concerts and protests, weddings, and marathons. Like New York City, it is a bit of a melting pot, but always a green and peaceful spot in the middle of this bustling city.

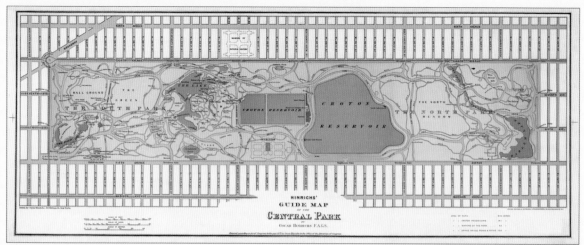

This 1875 map of Central Park shows the original Croton Distributing Reservoir used with the first aqueduct system that supplied the city with drinking water during the 19th century. The man-made lake was 4 acres in area, surrounded by 25-foot thick granite walls.

The Empire State Building was completed in 1931 and was the world's highest structure until 1954.

THE ERIE CANAL

At the beginning of the 1800s, the Appalachian Mountains marked the country's western frontier. But travel beyond—and sometimes to—that frontier was difficult. The terrain was covered by mountains, forest, swamp, and deep underbrush. Opening the Northwest Territory (the lands that would become Illinois, Indiana, Michigan, and Ohio) to settlement and commerce was an expensive proposition that could slow the growth of the new nation.

A canal that would connect Lake Erie to the Hudson River (and therefore New York City and the Atlantic Ocean) was not a new idea. But until 1817 it was thought to be impossible. Enter DeWitt Clinton, former mayor of New York City and newly minted governor of the state. Clinton knew that such a canal would mean great things for his state and campaigned hard for the idea. After years of political wrangling, ground was broken for the project on July 4, 1817, and construction began simultaneously on the eastern and western ends.

Construction and digging of the 363-mile canal—which was performed largely by manual labor of men and horses—continued for eight years. During that time it was often referred to as "Clinton's Folly" and "Clinton's Ditch" by a wary press and public. Clinton was voted out of office in 1822 and even removed from the Canal Board by his political enemies.

But when the canal was completed in 1825 (and Clinton was reelected governor in time to preside over its opening ceremonies), its impact was nearly instantaneous and undeniable. Settlers poured into the newly accessible west. Freight rates between New York and Buffalo dropped dramatically, from $100 per ton by overland transport to $10 per ton via the canal. Movement of goods exploded: in 1829,.3,640 bushels of wheat were carried to New York City from Buffalo; by 1833 that number skyrocketed to 1 million bushels. And in less than a decade, the canal paid for itself with the tolls collected, and New York City became the nation's busiest port. "Clinton's Folly" became the "eighth wonder of the world."

Today, the canal is used primarily for recreation by paddlers, and by bikers and hikers, who enjoy the paths on either side of the waterway, but its legacy as the key to westward expansion lives on.

Locks on the Erie Canal allowed barges to move over different elevations.

New Jersey

Liberty and Prosperity

New Jersey is a state of contrasts: not only is it a center of heavy industries like petroleum refining, it's also known for its miles of beaches. New Jersey is a leading producer of fresh fruits and vegetables—and of chemicals. More than 42 percent of the state is forested, and yet it is the most densely populated and one of the most urbanized states in the United States. New Jersey is known for its casinos in Atlantic City, but it also has Princeton University and Revolutionary War history.

Northern New Jersey in particular is strongly affected by its proximity to New York City. Two of New York's professional football teams—the Jets and the Giants—play in New Jersey. Thousands of New Jerseyans commute by train daily into New York for work, and two iconic landmarks strongly associated with New York—the Statue of Liberty and Ellis Island—are technically within New Jersey.

Newark is the state's largest city and the third-oldest major metropolitan area in the United States; only New York and Boston are older. The city struggled through the last several decades as a result of urban renewal and the loss of manufacturing jobs. Racial tensions erupted in 1967 when rioting broke out after the arrest of a black cab driver. But today the city is experiencing a renaissance with a $180 million performing arts center, and new housing, office, and retail development in progress.

Jersey City, the state's second largest city, and one of the oldest settlements in the U.S., is known for its diverse population; it is home to residents of (among others) African, Arab, Dominican, Filipino, Jewish, and Puerto Rican descent. It is also a major seaport and transportation center.

Trenton, New Jersey's capital, was the site of an important Revolutionary War victory for Washington's army; it was also considered as a permanent site for the United States capital after the war. Today, Trenton is a center of manufacturing (electrical goods and fabricated metal products), printing, publishing, and health care.

Besides its importance during the Revolution, New Jersey served as a home base for several renowned inventors. Thomas Edison, although born in Ohio, moved to New Jersey in 1870. In 1876 he built a research lab in Menlo Park, from which he gave the world the phonograph and electric light.

It's no secret that the Garden State has been the brunt of jokes throughout the years; yet its history and present bode well for its future.

Sandy Hook Lighthouse in New Jersey is the oldest operating lighthouse in the United States.

New Jersey State Facts

Full Name: State of New Jersey
Meaning of Name: From the English Channel isle of Jersey
Admitted to the Union: December 18, 1787 (3rd state)
Inhabitant: New Jerseyan
Capital City: Trenton

Flower: Purple violet
Tree: Red oak
Bird: Eastern goldfinch

Geography and Ecology

Despite the state's small size, New Jersey's landscape is quite varied. The far northwestern part of the state is composed of the mountainous area called the Appalachian Valley and the Kittatinny Ridge and Valley. This area is home to the state's highest peak, High Point (1,803 ft.). This area is also the site of the Delaware Water Gap, a scenic area where the Delaware River slices through the surrounding mountains. It is a favorite destination for canoeing, tubing, hiking, and fishing.

Southeast of the Appalachian Valley is the Highlands region, notable for its many steep, ragged ridges and lakes. The Ramapo Mountains, which are part of the Appalachian Mountains, run through the region.

The Piedmont is a flat region in northern New Jersey. Its expanse is broken by the low ridges of the Watchung and Sourland mountains and of the Palisades—steep cliffs of dark, fine-grained igneous rock that rise 500 feet above the Hudson River.

Pine Barrens

The Atlantic Coastal Plain is an area of sand beaches and swamps in the southern portion of New Jersey. The most interesting feature of the plain is perhaps the Pine Barrens. This wilderness area on New Jersey's southern coast is notable for its swamps, bogs, and expansive stands of pine trees, including the rare pygmy pitch pine. The area, which covers nearly 1,000 square miles, takes its name from the soil there, which European settlers found to be poorly suited to farming.

Rivers, Lakes, and Ocean

The Raritan River is the longest river entirely within the state of New Jersey. In addition to its popularity for recreational activities, the river is also an important source of drinking water for the central part of the state. The Hudson and Delaware rivers are also important in the

Although it is close to major population centers, New Jersey's Pine Barrens is almost completely undeveloped.

state; the former forms the border between New York and New Jersey near its southern end, and the latter forms the border between Pennsylvania and New Jersey. Most of New Jersey's 800-plus lakes and ponds are found in the northern part of the state. Lake Hopatcong is the largest and is popular for boating and fishing.

New Jersey's coastline is perhaps the state's best-known recreational area. The 130-mile ocean-facing shore features sandy beaches and resort towns with boardwalks, arcades, and amusements. The shore has been a popular vacation destination since 1801, when the town of Cape May started advertising itself as a resort area.

Climate

New Jersey has humid and warm to hot summers and cold winters. Along the coast, temperatures are moderated by ocean breezes year-round. Average temperatures in July range from 70° F to 76° F. In January temperatures range from 26° F to 34° F. The state receives from 13 to 50 inches of snow each year, depending on location.

"Although New Jersey, ever since her admission into the Union, has been the butt for the sarcasm and wit of those who live outside her borders, the gallant little state has much to be proud of."

—William Cullen Bryant, *Picturesque America*, 1874

The Garden State

The Lenape, or Delaware, Indians inhabited the area that is now New Jersey for at least 10,000 years before Europeans arrived on the scene. Giovanni da Verrazano was the first European to visit the area, around 1524. Later, Henry Hudson, an English captain working for the Dutch, claimed the land for the Netherlands, which established small trading settlements where today Hoboken and Jersey City are located. In 1660 Bergen—the first permanent European settlement—was established.

TURNING POINT OF THE REVOLUTION

Emmanuel Leutze's 1850 painting, Washington Crossing the Delaware.

Late 1776 saw the British gaining control of New Jersey and forcing General George Washington and his troops to retreat to the forests of Pennsylvania. Confident that fighting would be unlikely until the spring thaw, Colonel Johann Rall and his three Hessian regiments dug in, settling into three camps to wait out the winter. Rall and his regiments did not chase Washington across the Delaware, nor did they patrol its shores, because large blocks of unstable ice made the crossing treacherous and would surely deter Washington and his troops.

But in December, Washington and his men did make their way back across the Delaware and into New Jersey. Washington split his troops into two groups and surprised the Hessians from the west and the north, capturing 900 prisoners. Only four American soldiers were wounded in the attack.

Many experts consider this, the Battle of Trenton, the turning point of the war. Immediately after Trenton, Washington took Princeton, and the routed British fled into New York. The colonies were on their way to victory.

British Rule and the Revolution

In 1664 the British took control of New Netherland, as it was then called, from the Dutch. It was then that the land was officially called New Jersey, for the Isle of Jersey in the English Channel.

In 1776 New Jersey joined the colonial side in the War for Independence. Its location—between New York and Philadelphia—gave New Jersey grave importance during the war. Countless battles and skirmishes on its soil later earned New Jersey the moniker, "Crossroads of the American Revolution."

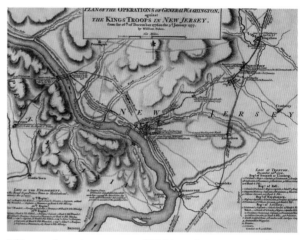

This map shows the movement of Washington's troops against the British during late 1776 into early 1777—a crucial time during the war.

The 1800s

New Jersey grew rapidly during the 1800s. Factories were centered in the northern part of the state. They produced silk, clay products, iron, and steel. The Industrial Revolution of the late 1800s spurred continued growth. Immigrants came from Ireland, Germany, and then Italy in search of jobs. By 1910 half of New Jersey's population was either born or had parents who were born outside the United States.

The 1900s and Beyond

Growth continued in New Jersey until the Great Depression caused massive unemployment. World War II helped the state's economy rebound; after the war, the economy continued to recover as factories turned to the production of electronics and chemicals—two products that remain important to the state's economy.

Newark, New Jersey, in 1916, the date this map was published, was a bustling city. Insurance, as well as the manufacture of leather, iron, celluloid, and electric lamps helped the city grow and thrive.

During the 1960s some of New Jersey's urban areas confronted the problem of spreading slums. Racial tensions mounted as rioting broke out in black neighborhoods of many cities. Newark experienced the worst of the rioting in July 1967, as 26 were killed and damage exceeded $10 million.

In its continued search for new sources of revenue, the New Jersey legislature adopted a personal income tax in 1976. Also that year, voters in the state approved legalized gambling, paving the way for the opening of Atlantic City casinos. Just three decades later, however, Atlantic City began a rapid decline as neighboring states jumped on the bandwagon and newer gambling facilities drew business away. The future of the "East Coast Las Vegas" may be uncertain, but if there's one thing New Jersey is known for, it's always coming out ahead.

The approval of legalized gambling in the state, in 1976, opened the door to the growth of Atlantic City as a gaming center.

Pennsylvania

The Keystone State

Virtue, Liberty, and Independence

Pennsylvania has seen more history than most states: the nation's first statute outlawing slavery was enacted there in 1780. Both the Declaration of Independence and the United States Constitution were written and signed in Philadelphia. Troops from the state participated in nearly every battle of the Revolution. And the Battle of Gettysburg—the turning point of the Civil War—was fought here. So many of the crucial events in the birth of our nation occurred in Pennsylvania, it's no wonder that its nickname is the Keystone State.

Philadelphia, the state's largest city, witnessed a large portion of those historic events. It was the site of the nation's first public hospital, law school, newspaper, public bank, public library, and volunteer fire department. Benjamin Franklin—the country's greatest statesman—lived and worked there, inventing the Franklin stove and lightning rod and conducting experiments proving that lightning is an electrical current. Philadelphia was also the nation's capital for a decade, beginning in 1790.

Today, Philadelphia remains a vital metropolis in Pennsylvania. It is not only the state's leading manufacturing city, but also a center of culture and education. Pittsburgh, in western Pennsylvania, is the state's second-largest city. For nearly 150 years, it was driven by steel production, but during the 1970s the industry collapsed as cheap steel imports poured in from overseas. Over the next two decades, the mills and the belching smokestacks that once pierced the sky were torn down. Thousands lost jobs. But Pittsburgh's economy showed its resilience by diversifying, and today the city is a center of health care, education, and technology.

Tourists who visit Pennsylvania can enjoy any number of options, ranging from the cultural to the outdoorsy. Fallingwater—one of Frank Lloyd Wright's crowning works—is the only Wright home with its original setting and furnishings intact. The Delaware River, which forms the state's eastern border with New Jersey, was the site of Washington's famous crossing during the Revolutionary War. Today, it's popular with aficionados of boating, fishing, and swimming. Hershey, a town that bills itself as the Sweetest Place on Earth, is famous for its amusement park, and for being home to the world's largest chocolate factory. All of which goes to show that even fun in Pennsylvania can be packed with history.

The Liberty Bell in Philadelphia was rung to signal the first public reading of the Declaration of Independence.

Pennsylvania State Facts

Full Name: Commonwealth of Pennsylvania
Meaning of Name: Literally, "Penn's Woodland." The state was named for the father of the state's founder, William Penn.
Admitted to the Union: December 12, 1787 (2nd state)

Inhabitant: Pennsylvanian
Capital City: Harrisburg
Flower: Mountain laurel
Tree: Hemlock
Bird: Ruffed grouse

Geography and Ecology

Pennsylvania's topography varies widely from region to region—from rolling hillsides and deep, narrow valleys to rocky ridges and mountains. But the landscape is largely defined by several mountain ranges that run through the state. They include the Allegheny, the Appalachian, and the Pocono mountains.

The 500-mile Allegheny Mountain range runs from north-central to southwestern Pennsylvania and is part of the Appalachian Mountain chain.

The Poconos, in the northeast, have been a popular resort destination since the mid 1800s. During World War II many GIs took their wives or girlfriends to the area before they shipped off; it was then that the area became known as the Honeymoon Capital of the World. Today, the Poconos are popular year-round, offering skiing in the winter and attractions like water parks and golfing in summer.

Spectacular Waterfalls

In eastern Pennsylvania, especially the Pocono region, are found some of the most impressive waterfalls in the country. The Delaware Water Gap National Recreation Area is home to Bushkill Falls, formed where Bushkill Creek flows over a 100-foot cliff to the Delaware River below, and Raymondskill Falls, the highest in the state at 105 feet. Both falls are popular with visitors and are accessible by hiking paths.

Caves and Caverns

Pennsylvania is home to eight commercial, or "show" caves open to the public. These caves give visitors an opportunity to safely explore areas that are normally open only to those who have been trained in spelunking. At Penn's Cave, in central Pennsylvania, visitors tour a limestone cavern via boat to see stalactites, stalagmites, pillars, and columns.

Climate

Pennsylvania's climate is one of cold winters and warm, humid summers. Northern and western areas are generally colder than elsewhere in the state. Average January temperatures range from 26° F to 34° F. Average July temperatures range from 70° F to 77° F. Annual snowfall in Pennsylvania averages 20 inches in the southeastern part of the state to approximately 90 inches in the northwest.

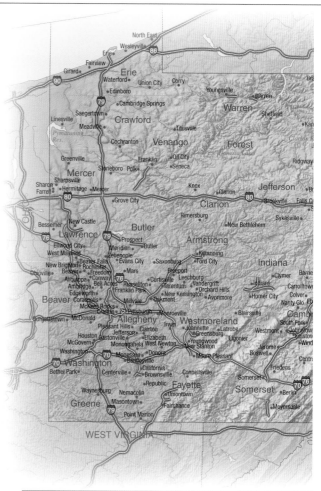

MINING IN PENNSYLVANIA

Mining has been an important industry in Pennsylvania since the mid-18th century. Coal from Pennsylvania fueled America's Industrial Revolution and made possible Allied victory in World War II. It has powered steel mills and power plants and heated homes for hundreds of years.

Pennsylvania is the fourth-largest coal-mining state in the nation, running behind Wyoming, West Virginia, and Kentucky. Two types of coal are mined in the state: bituminous, or soft, coal, which is used to generate electricity; and anthracite, or hard, coal, which is used for commercial and residential heating.

Bituminous coal is found in large portions of western Pennsylvania. Anthracite coal is mined in eastern Pennsylvania; in fact, almost all the nation's hard coal comes from that area.

Mining is routinely recognized as one of the most dangerous industries in which to work. Hazards include roof collapses and gas explosions; however, technological advances have made the work substantially safer than in centuries past.

The hills around the Delaware Water Gap in eastern Pennsylvania have many waterfalls.

The Delaware River, which forms the border between Pennsylvania and New Jersey, is a major recreation area.

The Keystone State

Before Europeans arrived in the area that is now Pennsylvania, the region was inhabited by Algonquian and Iroquoian Indians. The first permanent settlement in the area was established by the Swedes around 1643. A dozen years later the area was captured by the Dutch; in 1664 it was again captured by the English. The land changed hands several times over the next hundred years until the Treaty of Paris, in 1763, ended the French and Indian War and the land was ceded to the British.

The First Continental Congress

In the mid-18th century, Britain began imposing new restrictive regulations and new taxes on the colonies. Pennsylvanians were especially incensed by some of these developments. The Proclamation of 1763 prevented settlement beyond the Alleghenies. Western Pennsylvanians felt this was an attempt to keep the colonies hemmed in along the eastern seaboard and therefore easier to regulate. The Stamp Act, the Townshend Acts, and the Tea Acts—all of which placed taxes on imports—infuriated Philadelphians and Bostonians. In response, colonial leaders met in Philadelphia on September 5, 1774, to discuss their options. The outcome of this First Continental Congress was a cessation of trade with Britain.

Revolution and Statehood

One month after the Revolutionary War began in April 1775, the Second Continental Congress met in Philadelphia and voted to declare independence from Britain. In July 1776 the final draft of the Declaration of Independence was adopted in the Pennsylvania State House, now known as Independence Hall.

This view of Pittsburgh, with the Monongahela River in the foreground, was published in 1874. The Industrial Revolution was in full swing then, and Pittsburgh was one of the nation's chief industrial cities.

This modest building was George Washington's headquarters at Valley Forge during the winter of 1777.

The Declaration of Independence and the Constitution were both adopted at Independence Hall in Philadelphia.

After the war the Constitutional Convention met in Philadelphia in 1787 to approve the United States Constitution. Pennsylvania was the second colony to do so, becoming the fledgling nation's second state.

Pennsylvania's great coal stores made its economy strong from the state's birth. After the war, the state became the center of industry in the new nation.

In the years leading to the Civil War, coal fueled the state's iron industry. In 1859 the nation's first successful oil well was drilled in the northeastern part of the state. And by 1860 Pennsylvania was a leading producer of textiles, leather, iron, and glass.

Civil War and Growth

During the Civil War only New York sent more troops into battle for the Union cause than Pennsylvania. The three-day Battle of Gettysburg was a turning point in the war. General George Meade's men—a third of whom were from Pennsylvania—defeated the Confederate forces. The defeat sent General Robert E. Lee retreating to Virginia. President Lincoln's short speech at Gettysburg is one of the most eloquent and well-known addresses in history.

After the Civil War, Pennsylvania's economy diversified, although mining remained vital. In fact, during the

Benjamin Franklin may be Pennsylvania's best-known citizen. He moved to the state at age 17 from Boston and became the nation's foremost statesman.

final decade of the 19th century, Pennsylvania was the young nation's leading producer of coal, iron, and steel.

Organized Labor

The Wall Street crash of 1929 and the Great Depression that followed had devastating effects across the entire country, and Pennsylvania was no exception. In fact, many of the state's key industries, such as mining and lumber, were hit particularly hard, and thousands lost their jobs. But it was also during this time that organized labor unions emerged, empowering workers in the coal and steel industries to fight for fairer wages and working conditions.

As it had in other parts of the country, World War II helped trigger a recovery in Pennsylvania. Factories in the state came alive, producing all manner of war materials such as cement, clothing, ships, steel, and weapons. Along with the strong effort at home, the Keystone State also sacrificed thousands to the battlefields overseas.

The mid- to late-20th century was a difficult period for Pennsylvania. The steel industry all but collapsed as cheaper imports and lighter materials gained in popularity with manufacturers. Demand for coal decreased as well, throwing many miners out of work. Textile workers were hard hit as well, as jobs went to the South, where labor was less expensive and mills more modern. As if these developments weren't bad enough, Pennsylvania would face a near catastrophe in the late 1970s.

Three Mile Island

Dauphin Country, near Pennsylvania's capital of Harrisburg, was the scene of the most serious nuclear power accident in the nation's history. On March 28, 1979, one of the two nuclear reactors at the Three Mile Island experienced a partial meltdown when pumps supplying water to the reactor failed. As one account described it, the reactor was like "an automobile with a hole in its radiator." It overheated, leading to a partial meltdown of its core. This could have led to dangerous amounts of radioactive materials being released into the atmosphere, but in fact no immediate deaths or injuries were attributed to the accident.

After the accident at Three Mile Island, polls indicated that public support for nuclear power—around 70 percent in favor before the accident—fell to 50 percent, where it remained for decades. No-Nukes protests and concerts abounded, helping to fuel anti-nuclear-power sentiment. It was not until early in the new century that public sentiment about nuclear-powered energy began to turn more positive.

Recovery

Although the outlook for this historic state seemed bleak, the 1990s brought renewed growth and vitality to Pennsylvania. The economy rebounded as it began to achieve a balance between manufacturing and service industries such as education, finance, pharmaceuticals, and health care. A state program was instituted that would help manufacturing companies to retrain workers. And a renewed interest in the state's history led to the restoration of many historic sites, which in turn helped

Harrisburg has been the capital of Pennsylvania since 1812. Today, it is the fourth-largest city in the state.

to develop Pennsylvania's tourism industry. By the year 2000, the state's once-ailing economy had made a complete turnaround, being described by one newspaper as "relentlessly strong."

COMMONWEALTH OR STATE?

Pennsylvania is one of the four U.S. states (the others being Kentucky, Massachusetts, and Virginia) that designates itself as a "commonwealth." There is no legal difference in the United States between a commonwealth and a state. The word "commonwealth" simply emphasizes that the government is based on the "common consent of the people" rather than by an edict imposed by one person such as a king.

THE PLAIN PEOPLE

For many tourists, a trip to Pennsylvania includes a visit to the so-called Pennsylvania Dutch country. That's an area in the southeastern part of the state where some Mennonite and Amish groups (among others) make their homes. One theory is that the term "Dutch" came about because many of the people are of German descent, and the word *Deutsch* was mispronounced as *Dutch*.

These devout groups live in communities separated from the rest of society and shun most modern conveniences. Most live without electricity or electrical appliances, automobiles, and telephones. Farming is the most common occupation among the Plain People—a name given to them because of the plain clothing they wear. Men usually wear dark suits with no lapels, collars, or pockets. Pants are worn with suspenders; they have neither creases nor cuffs. Amish women wear dresses made of a solid fabric. The skirts are full and long, and the women wear no jewelry.

It's not unusual to see a family traveling local roads in a horse-drawn buggy in parts of Pennsylvania, yet it's important to remember that these people are not tourist attractions; rather, the Amish and Mennonite wish only to live their lives in peace.

THE JOHNSTOWN FLOOD

The final days of May 1889 had been rainy all over western Pennsylvania. A storm moving in from the Plains had dumped 6 to 10 inches over the area. The residents of Johnstown, a coal-and-steel town of 30,000, were accustomed to the minor flooding that sometimes accompanied heavy rains; after all, the town was built in a river valley. And so when May 31 broke heavy and wet and a few inches of water flowed in the streets, they did what they had always done when the Little Conemaugh or the Stony Creek rivers overflowed their banks: moved furniture and stowed belongings on higher shelves, away from harm.

But the minor street flooding that morning was only a presage of the devastation to come. Fourteen miles upstream on the Little Conemaugh River, an overtaxed and under maintained earthen dam was about to give way.

The dam, which held back the waters of Lake Conemaugh, had originally been built nearly 40 years earlier by the state. But the earthen structure had changed hands several times, ending up the property of the South Fork Hunting and Fishing Club—a private lodge with an elite membership that included the likes of Andrew Carnegie, Henry Clay Frick, and Andrew Mellon. Over the years, repairs to the dam had been made in haste, and with inadequate materials like straw and mud.

At 11:30 that Tuesday an engineer employed by the club, fearing that the dam would fail, attempted to send a message to the valley towns below via telegraph, but it was too late. At 3:10 p.m. the dam burst, sending 20 million tons of water down the winding valley. By 4:07 people in Johnstown heard a thunderous roar. A 60-foot wall of water moving 40 miles an hour slammed into the town, carrying with it 14 miles of debris: trees, houses, animals, and barbed wire from the villages farther up the valley. Witnesses described the torrent breaking off "trees like pipe stems" and crushing houses as though they were "eggshells."

By the time it was over, 2,209 people were dead; entire blocks had been razed, and damage totaled more than $17 million ($450 million in 2015 dollars). During the following days and months, relief poured in from every state and several foreign countries as tent cities were constructed for the victims. Led by Clara Barton, The American Red Cross, in its very first peacetime relief effort, came to the aid of the town, organizing thousands of volunteers and helping hundreds of residents.

Five years later Johnstown had mostly recovered. Despite evidence that the private club was at least partially responsible for the poor upkeep of the dam, the flood was deemed an "act of God," and no monetary compensation was awarded to the victims. However, members of the club did donate to relief efforts.

Today, the Johnstown Flood Museum honors the victims of the disaster and offers visitors an opportunity to see contemporary accounts as well as artifacts and exhibits of the flood.

This historic photo from 1889 shows damage to the John Schultz House after the Johnstown Flood. Six people were in the house as it was carried through the streets by the water. Incredibly, all six people survived, but not everyone in the area was as fortunate. More than 2,200 people lost their lives. In only minutes, the town was almost completely wiped out.

Delaware

The First State

DECEMBER 7, 1787

Liberty and Independence

Comprising only three counties—the lowest number of any state—Delaware is the second-smallest state in the nation, but is one of the most densely populated and one of the wealthiest. Sandwiched between the Delaware Bay and the Atlantic Ocean on the east and Maryland on the west, Delaware has benefited economically and culturally from its coastal location and proximity to several major cities. Wilmington, Delaware's largest city, lies within commuting distance of both Philadelphia and Baltimore, and the state's sports fans are divided between the teams of those two cities, lacking professional teams in-state.

Although Delaware cannot boast of any national monuments, parks, or battlefields, it can claim several National Historic Landmarks, including the house of John Dickinson (the "Penman of the Revolution") and Holy Trinity (Old Swedes) Church, the last remnant of the early-17th-century Swedish colony. It also contains the longest twin span suspension bridge in the world. The Delaware Memorial Bridge crosses the Delaware River, connecting Delaware and New Jersey, and measures 10,765 feet across its eastbound span and 10,796 feet across its westbound span. On the Delaware side is a memorial honoring soldiers of both states who found in World War II, the Korean War, the Vietnam War, and the Gulf War.

Currently, the state's population continues to rapidly grow, particularly along the coast and in the capital city of Dover. This may be due in part to Delaware's reputation for a business-friendly legal system and infrastructure; banking, chemical, and pharmaceutical companies are all very active in the state. It is not for this economic reason, however, that Delaware is sometimes called the "Diamond State." It was allegedly given that particular nickname by Thomas Jefferson, who thought of Delaware as a "jewel" because of its strategic location along the eastern coastline.

Uniquely, in addition to a state flower, tree, and other usual state symbols, Delaware claims a state star. Located in the Ursa Major constellation, the "Delaware Diamond" is registered on the International Star Registry. Also unusual is its centralized governmental structure; perhaps due to its small size, the state has a surprisingly simple hierarchy, with most power resting with the state government. In 2000 Delaware elected its first female governor, Ruth Ann Minner (Democrat), who served two terms, ending in 2009. In many ways still a border state, Delaware tends to vote Democratic, but only by slim margins. A little state with a lot of history, Delaware has something for everyone; simply put, a jewel indeed.

The Brandywine River, once harnassed for water power in numerous mills, is now a tourist attraction for its gentle beauty.

Delaware State Facts

Full Name: State of Delaware
Meaning of Name: From Thomas West, 3rd Baron De La Warr
Admitted to the Union: December 7, 1787 (1st state)
Inhabitant: Delawarean

Capital City: Dover
Flower: Peach blossom
Tree: American holly
Bird: Blue hen chicken

Geography and Ecology

Delaware is longer than it is wide, at its narrowest point measuring only 9 miles from east to west. Nevertheless, it hosts a surprisingly varied ecology along its 96-mile length, transitioning from a southern, humid subtropical climate to a cooler northern one, more akin to a continental climate. The southernmost county, Sussex, benefits from a long growing season and mild winters, and even possesses a lonely stand of bald cypress trees—a sight far more typical of the Deep South. New Castle County, at the northern tip of the state, receives colder winters and accordingly more snow, although it is still beset by hot, humid summers. The entire state is uniformly flat, and its climate moderated by the Atlantic Ocean.

River Rights

The Delaware River has, from the very first, been a focus of development. Soon after European settlement, control of the river's port became a point of contention, a history whose effects are still felt today. The state's northern border is defined as an arc extending 12 miles from the cupola of New Castle's courthouse. This definition left a small portion of land just to the west of the arc under debate, and not until 1921 was it decided in Delaware's favor. A more recognizable geographic divide—this one with ramifications for the whole country—was the creation of the Mason-Dixon Line.

The largest freshwater pond in the state, Lums Pond is the centerpiece of the 1,790-acre Lums Pond State Park.

Borders and Boundaries

Although never officially part of Pennsylvania, the three counties of what would become Delaware were held by lease by William Penn, who was aware of the river's significance in Philadelphia's development. The boundaries were disputed by Maryland, however, and not until the eve of the Revolution was the matter settled. All parties agreed to submit to the work of a surveyor, Jeremiah Dixon, and an astronomer, Charles Mason. These two Britons tarried for 4 years to establish the boundaries of Pennsylvania, Maryland, and Delaware. In later years the line was used to delineate free and slave states, and is still today taken as a cultural divide between the North and South.

Peculiarities in Delaware's boundaries also beset the southern boundary, the so-called Transpeninsular Line. Early inaccuracies in maps and competing bids for land among European families left the issue confused until 1751, when an east-west line was drawn across the Delmarva Peninsula. The line later served as the southern end-point of the only north-south portion of the Mason-Dixon line (the Tangent). The political demarcation has resulted in some curiosities on the border, including the town of Delmar. Split between Delaware and Maryland, the town operates a single government and services, but requires two postal codes and tax systems. It has adopted the motto, "The Little Town Too Big for One State."

Traps Pond in southern Delaware may be home to the northernmost strand of bald cypress tress in the United States.

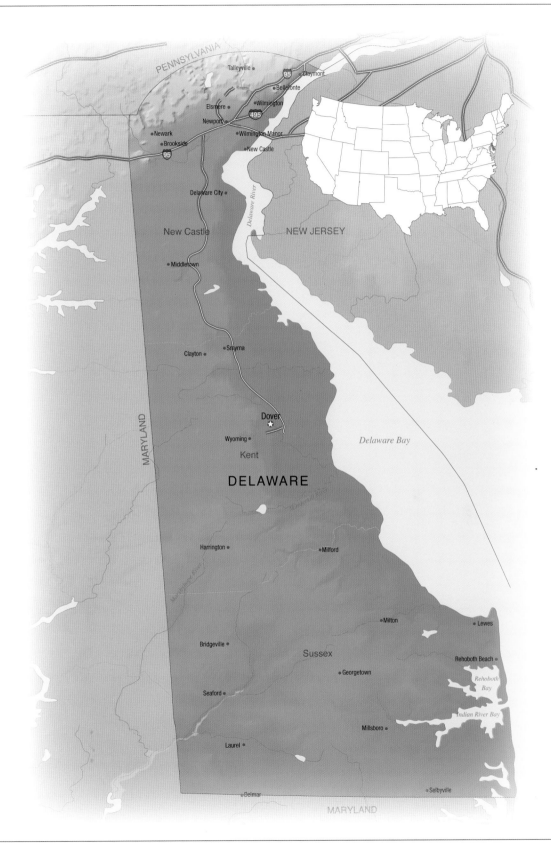

PENNSYLVANIA

Talleyville

95 Claymont

Bellefonte

Elsmere Wilmington

Newport 495

Newark

Brookside Wilmington Manor

95 New Castle

Delaware City

New Castle

Delaware River

NEW JERSEY

Middletown

Clayton Smyrna

Dover

Wyoming

Kent

DELAWARE

Delaware Bay

MARYLAND

Harrington Milford

Milton Lewes

Bridgeville Rehoboth Beach

Sussex Rehoboth Bay

Georgetown

Seaford

Indian River Bay

Millsboro

Laurel

Delmar Selbyville

MARYLAND

The First State

One of the most prominent American Indian groups living in the region when Europeans first arrived were the Lenni Lenape Indians, sometimes called simply the Lenape. Among other Algonquian Indians, the Lenape held an elevated status and were given preferred treatment at intertribal councils. By the time of the American Revolution, many of the Lenape tribes had moved, voluntarily or otherwise, but those that remained were the first American Indians to ally themselves with the fledgling nation against the British. The promise they received of an ultimate Indian state went unfulfilled, however, and today only one Lenape tribe—the Nanticoke Indians—remains in Delaware.

Caesar Rodney

Early Occupation

The first Europeans to establish a presence in Delaware were the Dutch, who set up a trading post in 1631. Problems with American Indians, as well as friction within the Dutch West India Company, forced the Dutch to temporarily withdraw, whereupon Sweden moved in with a new trading post called Fort Christina (present-day Wilmington) and established a colony there. The Swedish presence lasted from 1638 to 1655, when the Dutch, under Peter Stuyvesant, recovered

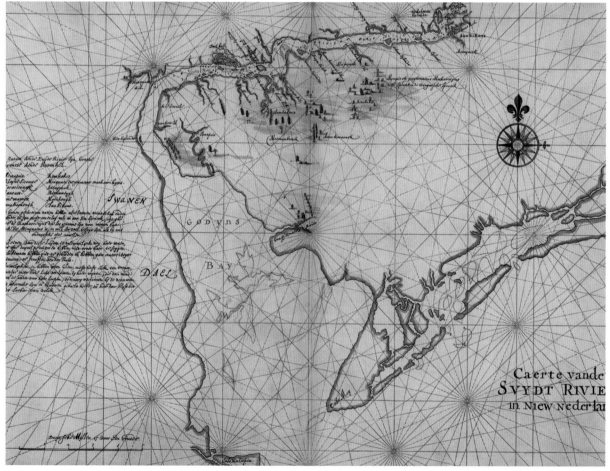

Delaware Bay, as it was known to the settlers of New Netherland in 1639.

the territory. This too was short-lived, for in 1664 James, Duke of York, led a British force to conquer the area. Still, the area remained in dispute, this time between two English factions; Cecilius Calvert, 2nd Lord Baltimore, held a rival claim to that of James, Duke of York, who had leased the territory to William Penn. The resulting contention continued for generations, ending finally in 1921 when the last boundary between Maryland and Delaware was settled.

THE DU PONT FAMILY

In few places can one find the history of a city so intertwined with that of a single family. In 1802 a French immigrant named Eleuthère Irénée du Pont set up shop near Wilmington, making gun- and blasting powder along the banks of the Brandywine River. His descendants expanded the successful DuPont Company and became not only extraordinarily wealthy but community leaders. When the company moved downtown in 1905, Du Pont family members and executives worked closely with city officials to develop Wilmington, building roads, a grand hotel, the courthouse, and public parks. Today, the DuPont Company is a global science firm, but the family's dedication to the city is still very much in evidence.

Eleuthère du Pont

The War of Independence

Delaware declared its independence from both Britain and Pennsylvania simultaneously, on June 15, 1776, but remained relatively lukewarm toward the Revolutionary War. On June 30, 1776, the Continental Congress convened in Philadelphia to vote on declaring independence from Great Britain. By the end of the next day, nine states had voted in favor and two against, with New York abstaining and Delaware evenly split, because only two of Delaware's three representatives—George Reed and Thomas McKean—were present. Caesar Rodney, the third, had been called away to put down a Loyalist riot, but received an urgent message from McKean, telling him his vote was needed in Congress. Not unlike the more famous midnight ride of Paul Revere, Rodney rode all night, through a thunderstorm, to arrive at Independence Hall in Philadelphia, 80 miles away, in time to cast the deciding vote on July 2, 1776.

The scenic vista of the marshy region near the Delaware Bay has changed little since Henry Hudson first sailed there in 1609.

Delaware played a vital role in the fighting of the Revolution, with its Continental regiment distinguishing itself in many of the war's most famous engagements. After the war, Delaware was the first to ratify the U.S. Constitution, on December 7, 1787. The event is memorialized in the state's official nickname, the First State.

On the Edge

Despite its small size Delaware has always presented a cultural and ideological mix. At no point was Delaware's borderline status more noticeable than during the Civil War, when, despite its slave-owning laws, it stayed in the Union. It was in fact the only slave state that did not officially organize Confederate troops, although certainly many Delawareans sympathized with and, as individuals, joined the Confederacy.

Delaware's tradition of being culturally in the middle of North and South continued in the Civil Rights Movement of the 1950s and 1960s, when one of its court cases, *Belton v. Gebhart*, was appealed and folded into the famous U.S. Supreme Court case *Brown v. Board of Education*. Of the four such initial cases, *Belton v. Gebhart* was unique in that the state courts had found in favor of the plaintiffs—a ruling that was upheld when the Supreme Court ruled segregated schools unconstitutional. Today, Delaware's "border" standing is reflected in its close political battles and its usual bellwether role in predicting national elections, although recently that phenomena has proved less reliable than in the past. As always, this mid-Atlantic jewel is hard to pin down.

Maryland

Old Line State

Fatti Maschii, Parole Femine (Manly deeds, womanly words)

Maryland, surrounding the Chesapeake Bay and squeezed between Pennsylvania and West Virginia in the west, is almost precisely in the middle of the eastern coast of the United States. It has been the wealthiest state in the country for some time, boasting the highest median household income and the lowest poverty rate. Its good fortune is due in part to its proximity to Washington, D.C., which has encouraged the proliferation of industries related to defense, aerospace, and bio- and medical research, as well as staffing of government agencies. Over 350 biotechnology firms contribute to the region's prosperity.

Most of this activity is centered on the densely populated central regions, in and around Baltimore and its heavily frequented port. The eastern region, on the Delmarva Peninsula, and the western region are more sparsely populated, more rural, and tend to vote Republican, although the state has been staunchly Democratic since before the Civil War. The state has two official nicknames, the Old Line State and the Free State. The former refers to its role in the Revolutionary War, when Maryland soldiers were known as the Maryland Line (allegedly, George Washington himself christened the state with the term). The latter is a more recent appropriation dating to the early 1920s, when Hamilton Owens, editor of the *Baltimore Sun*, began referring to Maryland as "the Free State" for its refusal to adopt prohibition laws.

Maryland, which enacted one of first laws of religious toleration in 1649, today houses one of the largest Catholic populations in the United States, and a large proportion of racial minorities. Chesapeake Bay is an extremely popular destination for vacation-goers and fishermen, as well as providing the nation with fully half its supply of blue crabs. It can even claim its own dog breed, the Chesapeake Bay retriever. Maryland also plays a role on the international stage, as the presidential retreat Camp David (properly the Naval Support Facility Thurmont) is located in scenic Frederick County. Johns Hopkins University and its affiliated hospital, one of the country's finest medical facilities, were founded in the late 19th century with the bequest of the Baltimore philanthropist whose name they bear. Thus, although the geographic center of the country has by now shifted far from Maryland, the nation's other "bay state" remains nationally central.

Baltimore's harbor has been a thriving place of business and commerce since the early 1700s.

Maryland State Facts

Full Name: State of Maryland
Meaning of Name: From Queen Henrietta Maria, wife of Charles I of England
Admitted to the Union: April 28, 1788 (7th state)
Inhabitant: Marylander

Capital City: Annapolis
Flower: Black-eyed Susan
Tree: White oak
Bird: Baltimore oriole

Geography and Ecology

Despite its small size Maryland can be roughly divided into three geographic regions. The eastern and southern regions of Maryland—that is, the area surrounding the Chesapeake Bay—are part of the Atlantic Coastal Plain. Flat topography and sandy soil mark this region, which falls within a humid subtropical climate. Temperatures there are moderated by the Atlantic Ocean, with long, hot, humid summers and brief, mild winters. With some frequency the region experiences the remnants of tropical storms and hurricanes, although the state is protected from hurricane devastation by the Delmarva Peninsula (the western half of which makes up Maryland's so-called Eastern Shore) and North Carolina's Outer Banks.

The Narrowest State

The middle of the state comprises a region known as Piedmont or Appalachian Piedmont. Strictly speaking, three distinct geological areas can be discerned in this region: true Piedmont in the northeast/central part of the state; the Blue Ridge, a tiny band stretching north-south across Frederick and Washington Counties; and the Appalachian Ridge, covering the rest of Washington County and nearly all of Allegany County. This region becomes progressively more mountainous, oak forests giving way to pine, and low, rolling hills becoming peaks more than 2,000 feet in height. The climate is also transitional, from the humid subtropical to humid continental more typical of Northeast states. At one point in this region the state is squeezed between its

boundaries of the Potomac River and the Mason-Dixon Line to barely one mile wide, giving it the dubious distinction of "narrowest state."

Where the Wild Things Are

The westernmost portion of the state lies fully within the humid continental climate zone and is mountainous, forested, and sparsely settled. Snowfall averages reach above 100 inches a year here; the coast can expect only 9 inches. Total amounts of precipitation are nonetheless fairly even across the state, with a liquid statewide average around 40–45 inches. There is an overabundant deer population across the state, particularly in the west, where humans decimated the deer's natural predators. Black bears, however, are beginning to

An Assateague pony browses contentedly in its adopted home.

PONIES NOT FOUND AT PIMLICO

A rare band of ponies lives free on Assateague Island off the coast of Maryland. Though often called wild, they are actually feral—the descendants of domesticated horses brought by European settlers. Because the ponies are, in fact, an invasive species, the National Park Service has taken steps to limit their impact on the island's native ecology. Their primary goal is to keep the little herd between 120 and 150 individuals, accomplished through contraception. The ponies have shrunk in size from their ancestral lineage (hence they are ponies, not horses) and have a "twin" feral herd on the Virginia side of the island. A fence keeps the two herds apart.

reassert themselves in the west, and there have even been much-debated reports of cougar sightings.

This varied topography has earned Maryland a third, unofficial, nickname: America in Miniature. However, by far the most obvious geographic feature of the state is the Chesapeake Bay, which nearly splits the state in half, and which many Marylanders believe ought to earn their state yet another nickname, the Bay State. The Chesapeake Bay is the world's largest freshwater estuary and—in terms of tourist dollars and commercial revenue—makes up for Maryland's unique lack of natural lakes.

Freshwater, brackish, and saltwater marshes line the Chesapeake Bay. All may be threatened by rising sea levels and human actions.

Old Line State

From the beginning Maryland was a battlefield for contesting cultures. While it was still a colony of Great Britain, the primary question was of religion; the founding Irish Catholic lords, the dominant Calvert family, wished to establish a safe haven for Catholics in the New World. The first settlers arrived in 1634, and Maryland passed an early act of religious toleration (extended only to Christians) in 1649, but Protestants quickly took over. Rebelling in the 1650s, they persecuted Catholics and took control of the government. The balance of power switched back and forth for the rest of the century, and although ultimately peace was restored, Catholics were not allowed to vote until after the American Revolution. Nevertheless, the only Catholic to sign the Declaration of Independence—Charles Carroll—hailed from Maryland.

Between the States

Maryland also housed conflicting northern and southern cultures. Cresap's War, a border conflict between Maryland and Pennsylvania in the 1730s, foretold the future North-South divide of the Civil War. In that War Between the States, Maryland—despite allowing slavery—remained in the Union. This unlikely alliance may have been, to some extent, forced; President Abraham Lincoln was warned in 1861 that his life was in jeopardy in the city of Baltimore, and the constitutionality of his actions in imprisoning Confederate sympathizers is still debated by scholars. Nevertheless, more than three-quarters of Maryland's fighting men joined the Union rather than the Confederacy.

In some ways the changing fortunes of Maryland's two most significant cities reflect the cultural divide. The capital city, Annapolis, had been primary in social significance, wealth, and political importance in the 18th century, when the area's economy was largely agrarian.

STAR-SPANGLED BANNER

During the War of 1812, invading British forces attacked Fort McHenry in Baltimore harbor for a full day without respite. Although the British had recently succeeded in burning and looting the capital city of Washington, D.C., Fort McHenry repelled them. Francis Scott Key, a lawyer negotiating for the release of an American prisoner, was so inspired by the stalwart defense that he wrote the "Star-Spangled Banner" on the spot, celebrating the American flag flying "through the perilous fight" despite the British "rockets' red glare." The song's enduring popularity led to its adoption as the official national anthem in 1931.

Francis Scott Key, a Marylander by birth, gestures toward the American flag from his viewpoint on a British ship.

Founded in 1729, Baltimore took over much of the state's economy in the mid-18th century, largely due to the new railroads and other transportation systems, and remains

The view from the State House dome in Annapolis in 1911 shows the Naval Academy, founded in 1845, and the Chesapeake Bay beyond.

Maryland as it appeared in 1794, with an inset showing the newly developed capital city in the District of Columbia. Maryland agreed to give up the land for the capital—almost entirely uninhabited at the time, except for Maryland's Georgetown port—in 1790.

today Maryland's largest city and center of population. Culturally, Baltimore tends to resemble the northern states, while the eastern and western portions of the state tend to resemble their southern neighbors.

Of Blood and Battle

Not all Marylanders lived in the "land of the free" so proudly extolled by Francis Scott Key's "Star-Spangled Banner." Although generally treated better in Maryland than in the deeper South, slaves were much in evidence in Maryland right up until the Civil War—nearly 90,000 lived there in 1860. Frederick Douglass, the famous abolitionist, was born a slave on the Eastern Shore and lived there and in Baltimore under white masters. Highly unusually, the wife of his owner taught him to read and write, and Douglass spread literacy among his fellow slaves as well as he could. Eventually escaping to the North, Douglass became extremely active in abolitionist movements, even conferring with President Abraham Lincoln.

The Civil War tore Maryland apart, quite literally in some cases. The first blood of battle was shed in Baltimore when an angry mob attacked the Sixth Massachusetts Regiment. Maryland also saw some of the fiercest fighting of the war, when Major General George McClellan engaged General Robert E. Lee's Confederate troops near Antietam Creek on September 17, 1862. The Battle of Antietam is listed as the bloodiest in American history, claiming the lives of 23,000 Americans in a single day.

Maryland Justice

Because Maryland remained loyal to the Union, President Lincoln's Emancipation Proclamation did not apply to the state. Nevertheless, Maryland adopted a new state constitution in 1864 that condemned slavery to the past. The University of Maryland's School of Law anticipated the Civil Rights Movement in 1936, when it admitted its first African-American student, and in 1967 Marylander Thurgood Marshall became the first African American appointed to the U.S. Supreme Court. A state not unused to social upheaval, Maryland has shown how prosperity, truth, and justice can nevertheless thrive.

Thurgood Marshall

Virginia

Old Dominion

Sic Semper Tyrannis (Thus always to tyrants)

Early in the history of English exploration of North America, the name "Virginia" applied to virtually all the eastern seaboard; consequently, the state is sometimes called, with some justification, the "mother of states," since so many states were "birthed" from its once vast dominion. Equally valid is Virginia's other moniker, "mother of presidents," since it has contributed no fewer than eight U.S. presidents, including four of the first five.

The proud tradition of independence, cemented by revolutionaries like Patrick Henry and George Mason, is reflected in the state's unapologetic motto, "Sic Semper Tyrannis" (Thus always to tyrants). The phrase is famous for John Wilkes Booth's alleged use of it after assassinating President Abraham Lincoln; Booth's subsequent escape ended finally at a farm in northeastern Virginia, the site of which is marked today by a simple sign. Virginia's lead role in the Civil War firmly established it as a southern state, but in recent years a more varied culture, with both southern and northern elements, has emerged. Geographically located centrally along the east coast, the state abuts the nation's cosmopolitan capital toward the northeast, while much of the western and southern parts of the state are more rural and tend to be culturally more similar to the Deep South.

Today, although its formative cultural and political role on the national stage has diminished somewhat from its heyday in the early republic, Virginia remains the 12th most populous state, with a strong economy, contentious politics, and a vibrant, heterogeneous culture. Government and associated industries compete with more traditional economic mainstays of agriculture and manufacturing in economic importance; in 2006, computer chips became the highest-grossing export. Nine Fortune 500 companies grace the capital city, Richmond, and in 2013 the state ranked in *Forbes* magazine as the Best State for Businesses in the country. With the nation's largest technology workforce and concentration of federal government institutions, Virginia is subtly reasserting its leadership position among the states.

In 1969 the Virginia State Travel Service developed the catchy "Virginia is for Lovers" slogan, trying to appeal to the younger generation. It certainly worked; since then, Virginia tourism has contributed millions of dollars every year to the state's economy, and the slogan endures. With a broad range of attractions from sea to mountain, scenery to history, there's plenty to love about Virginia.

Including 101 miles of the Appalachian Trail, more than 500 miles of trails meander through Shenandoah National Park.

Virginia State Facts

Full Name: Commonwealth of Virginia
Meaning of Name: From "virgin," in reference to Queen Elizabeth I, who was known as the Virgin Queen.
Admitted to the Union: June 25, 1788 (10th State)
Inhabitant: Virginian

Capital City: Richmond
Flower: American dogwood
Tree: American dogwood
Bird: Cardinal

Geography and Ecology

There are five general geographical regions in Virginia, running in roughly northeast-southwest lines across the state. From east to west, they are: the Atlantic Coastal Plain, the Piedmont, the Blue Ridge, the Appalachian Valley and Ridge, and the Appalachian Plateau. The Coastal Plain and Piedmont regions share a humid subtropical climate and rise from flat, swampy areas in the Coastal Plain—also called the Tidewater for its tidal interactions with the sea—to rolling plains in the Piedmont. The Blue Ridge Mountains contain the highest peaks in Virginia (Mt. Rogers, at 5,729 feet, crowns the state), and mark a transition to a humid continental climate.

A DISMAL REFUGE

The Great Dismal Swamp of southern Virginia and northern North Carolina contains the larger of Virginia's two natural lakes and a vast variety of wildlife. It also possesses a rather unusual history. During the 1850s and 1860s escaping slaves would stop in the swamp on their way north, and some runaways managed to establish a hidden, relatively permanent community there. During the Civil War, U.S. Colored Troops discovered, freed, and in many cases recruited unknown numbers of Great Dismal Swamp runaways. Now a nationally protected wildlife refuge, the swamp is also listed as a site in the Underground Railroad Network to Freedom—one of the few places to have served as refuge for both people and animals.

Prior to the Civil War, some escaped slaves found the forbidding landscape of the Great Dismal Swamp a welcome boon.

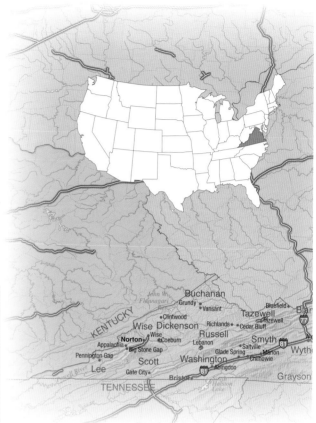

The Appalachian Ridge and Valley region to the west comprises a series of valleys, canyons, and limestone quarries. Sometimes the largest valley, Shenandoah, is listed as a separate region with its own microclimate. The westernmost part of the state covers the Appalachian Plateau, a broad, 2,000-foot-high plateau with thick forests and several rivers.

Home Away from Home

Inhabitants of the Appalachian Plateau have the peculiar distinction of living closer to eight other state capitals than to their own; Richmond lies in the Coastal Plain, roughly halfway up the length of the Chesapeake Bay. Similarly, Northern Virginians have a shorter trip to Annapolis, Dover, Philadelphia, and New York City than to the western panhandle, lending the area some "border state" characteristics culturally, demographically, and politically. Virginia also experiences a range of weather phenomena, dispersed unevenly across the state. While the eastern portion typically receives the remnants of hurricanes and tropical storms, the western, mountain regions may receive extreme snowfalls in the winter.

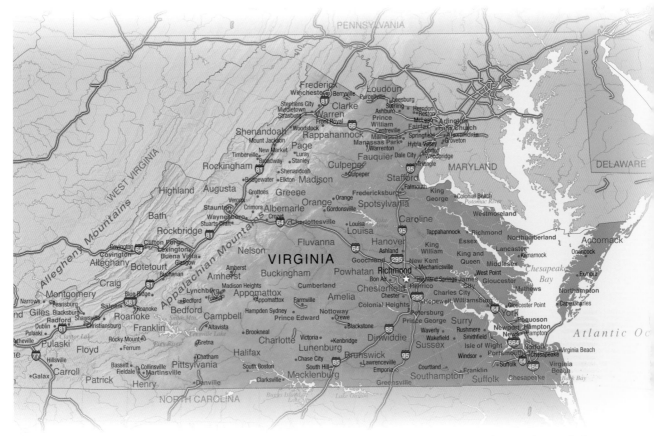

Fortunately, the state is reasonably well protected from major hurricanes, and although an average of 18 tornadoes per year appear in the state, most are weak.

Virginia Parks

In addition to Shenandoah National Park, located barely 75 miles west and south of Washington, D.C., Virginia houses no fewer than 37 state parks. It also boasts several battlefields and monuments, and portions of several other national historical parks, plus sections of the Appalachian and Potomac Heritage trails. In Fairfax County—the state's most populous area—is the nation's only national park dedicated to the performing arts, Wolf Trap National Park. Purportedly, the name derives from the 17th and 18th century preponderance of wolves in the region and the methods settlers undertook to eradicate them. Unfortunately for the wolves, the settlers were entirely successful, and now no wild wolves roam anywhere in the state.

A misty day shows clearly how the Blue Ridge Mountains earned their name. Their distinctive color is best viewed at a distance.

Old Dominion

Soon after Sir Walter Raleigh returned to England from his 1584 explorations of North America, the name "Virginia" was suggested in honor of Queen Elizabeth I, who was known as the Virgin Queen for her refusal to marry. The name was indiscriminately applied to much of North America, whose geography was only roughly understood by the enterprising English. Nevertheless, only a year after Raleigh's travels, 108 settlers arrived on Roanoke Island (in modern-day North Carolina) to colonize Virginia, although the little colony quickly failed.

Major conflicts quickly erupted between the early settlers and the indigenous peoples; soon after the first permanent English colony of Jamestown was founded in 1607, some 200 Indians attacked the settlement. Three years later the English virtually destroyed the nearby Paspahegh Indian village.

War and Peace

In part due to Indian raids and halted trading, the winter of 1609–10 killed more than four-fifths of the Jamestown settlers. Rescue from a new influx of settlers failed to improve relations with Indian chief Powhatan, who told the settlers they could remain only at their own risk. Ultimately, peace was achieved by the marriage of Powhatan's daughter, Matoaka—better known as Pocahontas—to John Rolfe in 1614. Three years previously Rolfe had imported tobacco seeds, and the success of the plant in Virginia was to endure and bolster the state's economy for centuries.

Pocahontas

Toward the end of the 17th century, the price of tobacco had fallen, and poorer colonists, their lot aggravated by the unbalanced aristocratic society, rebelled under the leadership of Nathaniel Bacon. Bacon succeeded in burning much of Jamestown in 1676 before the royal governor restored order. By 1698 Jamestown had seen four statehouses, each of which had been destroyed, and the capital was moved to Williamsburg.

Give Me Liberty

Virginia's long history as an English colony did not prevent intense anti-British sentiment in the years leading up to the Revolutionary War. The rebellious rhetoric of men like George Mason and Patrick Henry—who famously incited Virginians to take arms against the British with his legendary "Give me liberty, or give me death!" speech—inspired revolutionaries across the country. On May 15, 1776, Virginia declared its independence from Great Britain, after already having joined its fellow colonies in the Revolutionary War.

In 1780 then-governor Thomas Jefferson moved Virginia's capital from Williamsburg to Richmond, fearing that Williamsburg was too vulnerable to British attack. The war culminated at the siege of Yorktown in the fall of 1781, which ended in General Cornwallis's surrender. The American victory was the last major battle of the war.

Popular events in the open-air museum of Colonial Williamsburg include reenactments, such as this American militia parade.

Patrick Henry, a Virginian firebrand of the American Revolution, is famous for his impassioned oratory and radical politics.

Producer of Presidents

By the end of the 18th century, five future U.S. presidents had been born in Virginia. This distinguished group included the fledgling nation's first president, George Washington, who was widely credited for militarily defeating the British. Thomas Jefferson and James Madison, the third and fourth presidents, had significant roles in the Declaration of Independence and the Constitution respectively. Rounding out the list were William Henry Harrison, the first president to die in office, and his successor John Tyler. On top of this impressive litany, Virginia held a majority of representatives in the House, leaving little doubt as to the state's influence on the early republic.

Early Abolitionist Movements

Virginia's fortunes began to falter in the 19th century. A slow western migration, encouraged in part by the exhausted soil in the eastern part of the state, resulted in a proportional population loss; by 1860 Virginia—at the beginning of the republic the most populous state—ranked fifth. As early as 1792 Kentucky separated from Virginia and joined the Union independently.

The northeastern section of Virginia along the Maryland border. Since rivers were most conducive to travel in the colonial period, settlement tended to extend along waterways first.

One of the most violent slave rebellions in American history occurred on Virginia soil in 1831. Nat Turner led approximately 70 escaped slaves and free blacks in an uprising in Southampton County, freeing slaves and killing 55 white people. The retribution killed at least twice as many black people. The violence on both side was indiscriminate.

THE CURIOUS CASE OF WILMER MCLEAN

In one of the most curious coincidences of American history, the simple farmstead of a Virginian grocer named Wilmer McLean played an odd double role. On July 18, 1861, Union artillery fire aimed at McLean's house, where Confederate general Beauregard was headquartered. This salvo announced the beginning of the First Battle of Bull Run, the first major confrontation of the Civil War. Four years later, on April 9, 1865, the McLean farm hosted Generals Robert E. Lee and Ulysses S. Grant while the former surrendered his army and, by extension, the South. Thus it is said that the Civil War began in Wilmer McLean's backyard and ended in his front parlor.

The home of Wilmer McLean in 1865, unremarkable except for the strange confluence of Civil War events that occurred here.

Perhaps of greater national import was an attempted slave rebellion led by John Brown on Harpers Ferry (now part of West Virginia) in 1859. Brown raided the federal arsenal, killing several people in the process, in an attempt to arm slaves and lead a revolt. Although his plan failed, the incident ignited abolitionist sentiment throughout the country, pushing it closer to the Civil War.

Embattled Virginia

Despite initial opposition to secession by some of Virginia's leading men—including Robert E. Lee—the state joined the rest of the South in breaking with the Union in 1861. The Confederate States of America moved their capital from Montgomery, Alabama, to Richmond, and Robert E. Lee (who had previously declined President Abraham Lincoln's offer to command the Union forces) became one of the Confederacy's most successful generals. More battles were fought on Virginia's contested soil than anywhere else during the Civil War, including major contests like the First and Second Battles of Bull Run (often called the First and Second Battles of Manassas for their proximity to Manassas, Virginia), the Battle of Fredericksburg, and the Battle of Chancellorsville. It was during the First Battle of Bull Run that Confederate Colonel Thomas J.

Jackson earned his enduring nickname, "Stonewall," for his staunch defense of the Confederate position. Both Chancellorsville and Fredericksburg also proved to be major victories for General Lee's army.

Nevertheless, Virginia also saw General Lee's ultimate surrender at Appomattox Court House, on April 9, 1865. The town is now a national historic park. The state rejoined the Union on January 26, 1870; six years later the discovery of coal in southwestern Virginia

Approximately 4 million people visit Arlington National Cemetery every year. Combatants from every American military conflict from the Revolutionary War on are buried here.

The National Battlefield of Manassas may be quiet and beautiful now, but in 1861 and again in 1862 Confederate and Union soldiers clashed violently in the bloody First and Second Battles of Bull Run (also called the First and Second Battles of Manassas).

Richmond, above, founded in 1737, is Virginia's capital city and is today a thriving economic center.

Arlington County has benefited from its proximity to Washington, D.C., as major federal institutions like the U.S. military's head-quarters at the Pentagon, right, are based there.

helped relieve some of the economic pressures wrought by the war and Reconstruction. The constitution of 1870, which allowed all men to vote, held until the Jim Crow era. The 1902 constitution, which replaced it, effectively disenfranchised Virginia's black population, a regression not redressed until the Civil Rights Act of 1964. In 1989, however, Virginia was the first state in the nation to elect a black governor, Douglas Wilder.

Moving Forward

Economically, the state revived somewhat in the second half of the 20th century. The Pentagon, the headquarters of the federal Department of Defense, was constructed in 1941–43 in Arlington (the nation's smallest self-governing county), while the Central Intelligence Agency built its own headquarters in nearby Langley. The state also currently houses a thriving military-industrial economy. Tourism plays a major role in the state's economy as well, not least because of Virginia's wealth of historic landmarks. The "Historic Triangle" formed by Jamestown, Colonial Williamsburg, and Yorktown is a premier destination. Virginia's formative role in early American history may be the state's best-known asset, but the state's recent economic and cultural developments are encouraging signs of resurgence from America's "mother of states."

West Virginia

The Mountain State

Montani Semper Liberi (Mountaineers are always free)

The five states of Pennsylvania, Ohio, Kentucky, Maryland, and Virginia border West Virginia, highlighting some of the difficulty in classifying it. Because most of the state lies below the Mason-Dixon Line, it is often considered southern, and indeed many West Virginians in the southern portions consider themselves part of the neighboring South. However, parts of West Virginia reach as far north as Pittsburgh, Pennsylvania, so that the state can reasonably be called a Border State as well. Geographically, it is most certainly an Appalachian state, as it is the only state to lie entirely within the region designated "Appalachia" by the Appalachian Regional Commission.

In 1928 two members of a local family in Monroe County at the southern border of the state accidentally discovered one of the largest diamonds ever found in America, the 34.48-carat Jones Diamond. However, the state is better known—and owes far more economic stability to—the coal-rich fields covering much of the state's rugged mountain territory. Beginning soon after the Civil War and continuing to the present day, West Virginia has depended largely on coal production, a fact that has influenced much of the state's history and culture.

Coal also played a big role in the state's politics, as industrialization encouraged large-scale union membership. Today, the state suffers somewhat from its dependence on its lone export, ranking 48th in per capita income and last in median household income.

Nevertheless, the state's unique history (it is the only state to have formed out of a Confederate state during the Civil War) and mountainous beauty draws visitors from around the world, allowing it a stable and lucrative tourist industry. The state's rough alpine topography makes it the highest state east of the Mississippi River. But these scenic mountains have been a double-edged sword from the region's earliest colonial history. The first settlers in this region found travel in and out of the area quite difficult. As a result of this troublesome terrain, West Virginia today hosts a number of bridges and tunnels disproportionate to its size. All of this notwithstanding, the sheer beauty of this state is a sight to behold. In fact, in tribute to their state's famous landscape, many West Virginians refer to it as "almost heaven."

Tourists and locals alike flock to New River Gorge National River for white-water rafting, its popular recreational activity.

West Virginia State Facts

Full Name: State of West Virginia
Meaning of Name: From "virgin," in reference to Queen Elizabeth I, who was known as the Virgin Queen.
Admitted to the Union: June 20, 1863 (35th state)
Inhabitant: West Virginian

Capital City: Charleston
Flower: Rhododendron
Tree: Sugar maple
Bird: Cardinal

Geography and Ecology

Alone among the states, West Virginia is mountainous in its entirety. The mountains are covered mostly in hardwood forests that give way to spruce in the highest places, and traversed by many rivers and countless streams. The Appalachian Mountain Range is one of the oldest on earth, and while its weathered peaks do not rise as high as those of younger mountain ranges, they are just as dramatic. Because of the elevation—West Virginia's highest peak, Spruce Knob, rises 4,863 feet above sea level—the state is cooler than the other southern states. The capital city of Charleston sees an annual average snowfall of 34 inches, while the Monongahela National Forest has a climate resembling northern New England's.

Natural Beauty

The Monongahela National Forest, established in 1920, represents much of the best of West Virginia. Since its formation, the forest has grown to encompass more than 900,000 acres, and it offers a variety of leisurely pursuits. Its accessible location allows 3 million people to visit each year, and it boasts a wide variety of endangered or threatened plants, animals, and birds. No fewer than five federally protected wilderness areas can be found within Monongahela.

Weather Conditions

West Virginia has two climatic zones, transitioning from a humid subtropical climate in the southwest and eastern panhandle to a humid continental climate. Precipitation averages rise with elevation, from 32 inches annually in the southwest to 56 inches in the high mountains. Average temperatures cover a similar wide range, with extremes on both ends; the highest recorded temperature climbed to 112° F on July 10, 1936, while the lowest temperature was -37° F on December 30, 1917.

"The views are magnificent, the valleys so beautiful, the scenery so peaceful. What a glorious world Almighty God has given us . . . and how we labor to mar his gifts."

—General Robert E. Lee

Crossing the New River Gorge Bridge provides spectacular views of the surrounding Appalachian countryside from nearly 900 feet up.

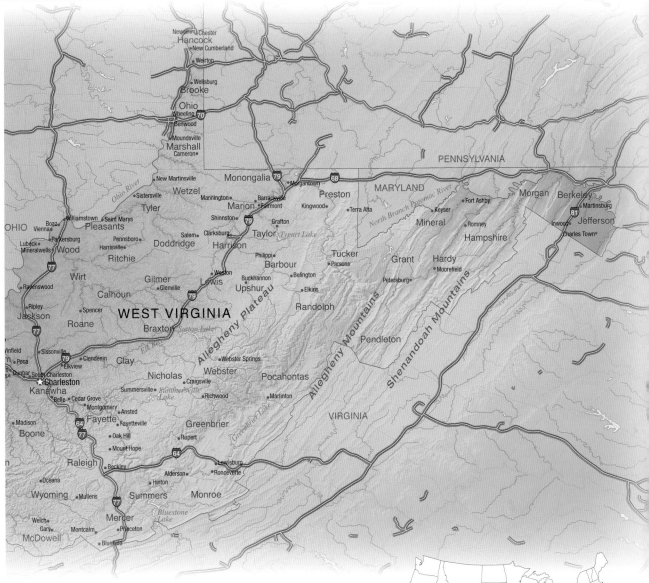

River Deep, Mountain High

Of the several rivers in West Virginia, one of the best known is the New River (an inappropriate name, since in geologic terms it is one of North America's oldest) and its emblematic bridge. New River is one of only 15 rivers in the United States given federal protection as a National River, in tribute to its unique ecological and scenic role. The river acts as a natural ecological east-west barrier and, conversely, as a north-south corridor, and several endemic species of fish have evolved in the course of the river's 500-million-year history. The river has carved a spectacular gorge, falling to a depth on average of 1,000 feet and in one place 1,500 feet. The gorge is crossed by one of the world's tallest and longest single-arch bridges, with 1,700 feet of a total 3,030-foot span crossing 876 feet above the river.

The mountains that give West Virginia its character also house the state's most significant natural resource, instrumental throughout virtually all its modern history: coal. Formed deep within the mountain's craggy ridges, coal has been West Virginia's economic mainstay since the 19th century, despite the rigors and dangers of mining.

The Mountain State

The last remnants of ancient cultures indigenous to the region are impressive mounds, which scholars believe were burial places for honored dead. The largest such mound in the United States rises 69 feet high near the aptly named city of Moundsville, West Virginia. It is estimated that this burial site was constructed between 250 and 150 BCE.

Lord Dunmore's War

By the time Europeans arrived, the Adena culture that had built the enormous Grave Creek Mound had long since vanished, replaced by several later-day American Indian tribes who used the region primarily as a hunting ground. The first white settler, a Welsh immigrant improbably named Morgan Morgan, built a simple log cabin between 1728 and 1734, which still stands to this day. European settlement, however, was met with considerable American Indian resistance. These disputes all came to a head in 1774 when colonial militia won a decisive battle in a war named for Virginia's soon-to-be-ousted British governor, Lord Dunmore. Lord Dunmore's War seemed fortuitously timed for burgeoning American patriotism. By the time George Washington issued a call for Virginians to take up arms against the British, western Virginians Hugh Stephenson and Daniel Morgan were free to lead a company of frontiersmen to Cambridge, Massachusetts, covering more than 600 miles in only 24 days. Their starting place—Morgan's Grove Park—is today listed in the National Historic Places register.

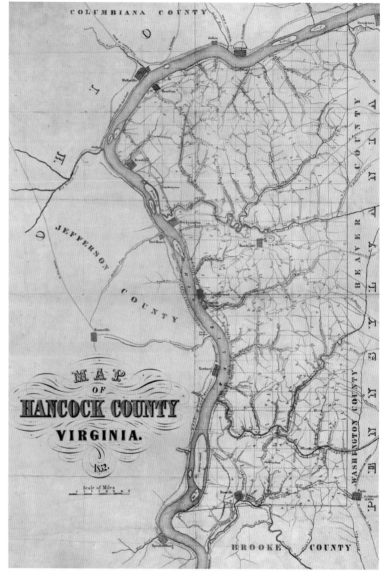

The northernmost county in West Virginia, Hancock voted almost unanimously to stay in the Union when the Civil War broke out.

Clash of Cultures

Even before the American Revolution, a discernable gap in culture, politics, and economics was growing between eastern and western Virginia, between the broad, fertile eastern plantations and the rugged western frontier. The indomitable mountains presented not only a very real physical barrier, but also produced dramatically different societies and inspired very different types of settlers. By the time of the Civil War, the two regions had grown almost irreconcilable, with westerners begrudging a state government that seemed to unfairly favor easterners and embedded eastern social customs—most notably the incendiary issue of slavery—that were out of place in the west.

Excavations in 1883–84 revealed 13 skeletons and numerous artifacts in Criel Mound. The largest of some 50 mounds in the immediate area, and behind only Grave Creek Mound in West Virginia, Criel Mound may have been the center of a large Adena culture grave complex.

Statehood at Last

When Virginia seceded from the United States in 1861, a convention held by discontented west Virginians declared Virginia's act of secession null and void, and eventually, on June 20, 1863, West Virginia was admitted to the Union as a separate state. After the Civil War Virginia protested the formation of the new state. Although the U.S. Supreme Court decided in favor of West Virginia in 1870, in some ways the issue was not truly settled until 1939, when West Virginia paid off its pre-Civil War debt to Virginia in accordance with a separate Supreme Court case.

Coal-oriented Society

Beginning soon after the Civil War and continuing through most of the 20th century, the fortunes of West Virginia rose and fell with the coal-mining trade. The proliferation of railroads in the state after the war suddenly turned coal into gold, as industrial markets in the east and overseas were opened up to the coal-rich state. However, the dangers of coal mining produced a strong labor movement in the first half of the 20th century, starting a tradition of labor unions that continues today. As recently as January 2, 2006, 12 of 13 miners died in an accident in a Tallmansville mine; similar tragedies mar the state's long history in the coal mines. Concerns over ecological and

environmental damage caused by the burning of coal, as well as the waste and damage produced by mining itself, have also been growing over the years.

Nevertheless, West Virginia continues to honor its traditions, embodied in the coal mines, its lively Appalachian music, and its residents' enduring appreciation for the state's wild beauty, even as it turns its eyes to the future—which will no doubt continue to be shaped by its ancient mountains.

West Virginia laborers and coal companies engaged in open hostilities during the 1920s, highlighting the significance of the industry.

Kentucky

The Bluegrass State

United We Stand, Divided We Fall

Home to bourbon, horse races, and the world's largest system of natural caves, Kentucky rests between the two largest rivers in North America in the middle of the United States. Once fiercely contested between westward-moving American pioneers and American Indian tribes, Kentucky was an early frontier and still displays its traditional individualistic streak.

One of only four commonwealths in the nation, Kentucky has the third-largest number of counties in the country, despite ranking only 37th in size. The proliferation of counties in the 19th century was due largely to roiling political disagreements, encouraging the dissatisfied to form new local governments. Today, no more counties can be legally formed without severe restructuring, and the count stands at 120.

Most of the nation's gold reserves can be found at Fort Knox, near the center of Kentucky's northern border, but the state's economy is largely driven by agricultural products, especially tobacco, and manufacturing. In the past some regions of Kentucky relied heavily on coal mining, and it is still a significant industry today. Kentucky also has a long tradition of stubbornly producing illegal products; the state's famous bourbon-making went underground during Prohibition, and today well-hidden fields cultivate large amounts of marijuana. Alcohol remains a vital source of income in Kentucky today, as the state produces the vast majority—about 90 percent—of the nation's bourbon.

Traditionally a frontier state, Kentucky has a unique culture blending southern and midwestern attributes. One of its most famous homegrown products shares its name with the state's nickname: bluegrass music traces its origins to Kentuckian Bill Monroe and has since become popular throughout much of the nation. The state may be even more well known for its horses; while the horse's economic importance to agriculture declined throughout the 20th century, Kentuckians focused on breeding phenomenal racehorses, and their success is well-documented in the annual Kentucky Derby, the oldest continuous sporting event in the United States.

The horses roam through one of the nation's most fertile states, with fields of its trademark bluegrass fed by the largest system of waterways in the contiguous United States. The state's natural beauty, much of which is protected at the state or federal level, generates a significant tourist industry; Mammoth Cave National Park alone draws more than 650,000 visitors every year. Other frequented parks include Daniel Boone National Forest, named for the state's most famous frontiersman, and Cumberland Gap National Historical Park, through which Boone himself traveled.

Curious horses crowd close to a fence in Lexington, Kentucky. The state is as recognized for its horses as it is for its bluegrass ranges.

Kentucky State Facts

Full Name: Commonwealth of Kentucky
Meaning of Name: Disputed; possibly from Iroquoian "meadowland"
Admitted to the Union: June 1, 1792 (15th state)
Inhabitant: Kentuckian

Capital City: Frankfort
Flower: Goldenrod
Tree: Tulip poplar
Bird: Cardinal

Geography and Ecology

Five geographic regions endow Kentucky with a range of natural attributes, from the mountainous Cumberland Plateau in the east to the low floodplains of the western Jackson Purchase (so called because future president Andrew Jackson procured the area from Chickasaw Indians in 1818). Between are the Bluegrass Region in the north, named for its flowing fields of bluegrass, the rocky Pennyroyal Region set between the Bluegrass and the Purchase, and the appropriately named Western Coal Field, set like a gem in the middle of the Pennyroyal Region on the Indiana border.

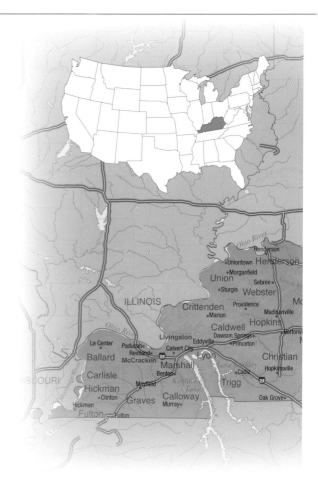

When the stem is fully grown (up to three feet), bluegrass seed heads display their characteristic color.

Mammoth Cave National Park

Below the Pennyroyal Region is one of the world's most unusual natural wonders. Mammoth Cave is the largest cave system ever discovered; to date, more than 400 miles of caves have been mapped, with some sections as deep as 360 feet. There are hundreds more miles of unexplored caverns, however, as well as lonely caves with no passageways to allow their discovery. First explored thousands of years ago by early miners, the caves have been visited continuously since 1816. Established as a national park in 1941, they have since been named both a World Heritage Site and an International Biosphere Reserve.

Rivers, Earthquakes, and the Kentucky Bend

Not only is Kentucky blessed with 90,000 miles of flowing waterways—besting all but Alaska for miles of navigable streams and rivers—but it is unique with three borders formed by rivers. To the east are the Big Sandy and the Tug Fork rivers, together forming the border with West Virginia. The entire northern border is determined by the course of the Ohio River; the short western border follows the Mississippi River.

This western section is the site of one of the oddest pieces of state geography in the country. A series of earthquakes in 1811 and 1812 in what is now Missouri culminated in the worst earthquake in the lower 48 states in history. The New Madrid Earthquake, as it was called,

An old stone bridge crosses the Cumberland River in the picturesque and historic Daniel Boone National Forest.

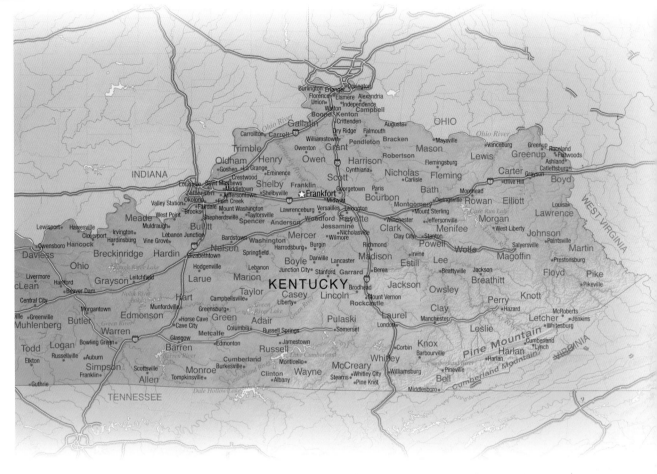

probably would have measured 8.0 on the Richter scale and reputedly was felt over a 50,000-mile radius, ringing church bells as far away as Boston, Massachusetts. The disrupted Mississippi River appeared to reverse its course temporarily, and in fact did create new enclaves as it found new paths. One of these enclaves was the "Kentucky Bend," a hairpin turn in the river that isolated one 18-square-mile part of the state. It is accessible only through Tennessee or Missouri, and is the only such case of an isolated portion of a state in the country.

RESTORING NATURE

Once, Kentucky teemed with vast herds of elk, but over hunting by Anglo-American settlers drove the species to extinction in the state by the mid-19th century. In 1997 the Department of Fish and Wildlife Resources began importing elk, and have reached their goal of maintaining a herd of 10,000 animals. Currently, Kentucky has the largest elk herd in the eastern United States. Because the original target was only 7,400 elk, the project is hailed as one of the most successful reintroduction efforts in American history. Since natural predators are in short supply, efforts to maintain a healthy population will depend on human hunters, rendering the project economically viable and a sportsman's favorite.

An elk, part of Kentucky's thriving herd, forages in the natural habitat long denied to the species.

The Bluegrass State

By the time European explorers arrived, Indians used the region largely as hunting grounds, although thousands of years ago settlements had thrived. Until the late 18th century the eastern mountains provided an effective barrier to westward expansion, but after Dr. Thomas Walker explored in 1750, settlers began considering the new western wilderness.

On the Frontier

Dr. Walker traveled through a natural break in the Appalachian Mountains called the Cumberland Gap, long used by American Indians. In 1775 Daniel Boone followed Dr. Walker through the gap and became one of Kentucky's earliest frontiersmen, blazing the "Wilderness Trail"

Daniel Boone

deep into the territory. Today, Cumberland Gap National Historical Park commemorates his journey and those of the people who followed. At the time the region was part of Virginia, but difficulties in traveling to the state capital, among other factors, prompted settlers to push for separation, and on June 1, 1792, Kentucky joined the Union as its own state.

Life on the frontier was not easy for settlers. The region was isolated, sparsely inhabited, and populated by wolves and bears. Several Indian tribes in the region resented the settlers' uninvited incursions and allied themselves with the British during the Revolutionary War. Kentucky fought few battles in the war, but skirmishes with Native Americans lasted for decades.

Louisville and the Southern Exposition in 1883. The city held the exposition for five years running and introduced the first large space lit with electric bulbs since their invention by Thomas Edison, himself a sometime Louisville resident.

Divided We Fall

Henry Clay may be Kentucky's most famous statesman. He served in both the House of Representatives and the Senate and ran for president five times. A member of the Whig party, he played instrumental roles in most national events from the War of 1812 to the Compromise of 1850. Despite a long-lasting dispute with Andrew Jackson and his followers, Clay earned a reputation as a compromiser, twice helping to avert civil war by finding a balance of power between slave and free states. Ultimately, of course, Clay's best efforts were unsuccessful, and barely a decade after his death the country spiraled into war.

Although Kentucky was a slave state, most residents sympathized with the Union, and the state did not secede. A movement to do so resulted in a brief double government, but the Confederate sympathizers found themselves outnumbered and outmaneuvered. After the war Kentucky still found itself somewhat divided, and racial violence spiked.

Right at the turn of the 20th century, Kentucky virtually disintegrated. A contested election resulted in an armed takeover of the capitol; the Democratic governor, William Goebel, was shot as he attempted to take his oath. For some months thereafter, Goebel's running mate, J. C. W. Beckham, and his opponent, William Taylor, both proclaimed themselves governor. The case went before the U.S. Supreme Court, where it was decided in favor of Beckham; Taylor took himself to Indiana and was indicted in his absence of conspiring to kill Goebel.

The Kentucky Derby attracts approximately 170,000 spectators every year. Only 3-year-old horses are permitted to race in the Derby.

and power lines. An enormous Ohio River flood in 1937 devastated several counties, but industry spawned by World War II helped the state recover.

Today, the vast majority of Kentucky's population lives in Louisville and its surrounding areas. Manufacturing, trade, and transportation account for much of the state's economy. But Kentucky retains its agrarian past, hosting the fifth-largest number of farms in the country and monopolizing certain niche areas—including the omnipresent bourbon and thoroughbred horse industries. No matter what the pursuit—from its bluegrass music to its barbecues—the independent, frontiersmen-like character of Kentucky comes shining through.

United We Stand

Although coalfields and railroads generated a mining industry in the 19th century, Kentucky remained largely agricultural throughout the 20th century. It suffered greatly even before the Great Depression struck, as inflation and Prohibition took their toll on manufacturing and alcohol production, respectively. The silver lining of the Great Depression, however, brought a number of New Deal programs to Kentucky, improving infrastructure, public education,

Kentucky's tradition of producing fine thoroughbred racehorses continues today, as Kentucky has avoided most of the industrialization common in other border states and devotes large ranches to horses.

North Carolina

Esse Quam Videri (To be, rather than to seem)

The pristine beaches, fertile lowlands, and scenic mountains of North Carolina draw as much admiration today as they did when Europeans first discovered them. The first English colony in North America was established on Roanoke Island off the Carolina coast, and although the colony mysteriously disappeared, it was only one of a long line of state firsts. North Carolina saw the first English child born in North America, the first public university at Chapel Hill in 1795, and, most famously, the Wright brothers' successful flight of the world's first manned heavier-than-air plane near Kitty Hawk, on North Carolina's Outer Banks.

Less convivially, the Outer Banks are known as the Graveyard of the Atlantic; the wrecks of more than 600 ships that foundered on this lovely string of islands are popular with scuba divers and treasure hunters. Once harboring the infamous pirate Blackbeard, the Outer Banks are currently experiencing a building boom as a vacation destination, despite taking the brunt of North Carolina's frequent hurricane strikes. North Carolina shares the nation's most visited national park with Tennessee; the Great Smoky Mountains attract 10 million people every year. One of America's most popular roadways, the Blue Ridge Parkway snakes its way from Virginia through North Carolina, accumulating a yearly average of 16 million drivers.

In this western part of the state, tourism leads the economy, although agriculture is making something of a comeback, particularly by exploiting the region's potential for growing Christmas trees. Although the traditional mainstay of textile manufacturing has slipped into decline, the populous, central Piedmont region—particularly the city of Charlotte—is a haven for the financial industries. Although in recent years the old standby of tobacco farming has encountered an uncertain market, North Carolina remains the nation's foremost producer of the plant, continuing a long history of tobacco production.

Currently, North Carolina is experiencing a rapid population boom and an accompanying political shift due largely to recent influxes of Latinos and Asians into the state. While North Carolina has voted Republican in every presidential election but one since 1968, the state gocernment is under divided partisan control. Once the state's political divide followed geographic lines between the lowlands and the mountainous west; now, as in much of the rest of the country, there is a growing urban-rural divide. Due in part to the boom, North Carolina is beginning to emerge as a national leader in culture and economics.

Fog filters through the Black Mountains in western North Carolina. Many people are now moving into this lovely region.

North Carolina State Facts

Full Name: State of North Carolina
Meaning of Name: From King Charles I of England
Admitted to the Union: November 21, 1789 (12th state)
Inhabitant: Carolinian
Capital City: Raleigh

Flower: Dogwood
Tree: Pine
Bird: Cardinal

Geography and Ecology

In the Appalachian western portion of North Carolina, the Black Mountains rise to the highest point east of the Mississippi River, 6,684 feet at the peak of Mt. Mitchell. The climate in this region is humid continental, much colder than the rest of the state. While the middle region, the Piedmont, can expect only 3 to 8 inches of snowfall per year, snowfalls of more than two feet are not uncommon in the west.

Central Population

Moving east, the Appalachian Mountains fall off to the rolling plains of the Piedmont region, which generally has hot summers and cold winters, and although precipitation averages here are the lowest in the state, inhabitants can still expect 40 inches or more per year. The Piedmont is the most urban part of the state, with most of the state's population centered in this region.

Most of North Carolina consists of the easternmost section, the Coastal Plain. Flat and sandy, this region is the most rural section of the state, with agriculture still economically dominant. The Atlantic Ocean moderates the humid subtropical climate here, so that summers are warm and winters mild.

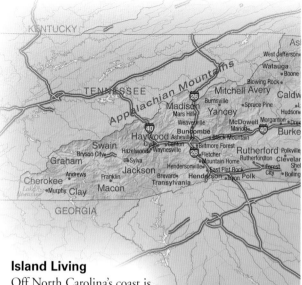

Island Living

Off North Carolina's coast is a long, thin string of barrier islands known as the Outer Banks. They form the two largest landlocked sounds in the country, Albemarle and Pamlico. The islands protect the mainland from storms, and one sand dune called Jockey's Ridge is the highest in the eastern United States, rising 138 feet high. Only Florida and Louisiana rank above North Carolina in number of hurricane strikes.

The Outer Banks are extremely popular with vacationers, not only for their beaches, but also for historic areas, including Fort Macon, which withstood 11 hours of Union bombardment during the Civil War before surrendering, and Fort Raleigh National Historic Site. Ocracoke's lighthouse first opened in 1823 and is the oldest operating lighthouse in the state, while Cape

THE LAST OF THE RED WOLVES

Although once they were native to all of southeast North America, today only a tiny population of endangered red wolves roams free, all of them in federal wildlife refuges in North Carolina. Most members of this critically endangered wolf species are held in captivity, to increase their chances of survival; only 50–75 or so can be found in the North Carolina wilderness.

A red wolf makes its way through a clearing.

Tobacco plants fill a North Carolina farm's fields. Tobacco has been a significant crop in the state's economy since the 17th century.

Hatteras is crowned with the tallest lighthouse in America at 198 feet. Two federally protected areas, Cape Hatteras National Seashore and Cape Lookout National Seashore, prevent too much activity from harming these delicate, ecologically crucial islands.

North Carolina Parks

Thirty-four state and 14 national parks grace the state, including the nation's most popular national park, which North Carolina shares with Tennessee. Great Smoky Mountains National Park spreads over 800 square miles and showcases a wide variety of wildlife, including black bears, bobcats, and eagles. It also contains thousands of species of plants, some of which are endemic to the region. In recognition of their unique ecology, the Smoky Mountains have recently been declared an international biosphere reserve.

The distinctive Cape Hatteras lighthouse flashes a warning to ships traversing the tricky waters of the Outer Banks. The current tower, built in 1870 and rising 198 feet, is the tallest in the United States and can be seen from 24 nautical miles away.

The Tar Heel State

Giovanni da Verrazzano, exploring the New World for France, reached Cape Fear in 1524, but it was not until 1584 that Europeans attempted to settle in North Carolina. The first English colony in North America was established on Roanoke Island under the jurisdiction of Sir Walter Raleigh, after whom North Carolina's capital is named, but lasted only a few years before vanishing. The "lost colony" has since become one of America's most investigated mysteries.

During the 18th century North Carolina began to attract different types of settlers. At first most had migrated south from Virginia, but a rift began to grow between the eastern plantation owners and western yeomen. During the Revolutionary War, this rift resolved itself into Loyalists and Revolutionaries, and although North Carolina saw few major battles, fierce guerrilla warfare between the two factions created mutual distrust that lasted through the 19th century.

A 1767 map of Great Britain's southeast colonies, including North Carolina, South Carolina, and Georgia, particularly notes the Cherokee Nation and its "warlike" character.

First, Farthest, Last

By the time of the Civil War, fully one-third of the population were slaves, most of them on eastern plantations. Nevertheless, this extremely rural state (only Wilmington's population topped 10,000) hesitated to join the Confederacy, not least because of western discontentment with eastern society. Once North Carolina joined, however, it threw itself into the war effort, providing nearly a fifth of the total Confederate army, or 125,000 men. Forty thousand of them never came home—the highest losses of any southern state.

During the war, North Carolina furnished the first soldier killed in action (Private Henry Wyatt at the Battle of Big Bethel), pushed the farthest into Union lines at the Battle of Gettysburg, and fired the final shots at the war's ultimate battle at Appomattox Court House. The litany earned the state an oft-recited motto, "First at Bethel, Farthest at Gettysburg, and Last at Appomattox."

Lunch Counters and Equal Rights

After the war North Carolinians fell back on their old economic standbys of cotton and tobacco farming and quickly became part of the "Solid South," referring to Democratic party loyalty. During Reconstruction African Americans not only voted, but also held public office. However, an 1898 Democratic campaign advocating white supremacy helped establish a racist pattern that lasted for most of the 20th century; North Carolina elected no African Americans to national office between 1898 and 1992.

In 1960 the Civil Rights Movement gained traction in Greensboro, North Carolina, when four African American college students orchestrated a six-month-long protest at a local Woolworth's lunch counter. Refusing to give up their seats or obey store policy that they must

Located in south-central North Carolina, Fort Bragg is a major U.S. Army base with a population of about 30,000. It stations many units and is an important regional employer.

stand to eat, their nonviolent protest inspired similar sit-ins throughout the nation and attracted so much publicity that local stores eventually reversed their policies. The instrumental Student Nonviolent Coordinating Committee was founded in Raleigh the same year.

Changing North Carolina

Today, North Carolina is moving rapidly, and in some cases painfully, away from its agrarian past. The city of Charlotte is now the nation's second-largest banking center, behind only New York City. Information and biotechnology industries are booming, particularly in the so-called Research Triangle area that includes Raleigh, Durham, and Chapel Hill. Culturally, North Carolina is shifting, as its Piedmont cities are growing and the region becomes increasingly suburban. Nevertheless, even while

FIRST IN FLIGHT

On December 17, 1903, Wilbur and Orville Wright ushered in a new age of transportation, flying their Wright Flyer four times on North Carolina's Outer Banks, near Kitty Hawk. The Flyer was the world's first manned, heavier-than-air, powered aircraft to sustain flight and make a controlled landing by a pilot. Although the best of their test flights lasted for only 59 seconds, the feat heralded a technological revolution, with long-lasting communications, transportation, economic, and military ramifications.

Wilbur Wright runs alongside the Wright Flyer as his brother Orville pilots their innovation into history.

some regions are booming, others are suffering as the textile industry falters in smaller communities. As North Carolina navigates the choppy waters of transition, there still appears to be a bright future on the horizon.

Charlotte is one of the nation's fastest-growing cities, thanks in large part to the financial industry, which dominates the growing downtown.

Tennessee

The Volunteer State

Agriculture and Commerce

Somewhere between the high mysteries of the Great Smoky Mountains and the broad, thick soils of the Mississippi River floodplains was born Tennessee. Fiercely independent, with a frontiersman's spirit and a farmer's ingenuity, Tennessee was the first state to declare itself part of America from the western wilds. It was also the last to join its Confederate sisters in their struggle for secession, and the first to rejoin the Union after that struggle faltered and failed.

Three lands pressed into one, Tennessee ranges from mountains to rolling hills and plateaus—where stands the capital city both of Tennessee and country music, Nashville—to fertile low-lying regions watered by the Mississippi River. The state's nature is reflected in its flag, whose three stars represent the three geographic and cultural regions. They may just as well, however, represent Tennessee's broad history of struggles, from the early days when settlers and American Indians sparred constantly for land, to the Civil War when North and South, mountaineer and plantation-owner, turned against each other, to the long, drawn-out struggle of Tennessean African Americans to truly win their rights and liberty.

Perhaps it is no wonder that out of such history some of America's greatest sounds were born, from Memphis blues to Nashville's honky-tonk. At once a vindication and a mourning, Tennessean music reaches deep into the American soul, and it is here that many American music legends flowered. The Carter Family, Merle Haggard, B. B. King, Johnny Cash, and Roy Orbison all found their sound in Tennessee. Perhaps most famous of all, Elvis Presley recorded his first album in Memphis, and later settled into Graceland, an estate on the southern side of the city.

In some ways Tennessee encapsulates the southern United States, both geographically and culturally, even as it sings its soul to the rest of the nation. Today, the state is known for log cabins preserved in its numerous parks, its friendly traditional barbecues, and its dedication to American music. But in these things can be heard the echoes of rougher ages, when men armed with muskets probed the dense forests, when slaves sang their discontent while working in the cotton fields of the west, and when cowboys drove their cattle to market along the mighty Mississippi. The Tennessee Valley Authority began the state on its increasingly industrial road, but Tennessee's sights and sounds preserve the American South in ways few other places can claim.

Tennessee still supports a variety of pastoral scenes. Here, an old fence marks off a meadow in view of the Great Smoky Mountains.

Tennessee State Facts

Full Name: State of Tennessee
Meaning of Name: From Tanasi, Cherokee towns along Little Tennessee River
Admitted to the Union: June 1, 1796 (16th state)
Inhabitant: Tennessean

Capital City: Nashville
Flower: Iris
Tree: Tulip poplar
Bird: Mockingbird

Geography and Ecology

Shaped like a distended parallelogram, Tennessee is far longer than wide, measuring approximately 440 miles east-west and only 120 miles north-south. It crosses six distinct geographic regions, although several of these are quite small. Generally speaking, the landscape falls off from the high points in the Blue Ridge Mountains on the eastern border (the highest point in the state, Clingman's Dome at 6,643 feet, is here) to the lowest point at 178 feet in the Alluvial Plain next to the Mississippi River.

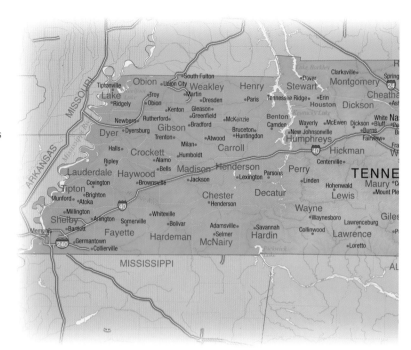

Tennessee Topography

Next to the Blue Ridge range is the Ridge and Valley region. This area is forested and divided by several streams and rivers, which flow into the 652-mile-long Tennessee River. Middle Tennessee consists of the high, flat Cumberland Plateau and the Nashville Basin. The fertility of this region was recognized early on by settlers, and it is still a lucrative area for tobacco growers, although most of the region's population is centered in the city of Nashville.

The distinctive skyline of Tennessee's capital city, Nashville, is much changed from the city's early years as a remote trading post.

The flat, fertile Gulf Coastal Plain takes up the majority of West Tennessee. The city of Memphis marks the sharp transition between the Coastal Plain and the Alluvial Plain, an area of swampy, low-lying floodplains sometimes referred to as the Delta. The western part of Tennessee receives most of the state's tornadoes, averaging 26 tornadoes per year.

Trails and Tears

A path called the Natchez Trace used by Indian traders and, later, incoming settlers, stretched all the way from Natchez, Mississippi, to central Tennessee, linking the Cumberland, Tennessee, and Mississippi Rivers. Today the trail is commemorated in the Natchez Trace Parkway,

AMERICAN CHESTNUT

Once, there were perhaps 4 billion American chestnut trees throughout the eastern United States. Today, there may be fewer than 100. The culprit behind the disappearance of these mighty, 100–150 foot trees is a fungus, first observed on an American chestnut in 1904. One of the few places where mature American chestnuts still survive is Jackson County, Tennessee. Two of the largest remaining trees grow here, and botanists often come to observe and study their success.

which allows visitors to traverse all 444 miles of the trail with ample recreational stops along the way.

Another trail that wends its way through Tennessee (and eight other states, as well) has a far sadder history. In 1838 federal troops escorted thousands of Cherokee Indians out of their traditional lands, removing them to the west in order to open up the area for white settlers. More than 16,000 Cherokees walked the so-called Trail of Tears. Approximately 4,000 of them died along the way. Today, all 2,200 miles of their path are recognized as a National Historic Trail.

AN AMERICAN HERO

Deliberately introduced in America in 1876 from Asia, kudzu—a rapidly growing vine—has established itself throughout nearly the entire South. Grown far out of control, the plant chokes natural vegetation and destroys crops, costing the nation millions of dollars every year. Chattanooga, Tennessee, employs a unique and so far effective kudzu-killing machine: goats. Good for the native plants, good for the goats, and good for the environment, the animal solution may soon be adopted by other regions.

Once welcomed as a bulwark against soil erosion, kudzu runs rampant throughout the South, strangling vegetation.

TVA built its first dam along the Clinch River in 1933–36. Today, visitors travel to Norris Dam for recreation and the scenery.

The Volunteer State

Although their destination was officially designated as "Indian territory," Anglo-American settlers began crossing over the mountains in the mid-18th century. These "overmountain men" attempted to create a 14th state soon after the American Revolution. Hardships and failures did not prevent settlers from pushing west, despite clashes with Cherokees. One of these pioneers was the American folk hero Davy Crockett, who served in Congress for three terms. Finally North Carolina—which technically controlled the land—handed it over to the federal government. Tennessee became the first state to apply for admission from a territory, a wish granted on June 1, 1796.

Volunteers

Tennessee earned its nickname either during the War of 1812 or in the Mexican War of the 1840s, when the state called for volunteers to fight. In either case, Tennessee provided so many fighters that it became known as the Volunteer State. In the early 19th century, some

In one of the bloodiest battles in American history, the fierce fighting at Shiloh resulted in a Union victory, but not without a heavy toll.

Tennesseans, including future president Andrew Jackson, forced American Indians out, and new settlers established large plantations in west and middle Tennessee. East

Nashville held the Tennessee Centennial and International Exposition, celebrated in fact one year late for the centennial, in 1897. By the time of the fair, Nashville had largely recovered from the Civil War, with manufacturing and commerce booming.

Tennessee remained the home of mountaineers and small farmers. The Indians had all but vanished, but in the west the number of enslaved African Americans rose precipitously, so that by 1860 fully a quarter of the state's population were slaves.

Although it was the last state to secede and join the Confederacy, Tennessee fought a number of battles. One of the worst of these—and indeed of the war—was at Shiloh. At the time, it was the bloodiest battle in American history. The more than 23,000 men killed or wounded at Shiloh exceeded that of all previous American wars combined.

Reconstruction

Tennessee fell early to the Union, and its compliance in ratifying the 14th Amendment allowed it to escape military governance after the war, the only former Confederate state to do so. Although Tennessean Andrew Johnson became president upon President Lincoln's assassination, the state nevertheless suffered economically and socially after the war. A few ex-Confederates founded the Ku Klux Klan as a social club in 1865. The Klan's birthplace of Pulaski now hosts a parade on Martin Luther King Day, celebrating the triumphs of the Civil Rights Movement.

The Authority in the Valley

The state was struck badly by the Great Depression, and in 1933 the Tennessee Valley Authority was created as a way of bringing electricity and jobs to the region. By 1945 the TVA had become the largest utility in the nation.

Andrew Johnson

Harnessing and taming the mighty Tennessee River with a series of dams, the TVA reduced flooding and provided cheap, renewable energy, besides generating industry. The project was so successful that the region was chosen to house a town devoted to the clandestine Manhattan Project; by 1945 the planned military-industrial community of Oak Ridge had swelled to some 70,000 people.

Fighting for Rights

Tennessee has a long history of independent thinkers. Early settlers fought for land; soon after the turn of the 20th century the region became a hotbed for women's suffrage; and in the mid-20th century civil rights activists gravitated to its cities. The movement won an early victory in the state when students, using nonviolent methods, succeeded in desegregating lunch counters. Sadly, it was in Memphis that the most tragic act of the era played out, when Dr. Martin Luther King Jr. was assassinated on April 4, 1968.

Despite this tragedy, Tennessee is remembered at the forefront of the Civil Rights Movement, and today Memphis hosts the largest percentage of African Americans of any major metropolitan area in the nation. The unique intersection of African American, country, and mountaineer influences gives Tennessee one of the most vibrant and dynamic cultural blends in the nation. Visiting the haunted fields at Shiloh or walking the echoing halls of the Country Music Hall of Fame, one cannot help but respond to the depth of Americana that Tennessee so proudly displays.

A guide demonstrates the functioning of a Tennessee Valley Authority dam to visitors. TVA projects revolutionized Tennessee in the 1930s.

The 13.8-acre estate of Graceland, home to rock-and-roll legend Elvis Presley, is now a National Historic Landmark.

South Carolina

The Palmetto State

Dum Spiro Spero (While I breathe, I hope)

The smallest of the Deep South states, South Carolina stretches from its long beaches on the Atlantic Ocean, with waters kept warm by the passing Gulf Stream, to a northwestern tip in the Blue Ridge Mountains. Its warm, humid climate produces lush vegetation, while its swamps and waterways teem with wildlife—including the voracious American alligator. Its climate has also heavily influenced the state's history, which from the first benefited from crops on large plantations, and the architecture, which adapted to the heat and humidity with graceful piazzas and large windows.

Although small, ever since it separated from North Carolina in 1729, South Carolina has played a large role on the national stage, contributing rowdy sharpshooters to the Revolutionary War and firing the first shots of the Civil War. South Carolina's early fortunes rose and fell along with cotton and indigo; still largely agrarian, today the state focuses on tobacco and various livestock products. In addition, South Carolina has a large textile-manufacturing sector, although in recent years the industry has suffered somewhat.

South Carolina also hosts a bustling tourism industry, attracting beachgoers, history buffs, and water-sport enthusiasts of all types. One of the nation's most celebrated zoos, Riverbanks Zoological Park, is located in South Carolina's capital, Columbia, which doubles as the state's largest city. A gorgeous array of grand antebellum houses grace the streets of Charleston, historically South Carolina's most prestigious city, and home to Fort Sumter National Monument. It was here that the Civil War opened, and the fort is now a popular tourist attraction.

Arguably, however, South Carolina's greatest attractions are its beaches, rivers, and biologically rich swamps and forests. The Grand Strand is an exceptionally long string of virtually uninterrupted beaches, covering nearly 60 miles along US 17. Its primary attraction is Myrtle Beach, a city synonymous with summer vacation activities. Nearby Hilton Head Island, the largest sea island between New Jersey and Florida, is famous for its luxury resorts and ideal beaches. On the other side of the state, the Chattooga River snakes its way through Sumter National Forest, and its rapids prove an irresistible attraction to kayakers and white-water rafters every year.

Despite the cultural, political, and economic transitions of the last half-century, South Carolina still proudly displays its rich past. Instrumental in so many of the country's formative events, the state still has much to offer to the nation it helped to found.

Charleston's coastal beauty, historic buildings, and oak-lined streets produce a healthy tourist industry in this rapidly growing port city.

South Carolina State Facts

Full Name: State of South Carolina
Meaning of Name: From King Charles I of England
Admitted to the Union: May 23, 1788 (8th state)
Inhabitant: South Carolinian

Capital City: Columbia
Flower: Carolina jessamine
Tree: Palmetto
Bird: Carolina wren

Geography and Ecology

Historically, South Carolinians have divided themselves into "uplanders" and "lowlanders," although there are, strictly speaking, three disparate geographic regions. The majority of the state belongs to the low, flat, Coastal Plain (the "lowland"), stretching from the Atlantic Ocean inland to a string of low, sandy hills. This unlikely ridge, known as the Sandhills region, may be the remnants of an earlier age, when the Atlantic covered the entire Coastal Plain. The rest of the state (the "upland") rises through the hilly Piedmont up to the state's highest elevations in the Blue Ridge Mountains, which are lower and rounder here than farther north.

Regional Differences

South Carolina's most fertile land can be found in the Coastal Plain. Piedmont farmers never had much success, and now the region is largely reforested, except for the increasingly suburban areas around cities like the capital, Columbia. The Piedmont's southeastern border is the fall line, the place at which rivers fall to the Coastal Plain below. Because rivers became increasingly difficult to navigate inland from that point, the northwest portions of the state developed somewhat differently from their eastern cousins. The geography contributed to a mutual dislike between uplanders and lowlanders. Those hard feelings were somewhat resolved when the site of the state capital (Columbia) was agreed upon to rest in the center of the state.

CONGAREE NATIONAL PARK

Few forests are taller than Congaree in central South Carolina. Although it is one of the nation's smallest national parks, it is the largest section of old-growth floodplain forest in North America. Once these forests covered huge swaths of land, but prolonged logging threatened their survival. A grassroots movement succeeded in naming the area as a national monument in 1976; in 2003 recognition of the area's value in terms of ecology and recreation prompted the National Park Service to designate it a national park.

Bald cypress trees feast in the nutrient-rich swamps of Congaree National Park, one of the last holdouts of virgin floodplain.

A pair of live, or evergreen, oaks thrive in a field of wildflowers. They owe their names to the fact that they are green year-round.

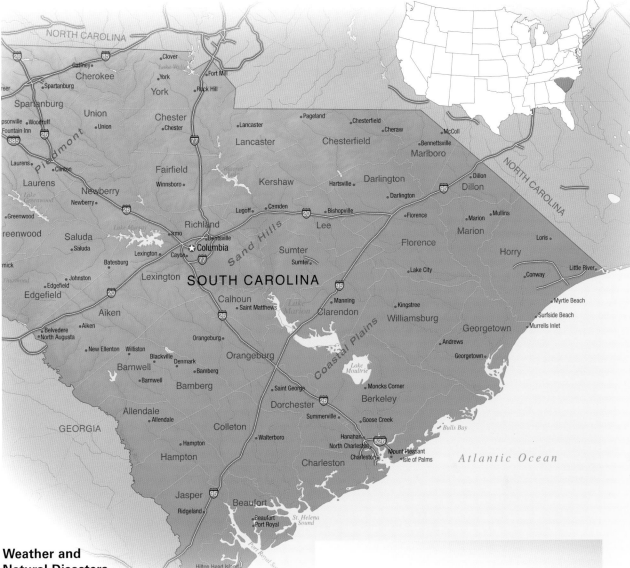

Weather and Natural Disasters

South Carolina's climate is fairly uniform, humid subtropical except in the very western tip, where it shows characteristics of humid continental. The state is subject to hot, humid summers and mild winters, with little appreciable snowfall anywhere. Tropical storms and hurricanes strike the state with some regularity. Although South Carolina suffers less frequently from severe thunderstorms and tornadoes than other Deep South states, it has its fair share of bad weather, particularly freezing rain. It also experiences the occasional earthquake, the worst of which measured 7.2 in magnitude and killed 60 people in Charleston in 1886.

Pawley Island, one of the Grand Strand islands along the North and South Carolina coasts, is a popular tourist destination.

The Palmetto State

More than 30 American Indian tribes of the area were present when the first permanent English settlers arrived in 1670. The Indians' trails became the fledgling colony's roads, and are still used today; several sections of the Cherokee Path are now paved as South Carolina Highway 11 and US Interstate 26.

Situated strategically on a natural harbor, the one-time capital city of Charleston quickly blossomed into one of the busiest and richest towns in the American colonies. The fertile Coastal Plain was ideal for growing crops of rice, cotton, and, thanks largely to the enterprising Eliza Lucas (the daughter of a British army officer), indigo. Unfortunately, such crops encouraged the institution of slavery. Almost immediately, enslaved Africans or people of African descent outnumbered white colonists in the Palmetto State. This situation persisted until the 20th century, when African Americans began moving north in large numbers. Unsurprisingly, one of the nation's earliest slave insurrections occurred on South Carolina soil in 1739.

The Nullification Crisis

Charleston's fortunes—and, by extension, all of South Carolina's—began entering a long decline soon after the Revolutionary War. Charleston's elite had come to depend almost exclusively on cotton, allowing other commercial sources of wealth to decline. During this period, the federal government enacted tariffs on imported goods, designed to bolster the North's growing industries; as South Carolina's agricultural economy began to suffer, state leaders began to vigorously object, claiming that the tariffs unfairly favored the northern economy. The issue

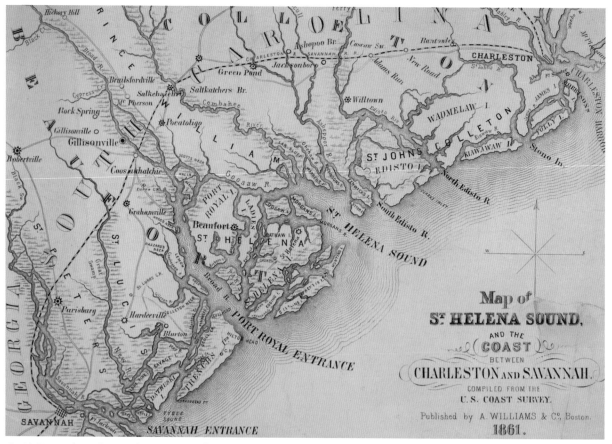

An 1861 map shows the central-eastern coast of the Confederate States of America, from Charleston in the north (where the first shots were fired) to Savannah, Georgia, in the south (where General Sherman ended his infamous march to the sea).

came to a head when South Carolinian John C. Calhoun nearly brought his state to blows with the federal government, despite serving as vice president of the United States at the time. Although South Carolina did not, in the end, declare the tariff void, the "Nullification Crisis" foreshadowed the dramatic events of April 12, 1861.

Today an oft-visited national monument, Fort Sumter retains the trappings of its former role as a military stronghold.

Civil War and Its Aftermath

Wade Hampton

Frustrated with federal power, South Carolina seceded from the Union on December 20, 1860, starting a wave of secessions throughout the South. In April Confederate forces fired on Union-held Fort Sumter in Charleston harbor; although no one was killed, the event sparked the Civil War. South Carolina contributed much to the ensuing war effort, including 44,000 troops and the celebrated general Wade Hampton III. The state suffered horribly, however, particularly the city of Charleston, which was choked by a Union blockade.

Virulent resentment of Reconstruction and economic desolation, worsened by a general decline in agriculture and the 1920s boll weevil plague, left much of South Carolina destitute until World War II. During that time the Ku Klux Klan became powerful in the state, contributing to periodic spikes of racist violence. The extent of 20th-century discrimination was significant; after the Voting Rights Act of 1965 the number of registered African American voters in South Carolina more than tripled.

Old Wounds, New Directions

South Carolina's early dependence on plantations and an accordingly large slave population caused repercussions still felt today. Its role in the Civil War, the ensuing economic devastation, and the institutionalized segregation that followed have left an indelible mark on the state. But today South Carolina is slowly transforming into a vibrant culture and diverse economy, capitalizing on its wealth of natural beauty and historical sites. Doubtless the state will be well-served by its tradition of stubborn perseverance, as suggested by both of its mottos, "While I breathe, I hope," and "Ready in soul and resource."

"SHOELESS" JOE JACKSON

Born in Pickens County, "Shoeless" Joe Jackson became one of baseball's best hitters and most controversial players. Along with seven teammates of the Chicago White Sox, he was accused of throwing the 1919 World Series, although his culpability remains in doubt. He earned his nickname in his hometown, during a company game when he got such a painful blister that he played without his shoes.

"Shoeless" Joe Jackson in his Chicago White Sox outfit. Along with several teammates, he was banned from baseball in 1921.

Georgia

The Peach State

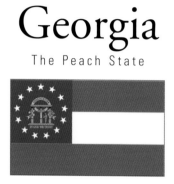

Wisdom, Justice, and Moderation

Famous for its peaches, graceful coastal architecture, and sprawling old plantations, Georgia is today one of the nation's most rapidly growing states. Its capital city, Atlanta, is a bustling hub and home to such companies as Coca-Cola and Home Depot. Once dependent on its thick soil for a cotton-heavy agricultural economy, Georgia has recently emerged as a leader in manufacturing, trade, and financial services; 5.13 million people—more than half the state's total population—live in Atlanta's metro area.

Its population and business booms notwithstanding, Georgia suffered from a historic drought in 2007–8 that threatened not only agricultural areas and ecosystems, but also urban and economic growth. While there are no easy solutions to such environmental pressures, the state set about tackling these issues through various conservation programs and laws restricting water usage.

Historically, Georgia has succeeded admirably in recovery. After General Sherman destroyed Atlanta in the Civil War, the city adopted the image of a phoenix—a mythic bird that rises from its own ashes—and has since become one of the nation's most influential cities. After decades of suffering under Jim Crow laws, African Americans triumphed and Atlanta elected the first African American mayor in any major southern city in 1973.

The state has also recovered and preserved much of its history and natural beauty, showcased in more than 60 state and 10 national parks, ranging from prehistoric mounds to the largest swamp in the country. Some of the state's most visited and lovely areas include the historic districts of Atlanta and Savannah, whose 19th-century architecture was fortuitously saved from destruction and is now protected by law and custom.

Savannah's unique culture and history were showcased in the novel and movie of the same name, *Midnight in the Garden of Good and Evil*, but the state's most famous bestseller-turned-blockbuster is undoubtedly *Gone With the Wind*. The author, Margaret Mitchell, is one of many celebrity or musical giants native to Georgian soil. Others include Alice Walker, Otis Redding, James Brown, Gladys Knight, and President Jimmy Carter. Also emerging from this increasingly diverse state are rock bands such as R.E.M. and The Black Crowes.

It is clear that Georgia is in a period of transition, becoming culturally more vibrant, politically more competitive, and demographically more urban. The drought proved that it has much to do to ensure its future, but if it dedicates itself to the state motto, "Wisdom, justice, and moderation," undoubtedly it will emerge as a national leader in the years to come.

Georgia is famous for its peaches, to which it dedicates 15,000 acres statewide. It ranks third in peach production nationwide.

Georgia State Facts

Full Name: State of Georgia
Meaning of Name: From King George II of England
Admitted to the Union: January 2, 1788 (4th state)
Inhabitant: Georgian

Capital City: Atlanta
Flower: Cherokee rose
Tree: Live oak
Bird: Brown thrasher

Geography and Ecology

Georgia's terrain falls from north to south through five distinct geographic regions. In the extreme northwest, a tiny piece of the Appalachian plateau hosts the popular tourist destination Lookout Mountain. Next to it, to the east, is a slightly larger section of the Appalachian Ridge and Valley, and in the north/northeast is the southernmost tip of the Blue Ridge Mountains. It is here that Georgia's highest elevations can be found, culminating in Brasstown Bold at 4,784 feet.

Before the Falls

From these three northerly regions, forested and mountainous, the land falls steadily across the broad, hilly Piedmont region. At the fall line—where the rivers tumble to the plain below—the land rises only 400 feet or so above sea level. Atlanta, located in the northern section of the Piedmont, is the highest major city east of Denver at more than 1,000 feet. Several of Georgia's most significant cities, including Augusta, Macon, and Columbus, are located along the fall line. In the past these areas marked the end of navigable waterways for merchant ships as they approached waterfalls and rapids.

Fog drifting through Chattahoochee National Forest lends the Appalachian Mountains an ethereal, aloof air.

Trouble with Trees

Below the fall line, the vast coastal plain spreads south and east. Taking up fully half of the state's landmass, the coastal plain can actually be split in half: the East Gulf Coastal Plain in the west and the Atlantic Coastal Plain

Georgia is known for its magnolia trees, which put on a brilliant display throughout the state every spring.

in the east. Both are flat and fertile, although much of the native ecology has been threatened by centuries of agriculture and logging. Forests of longleaf pine with their attendant ecosystems have all but disappeared, although Georgia—and other southern states—is now making a concerted effort to restore this fire-resistant type of forest.

Logging also threatened one of Georgia's most astonishing natural wonders: the Okefenokee Swamp, the largest swamp in North America, covering 700 square miles of southeastern Georgia. The lumber business expanded rapidly after the Civil War, and incursions into the swamp destroyed some of the nation's most impressive trees. Fortunately, the danger to the area was recognized fairly early, and the Okefenokee National Wildlife Refuge was established in 1936. In 1974, 350,000 additional acres were declared a national wilderness area. Among the swamp's rich wildlife can be seen wild turkeys, alligators, otters, and black bears.

Boundaries and New Issues

Although the colony of Georgia was established in 1733, the state's borders are still under debate. Georgia has the largest land area of states east of the Mississippi River, and rivers determined several of its boundaries. However, some of these borders no longer follow the rivers exactly, because over time the rivers' courses have changed. One

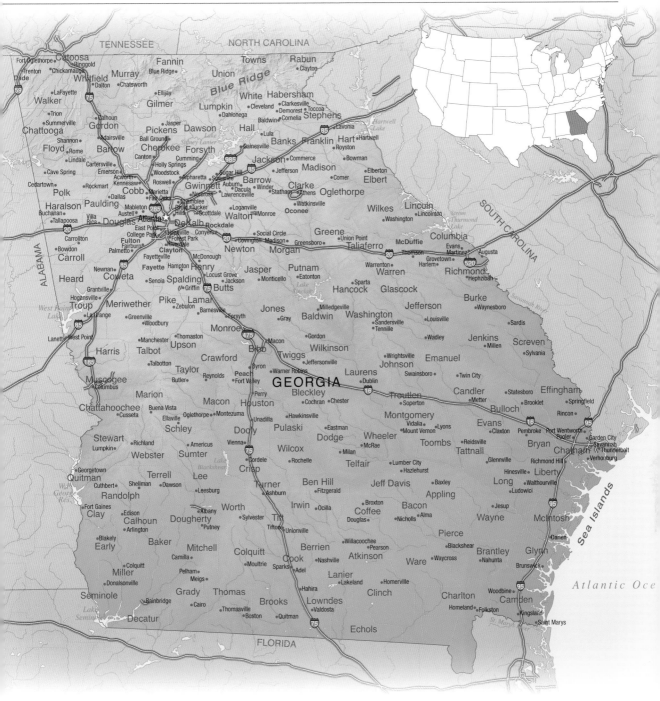

of the most debated borders concerns the Savannah River, which lies between Georgia and South Carolina; the issue was not settled until 1989.

More recently the severe drought conditions throughout Georgia have prompted the state to take another look at its borders. It has been argued that a cartographical error made 190 years ago unfairly denied the state access to the Tennessee River, and that the border should be reassessed. Severe restrictions on water use due to droughts take their toll across the state, and leaders worry about the effects such shortages will have on the state's economy and health. Although a variety of measures have been implemented for these conditions, long-term solutions have yet to be found.

The Peach State

Georgia has a long history of inhabitation, with an archaeological record dating back some 12,000 years. The earliest European presence in the region was Spanish, as explorers pushed into Creek and Cherokee lands from Spanish Florida. When James Oglethorpe, an English philanthropist, settled Savannah in 1733, the British crown welcomed it as a buffer against Spanish expansion. Oglethorpe planned Savannah to reflect his ideals of grace and equanimity, hoping to relieve England of its debtors and allow them to become productive members of society. He did not allow slavery, alcohol, or lawyers.

As admirable as Oglethorpe's vision was, it did not take long after Georgia became a crown colony in 1752 for economic and social reality to set in. Eventually, however, Georgia's rich soil proved ideal for the cash crops of the colonial and antebellum period. In fact, it was near Oglethorpe's Savannah that Eli Whitney invented his famous cotton gin, the machine that allowed the plant to boost the South in both economic and cultural importance.

A statue of James Oglethorpe presides over Augusta Common in Augusta, Georgia.

From Atlanta to the Sea

Although the last of the 13 English colonies in North America, Georgia was the fourth to ratify the Constitution, and the first southern state to do so, on January 2, 1788. Its economy soon came to rely heavily on cotton, although it also witnessed the first of many gold rushes in the United States when the precious metal was discovered in Dahlonega in 1828. Soon afterward the Cherokee were forcibly removed and Atlanta was founded in their former territory—a location ideal for the railroads suddenly sprouting all over the country. Atlanta quickly grew into a major transportation and manufacturing center, a reputation it had cause to regret during the Civil War.

By 1860 nearly half of Georgia's population were slaves, and the state emphatically supported the Confederacy. Few battles were fought in Georgia in the early years of the war, but it was the site of one of the last major Confederate victories, at Chickamauga in 1863. This battlefield and the neighboring battlefield of Chattanooga compose the largest military park in the nation; formed in 1890, it is also the oldest. More

Union picket soldiers near Atlanta in 1864. The picket typically built a low defensive structure as near to Confederate lines as possible and reported on enemy movements.

Ivy drenches the stairs of a classic Savannah home. Resplendent with vegetation, Savannah sometimes suffers the adverse effects of plant life thriving on its subtropical climate.

famously, Georgia suffered one of the most ruthless of Union campaigns in 1864. General Sherman burned a large swath of the state on his March to the Sea, starting with the vital city of Atlanta and ending in Savannah.

Cotton and Civil Rights

Georgia pulled itself through Reconstruction and the devastation with stubborn perseverance. Some areas began switching from cotton to fruit crops; others invested in lumber. Atlanta's population reemerged almost overnight, and by 1880 it was the state's largest city. However, cotton still reigned in many regions, including northern Georgia, and first the Ku

Born in Atlanta in 1929, Martin Luther King Jr. became a prominent leader in the American Civil Rights Movement.

Klux Klan and later Jim Crow laws threatened the new-found freedom of Georgian African Americans. When the boll weevil struck the cotton fields in the 1920s, the state slipped into economic depression early.

The Great Migration of the 20th century stripped Georgia of much of its African American population, as the disenchanted and disenfranchised left for the North. But the state birthed one of the Civil Rights Movement's greatest figures in 1929. Martin Luther King Jr. rallied not only his Baptist congregation but also much of the nation, leading the way in one of the most meaningful cultural and political shifts in American history. Both his birth-place and his gravestone can be seen in Atlanta today.

Just an Old Sweet Song

Currently, Georgia is one of the nation's most rapidly expanding states. Atlanta is internationally recognized and hosts more Fortune 500 companies than any city besides New York and Houston. An increasingly diverse culture has endowed the state with a series of national-ly famous artists, many of whom seem to return to the state's voluminous beauty, lush society, and complicated history for inspiration. Assuredly, Ray Charles was not the only Georgian for whom "Just an old sweet song / Keeps Georgia on my mind."

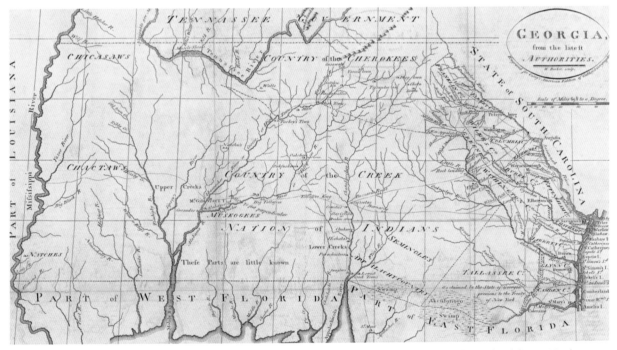

In 1795 American Indians were much in evidence in Georgia. Some of the groups identified here include the Creek, Chikasaw, Natchez, Muskogee, and Seminole peoples.

Mississippi

The Magnolia State

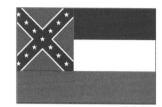

Virtute et Armis (By valor and arms)

Sandwiched between Alabama and the Mississippi River, the state of Mississippi in many ways typifies the Deep South. Characterized by low, fertile river lands and dense swamps, Mississippi still grows copious amounts of cotton, once the reigning crop not just of the state but also of the American South. The state has struggled since the Civil War with poverty, race relations, and environmental disasters but is beginning to recover economically. Still one of the most rural states in the South, Mississippi is home to vast cultivated fields, mighty forests of pine and oak, and fleets of shrimp boats, that trawl the Gulf of Mexico.

The state is named for the mighty river that dictates its western border. In the past the river's role as the nation's primary internal transportation route enriched Mississippi, encouraging cities and ports to emerge along its banks. Located along what may be the most fertile river valley in the world, Mississippi saw its golden age in the pre–Civil War period of sprawling plantations and king cotton. In the long hard years after the war, cotton and Mississippi fell from grace. However, cotton is still the state's most important crop today.

Significant social inequities culminated in the Civil Rights Movement of the mid-20th century, when violence against activists helped spark a national movement toward equality and desegregation. When James Meredith, the first African American student at the University of Mississippi enrolled, federal marshals were required to protect him; today, race relations have seen a marked improvement.

The economy, too, has revived, with agriculture, lumber, and tourism—particularly the newfound casino wealth along the coast—leading the way out of poverty. Unfortunately, the casinos' coastal location exposes them to the hurricanes that occasionally ravage the Gulf Coast. In 2005 Hurricane Katrina wreaked devastation upon the area and the industry, which have yet to fully recover.

Ecological disasters like hurricanes and floods have played major roles in Mississippi's history and development, slowing recovery after the Civil War, heralding the Great Depression in 1927, and restricting coastal development today. Moreover, all attempts to rein in the mighty Mississippi River have proved insufficient. Concern is growing that obstructing the river's natural development may ultimately harm its dependent ecological systems, including swamps and wetlands. Solutions to these and other issues still facing Mississippi will go a long way in helping the state continue to redeem its troubled past.

Apparently unchanged in the centuries since European discovery, the Pearl River curves through a forest not far from Jackson, Mississippi.

Mississippi State Facts

Full Name: State of Mississippi
Meaning of Name: From American Indian word
  meaning "great river" or "gathering-in of all waters"
Admitted to the Union: December 10, 1817 (20th state)
Inhabitant: Mississippian

Capital City: Jackson
Flower: Magnolia
Tree: Magnolia
Bird: Mockingbird

Geography and Ecology

Rising on average only 300 feet above sea level, Mississippi almost uniformly consists of fertile lowlands and gentle hills, culminating in the inaccurately named Woodall Mountain—at 806 feet the highest point in the state. Settled slowly and industrialized late, Mississippi remains heavily forested, with vast woodlands of pine, elm, and oak trees covering more than half the state's 45,000 square miles of land. Several rivers wend their way through Mississippi, fertilizing the earth as they travel and watering two of the most productive river valleys in the nation along the Pearl and Tombigbee rivers.

The rivers and the resultant nutrient-heavy soil enriched Mississippi for much of its state history. The soil is particularly conducive to growing cotton. Even today the state is one of the largest producers of cotton in the nation, and Greenwood follows only Memphis as a cotton exchange. However, Mississippi pays a heavy price for its lovely rivers, which tend to overflow their banks. Although such floods bring valuable nutrients to the state's fields and crops, they wreak destruction and cost millions of dollars in rescues and repairs.

Rising Waters

Successive Mississippi River floods in the years following the Civil War, when many of the laboriously built levees were damaged or destroyed, devastated much of the region and slowed the state's recovery. The worst of the floods, however, struck at a time when the U.S. Army Corp of Engineers had taken over levee building. Overconfidence in their accomplishment resulted in hundreds of deaths as the Great Mississippi River Flood of 1927 inundated 27,000 square miles—roughly the size of New England, excluding the state of Maine.

Hurricane Exposure

More recently, Mississippi has suffered from violent hurricanes, notably Camille in 1969 and Katrina in 2005. Direct strikes are less common than secondary hits as storms move in after making landfall in neighboring states. However, two of the three most populous cities, Biloxi and Gulfport, lie vulnerable on Mississippi's slim strip of coast, protected only somewhat by barrier islands in the Gulf of Mexico. These draw thousands of visitors to their sandy beaches and wild areas, protected by the

The Mississippi River still serves as a major inland waterway and a crucial source of water for farms and cities.

National Park Service as part of the Gulf Islands National Seashore. In addition, the coastal areas have recently become heavy with casino traffic; in 2005 Mississippi was the second-largest gambling state, trailing only Nevada, although the industry suffered from Hurricane Katrina later that year.

THE SINGING RIVER

Visitors to the lower stretches of the Pascagoula River may notice something strange: an eerie, low humming sound, beckoning from the dark waters. The unusual sound, sometimes described as similar to that of a swarm of bees, is said locally to be the last haunting refrain of the vanished Pascagoula Indians, who marched into the river to drown, singing as they went, rather than fight or be enslaved by the invading Biloxi Indians. In tribute to the tragic legend and the strange echoes of this faded past, locals often refer to the buzzing waters as the Singing River.

TENNESSEE

Southaven
Olive Branch
Benton
Corinth
Burnsville
Iuka
DeSoto
Marshall
Tippah
Alcorn
Tishomingo
Hernando
Holly Springs
Ripley
Booneville
Tunica
Coldwater
Union
Prentiss
Tunica
Tate
Senatobia
New Albany
Baldwyn
Belmont
Crenshaw
Bardis
Lee
Saltillo
Itawamba
Friars Point
Panola
Oxford
Pontotoc
Tupelo
Fulton
Coahoma
Jonestown
Batesville
Lafayette
Plantersville
Marks
Water Valley
Pontotoc
Verona
Clarksdale
Lambert
Shannon
Nettleton
Quitman
Charleston
Yalobusha
Bruce
Okolona
Amory
Tutwiler
Calhoun
Houston
Monroe
Shelby
Tallahatchie
Calhoun City
Chickasaw
Aberdeen
Rosedale
Mound Bayou
Grenada
Cleveland
Ruleville
Grenada
Webster
Clay
West Point
Bolivar
Leflore
Montgomery
Columbus
Shaw
Sunflower
Itta Bena
Greenwood
Eupora
Metcalfe
Indianola
Moorhead
Winona
Starkville
Greenville
Leland
Carroll
Oktibbeha
Lowndes
Inverness
Choctaw
Washington
Ackerman
Brooksville
Hollandale
Belzoni
Tchula
Attala
Louisville
Macon
Humphreys
Lexington
Kosciusko
Winston
Noxubee
Holmes
Goodman
Rolling Fork
Pickens
Sharkey
Yazoo City
Leake
Philadelphia
De Kalb
Yazoo
Carthage
Neshoba
Kemper
Issaquena
Madison
Union
Flora
Canton
Scott
Newton
Collinsville
Warren
Madison
Decatur
Nellieburg
Marion
Vicksburg
Ridgeland
Morton
Meridian
Edwards
Clinton
Forest
Pelahatchie
Newton
Lauderdale
Jackson
Pearl
Brandon
Raymond
Richland
Rankin
Stonewall
Hinds
Florence
Jasper
Quitman
Utica
Raleigh
Bay Springs
Clarke
Claiborne
Crystal Springs
Mendenhall
Smith
Port Gibson
Copiah
Simpson
Magee
Taylorsville
Hazlehurst
Jefferson
Covington
Laurel
Waynesboro
Fayette
Wesson
Collins
Ellisville
Wayne
Lawrence
Prentiss
Jones
Natchez
Brookhaven
Monticello
Adams
Franklin
Lincoln
Jefferson Davis
Sumrall
Petal
Richton
Marion
Hattiesburg
Summit
Columbia
Lamar
Wilkinson
Gloster
McComb
Walthall
Purvis
Beaumont
Leakesville
Woodville
Magnolia
Tylertown
Forrest
Perry
Greene
Amite
Centreville
Pike
Lumberton
Lucedale
Poplarville
Wiggins
George
LOUISIANA
Pearl River
Stone
Picayune
Harrison
Jackson
Lyman
Hancock
Ocean Springs
Escatawpa
Long Beach
Biloxi
Gautier
Moss Point
Bay Saint Louis
Gulfport
Pascagoula
Waveland
Pass Christian
Mississippi Sound

ARKANSAS
Mississippi River
The Delta
Tallahatchie River
Sardis Lake
Enid Lake
Greenleaf
Yalobusha River
LOUISIANA
Ross Barnett Res.
Okatibbee Res.
ALABAMA
Homochitto River
Pickwick Lake
Mississippi Sound
Gulf of Mexico

MISSISSIPPI

State History

Mississippi

The South

The Magnolia State

Inhabited since 10,000 BCE, Mississippi has been home to numerous peoples over the years and retains signs of many of them, from prehistoric mounds to modern architecture. The first European to explore the area, Hernando de Soto, arrived in 1540, but it took another century and a half for Europe to establish a presence there. This was the 1699 French settlement of Fort Maurepas, on the site of today's Ocean Springs. For more than 100 years, Europeans, Americans, and Choctaw, Chickasaw, and Natchez Indians fought and traded with each other in the disputed territory.

Cotton is King

Anglo-Americans started moving to the area in large numbers in the 1830s, although the region remained only sparsely settled throughout most of the 19th century. When farmers recognized the land's potential, the state developed a large-scale cotton economy almost overnight, with enormous plantations shipping cotton by steamboat and railroad. By 1860 slaves accounted for more than half of Mississippi's population, and the state became the second to secede after South Carolina.

A replica of the 1699 Fort Maurepas stands at Ocean Springs. Sadly, Hurricane Katrina badly damaged the rebuilt fort.

From Riches to Rags

Mississippi fought hard for the Confederate cause, losing 30,000 men and contributing President Jefferson Davis, whose two Mississippi homes are open to the public. The state didn't see significant action on its home soil until the second and third year of the war, but it

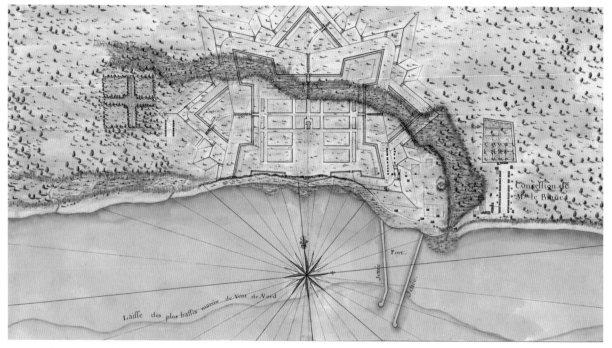

A plan of a new fort at Biloxi in 1721. France had moved the administrative center of French Louisiana to Biloxi from Mobile the year before, but fears of floods and storms prompted the removal of the capital to New Orleans shortly afterward, in 1723.

TOY STORY

In 1902 President Theodore Roosevelt went on a bear-hunting trip to Sharkey County, Mississippi. His companions tied an exhausted old bear to a tree for the president to shoot, but Roosevelt, touched by the animal's plight, refused. Immortalized in a political cartoon, the event sparked a craze evident to this day: the cuddly children's teddy bear.

Known as a hunter and naturalist, President Theodore Roosevelt dedicated 42 million acres of federally protected areas.

Race Relations

Mississippi was a major battleground in the African American Civil Rights Movement. Some of the worst offenses of racial violence occurred here, notably the murders of 14-year-old Emmett Till in 1954 and National Association for the Advancement of Colored People (NAACP) leader Medgar Evers in 1963. Not until 1995 did Mississippi formally ratify the 13th Amendment to abolish slavery, but race relations have improved dramatically since the 1960s.

On October 1, 1962, James Meredith became the first African American student of the University of Mississippi. His protection was ensured by U.S. marshals, but ensuing riots killed two people.

was forced to concede Vicksburg in what was to prove the beginning of the end for the Confederacy. Today, Vicksburg National Military Park and its associated cemeteries are popular destinations, especially during its annual Civil War reenactment.

Before the war, Mississippi ranked as the fifth-wealthiest state, in part due to its large, expensive concentration of slaves. After the war, emancipation, falling cotton prices, shattered infrastructure, floods, and a sort of cultural reticence concerning development impoverished the state to an extent that it has yet to fully recover from; today, Mississippi is the poorest state in the Union. Race relations rapidly became strained as whites wrested political power back from newly freed blacks. Although African Americans achieved startlingly high land-ownership rates immediately after the war, by the turn of the century most of the black population was mired in poverty.

Perhaps a silver lining to the state's impoverishment and troubled culture is the astounding array of literary figures, musicians, and actors who hailed from Mississippi in the 20th century. Among the most influential are Tennessee Williams, William Faulkner, Shelby Foote, Muddy Waters, B. B. King, Jimmy Buffett, Morgan Freeman, and Oprah Winfrey.

The Hospitality State

In the last quarter-century, industry has finally made inroads, and more recently still, new casinos are contributing to the economy. Tourism has also become economically significant. These economic changes encourage immigration and cultural renewal and have revitalized Mississippi's other nickname, "the Hospitality State." Whether Mississippi will heal all its wounds remains to be seen, but assuredly this "late bloomer" has yet to fully tap its own potential.

Alabama

The Heart of Dixie

Audemus Jura Nostra Defendere (We dare defend our rights)

A fertile land of humid summers, mild winters, and lush scenery, Alabama is a state where history is closely tied to geography. The north hides large mineral deposits in its rocky and forested depths, bestowing a heavy industrial flavor to Birmingham and its surrounding areas. In the past the nutrient-rich soils of central and southern Alabama gave rise to sprawling plantations and the attendant "peculiar institution" of slavery—a social reality that still echoes in the state's culture, society, and politics today.

Only a thin tab of land connects Alabama to the Gulf of Mexico, and it was not until General Andrew Jackson won the land in a bloody Indian war that Alabama became a state. The city of Mobile on the bay still reflects its unique history, with colonial architecture, Civil War memorabilia, and the oldest celebration of Mardi Gras in the country, stretching back to 1704. Mobile's Bellingrath Gardens, 27-mile Azalea Trail, and beachside resorts all show the softer side of Alabama.

Sadly, Alabama is better known for its hard-fought and sometimes violent battles in the Civil Rights Movement. Although race relations have improved dramatically since then, there is no denying the indelible and sometimes bru-tal effects of racism on Alabama's history. Still, in 2008 the overwhelmingly white county of Cullman voted an African American, James Fields, into Congress, an election that can be taken as one of many signs that the old social order is slowly fading.

Today, Birmingham is the undisputed center of Alabama. With a population of over a million, it is by far the largest city, the center of the state's industrial economy, and the point where interstates I-65, I-59, and I-20 meet. The former of these neatly bisects the state along its north-south axis and will take drivers through nearly all of Alabama's varied geography, from its mountainous north through the hills of Birmingham, to the broad fertile plains of the south and ending in the coastal, historic port city of Mobile.

Alabama has produced many Americans of note, including Booker T. Washington, Helen Keller, Hank Williams, Hank Aaron, Nat King Cole, Jesse Owens, and Rosa Parks. The list of sports achievers, rights activists, and artists stands testament to the same stubborn pride and ingenuity of Alabamians for which its early settlers were once praised.

Although cotton has not reigned for many years, fields still grow thickly throughout Alabama's fertile Black Belt.

Alabama State Facts

Full Name: State of Alabama
Meaning of Name: From Native American tribe Alabamas or Alibamons
Admitted to the Union: December 14, 1819 (22nd state)
Inhabitant: Alabamian

Capital City: Montgomery
Flower: Camellia
Tree: Southern longleaf pine
Bird: Yellowhammer

Geography and Ecology

Most of Alabama consists of the broad, flat, fertile Coastal Plain stretching north through the state nearly to Birmingham and even farther north along the western edge. Although not all of the region is perfectly suited to agriculture, it does include the famous "Black Belt" or "Black Prairie," so named for its rich, dark soil. Anglo-American settlers soon realized that the area was ideal for growing cotton, and cotton plantations sprang up everywhere in the 18th and 19th centuries. Today, the slim strip of Alabama on the Gulf Coast is a more attractive draw, with its luxurious resorts and lovely beaches.

North of the Coastal Plain are hillier regions, flat plateaus and, in a northeast–southwest strip ending near the center of the state, the southernmost tip of the Appalachian Mountains. Just to the south and southeast of the mountains, some of Alabama's most significant natural resources, notably coal, iron, and limestone, can be found in the Piedmont Plateau. Here, Cheaha Mountain rises to 2,407 feet, making it the highest point in the state. The Cumberland Plateau and Highland Rim extend from the mountains north-northwest, cut into sections, sometimes drastically, by rivers.

Natural Disasters

Only the small stretch of Alabama that reaches the Gulf of Mexico in the Mobile area is seriously vulnerable to hurricanes, as the state is protected for the most part by Florida's panhandle. Still, it is not uncommon for the state to suffer damages from hurricanes and tropical storms. A greater danger are the frequent violent tornadoes, tying the state for the most F-5 tornadoes—the most powerful category—with Kansas. The northern portion of the state

"From thy prairies broad and fertile, / Where thy snow-white cotton shines. / To the hills where coal and iron / Hide in thy exhaustless mines."

Alabama (state song), by Julia S. Tutwiler

Tornadoes are Alabama's most feared natural disaster; the state is located in the tornado-ridden "Dixie Alley" of the South.

is subjected most frequently to this hazard. Only Texas, Arkansas, and neighboring Mississippi have suffered more tornado-related fatalities than Alabama.

Meteor!

The worst natural disaster to strike Alabama, however, came not in the form of a tornado or hurricane but as a meteorite, some 83 million years ago. Only a few miles north of Montgomery, a 5-mile wide crater disrupts the natural landscape, and indeed some evidence of the impact is visible even to the untrained eye from US 280. Here, the rocky impact rim rises above the surrounding plain, stark evidence of an ancient collision that would have devastated the landscape for miles around.

RUSSELL CAVE NATIONAL MONUMENT

Located near Bridgeport in northeast Alabama, Russell Cave gives one of the most comprehensive archaeological records in the United States, providing numerous artifacts over a 10,000-year period of continuous habitation. It is the third-longest cave system in Alabama, but it is the abnormally large front entrance that attracts the most attention, for it is here that people frequented the cave from 6,500 BCE right up until European settlement in the 18th century. A natural as well as archaeological wonder, the cave system features wildlife such as an endemic scorpion, a cave length of more than 7 miles, and a natural spring, whose existence doubtless helped sustain the countless generations of inhabitants.

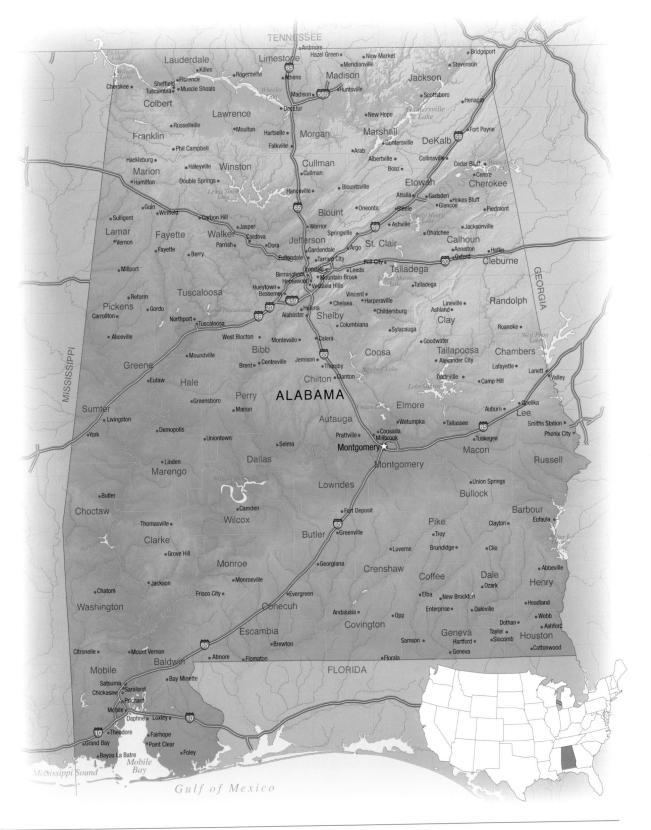

The Heart of Dixie

In the 17th and 18th centuries, Alabama territories changed hands repeatedly between Indian tribes, France, Spain, Britain, and the United States. Finally, future president Andrew Jackson, with his team of Tennessee militiamen, threw the remaining Creek Indians out after a bitter battle at Horseshoe Bend—today a popular national military park. Jackson's successes opened the region to Anglo-American settlement, and in 1819 Alabama joined the Union as the 22nd state.

Cotton Trade

In the 19th century Mobile emerged as a significant southern port, which allowed the shipment of the state's most lucrative export, cotton, to foreign markets. Also essential to the cotton market was Montgomery, which—after the invention of the steamboat—became a central transportation hub and subsequently the state capital. Arguably the most crucial aspect of cotton production, however, were Alabama's slaves, who by 1860 numbered 433,890, or nearly half the state's total population.

For a short time Montgomery functioned as the capital of the Confederate States of America: a star on the steps of the Capitol marks where Jefferson Davis stood during his inauguration as the Confederate president. It is for this reason that Alabama became known as the Heart of Dixie. Fairly few Civil War battles were fought on Alabamian soil, but nearly all of Alabama's population of white, able-bodied men enlisted, some 120,000 in all. Countless numbers of slaves were pressed into service as well, although many thousands escaped to join the Union army. Alabama's most prized service to the Confederacy, however, was its reserves of iron and its munitions factories in Selma. It was here that the Union aimed—and found—its crucial Alabamian target in 1865.

Iron and Industry

Alabama suffered badly in the long years between the Civil War and World War II. Poverty, corruption,

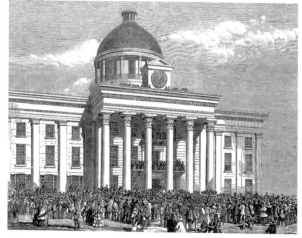

This wood engraving depicts the inauguration of Jefferson Davis on the steps of Montgomery's Capitol in 1861.

Despised by southern gentry, northerns who moved south after the Civil War were derisively called "carpetbaggers" for their trademark carpetbags and accused of economic predation.

and racial violence took a heavy toll on the state. Cotton still reigned in the fields, though the market had all but vanished; when the boll weevil struck in 1915 it proved to be the death knell to the cotton economy.

In 1871 investors founded Birmingham where two railroad lines met in the mineral-rich Jones Valley. The city's investors had high hopes of massive steel production. Instead, the city's mainstay proved to be iron, and the industry's promise helped the city grow explosively, reaching a population of 132,000 by 1910. It is still the state's largest city today.

Nevertheless, Alabama as a whole suffered vast social problems. Rampant racism encouraged thousands of African Americans to move north, denuding the state of much of its population and slowing its urbanization. The state remained mostly rural until 1960, despite the beneficial effects of Tennessee Valley Authority projects and industry in Birmingham and Huntsville, where the U.S. Army and later NASA set up shop.

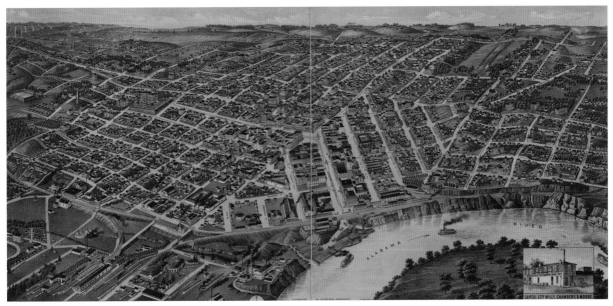

The city of Montgomery as it appeared in 1887.

Civil Rights Unrest

Slavery transitioned easily into institutionalized segregation in Alabama, and by the 1950s the state had earned a reputation for its troubled race relations. George Wallace, one the era's most divisive figures, vowed to retain segregation as he took his oath as governor on the star where Jefferson Davis once stood. Rosa Parks instigated the famous Montgomery bus boycotts by refusing to give up her seat to a white person; church bombings and televised police beatings of peaceful protesters horrified the nation and brought newfound momentum to the Civil Rights Movement.

Looking Toward the Future

Today, the state is recovering from the injustices of the past. Its economy has diversified and is expanding, particularly in automotive manufacturing. The sandy beaches of Mobile Bay draw tourist dollars, while a steadily increasing industrial economy in the north invigorates cultural change. The passage of a resolution signed by Governor Bob Riley in 2007 formally expressing regret for slavery and its repercussions indicates that the state is beginning to heal its internal wounds. Finally, Alabama is re-emerging with a new face on the national stage.

Above, Vivian Malone's entrance to the University of Alabama in 1963 was heavily publicized. Below, the bus where Rosa Parks refused to give up her seat is now a museum attraction.

Florida

The Sunshine State

In God We Trust

A curious intersection of old and new, Florida hosts both the oldest city in the United States and the third-fastest growing population; it provides the last chance for the crucially endangered Florida panther and the best chance (NASA hopes) for launching men to Mars. Orchard trees and neon lights, Spanish cuisine and southern music, immigrants from South and Central America and migrants from the North: all meet in Florida.

One of the most distinctively shaped states in the nation, Florida is mostly a peninsula, dividing the Atlantic Ocean on the east from the Gulf of Mexico on the west. With a thin panhandle reaching nearly to Mississippi in the northwest, Florida has more miles of coastline than any state besides Alaska—but unlike Alaska's, Florida's waters are warm and welcoming. Eight hundred miles of beaches, a concentration of amusement parks, and an inviting climate have conspired to make Florida one of the world's premier vacation destinations, attracting some 60 million people every year.

The year-round population is also growing at an astonishing pace. Ranked 20th in population in 1950, Florida is now the third-most populous state behind Texas and California. As the population has grown, so too has the economy, which has diversified from its traditional citrus farming, tourism, and phosphate mining to include aerospace, medical research, and biotech industries. Florida is still known for its oranges, however, and for good reason: over 60 percent of the nation's orange juice is produced in the Sunshine State.

Despite its nickname, Florida weathers more thunderstorms than any other state, and Tampa, which means "lightning" in the Calusa Indian tongue, is called the "lightning capital of the world." Hurricanes also land in Florida with more regularity than any other state, though this has yet to dampen the tourist industry. In recent years Florida has also gained infamy for its politics, becoming the eye of a different kind of storm. Between 2000–2010, Florida topped all other states in convictions on broken federal corruption laws.

With its vibrant, diverse culture ranging from nightclubs to orange groves, its extraordinary ecosystems, and its rich history, all of Florida may well deserve the name given to its most famous amusement park, Walt Disney World, for this unique state truly appears as a Magic Kingdom.

High-rise apartment buildings and luxury hotels crowd Miami Beach, one of the most popular vacation spots in the world.

Florida State Facts

Full Name: State of Florida
Meaning of Name: From *pascua florida*, "Flowery Easter" in Spanish
Admitted to the Union: March 3, 1845 (27th state)
Inhabitant: Floridian

Capital City: Tallahassee
Flower: Orange blossom
Tree: Sabal palmetto palm
Bird: Mockingbird

Geography and Ecology

Most of Florida consists of a long peninsula in the far southeastern tip of the mainland of the United States. When humans first migrated into Florida some 12,000 years ago, the peninsula covered twice as much land as it does today; when sea levels rose, some fascinating undersea environments were created, many of which are protected by underwater national parks. High land to the south became the Florida Keys, a string of islands curving southwest; one of these, Key West, is the southernmost city in the United States. To the east of the keys can be found the only living coral reef in the continental United States.

Topography and Temperature

Florida is largely flat, and its porous limestone foundation and humid climate place it behind only Alaska and Michigan in terms of water area. Lying flat between the Atlantic Ocean and the Gulf of Mexico, Florida rises to only 345 feet above sea level at its highest point, Britton Hill—the lowest high point of any state. Most of Florida is subtropical, but southern Florida (including the Keys) swelters under a true tropical climate.

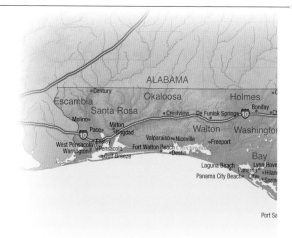

Sunshine under Storm

Florida's location and climate expose it to more hurricanes and more tornadoes per square mile than any other state. Tornadoes, while frequent, are typically quite weak, but Florida's hurricanes are both strong and regular. Until Hurricane Katrina devastated New Orleans, Hurricane Andrew ranked as the costliest hurricane in American history to the tune of 25 billion dollars in southern Florida in 1992.

One benefit of hurricanes is their torrential rain. While residents don't welcome the flooding, the rain restores reservoir levels (at a time when water consumption is a rising concern) and replenishes ecosystems, such as Florida's famous Everglades. Here, the subtropical climate produces two seasons: wet (spring and summer) and dry (fall and winter). Nowhere else is water management a larger issue, as this unique ecosystem—once called the "River of Grass" by American Indians—depends entirely on the natural and fragile water systems of the state. Some 1.5 mil-

---

LAST OF THE PANTHERS

On the southern tip of Florida's peninsula, the only breeding population of Florida panthers struggles to survive. Less than 100 of these big cats, once common across the Southeast, may roam their remaining wilderness, making them one of the most endangered species of cats on the planet. In recognition of their plight, Florida adopted the panther as its state animal in 1982.

Flordia panthers are one of the smallest of the big cats. Adult males weigh only 150 pounds but are still quite dangerous.

Lightning crashes in the Gulf of Mexico off the Florida coast. The sight is quite common for the state's inhabitants.

lion acres of a total of 5,000 square miles of the Everglades are protected by a national park, but actions outside the park still threaten the environment.

Red Tide

In addition to these concerns, there is growing pressure to begin drilling for oil in the Gulf of Mexico, and natural resources are beginning to feel the strain of 18 million people. The unsightly phenomenon called "red tide"—the rapid accumulation of reddish algae—affects not only the ocean's health, but also tourist industries that rely on coastal appeal. Addressing these issues will be crucial for Florida's continued growth and well-being, and efforts are growing to keep Florida as attractive and unique today as it was when Europeans first arrived.

The clear, warm waters surrounding the Florida Keys—actually the exposed remnants of an ancient reef—draw thousands of tourists.

The Sunshine State

According to legend, Spanish explorer Juan Ponce de León came to Florida's shores in 1513 to search for the Fountain of Youth, whose waters reputedly returned beauty and youthful vigor. He discovered a flowering land of dense forests, thick swamps, and an amazing array of wildlife, as well as over 100 distinct American Indian groups. Neither the fountain nor any other treasure appeared, but the land impressed de León, and he returned in 1521 to start a colony. This failed quickly, in large part because the region's inhabitants—whose largest groups included the Apalachee, Ais, and Calusa peoples—did not appreciate the uninvited neighbors.

Juan Ponce de León

Early Settlements

Spain did not show real determination to settle the region until France's René Goulaine de Laudonnière established a refuge for Hugenots at Fort Caroline, modern-day Jacksonville, in 1564. In response to the perceived French threat, Pedro Menéndez de Avilés founded the first successful Spanish colony in Florida, San Augustín. Known today by its Anglicized name, St. Augustine is the oldest continuously inhabited European settlement in the United States.

For the next two centuries, the Spanish, French, British, and various American Indian groups traded blows and territorial control of

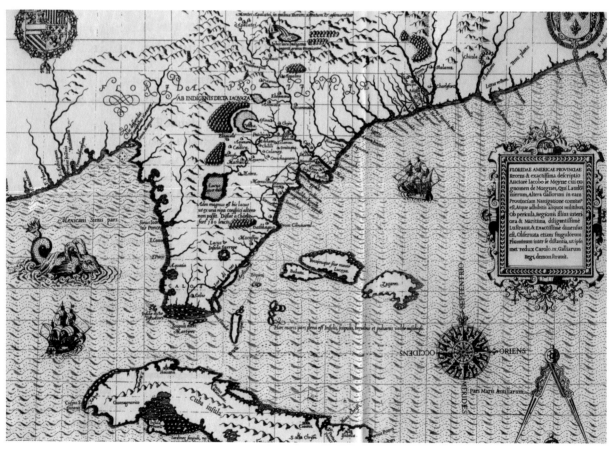

A 1591 map of Florida, engraved by Jacques Le Moyne de Morgues. In this early period the geography was poorly understood, with the shape of Florida's peninsula and Caribbean islands only barely recognizable. Several American Indian tribes are identified.

Florida. In the early 18th century, the British colony of Georgia and French Louisiana jeopardized Spanish control, and in 1763 Spain ceded Florida to Great Britain. Around the same time, a group of Creek Indians, called Seminoles, moved into the area.

Two Floridas

Great Britain divided the region, centering West Florida on Pensacola, a Spanish settlement nearly as old as St. Augustine, and East Florida on St. Augustine itself. The English fared poorly in Florida, however, finding the soil too sandy and the Indians too hostile. Great Britain would claim Florida for only 20 years; after the American Revolutionary War, Spain again took over.

The second Spanish period lasted only until 1819. Spanish in name only, the period saw significant American immigration, so that by its end, Florida looked more like an American territory than a Spanish colony. The Seminoles, supposedly allied with the Spanish, began raiding Georgian towns over the border. Provoked, future president Andrew Jackson led an invasion in 1817–18, a campaign later known as the First Seminole War. The Adams-Onís treaty, signed two years later, formalized what was already true in practice, and Florida entered American jurisdiction.

Culture and Clashes

The United States combined East and West Florida and established a new capital, Tallahassee. American settlers came largely from southern states, and as a result the culture and politics closely resembled those of the Deep South. The settlers built large plantations in central Florida, and by 1860 nearly half the population consisted of African American slaves.

Relationships with the Seminoles deteriorated. Not only did settlers wish the American Indians removed from Florida to facilitate white settlement, but the Seminoles welcomed escaped slaves. A fair number of Seminoles agreed to leave after signing the Treaty of Payne's Landing in 1832, and moved west of the Mississippi River like so many other American Indian tribes. Many others, however, refused, and in 1835 the United States Army arrived to force them west.

The Unconquered Tribe

On December 28, 1835, a band of Seminoles ambushed 108 American soldiers under the command of Major Francis L. Dade, and all but one were killed. This, the Dade Massacre, started the Second Seminole War.

Eight years, 20 million dollars, and thousands of deaths later, the war ended, seemingly out of exhaustion. Osceola, the charismatic and indefatigable Seminole leader, had been captured (malaria killed him shortly afterward). The remaining Seminoles retreated to the vastness of the Everglades, and there matters stood until 1855. Once again, the United States attempted to force the Seminoles out, and once again the army failed—although it is possible that at the end of the Third Seminole War in 1858 as few as 100 Seminoles remained. Their numbers gradually increased, and the Seminoles today call themselves the "Unconquered," for theirs is the only Indian tribe never to have signed a peace treaty with the United States.

Florida, My Southern Home

Florida seceded with the rest of the South in 1861 and contributed some 15,000 troops to the Confederacy (and some 2,000 to the Union). A Union blockade stymied shipping, but on the whole Florida suffered fairly little; Tallahassee was the only Confederate capital east of the Mississippi River to escape Union capture.

Osceola led Seminole resistance to American troops in the Second Seminole War, which lasted from 1835 through 1842.

Similarly, Florida avoided much of the social and economic upheaval experienced in the rest of the South in the last quarter of the 19th century. Although agriculture suffered, the plantation economy had never been as dominant in Florida as it had been elsewhere, and thus Florida's economy transitioned more easily. Lumber boomed, and ports like Pensacola accordingly thrived. In 1889 the first commercial phosphate mine opened, and the industry quickly became an economic staple. Perhaps of greater import, and certainly a more visible newcomer, were the railroads. By 1900 more than 3,000 miles of railroad track brought industry and—crucially—tourists.

Land speculators and developers followed the railroads, eventually creating a real estate bubble that reached its climax in the 1920s. The crash came in 1925 and accelerated the following year, when the 1926 Miami hurricane ravaged the city. That disaster was followed two years later by another hurricane, and one year after that—the same year of the Wall Street crash—the Mediterranean fruit fly discovered Florida's citrus orchards. The state sank into depression.

Florida's wet, warm climate is ideal for citrus trees, and today the state produces the majority of the nation's orange juice. The citrus industry has, however, been dwarfed by tourism.

Digging out of the Depression

New Deal programs modernized transportation, which in turn breathed new life into the citrus industry. Tourism buoyed the economy somewhat through the dark years of the Great Depression; Florida opened its first amusement parks in the 1930s, although they would not take off for another decade or more.

The economy did not truly recover until World War II. The nation's first aviation facility had opened in 1917 at Pensacola, and in the 1940s the war greatly expanded the military industry in the state. One of the more famous institutions to emerge was the aerospace center at Cape Canaveral, which in the 1960s drew the eyes of the world as NASA launched astronauts from Kennedy Space Center to the surface of the moon.

Flocking to Florida

Florida exploded in the second half of the 20th century, becoming the destination of choice for thousands of immigrants, vacationers, and retirees. The advent of air conditioning transformed Florida's climate into a boon, while theme parks like Universal Orlando Studios, Busch Gardens, and the largest amusement park in the world, Walt Disney World, entered their heyday.

Vibrant art deco buildings liven up the streets of Miami, courtesy of a short-lived construction boom in the 1930s.

With the state's burgeoning population came social, political, and environmental problems. Legal segregation of African Americans ended with the Civil Rights Movement, but ever since the Cuban Revolution of the 1950s, Florida has been a haven for immigrants from Cuba, the Caribbean, and South and Central America. The demographic shift has strained this politically turbulent state, while environmental issues continue to develop. How Florida addresses these issues will be crucial for its future, which certainly has the potential to be as sunny as the state's nickname implies.

THE LAND OF YOUTH

Early in its colonial-era history (and possibly even before) Florida became associated with a miraculous pool, known as the Fountain of Youth, whose waters reputedly restored youth and vitality. Although Ponce de León may not have been looking for it himself, as legend suggests, several explorers since then have scoured the landscape for the elusive spring. In a twist of fate, Florida today is famous as a destination for retirees. Hoping to escape the troublesome cold of northern winters, many find Florida's warmth and climate recuperative, so that even if no mystical fountain exists, the entire state may yet serve a similar function.

One of Orlando's major theme parks, SeaWorld focuses on marine life and hosts shows featuring the abilities of its inhabitants.

It seems that everybody wants to live in Florida these days, with its booming cities, sparkling nightlife, and range of natural attractions. Miami's 2008 building boom was the busiest of the nation, raising 20 skyscrapers that reach more than 400 feet high.

Arkansas

Regnat Populus (The people rule)

For centuries Arkansas has been famous for its wilderness. The earliest European settlers were drawn to its thick forests for their developing fur trade. Today, the state's unofficial designation as the "Razorback State" speaks to the dominance of those fierce feral pigs, which many Arkansas sports teams have adopted as mascots. Once derided as a stereotypically backwoods, uncultured state, Arkansas has embraced its frontier past, and a thriving tourist industry proves the state's success in producing an attractive and authentic image.

In the last half of the 20th century, however, Arkansas not only protected its natural beauty and its heritage, but also produced some of the country's most successful entrepreneurs, corporations, and politicians. Wal-Mart first opened its doors in Rodgers, Arkansas, in 1962, and the little retail store has now become a global giant. Elected five times as Arkansas' governor, Bill Clinton won the presidency and new renown for his home state in 1992.

Tourists flock not only to the historically important eastern Delta region, where antebellum plantations once dominated state politics, but also to the mountainous west. The Ouachita, Boston, and Ozark mountains stretch across much of the state and provide opportunities for many types of outdoor recreation, including hiking, hunting, and fishing. Popular national protected areas also focus on the state's wealth of peaceful scenery, including the Ozark National Forest, nestled around the highest point in the state, and Buffalo National River, which can still be traveled by canoe, as it had been for centuries by American Indians.

When the first European arrived on the scene, the inhabitants lived in a complex, highly developed society, but when the next wave of Europeans arrived more than a century later, this civilization had all but vanished. This strange pattern of cultures vanishing and new ones appearing continued as the colonial period faded and the cotton kingdom reigned. The demise of that culture in the Civil War produced a hodgepodge of farmers and mountaineers, progressives and social conservatives, in a cultural landscape as variable as the geography of Arkansas itself.

Today, Arkansas is a state of nuance and complexity: a socially conservative state that produced a moderate Democratic president, a state of forested mountains that still devotes itself to agriculture, and a traditionally rural state that houses two of the nation's largest corporations. This land of razorbacks, big-game bucks, and record-size fish is for outdoorsmen of all kinds, as well as students of the truly unique American story that is Arkansas.

The dense forests of the Ozarks show off early fall colors, threading golden trails through their usual green glory.

Arkansas State Facts

Full Name: State of Arkansas
Meaning of Name: From Quapaw American Indians, meaning "south wind"
Admitted to the Union: June 15, 1836 (25th state)
Inhabitant: Arkansan

Capital City: Little Rock
Flower: Apple blossom
Tree: Pine
Bird: Mockingbird

Geography and Ecology

Arkansas descends from its most famous geographic feature, the Ozarks in the west, to the broad, fertile alluvial plain (also called the Delta) along the Mississippi River, which marks the state's eastern boundary. Below the Ozark Plateau, running in parallel east-west lines, are the Arkansas River Valley, the Ouachita Mountains, and, covering most of the southern half of the state, the West Gulf Coastal Plain.

Historically, the Delta drove the economy as the state's agricultural powerhouse, but the decline of farming in the 20th century sank the area into a long depression. Today, the north and western portions of the state reign economically with corporate and diverse industrial interests driven partly by the profusion of lumber in the heavily forested Ozarks. The Ouachita Mountains host two of Arkansas' most famous features, the natural hot springs near their eponymous city, now a national park, and Crater of Diamonds State Park, the site of America's first diamond discovery and home to the world's only public diamond mine.

A NEW HOPE

The ivory-billed woodpecker once flew throughout the swamps and hardwood forests of the southeastern United States but was driven to extinction by a rapidly expanding lumber industry in the late 19th and 20th centuries. Or was it? In 2004 an observer in the Cache River National Wildlife Refuge in Monroe County, Arkansas, reported sighting a male bird. The report set off a frenzy of bird watching and recovery hopes, although the bird still proves elusive.

An illustration by John Audubon in 1830 provides a heartbreaking portrait of this glorious bird, feared to be extinct.

The clear, cold waters of the White River in northwestern Arkansas produce some of the world's largest trout.

Climate and Weather

Arkansas' humid subtropical climate transitions to a humid continental climate in the mountainous north and experiences significant seasonal variation, with monthly average highs ranging from 93.6° F to 26.6° F over the course of a year. The winter months usually bring some snow, although the yearly average measures only 5 inches. More problematic are tornadoes, which strike the state with some frequency and great strength: although Arkansas ranks only sixteenth in number of strikes, it ranks fourth in number of tornado-caused deaths.

The Great Outdoors

In the last half of the 20th century, Arkansas began advertising its scenic stretches of untouched natural

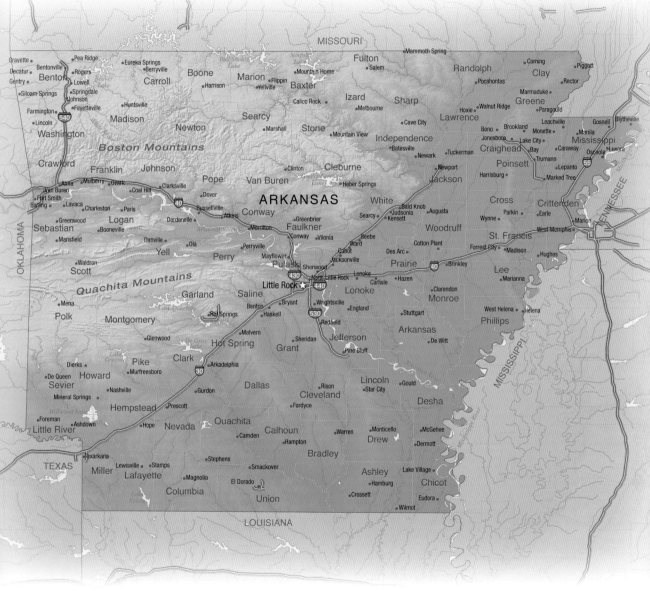

beauty. Protected by an economy slow to industrialize and a population predisposed to outdoor recreation and pursuits, Arkansas quickly capitalized with no fewer than 52 state parks. These parks showcase some of the most stunning natural features in the state, from the appropriately named Mammoth Spring State Park to the picturesque mountain scenery of Devil's Den State Park.

European interest in Arkansas was sparked in the 17th century by the area's fur-trade potential, and this early interest in hunting continues even today as sportsmen flock to take advantage of the state's rich fishing and hunting opportunities. The Game and Fish Commission demonstrated as early as the late 1940s that regulation could both protect a species and provide adequate hunting opportunities, as it helped the white-tailed deer population to recover and enacted hunting restrictions for the first time in the 1950s. Today, both big- and small-game hunters prowl Arkansas' wilderness, while the state's waterfowl have led to its unofficial designation as "the duck hunting capital of the world."

The Natural State

Arkansas has been inhabited since the Pleistocene epoch 13,500 years ago and consequently offers several archaeologically interesting sites. One of these dates to roughly 9,000 BCE and belongs to the hunter-gatherers of the Dalton period; the Sloan Site may be the oldest cemetery on the continent. By the time Europeans arrived, American Indian groups had established trading contacts that may have reached as far south as the Aztec Empire.

The first Europeans to visit were Spanish—the explorer Hernando de Soto died while traveling through Arkansas— and French, who allied themselves with the powerful Quapaw Indians. The fur and game meat trades dominated the region through the colonial period, but meager European interest produced a low population, while disease and warfare decimated various American Indian tribes, including the Quapaw. By the time the United States gained control of the region through the

Patrick Cleburne

Louisiana Purchase in 1803, the territory was only sparsely settled, with fewer than 500 non-Indian inhabitants.

Becoming Southern

Anglo-Americans began moving to the area in the 1830s, bringing a culture of plantations and slavery with them, although the northwestern "upland" regions retained the old hunting-and-trapping society of the colonial era. The state nevertheless became the northern boundary of the South, and although slaves accounted for only 26 percent of the population in 1860, their rich plantation owners controlled the government in what remained a thinly settled frontier state.

Neither objections to nor defense of slavery resonated in Arkansas the way they did in the rest of the nation, and Arkansas joined the Confederacy only when President Lincoln called for volunteers to suppress South Carolina. After seceding, however, Arkansans

Steamboats trudge along the Arkansas River next to Little Rock in this 1871 map, belying the poverty that beset many of the state's farmers.

threw themselves into battle, with Arkansan immigrant Major General Patrick Cleburne quickly gaining a reputation as the "Stonewall of the West." The site of numerous skirmishes, Arkansas descended into near anarchy during the war.

The Struggling Years

The Civil War left Arkansas in dire straits, killing more than 10,000, shattering the economy, and ushering in a grim social reality. Although lumber, coal, and railroads brought some prosperity, only a select portion of the population benefited. Left out were most farmers, the backbone of a still rural state. Racial problems intensified, and by 1906 the ruling Democrats had effectively disenfranchised the black population.

In the 1920s the cotton market collapsed, with other agricultural commodities not far behind; this financial disaster was exacerbated by the Mississippi River flood of 1927 and a severe drought in 1930. Nevertheless, Arkansas grew into a hotbed of progressivism: in 1920 Arkansas became the second state to ratify the 19th amendment, giving women the right to vote.

New Policies

Although Arkansas remained part of the "Solid South," for the most part the racially motivated social issues dominating the rest of the South were not as extreme in Arkansas. One exception came in 1957, when Governor Orval Faubus sent the state guard to prevent nine African American students from entering Little Rock's Central High. Segregationist fervor had reached a climax, and although President Eisenhower sent the 101st Airborne Division and later the National Guard to protect the students, the city closed its schools the following year rather than integrate.

Since then Arkansas has gone through several significant changes. A series of overdue governmental reforms began in the 1960s, and major corporations like Tyson Foods and Wal-Mart brought modern industry to the northwest. By 1970 more Arkansans lived in urban areas than rural ones. The state's national presence was cemented when former governor Bill Clinton won the presidency in 1992.

However, Arkansas also remains true to its past, embracing its rough frontier history with celebrations like the popular Arkansas Blues and Heritage Festival. Even entering the 21st century, Arkansas has become more politically conservative, and the old strains of bluegrass and country can still be heard throughout the state. In addition, Arkansas fought hard and early for environmental preservation, and as a result the state today has that rare quality of authentic heritage existing harmoniously beside modern development.

FAMOUS ARKANSANS

Johnny Cash (1932–2003), country music singer
Wesley Clark (b. 1944), U.S. Army general
Bill Clinton (b. 1946), 42nd U.S. president
John Grisham (b. 1955), author
Douglas MacArthur (1880–1964), U.S. Army general
Winthrop Rockefeller (1912–1973), philanthropist
Sam Walton (1918–1992), entrepreneur

Arkansans protest integration vigorously at a rally in 1959.

William J. Clinton, 42nd president of the United States.

Louisiana

The Pelican State

Union, Justice, and Confidence

Draped with hanging Spanish moss, oak trees line entrance pathways to stately plantations. Nearby, shifting bayous haunted equally by swift alligators and local legends swelter under a tropical sun. Far to the southeast, the queen city of the South shimmers with colorful festivals and equally colorful antebellum homes. Unfolding through the centuries along the mighty Mississippi, Louisiana's varied and sometimes impenetrably convoluted history has left it vibrant and storied, with a culture all its own.

In keeping with its nonlinear development, Louisiana has moved its capital several times. Currently, Baton Rouge, the second-largest city, serves. Its name dates to an alleged custom among local American Indians, recorded by Pierre le Moyne, Sieur d'Iberville, in 1699, of delineating tribal boundaries by staining cypress poles with animal blood. It is an excellent example of entwined American Indian and French histories; other influences can also be strongly felt in the state, including Spanish and African. In addition, several unique cultures have developed in Louisiana over the years, including Cajun, Creole, and Isleños.

It is this cultural mix, this uniquely Louisianan collection of cultures and peoples, that most definitively identifies the state. Although problems with poverty, race relations, and hurricanes have threatened Louisiana, every storm—both figurative and literal—has so far been weathered. The state is still recovering from Hurricane Katrina, which made world headlines when it swamped New Orleans and a broad surrounding area in 2005. But, in Louisiana's grand tradition of incorporating its tragedies and its social upheavals, doubtless Katrina too will become part of the shared state narrative.

Louisiana's dynamic culture expresses itself in different ways. Well known are jazz and Mardi Gras, but the state thrives on all performing arts, both historically—the first opera in the United States was performed in New Orleans in 1796—and today, with film becoming a major industry in New Orleans and Shreveport. These aspects of Louisianan culture, in addition to its wealth of historic sites, contribute to the importance of tourism in the state's economy, although oil and natural gas are economic front-runners. Also significant are shipping and transportation, with the Port of South Louisiana the largest bulk cargo port in the world. Agriculturally, Louisiana is the world's largest producer of crayfish, which play a major role in regional cuisine. Spicy, thick Cajun and Creole dishes are yet another draw to this textured state of colonial grace, time-honored legends, and modern music.

Slowly shifting waterways known as bayous slink through much of Louisiana. Their eerie atmosphere has generated many a popular tale.

Louisiana State Facts

Full Name: State of Louisiana
Meaning of Name: From King Louis XIV of France
Admitted to the Union: April 30, 1812 (18th state)
Inhabitant: Louisianan
Capital City: Baton Rouge

Flower: Magnolia
Tree: Bald cypress
Bird: Brown pelican

Geography and Ecology

Consisting entirely of low, flat coastal or alluvial plains, Louisiana rises only 90–100 feet above sea level on average, with a high point of 535 feet at Driskill Mountain in north-central Bienville Parish. Much of New Orleans actually lies below sea level, making the city especially vulnerable to flooding. At 8 feet below, part of the city is the second-lowest point in the United States, beaten only by Death Valley in California.

Resources and Wildlife

Well-known for its wealth of waterways, Louisiana proved conducive in the past to growing several of the great cash crops of the 19th century, including indigo, sugar, and cotton. In the 20th century its natural reserves of oil and natural gas have replaced agriculture as the primary economic mover. But in recent years tourists—drawn by Louisiana's unparalleled swamps and bayous—have contributed significantly to the state's economy as well. Visitors are also

The Mississippi Delta covers more than 11,000 square miles, but river management has caused ecologically troubling shrinkage.

drawn by Louisiana's rich and varied wildlife, including the ever-popular American alligator.

Warm and Wild Weather

All of Louisiana swelters under a humid subtropical climate, with the northern part of the state suffering under higher temperatures in the summer than the south. Normal high temperatures for most parts of the state in July and August are into the 90s, while winters are mild, with snowfall rare. The climate contributes to a long growing season, but heat produces its own risks, particularly for the elderly or very young. Moreover, the swamps host huge numbers of insects; in the past, yellow fever, cholera, small-

GATOR COUNTRY

Now fully recovered from their endangered species plight, American alligators can be found throughout the southeastern United States, including the entire state of Louisiana. Although they tend to attack smaller prey, they are perfectly capable of killing humans and should inspire caution in those traveling near their watery haunts. The larger of the two alligator species (its cousin lives in China), American "gators" may grow up to 19 feet long, although that size is highly unusual.

A group of American alligators lounges nonchalantly near a Louisiana bayou, warming in the summer sun.

Most of the damage caused by Hurricane Katrina resulted from extreme flooding caused by the storm, rather than the high winds.

pox, and malaria, spread by mosquitoes and poor sanitary conditions, killed thousands during numerous outbreaks. In 1853 an epidemic of yellow fever killed more than 12,000 in New Orleans alone, setting a national record for annual death rates in the 19th century.

Due to its long coast in the Gulf of Mexico, Louisiana is extremely vulnerable to hurricanes, and in the 20th century storms overtook disease as the primary environmental concern for inhabitants. Tornadoes and thunderstorms both take their toll on the state, but the worst offenders are hurricanes, which in addition to highly destructive winds can cause devastating flooding due to Louisiana's low-lying landforms. The dangers inherent to living on the Gulf Coast became an international news event when Hurricane Katrina struck the city of New Orleans in 2005. The city's protective levees failed, resulting in an enormous amount of devastation, and Katrina ranks as the costliest hurricane in United States history, killing nearly 2,000 people. The region, and New Orleans in particular, has yet to fully recover from the storm.

The Pelican State

Numerous American Indian tribes inhabited the region for thousands of years, with one culture leaving behind some of the largest prehistoric ruins on the continent, dating to 1700 BCE, at Poverty Point National Monument. Hernando de Soto became the first European to reach the Mississippi River in 1541, but Robert Cavalier, Sieur de la Salle, claimed the region in 1682 for France.

Louisiana subsequently changed hands several times, between France, Spain, and finally America in 1803, although full ownership was not achieved until 1815 when future president Andrew Jackson wrested New Orleans from the invading British at the end of the War of 1812. In the colonial period, Louisiana attracted a disparate group of settlers, bestowing a unique cultural heritage visible to this day. Most famous of these, and arguably most influential, are the Acadians, more typically known as Cajuns, and the Creoles.

Cajun and Creole Cultures

During the mid-18th century, thousands of French-speaking refugees from Acadia (modern Nova Scotia), expelled by the British, migrated to Louisiana. The southwest region of the state where they settled is still called Acadiana, but their descendants, owing to linguistic confusion, are called Cajuns. Elements of Cajun culture have become world famous and stereotypically Louisianan, including flavorful Creole-influenced dishes like jambalaya and gumbo.

Located near Baton Rouge, Myrtles Plantation (c. 1796) is reputedly one of America's most haunted houses, with purported visitations from numerous ghosts, ranging from slaves to Union soldiers.

The definition of "Creole" has changed over time, with meanings as disparate and fluid as the cultures that it came to define. Today, Creole usually refers to people of mixed race, descended from early Spanish, French, African, and American Indian inhabitants. In the colonial period (under Spanish and French government) it referred to anyone born in the colony, rather than an immigrant. As did Cajuns, Creoles developed a distinct dialect of French. Both vernaculars are still spoken in the state.

From Cotton to Oil

In the colonial period European influence produced an unusual, three-tiered society, which lasted to some extent until the Civil War. Distinctions were drawn between white, black, and free colored, though this

VOODOO IN LOUISIANA

Voodoo, loosely understood as a religion merged from African spiritualism and Catholicism, has been practiced in Louisiana for centuries. At first confined to Africans and their descendants, voodoo has a history that is convoluted and confused, as elites largely discouraged its practice. Associated variously with magic, Satanism, and related practices like hoodoo, voodoo has assumed a mysterious quality in American culture and appears in many horror films and literary works.

A depiction of voodoo celebrations from the late 19th century. The religion still struggles with negative associations.

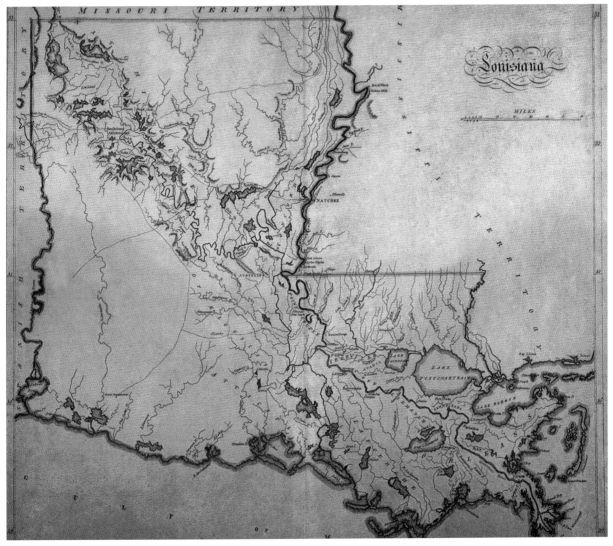

Louisiana from an 1814 atlas, on the cusp of transition to American control. Despite the Anglo-American newcomers, though, Louisiana retained its earlier French, African, Caribbean, and indigenous cultures—and in many ways still does.

did not prevent a widespread plantation culture and its incumbent societal strains from developing in pre-Civil War Louisiana. Cotton crops were common, but indigo, rice, and sugar, particularly in the south, kept the state's economy somewhat more diverse than its eastern neighbors.

Nevertheless, Louisiana and especially its major port, New Orleans, suffered badly during the Civil War. Although it escaped physical destruction, New Orleans still stifled under Union blockade and occupation. By the end of the war, with plantations and trade ruined, Louisiana ranked 17th in the nation by wealth and last

in the South. Prior to the start of the war, Louisiana had glittered as the second-wealthiest state in the nation.

Louisiana's economy recovered during the latter quarter of the 19th century, buoyed by some fortuitous discoveries. The oldest salt mine in the Western Hemisphere opened in 1862 on Avery Island, the state produced its first sulfur in 1869, and—most significant for the 20th century—inhabitants discovered Louisiana's first oil field in 1901. Oil and natural gas have been the mainstays of Louisiana's economy ever since, and it was in Louisiana that the world's first true offshore drilling occurred near Morgan City in 1947.

The Louisiana Purchase

In 1803 President Jefferson's representatives, Robert Livingstone and James Monroe, bought some 828,000 square miles of North America from the land's nominal owner, Napoleon Bonaparte of France. Arguably the largest—and cheapest, at 3 cents an acre—real estate deal in history, the Louisiana Purchase doubled the size of the United States overnight. Eventually, all or some of 15 states would emerge from the territory. The last of these was New Mexico in 1912; first was Louisiana itself, 100 years earlier.

Slow to Change

Shifting to American rule brought slow but significant economic and social changes, but cultural conservatism still preserves today some remnants of the state's European origins. Uniquely among the states, Louisiana is divided into parishes, reflecting its early Catholic influences, and its legal system more closely resembles that of France in some ways than that of the United States. The aftermath of the Civil War brought new rigidity to the state's racially stratified society, and although Louisiana gave African American men the vote and integrated public schools in the 1868 state constitu-

tion, Jim Crow laws reversed any progress, and racial violence spiked during Reconstruction. As in other southern states, it was not until the Civil Rights Movement of the 1950s and 1960s that African Americans began to achieve true political equality.

All that Jazz

Many African Americans moved north during the Great Migration of the 20th century. They spread one of New Orleans' most recognized indigenous sounds, jazz, which took root in many other American cities. Jazz flourished in the New Orleans speakeasies of the Prohibition era, and one of the genre's most famous members, Louis Armstrong, first played on the city streets in the 1910s. Today, visitors can attend the New Orleans Jazz National Historical Park year-round, or wait for the annual Jazz and Heritage Festival in April.

A Long Legacy

In the 20th century, native Louisianan Huey Long built one of the most powerful and controversial state governments in national history. Serving successively as governor and U.S. senator, Long won broad appeal with his populist program in a state struck by the

From the lovely buildings of the gracious French Quarter to the soft sounds of jazz still played on the streets, New Orleans bares its history and soul for all to rejoice in.

Great Depression. His drive to build new infrastructure (doubling the miles of road in the state and building the tallest southern building at the time, the new State Capitol) did provide much-needed jobs. However, his power in the government provoked dissension, and antagonist Dr. Carl Weiss fatally shot him on September 8, 1935. Accounts of both the assassination and the politician remain divisively controversial.

Mansions and Mardi Gras

The 34-story State Capitol Long built (and on whose steps he was killed) is a fabulous example of the art deco style, but it is outshone by the gracious plantations of rural Louisiana, including Nottaway, the largest in the South, and the famous colonial architecture of New Orleans' French Quarter. It is here, too, that the long colonial legacy displays perhaps its most famous expression: Mardi Gras. A Catholic festival just prior to Lent, Mardi Gras has been celebrated wildly in New Orleans since at least the mid-18th century. So far wars, poverty, and weather have yet to halt the massive parade that draws hundreds of thousands of tourists each year. Even despite the ravages of Hurricane Katrina, New Orleans celebrated Mardi Gras as usual. It is perhaps the surest

sign of the city's resilience and the state's dedication to its history and its culture. As Kim Priez, vice president of New Orleans' tourism bureau, once remarked: "Mardi Gras is in our soul." From the thick bayous to the stately plantations to the colorful relief of Mardi Gras, Louisiana certainly has a lot of soul, a trait for which it is renowned throughout the nation.

Traditionally, Mardi Gras celebrants dress in fabulous costumes, a custom found in similarly cathartic festivals around the world.

Mardi Gras (literally, "Fat Tuesday") marks the coming of Lent, when Catholics ritually mimic the fasting of Jesus Christ in the desert. As such, the festival swings in the opposite direction, marked by wild celebrations. In New Orleans the event annually draws huge crowds.

Oklahoma

Sooner State

Labor Omnia Vincit (Labor conquers all)

Oklahoma, rich in oil, ecological variety, and culture, went largely ignored by Europeans and Americans for centuries. Although Spanish explorer Francisco Vásquez de Coronado reached the region now known as Oklahoma in 1541, no European power established a firm presence. However, Spaniards routinely set out to discover the much-desired (and entirely fictional) cities of gold rumored to exist nearby, and French trappers established business relationships with American Indians in the forested eastern portions of the state.

For the most part the United States continued in the same vein, establishing the region as a sort of penal colony for the rest of the nation's unwanted American Indians. For most of the 19th century, Oklahoma existed as Indian Territory, and for a short time some Indian nations seemed on a track to join American culture and even harbored hopes for an Indian-only state. Later, the United States allowed settlers in the region and finally accepted it as a (decidedly non-Indian) state, disregarding the Indian nations' sovereignty. Nevertheless, Oklahoma American Indian cultures persist today, with 67 nations, 39 tribe headquarters, and more than 25 American Indian languages spoken in the state, far surpassing the rest of the country. Perhaps the most obvious, if somewhat discomfiting, influence of their long-established presence is the translation of Oklahoma's name, "red people."

Part of the initial willingness to allow American Indians to keep the region stemmed from negative assumptions about the landscape, which still have currency today. In reality, Oklahoma hosts an astounding array of terrains, and its broad, undulating plains shielded one of its most valuable resources; although it bore little resemblance to the gold sought by 16th-century Spain, oil quickly became the state's "black gold" and dominated the economy for much of the 20th century. More recently, related industries like natural gas and manufacturing have supplanted it.

Today, stereotypes formed in the 1930s by the poverty of Dust Bowl farmers still exist, but Oklahoma's economy is growing at one of the fastest paces in the nation, with a rapidly diversifying industrial sector and a steady agriculture base. Due to its central location and unique history, Oklahoma is a crossroads for the cultures of the Midwest, Southwest, Southeast, and Texas—not to mention myriad American Indians—that surround it. After the seesaw of the 20th century, which alternated between oil booms, social and demographic turbulence, and agricultural crashes, the Sooner State is ready to be discovered at last.

The 76-foot Golden Driller, standing in front of the Tulsa Expo Center, pays tribute to the importance of the petroleum industry.

Oklahoma State Facts

Full Name: State of Oklahoma
Meaning of Name: From Choctaw *okla* (red) and *humma* (people)
Admitted to the Union: November 16, 1907 (46th state)
Inhabitant: Oklahoman

Capital City: Oklahoma City
Flower: Mistletoe
Tree: Redbud
Bird: Scissor-tailed flycatcher

Geography and Ecology

Oklahoma was famous for its broad expanse of prairie and grasslands, frequented by American bison and, later, by herds of domesticated cattle on their way to market from Texas ranches. However, Oklahoma is in fact one of the most geographically diverse states in the nation, with 11 ecological systems within its borders (it is only one of four states to harbor more than 10). In terms of ecological regions per square mile, it is by far the most diverse, as it ranks only 20th in terms of size.

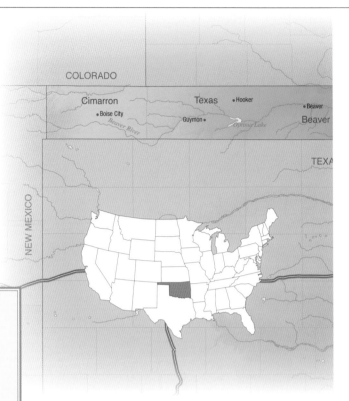

GLITTER AND PARKS

In north central Major County rise a series of strange mesas, which seem to sparkle in the sun. The appearance of the mesas (steep-sided, flat-topped hills) inspired the name Glass Mountains, although they are also called Gypsum or Gloss Mountains. It is the presence of gypsum, a very soft mineral, that makes this area glitter. Oklahoma has designated the region a state park. In addition to Gloss Mountains State Park, Oklahoma operates 49 other parks. Six national parks and the largest protected grassland in the world, the Tallgrass Prairie Preserve, can also be found throughout the state.

Glittering gypsum flakes beautify the strikingly red soil of Oklahoma, which ranges from brown to cinnamon in shade.

Grand Oklahoma

Six eco-regions crowd each other in eastern Oklahoma. In the south, cypress swamps and marshes resemble the Deep South; above them, the Ouachita Mountains rise eastward. Here is the world's tallest hill: at 1,999 feet tall, Cavanal Hill falls short by 1 foot of the designation "mountain." Hardwood forests, a small portion of Ozark woodlands, and Ozark highlands complete the Arkansas border, while various prairies stretch south from Kansas in the northeast corner. Most of the eastern third of Oklahoma consists of Crosstimbers, a region of prairie and woodlands. Tulsa lies on the edge of this region in the northeast.

The largest of Oklahoma's several eco-regions is the Great Plains. Here are the undulating grasslands of cattle-drives, land runs, and a late holdout of an Indian frontier. Oklahoma City lies on its eastern edge, and American bison, armadillo, and the vulnerable greater prairie chicken still roam through its fertile meadows. The state gradually becomes more arid to the northwest, where high plateaus and short-grass prairie take over the landscape. Prairie dogs are a common sight in Oklahoma's panhandle, which houses some of the country's largest "towns." Here, in the northwest corner of the panhandle, rises Black Mesa, which at 4,973 feet is Oklahoma's highest point.

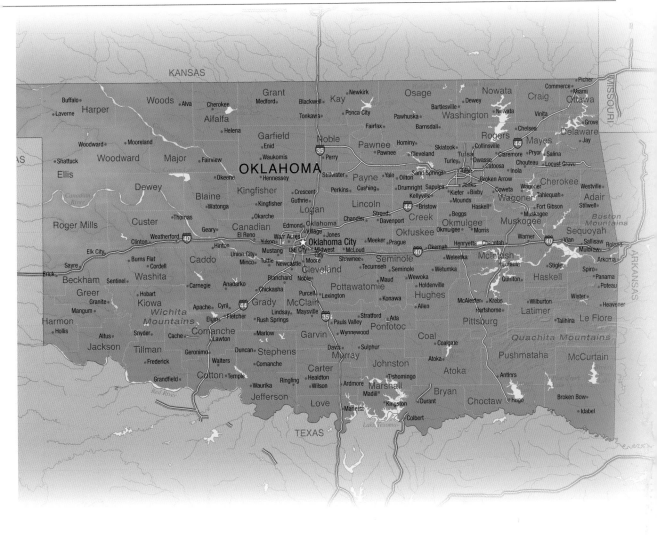

Dust and Tornadoes

Although precipitation levels vary widely throughout the state, with eastern portions falling into a humid subtropical climate, Oklahoma is known for its "Dust Bowl" days, when droughts dried up much of the state's agriculture. Indeed, the state does have a low proportion of water to land, with only 1,224 square miles of water to 68,679 square miles of land. Efforts to restore Oklahoma during the 1930s eventually bestowed some 200 man-made lakes and reservoirs on the state, more than in any other state.

Oklahoma's varied climates and flat terrain invite tornadoes, and indeed the vast majority of the state lies squarely within "Tornado Alley," the region where tornadoes appear most frequently in the United States. Unfortunately for Oklahoma, this means that it is struck more frequently than any state, except for Texas.

A tornado forms at the edge of a storm over Oklahoma. Tornadoes kill several people in the state every year, despite warning systems.

The Sooner State

Paleo-Indians hunted in Oklahoma perhaps 20,000 years ago, establishing a long-lasting way of life, at least in the western prairies. Numerous civilizations came and went in the following millennia, but as late as the 19th century inhabitants hunted American bison as a primary means of survival.

Indian Territory

Oklahoma changed little between European discovery and the Louisiana Purchase in 1803. Located at the far edge of both Spanish and French territories, it was of little interest to either European power.

Despite some initial favorable reports from American explorers, an expedition in 1820 led by Major Stephen Long sent back a depressing description of a hot, inhospitable desert, an impression that was to shape the area's history for the remainder of the century.

With a pressing need to relocate thousands of American Indians, the United States officially designated the region "Indian Territory" in the 1830s. American Indians were already living there, soon to be joined by the members of the "Five Civilized Tribes"—Cherokee, Chickasaw, Choctaw, Creek, and Seminole—removed by the government to the eastern portions of the state. Many, particularly the Chickasaw and Choctaw, adopted a southern way of life, complete with plantations and slaves.

American Indians moved into Oklahoma in large numbers in the 19th century, often compelled by the United States.

This short-lived state of affairs ended with the Civil War. Many American Indians joined the Confederacy, but Union sympathizers were plentiful, and soon Oklahoma descended into near anarchy. At the end of the war, the fragile society and economy that had existed before 1861 was no more. Thousands had been killed or displaced; ranchers had lost some 300,000 cattle, and the plantation was doomed here as elsewhere.

By 1918 oil discoveries and the foreign war had established Tulsa as the "Oil Capital of the World." The wealthy, culturally rich African American enclave of Greenwood became known as "Black Wall Street," but race riots in 1921 devasted the community.

Settling and Statehood

In the late 19th century, cowboys began crossing the state in large numbers, with even larger numbers of cattle. With the cowboys came other Americans, and their numbers only increased as railroads were built across Indian lands. In 1889 the United States reneged on its Indian treaties, creating Oklahoma Territory out of the central part of the state.

On April 22, 1889, some 50,000 hopeful settlers arrived for the first of several land runs. Some sneaked early into the country to stake a claim—these were called "sooners." Somewhat ironically, the name stuck to Oklahoma, despite the fact that the state was settled quite late, comparatively. The population boomed, reaching 722,441 in 1907. Attempts by the increasingly crowded American Indians to form an all-Indian state failed, and in 1907 Indian Territory was absorbed completely as Oklahoma became the 46th state.

The 20th Century

Oil prosperity in the early 20th century belied an unhealthy economic situation, as more and more farmers slipped into poverty. Along with the rest of the South, the state disenfranchised its African Americans and institutionalized segregation. By the end of the 1920s, poor farming practices, drought, and bad weather had taken a heavy toll on the region's agriculture. The Great Depression struck hard, with the "Dust Bowl"—a series of debilitating dust storms—centered on the panhandle. The plight of these unfortunate farmers was depicted in John Steinbeck's *Grapes of Wrath*.

Oklahoma's fortunes revived in World War II. Legal racial segregation ended with the Civil Rights Movement in the 1950s and 1960s, and for the most part Oklahoma avoided the violent clashes common elsewhere. The economy boomed in the 1970s, driven by thriving oil, natural gas, and subsidiary industries, although it suffered badly in the 1980s. One of the worst incidents in 20th century Oklahoman history occurred in 1995 in Oklahoma City, the capital and largest city. American terrorists detonated a bomb outside the Alfred P. Murrah Federal Building, killing 168 people.

Oklahoma is OK

Today, Oklahoma still focuses on its old standbys, oil, ranching, and agriculture. It is also expanding in the fields of manufacturing and aerospace, and maintains a niche market in weather research. Although its history has largely been one of adversity, from the Indian Removal Act to the Oklahoma City bombing, the state deserves appreciation for its unique culture, formation, and, rich environment. As Oscar Hammerstein wrote in the signature song to *Oklahoma!*, "We know we belong to the land / and the land we belong to is grand."

A farmer and his sons trudge through a dust storm in Cimarron County, 1936. Storms like these denuded farms, destroyed the agricultural economy, and led to the region's nickname, the Dust Bowl.

The Oklahoma City National Memorial and Museum remembers the tragic events of April 19, 1995. The chain-link Memorial Fence holds numerous personal remembrances from mourners and visitors.

Texas

The Lone Star State

Friendship

Although their state is often designated as southern, many Texans feel with some justification that theirs is a unique state, with a culture and history all its own. Spanish, French, and Anglo-American settlers clashed with Apache, Comanche, and other American Indians; Texas operated for a number of years under Mexico's jurisdiction and then for a short-lived (but much remembered) period as its own, internationally recognized country. The single star on the state flag recalls this period, and also reflects the individualism and self-sufficiency early Texans developed and later Texans espoused.

Many of Texas's formative peoples have left their marks on the state, from indigenous adobe architecture to legal codes descended from Spanish antecedents. Today, Texan culture has become a significant force on the national—and even international—stage, with homegrown "Tex-Mex" cuisine demonstrating the blend of nationalities so common to this border state. Most famously, the colorful language of the cowboy and his attendant trappings have become hallmarks of Texas and a broader American cultural linchpin.

Some of this recent exporting of Texan culture results from its rapidly expanding population, and the elections in 2000 and 2004 of Texan George W. Bush to the presidency. Until Alaska joined the Union in 1959, Texas enjoyed its status as the nation's largest state by area. Still associated with size, the state has found another source of prestige in recent years in its new rank as second in population, having overtaken New York in the 1990s.

Associated with the boom is a demographic shift from countryside to city and a changing economy. Traditionally reliant on cotton, ranching, and oil, Texas possesses a diverse economy today, making significant inroads in varied fields like health care, technology, and film. To some extent the demographic shift has blurred old geographic-cultural lines, although there are still significant differences between southern, western, northern, central, and eastern areas—as might be expected in a state covering 268,581 square miles and several distinct geographies.

Recent years have also continued a political trend that began in the 1920s. Although Texas continued to vote solidly Democratic for many years, Republicans gained a foothold in the middle of the century, and since then the political field has been shifting in their favor. The diverse economy and growing population have undoubtedly benefited the state, but they have also produced societal, political, and environmental problems. As always, Texas is facing these challenges head-on as it rides into the 21st century.

Santa Elena Canyon, carved by the Rio Grande as it travels through Big Bend National Park. The river divides Texas and Mexico.

Texas State Facts

Full Name: State of Texas
Meaning of Name: From Caddo word meaning "friends" or "allies"
Admitted to the Union: December 29, 1845 (28th state)
Inhabitant: Texan

Capital City: Austin
Flower: Bluebonnet
Tree: Pecan
Bird: Mockingbird

Geography and Ecology

Texas is so large and has such an irregular shape that geographic characterizations can be difficult. Generally speaking, the state may be divided up into five regions: the interior lowlands, demarcated roughly by Abilene, San Antonio, and Dallas; the northeastern Piney Woods; the Gulf Coastal Plain; the Rio Grande Valley; and the arid west, composed of plains, plateaus, and Texas's highest peaks.

Interior Lowlands and the East

Stretching west from the Louisiana border and the Sabine River, the Piney Woods continue a landscape that covers parts of Louisiana, Arkansas, and Oklahoma.

GALVESTON DISASTER

The city of Galveston, on a Gulf Coast barrier island, was once Texas's most important port, but in September 1900 a hurricane barreled in from the Gulf and tore the city to shreds. Owing to poor communications, inhabitants were woefully unprepared for the storm. Although later, more violent storms proved costlier elsewhere in the Gulf, the 1900 Galveston hurricane ranks as the worst natural disaster in North America due to the inordinately high death toll: as many as 12,000 people may have lost their lives to the raging wind and water.

Armed men guard relief supplies of food and goods for victims of the hurricane near Galveston's Commissary.

In Texas, the lumber industry started early and continues today, with the result that no virgin forest remains. All four of Texas's national forests can be found here, as well as 17 state parks. The region is subtropical and wet, and rice is one of the area's main crops, although reserves of oil—particularly the massive East Texas oil field near Tyler—are the economic mainstay.

The interior lowlands, also called the Blackland Prairie, end at the Edwards Plateau and the Great Plains. Although settled late, several of Texas's most populous cities are located here, including San Antonio, Dallas, Fort Worth, Waco, and the capital, Austin. Once a center of cattle, grain, and cotton industries, today the region is heavily industrial and increasingly urban.

The Coastal Plain and the Rio Grande

Texas's most humid region, the Gulf Coastal Plain once dominated the state's culture and politics as cotton plantations thrived in the antebellum period. Coastal cities are still important ports today, particularly Houston—the largest city in Texas and the fourth-largest nationwide. Industry, tourism, and aerospace concerns (particularly NASA) support the region's economy.

The Rio Grande forms the border with Mexico, and from early on the population has been heavily Spanish-speaking. Ranching remains the economic mainstay, although trade with Mexico is also important. Since the

Texas Revolution, international relations have been somewhat strained, and today the area is the epicenter of a border-fence debate.

The West

The southernmost tip of the Great Plains covers Texas's panhandle and continues until the Edwards Plateau on the Mexican border. Ranching took root in the late 19th century and is still common today. Tornadoes are most frequent in this area of the state (which ranks first nationally for number of strikes).

The western tip of Texas is arid and inhospitable, still sparsely settled except for El Paso. Fierce American Indian warriors once prevented Europeans from entering the region, which boasts some of the state's most spectacular scenery in two national parks: Big Bend in the south and Guadalupe Mountains in the north, where visitors can climb Guadalupe Peak, the state's highest point at 8,749 feet.

The Lone Star State

The history of human habitation in Texas begins 11,000 years ago in the Pleistocene epoch and is documented by hundreds of archaeological sites scattered around the state. Some aspects of life remained unchanged straight through to the modern era; Paleo-Indians were hunting bison as early as 6,000 BCE. By the time the Spanish arrived in the mid-16th century, American Indians had established trading routes that reached as far as Idaho to the north and central Mexico to the south.

Early Spanish Influences
Spanish control over Texas was sporadic and restricted to the southeast portion of the state. Although the first Spaniard (also the first European) to see Texas, Alonso Álvarez de Piñeda, arrived in 1519, it was not until the early 18th century that the Spanish attempted to colonize the region. Worried by a growing French presence in Louisiana, Spain sent wave after wave of missionaries to convert and soldiers to pacify the American Indians. Although the Spanish did prevent Texas from falling under French influence, they were largely unsuccessful at colonizing it, in part because Apache and Comanche warriors had moved south into the plains and were persistently hostile to the encroaching Europeans. However, by the time the Spanish left the scene in 1821, they had introduced several enduring features to the Texas landscape, including domesticated livestock (and ranching), Christianity, and Spanish city and location names.

Going it Alone
The first half of the 19th century saw Texans struggling in a rough frontier, which was politically tumultuous and still threat-ened by hostile Indians. Mexico, which had acquired the territory when it won its independence, had better luck than Spain in attracting settlers to Texas. This was due in large part to the favorable conditions they offered to Anglo-American immigrants. The most famous of these newcomers came from Missouri with 300 families in his company: Stephen F. Austin, after whom the city is named, and the Old Three Hundred signify the beginning of the shift to an American, southern culture.

Revolution
Mexico quickly began to harbor suspicions about the immigrants, and for good reason; chafing against Mexican transgressions, real or imagined, the rapidly expanding American population started agitating for independence. The rise of the centralist, aggressive Santa Anna to power proved the last straw for the Texans. When the Mexican army asked that a cannon in American-held Gonzales be

Mission Concepción, dedicated in 1755, is the only San Antonio mission to retain its original roof. San Antonio missions are recognized as some of the best examples of Spanish architecture in North America.

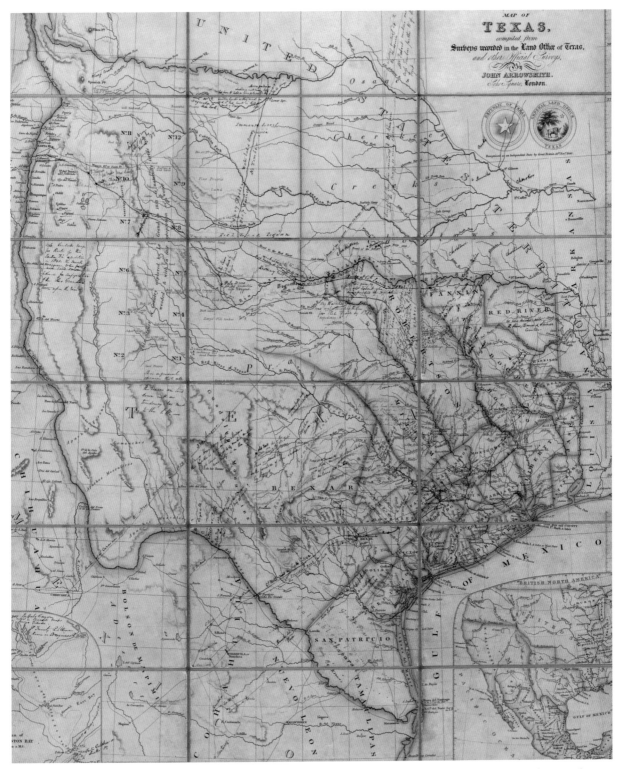

A map of the Republic of Texas, drawn in 1841. Visible in the upper right-hand corner are the Lone Star and an American bison, at the time a common sight in the broad Texas prairies. The volatile political situation made this map obsolete within five years of its printing.

returned to them, the citizens provocatively responded, "Come and take it." Shots were fired, and the Texas Revolution began.

A combination of luck, Texas sharp-shooting, and miscalculations on Santa Anna's part resulted in Mexican capitulation on April 21, 1836. Even so, Mexico refused to recognize the new Republic of Texas until 1845, by which time Texas was about to join the United States. As a republic, Texas had oscillated between two vastly different presidents, the hero of the revolution, Sam Houston, and Mirabeau Lamar, who took an aggressive stance against American Indians and fought against annexation by the United States, both positions antithetical to Houston's. Debts, Apache and Comanche raids, and the continuing threat of Mexican invasion drove Texas into the Union on December 29, 1845.

Sam Houston

Wild West in Texas

Most of the American settlers who flocked to Texas in the second quarter of the 19th century came from the South, and they brought their cotton, their plantations, and their slaves with them. As a result, Texas (particularly the

most heavily populated area, the east) quickly began to resemble its Deep South neighbors economically, socially, and politically. By the outbreak of the Civil War, only a few argued to stay in the Union (among them Sam Houston), and Texan cavalry rode in major battles throughout the war.

During Reconstruction, the federally imposed Republican government faced several problems. Despite laws protecting the rights of freed men, resentment, racism, and declining economic conditions kept most African Americans in a state of poverty. Violence, both racially motivated and otherwise, became an omnipresent issue. In addition, raids by American Indians began to increase again, leading to even more lawlessness.

The Cattle Drive

The Republicans were ousted in 1871 and would not return to the political stage for nearly a century. Taking control in the late 19th century, the Democrats benefited from the booming economy—although assuredly Texas bore little resemblance to the true Gilded Age powerhouses of the east. Agriculture benefited less, and as a result farmers began agitating against corporations such as railroads, which were spreading across the state and changing its culture, politics, and economics almost overnight. By 1900 nearly 10,000 miles of track connected Texans to each other and the rest of the nation.

During the same period, cattle driving took off. Although Texans had been herding their cattle across the landscape for decades, not until 1866 did large-scale, long-distance drives begin in earnest. That year, more than 260,000 Texas cattle traveled to market, some as far away as Denver. The golden age of cattle driving proved short, however, as the railroads soon took over cattle transportation. By 1890 the era was over, but the image of the cowboy has endured.

Oil Kingdom

In the 19th century cotton ruled, but the discovery of oil in 1901 at Spindletop inaugurated a new king, who would reign for much of the century. However, the dominance of oil grew slowly for the first half of the 20th

Texas longhorn cattle developed from three Spanish breeds and have been a familiar sight in Texas since the 18th century.

century; agriculture, including ranching, still controlled the state's economy. Faltering prices—and particularly the 1921 cotton crash—further rocked this broad section of the Texas population, and progressivism, particularly the prohibition movement, took hold.

Racial relations continued to decline. Along with the rest of the South, Texas effectively disenfranchised its black population. As elsewhere in the South, African Americans were segregated in increasingly official ways. Also discriminated against was Texas's other large minority population, Hispanics, who started to immigrate in large numbers in the 1920s. Briefly, the Ku Klux Klan and religious fundamentalists, who attempted to pass anti-evolution laws in the state, won significant influence in state politics.

Turbulent Times

The Great Depression struck Texas hard. Violence and lawlessness again infected the state, as the success of the famous bank-robbing duo Bonnie Parker and Clyde Barrow demonstrated. New Deal programs provided some relief, but it would be years before Texas fully recovered from the hardships of that time.

Beginning in World War II, Texas manufacturing, industry, and oil production began to boom. The state rapidly urbanized. Partially due to the new urban demographic, the Civil Rights Movement took hold in the state, and despite a drawn-out, bitter integration process, Texas avoided much of the violence prominent elsewhere in the South. For much of the rest of century, despite downturns in the 1970s, oil and associated industries exploded throughout Texas. The industry has declined somewhat since then but is still a significant part of a diversifying Texan economy.

Today, Texas has traded its old problems of Mexican threats, Indian raids, and fluctuating farm prices for new ones, among them water shortages, social turbulence, and a troubled educational system, but undoubtedly it will address these as it has in the past: with a steady eye and sure aim.

REMEMBER THE ALAMO

For 13 days in 1836, fewer than 200 Texans and Americans held off Santa Anna's assault force of some 1,800. Waiting for reinforcements that never came, the defenders of the Alamo died to the last man when Mexico finally overwhelmed the mission-turned-fortress. In the process of the siege, the Texan sharpshooters gave a good account of themselves, killing or incapacitating a full third of the attacking troops. The victory came back to haunt Santa Anna, who encountered cries of "Remember the Alamo!" throughout the remainder of the Texas Revolution. The phrase is still uttered today, and the Alamo attracts some 2.5 million visitors every year.

At one time a Spanish mission, the Alamo now evokes Texas patriotism more than religion.

One of the most infamous sites in Texas, the "grassy knoll" figures heavily in conspiracy theories surrounding the assassination of President John F. Kennedy in Dallas.

Michigan

The Wolverine State

Si Quaeris Peninsulam Amoenam Circumspice (If you seek a pleasant peninsula, look about you)

The Great Lakes state of Michigan is unusual in that it is composed of two peninsulas—the Upper Peninsula and the Lower Peninsula—that are linked by a 5-mile bridge that crosses the Straits of Mackinac. The Upper Peninsula is bordered on the south by Lake Michigan and Lake Huron, on the north by Lake Superior, and on the west by Wisconsin. The Lower Peninsula is bordered on the south by Indiana and Ohio, on the west by Lake Michigan, and on the east by Lake Huron and Lake Erie. Boasting 3,200 miles of shoreline, Michigan touches four of the five Great Lakes; no city or town in the state is more than 85 miles from one of those lakes.

Michigan is so associated with the automotive industry that it can be easy to overlook its many other facets. In fact, economically, the state is quite diverse. Tourism contributes more than $15 billion annually to the state's gross domestic product. And only Minnesota produces more iron ore than Michigan.

About a quarter of the land in Michigan is devoted to farming, most of it in the southern part of the state. Corn, beans, hay, and soybeans are the state's leading crops. In addition, Michigan is one of the country's top producers of Christmas trees. The area around Lake Michigan in the state's Lower Peninsula is also one of the nation's leading fruit-growing areas. Apples, blueberries, cherries, and grapes are just some of the products grown in this fertile region.

Of course, the automotive industry is important in Michigan. Detroit, known as both the Automobile Capital of the World and the Motor City, produces more cars and trucks than any other part of the country.

More than 80 percent of Michigan's population of 9.9 million live in one of the state's metropolitan areas. Detroit is Michigan's largest city, an important port city, and is also the birthplace of Motown Records, as well as the center of the automotive industry.

Lansing (pop. 113,972) has been the capital of Michigan since 1847. It is also a major industrial city, producing automobiles and automotive parts, as well as gasoline engines. Michigan State University, located in East Lansing, is just one of many institutions of higher learning in Michigan. Along with cars, Michigan's colleges and universities are also great sources of pride in the Wolverine State.

Lansing has been the capital of Michigan since 1847. The Renaissance-revival-inspired capitol building, completed in 1879, was designed by Elijah Myers.

Michigan State Facts

Full Name: State of Michigan
Meaning of Name: From the Indian word *michigama*, meaning "great or large lake"
Admitted to the Union: January 26, 1837 (26th state)
Inhabitant: Michiganian, Michigander

Capital City: Lansing
Flower: Apple blossom
Tree: White pine
Bird: Robin

Geography and Ecology

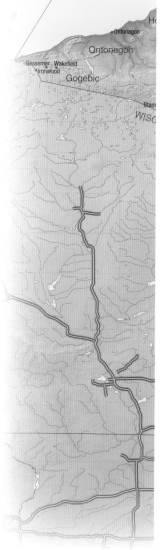

Michigan's landscape is divided into two primary regions: the Superior Upland and the Great Lakes Plains.

The Superior Upland covers the western portion of the Upper Peninsula along Lake Superior. This area is hilly and in some spots rugged—Michigan's highest peak, Mount Arvon (1,979 ft.) is in the Upland region—and has the highest concentration of the state's waterfalls. Iron and copper deposits here are some of the richest in the United States.

The Great Lakes Plains covers the eastern portion of the Upper Peninsula and all of the Lower Peninsula. In the Upper Peninsula the region is characterized in many areas by swampland. The Lower Peninsula, by contrast, is distinguished by a rolling landscape.

Lakes and Waterways

Michigan enjoys the unique distinction of touching four of the five Great Lakes, and so it is not surprising that the lakes provide the state with tourism income. But throughout history the Great Lakes have also been used extensively for transportation and shipping. Approximately 6,000 vessels have been lost in the Great Lakes, and an estimated 1,500 of them are in Michigan waters. Today, these wrecks are popular sites with divers and archaeologists for exploration and recreation.

The majority of ships have been lost to storms; November is an especially deadly month. Gale-force winds can cause ocean-size waves, some as high as 30 feet. The Great Lakes Shipwreck Museum, located at Whitefish Point on the Upper Peninsula, is the only museum dedicated to shipwrecks in the Great Lakes.

Michigan also has more than 11,000 inland lakes. Houghton Lake, in the north-central region of the Lower Peninsula, is the largest, at 31 square miles. The lake and its environs are popular for canoeing, fishing, boating, hiking, and hunting.

Michigan's longest river is the 260-mile-long Grand River. It flows from Jackson and empties into Lake Michigan.

Weather and Climate

Michigan's climate is temperate, with cold winters and warm summers. The state's position on the Great Lakes

---

MICHIGAN'S WATERFALLS

More than 200 waterfalls dot the Michigan landscape, most of them in the Upper Peninsula. With a drop of approximately 50 feet, upper Tahquamenon Falls on the Tahquamenon River (made famous by the Longfellow poem *The Song of Hiawatha*) is located near Lake Superior in the state's Upper Peninsula.

In spring, when snowmelt swells the river, up to 50,000 gallons spill over the falls every second, making the falls the third-most voluminous vertical waterfall east of the Mississippi.

Upper Tahquamenon Falls is the second-largest waterfall east of the Mississippi River.

means that it experiences many cloudy and partly cloudy days—approximately six out of ten days in summer and seven out of ten days in winter.

Generally, the Lower Peninsula is warmer than the Upper Peninsula. Average January temperatures range from 15° F to 26° F; in July temperatures range from 65° F to 73° F.

Michigan receives between 26 and 36 inches of precipitation a year. Average annual snowfall ranges from less than 40 inches to more than 160 inches. A record snowfall of 276.5 inches fell in Houghton during the winter of 1949–50.

More than 75 lighthouses dot the shores of Lake Michigan. Late fall storms can make navigation on the lake treacherous.

The Wolverine State

Approximately 15,000 Indians from tribes including the Chippewa, Ottawa, and the Potawatomi once inhabited the land that is now Michigan. The first European to arrive was Frenchman Étienne Brûlé, who explored the area in 1620. France controlled the region that now includes Michigan for nearly 150 years before ceding it to Great Britain after the French and Indian War. After the American Revolution the land was formally surrendered to the United States. Michigan became the 26th state in 1837.

Economic Growth

Michigan's early economy was based on agriculture—in 1850 roughly 85 percent of the population depended on agriculture for a living. But by 1870 lumber and mining had entered the mix, with the exploitation of the state's pine forests and the discovery of rich deposits of copper, iron ore, and salt.

The Industrial Revolution brought even more economic growth to the state. Although forests were being depleted, manufacturing exploded: paper and furniture production were leading industries. In the late 1800s such well-known companies as Kellogg and the Upjohn Company were established. But no other product had more impact on the state's economy than the automobile.

The Automotive Industry

In 1901 the popularity of the Oldsmobile Runabout—the first mass-produced motor vehicle in history—paved the way for other Michigan car companies. These new enterprises manufactured and sold affordable vehicles for the first time in America. By 1904 Michigan was the nation's leading automobile producer. Over the next 20 years, Michigan saw the birth of General Motors (1908), the development of Henry Ford's Model T (1908) and the assembly line (1913–14), and the Chrysler Corporation (1925).

During the late 1800s, Detroit was known as the Paris of the West because of its mansions. It was also an important hub of transportation because of its location on the Great Lakes.

The Model T Ford was not the first car to be manufactured in Detroit, but it was the car that made automobiles popular. The price: $850 in 1909.

In the early 1920s the decline of the lumber and mining industries of the Upper Peninsula left that area economically depressed. The Great Depression ravaged the automotive industry and the entire state's economy.

Depression and Recovery

Job losses brought about by the Depression led to the birth and growth of the United Auto Workers (UAW) union. After a contentious strike against General Motors in 1936–37 and negotiations with Chrysler (1937) and Ford (1941), the UAW's demands for higher pay and union recognition were won.

Economic recovery came in the form of the Second World War, when the entire automotive industry turned to the manufacture of war materials including airplanes, tanks, and ships.

Today, despite a more diverse economy with a strong and growing service sector, Michigan's economic health is still heavily dependent on the automotive industry.

This map of Michigan, published in 1877, shows the importance of the railroad in the 19th century. It was the major means of transporting goods such as lumber.

Ohio

The Buckeye State

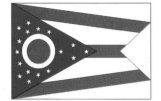

With God All Things Are Possible

Ohio lies north of the Ohio River and south of Lake Erie. This state, once part of the Northwest Territory, is steeped in history. Seven U.S. presidents were born in Ohio: Ulysses S. Grant, Rutherford B. Hayes, James A. Garfield, Benjamin Harrison, William McKinley, William Howard Taft, and Warren G. Harding. And although William Henry Harrison was born in Virginia, he was living in Ohio when he was elected president. Only Virginia has been home to more. And two of America's best-known astronauts—Neil Armstrong, the first man to walk on the moon, and John Glenn, the first American to orbit the Earth, were born in Ohio.

But it is not only its famous sons and daughters that make Ohio important. It is a leading industrial state, producing chemicals, motor vehicles and their parts, industrial machinery, and processed foods. Agriculture, too, is a vital source of income. Nearly half the land in Ohio is given to farming; the state is a major producer of both corn and soybeans. Most of the working population is employed in one of the service industries that thrive in the state, such as health care, finance, and education.

Ohio's location on Lake Erie gives it access to international trade through the St. Lawrence Seaway.

Ohio is a densely populated state, and most of its 11.5 million residents live in one of the several urban areas. Among the largest are Columbus, Cleveland, and Cincinnati.

Columbus, the largest city and the state capital, is home to the main campus of Ohio State University, one of the largest universities in the United States, as well as the Columbus Blue Jackets NHL team.

Cleveland is Ohio's second-largest city. In addition to being a major industrial center, it is well known as the home of the Rock and Roll Hall of Fame, plus the International Women's Air and Space Museum and several professional sports teams, including the Cleveland Browns football team and the Cleveland Cavaliers basketball team. The Cleveland Orchestra is regarded as one of the world's finest. In 1967 Cleveland became the first major city in the United States to elect an African American, Carl Stokes, as mayor.

Cincinnati enjoys the distinction of being the birthplace of professional baseball, in 1869, when the Cincinnati Red Stockings came into being. Today, fans in the city also support the Bengals football team. Football is also represented in Canton, home of the Pro Football Hall of Fame.

Cincinnati has come a long way since its founding in 1788. Today, it is a thriving city of 297,517.

Ohio State Facts

Full Name: State of Ohio
Meaning of Name: From the Iroquois Indian word meaning "something great" or "great water"
Admitted to the Union: March 1, 1803 (17th state)
Inhabitant: Ohioan

Capital City: Columbus
Flower: Scarlet carnation
Tree: Buckeye
Bird: Cardinal

Geography and Ecology

Ohio's topography is made up of three regions: the Appalachian Plateau, the Central Lowland, and the Interior Low Plateaus.

The Appalachian Plateau region (sometimes called the Allegheny Plateau) covers the eastern half of the state. The northeastern part of the plateau experienced glacial eroding during the last ice age, leaving it relatively flat. But glaciers did not reach the rest of the plateau, which is in southeast Ohio. As a consequence, the landscape there features ravines, steep ridges, and hills. Much of the area is also forested.

The western portion of the state lies in the Central Lowland region. This area is flat to gently rolling and is covered with rich soil. This area is the heart of Ohio's farmland.

The Interior Low Plateaus region is a small, triangle-shaped area in south-central Ohio. Also known as the Bluegrass region, this area is marked by deep valleys, steep cliffs, caves, and sinkholes.

Lakes and Waterways

The Ohio River, which forms Ohio's southern border, is important for both recreation and the transport of cargo in the state.

Lake Erie, the smallest of the nation's Great Lakes, gives Ohio access to the St. Lawrence Seaway and therefore international shipping. The state's 312-mile-long shoreline is rocky, with a few sandy stretches. The soil around the lake is famously fertile and has long been farmed. However, since the mid-1800s, waste from farming and industry polluted the lake to such an extent that in 1969 it

RIVER OF FIRE

The Cuyahoga River, which flows through Cleveland, was once little more than a dumping ground for industrial pollutants and debris. In 1969 national attention was turned to the river—and to environmental concerns in general—when the river caught fire. It is believed that sparks from a passing train may have ignited an oil slick on the river. The fired burned for only 30 minutes, but it sparked a nationwide movement that eventually led to the passage of the Clean Water Act of 1972.

The Cuyahoga River cleanup is considered one of the nation's environmental success stories.

Riverboats on the Ohio River were once a common sight in Cincinnati. Today, replicas make their way up the river.

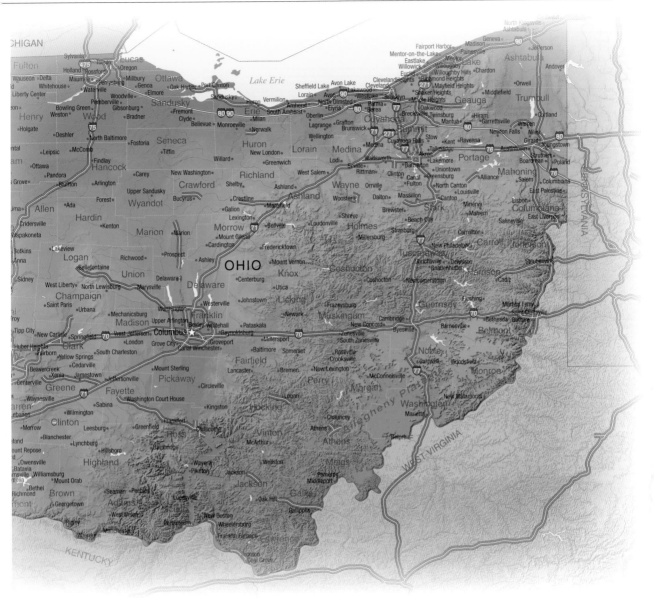

was declared "ecologically dead," unable to support most marine life. Although a few dead zones still exist, the health of the lake greatly improved in the decades since passage of the Clean Water Act in 1972. Today, fishing and boating are common recreational activities on the lake.

Natural Resources

Among Ohio's natural resources and minerals are oil, natural gas, clay, sandstone, and gypsum. Bituminous coal, a soft coal that contains large amounts of ash and sulfur, is Ohio's most important mined product. Salt is also plentiful in the state; in fact, it has been estimated that the entire country's salt needs could be supplied for thousands of years by Ohio alone.

Climate

Ohio's climate is temperate; in January the temperature averages 31° F. In July it averages 71° F. Annual precipitation averages 32 inches in the northern part of the state and 42 inches in the south.

The city of Cleveland lies in the snowbelt of the United States and receives what is known as lake-effect snowfall. Lake-effect snow is unique to only a few places in the world, including the Great Lakes. Cities in the snowbelt can receive up to 110 inches of snow a year.

The Buckeye State

Prior to European exploration the area that is now Ohio was inhabited by a series of different Indian tribes. Among the pre-Columbian peoples who lived there were the Adena (100 BCE–100 CE) and the Hopewell culture (100 BCE–400 CE), which constructed earthen burial mounds, some of which still exist today. In 1669–70, Frenchman Robert de La Salle may have been the first European to explore the region. During that time four Indian tribes, all of which were hunter-gatherers, inhabited the area: Wyandot and Delaware in northern Ohio, Miami and Shawnee in the south.

The Greek Revival State House in Columbus, Ohio. The building houses the only bust for which Lincoln sat during his lifetime.

Disputes and Bloodshed

Both the French and the English claimed the area, and disputes continued until after the French and Indian War (1754–63), when France ceded its possessions to Great Britain. After the Revolutionary War, Britain in turn handed over to the United States an enormous territory that included Ohio. From the time that France handed over the lands, through the War of 1812, Europeans came into conflict with the region's Indian populations. Hundreds of settlers and Indians died in numerous bloody battles. After the War of 1812 the tribes that had not fled the area were forcibly confined to tiny reservations. Eventually, even those lands were seized by the American government, and after 1843 no organized tribes remained in the state.

Unofficial Statehood

Ohio unofficially became the 17th state in 1803—unofficially, because Congress had not formally passed an act to admit the state. That formal resolution was passed on August 7, 1953. The years prior to the Civil War saw extraordinary growth. Immigration brought settlers from New England and the South, Germany, and Ireland. Canals, the National Road, and the railroad all increased access to and from the state for goods and people.

During the Civil War Ohio supported the Union. The state lost more than 35,000 men in the war, but also produced two of the era's Union heroes: both Ulysses S. Grant and William Tecumseh Sherman were born in Ohio.

Ulysses S. Grant

World Wars and Beyond

Ohio's economic fortunes rose and fell with world events in the century following the Civil War. A building boom in the 1920s crashed with the stock market in 1929. During the Depression, industrial workers suffered long periods of unemployment. During one especially embittered action against the rubber, steel, mining, and automotive industries, the Congress of Industrial Organizations (CIO) organized the first sit-down strike in history.

World War II brought with it economic prosperity as well as job opportunities for both African Americans and women. Ohio's population grew by more than 3 million over the 30 years after the war, but the economy again began to experience a decline as

Cleveland's population in 1887, the date this map was published, was 261,353, making it the 10th-largest city in the United States. Today, Cleveland's poplulation stands at approximately 396,815.

manufacturing jobs moved abroad or to other states.

In the last few decades, Ohio's economy has had its ups and downs, but it is a more metropolian state than most, having seven large metro areas to contribute to the GDP. In 2016 the state hosted the Republican National Convention, leisure and hospitality jobs were on the rise, and growth was robust in other sectors, giving hope that the state will soon recover its economy.

May 4, 1970

The social unrest of the 1960s did not spare Ohio. In one of the iconic events of the era, National Guardsmen shot and killed four unarmed students at Kent State University on May 4, 1970. Governor James Rhodes had called in the Guard during student demonstrations against the American invasion of Cambodia during the Vietnam War.

The Rock and Roll Hall of Fame opened in 1995 in Cleveland. Several artists are inducted each year.

Indiana

The Hoosier State

The Crossroads of America

This smallest of the midwestern states has a reputation as an agricultural and an industrial state—and both of those characterizations are accurate. Approximately 65 percent of Indiana's land is devoted to farming. It is the nation's second-largest producer of tomatoes and popcorn; it ranks fourth in production of peppermint and spearmint, and fifth in production of corn. Most of the farmland lies in the central part of the state, where the terrain is gently rolling and the soil rich.

At the same time Indiana is now the nation's top steel-producing state. Furniture, iron, and pharmaceuticals are other important manufactured products. Fort Wayne, South Bend, and Gary are among the state's major industrial centers. The latter two form a portion of an industrial belt that runs from Chicago into northwest Indiana.

Indiana natives are known as Hoosiers—one of the state's nicknames is the Hoosier State. The derivation of the word is lost to time, but residents of the state wear the badge proudly.

Indiana has a rich sports heritage; high school and college basketball are especially well loved. Indiana University, Purdue, and Notre Dame have consistently produced winning programs. The motion picture *Hoosiers*, which tells the story of an underdog high school basketball team, also won legions of fans across the state and around the world.

Indianapolis, Indiana's capital and the state's largest city, is home to the Indianapolis Motor Speedway, site of the Indianapolis 500 and the Allstate 400 NASCAR race. The city is also home to the NBA's Indiana Pacers as well as the NFL's Indianapolis Colts, who triumphed over the Chicago Bears in Super Bowl XLI in 2007.

Even though it is considered fairly conservative, the state has elected an almost equal number of Democrats and Republicans in both state and national elections. Another indicator of Indiana's independent spirit is that from the early 1970s until 2006, the state refused to recognize Daylight Saving Time. Today, 80 counties in the state are included in the Eastern Time Zone and 12 counties are in the Central Time Zone.

Although no American presidents have been born in the state, five vice presidents were born or lived a substantial part of their lives in Indiana: Schuyler Colfax (Grant); Thomas Hendricks (Cleveland); Charles W. Fairbanks (Theodore Roosevelt); Thomas Marshall (Hoover); and Dan Quayle (G. H. W. Bush). For this reason Indiana is sometimes called the mother of vice presidents.

Skyline of Indiana's state capital, Indianapolis.

Indiana State Facts

Full Name: State of Indiana
Meaning of Name: "Land of Indians"
Admitted to the Union: December 11, 1816 (19th state)
Inhabitant: Indianan, Hoosier
Capital City: Indianapolis

Flower: Peony
Tree: Tulip tree
Bird: Cardinal

Geography and Ecology

Indiana's topography can be roughly divided into three distinct areas: the Northern Lake and Moraine region, the Central Till Plain, and the Southern Hills and Lowlands.

The northern third of Indiana, which comprises the Northern Lake and Moraine region, was eroded by glaciers millions of years ago. The landscape here is dotted by bogs, marshland, and small lakes.

The Central Till Plain forms a band that stretches across the middle third of the state. Glaciers flattened the land in this area and deposited rich soil. Central Indiana terrain was formed by glacial movement as well; the glaciers also deposited the fertile soil in this area, which is today the heart of Indiana's farmland.

The Southern Hills and Lowlands region, in the southern part of the state, was almost completely untouched by glacial activity. The landscape was therefore not as eroded and is more rugged than other areas of the state, marked by streams, sinkholes, and caves. Many caves in southern Indiana are easily accessible to the public—these are called show caves. The largest of these, Wyandotte Caves, in Leavenworth, is a popular tourist attraction and the fifth largest cave system in the state.

Lake Michigan Shoreline

Indiana fronts Lake Michigan with a 43-mile shoreline. Much of the area is highly industrialized; Gary and Hammond, two of the larger industrial cities on the shorefront, are centers of steel production and oil refining. There is concern among many that the pollutants dumped into the lake are causing irreversible environmental damage.

Between Michigan City and Gary is the Indiana Dunes National Lakeshore. This 15,000-acre national park is home to dunes, swamps, bogs and marshes, rivers, and forests. Most notable is the biological diversity within the park: more than 1,100 species of plants and ferns grow there, and more than 350 bird species are found in the park, including great blue herons.

Climate

Indiana's climate is temperate; extremes—of precipitation and of temperature—are rare. In January the average temperature ranges from 25° F to 37° F; in July temperatures range from 73° F to 78° F. Winter in the state can bring significant amounts of snow, especially in the northwestern area of the state, where 100 inches in a single season is not unusual.

Springtime brings with it tornadoes; in fact, Indiana experiences tornadoes with similar frequency to Great Plains states such as Texas or Kansas. Indiana averages 20 tornadoes a year, generally between March and June—but the storms can and do occur in any month.

Indiana Dunes National Lakeshore.

INDIANA TORNADOES

On April 3 and 4, 1974, the worst tornado outbreak in U.S. history occurred. During those two days, a super-outbreak of 148 tornadoes touched down in 13 states, including Indiana. In 16 hours 330 people were dead, nearly 5,500 were injured, and the path of destruction covered more than 2,500 miles. In Indiana alone 21 tornadoes killed 48 people and caused $200 million in damage.

Indiana's deadliest tornado outbreak occurred on Palm Sunday, 1965, when 11 tornadoes left 137 people dead, more than 1,700 injured, and caused more than $30 million in damage.

On average, Indiana experiences 20 tornadoes each year.

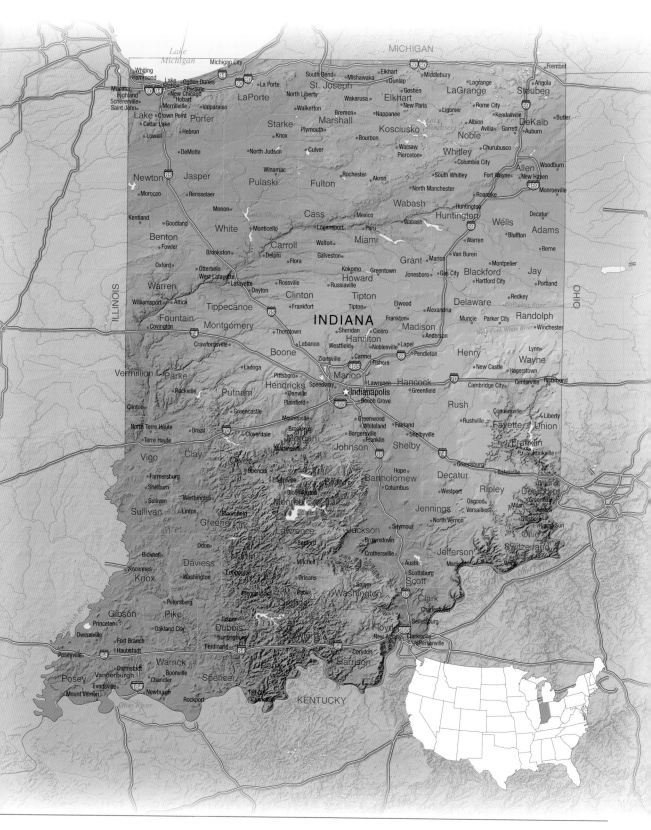

The Hoosier State

Before the first Europeans arrived to explore the area that is now Indiana, American Indians inhabited the area for thousands of years. From around 800 BCE until the early 1800s, Indians lived on the land, growing crops, hunting, and developing crafts. Some of the ceremonial burial mounds that they built remain on the state's landscape today.

The first European to arrive in the area was Jesuit missionary Jacques Marquette. Thereafter the French controlled the area; but in 1763, after the French and Indian War, the region was ceded to the British.

Statehood Achieved

After the Revolution, fighting between the Indians and Americans was common and frequent, until around 1815, when after battles and forced relocation the tribes no longer posed a significant threat to white settlers. In 1816 Indiana entered the Union with barely 80,000 residents.

After Indiana achieved statehood, pioneers poured into the state from New England and the South. European immigrants came primarily from Germany and Ireland. Agriculture drove the economy in those early days. From 1816 to the Civil War, the state experienced great growth in transportation and infrastructure. Roadways were built, as was a canal system that would link the state's rivers to the Great Lakes. And a railroad system also began to develop.

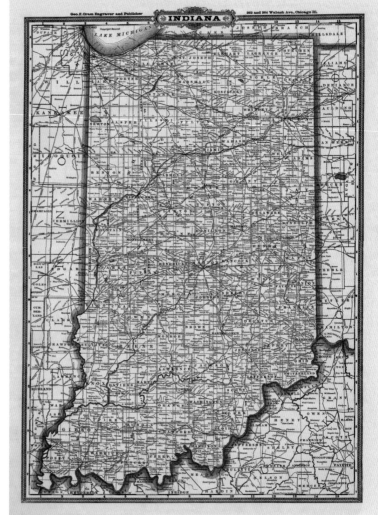

Indiana, 1888. The 19th century saw Indianapolis becoming the state's capital, and the founding of the University of Notre Dame.

Finding Economic Balance

Nearly 200,000 Indianans fought for the North during the Civil War. After the war, growth continued; in the 1880s the natural gas that had been discovered in the state lit homes in an increasing number of cities.

BUILDING A CAPITAL

The design for Indiana's capital city, Indianapolis, was based on Versailles, France, and Washington, D.C.

Over time Indiana's economy began to find a balance between industry and agriculture. By the early 1900s meat-packing, the milling of steel, drug manufacturing, and glass-making had become important industries; however, agriculture—with corn and hogs being the chief products—still formed the backbone of the state's economy.

Metropolitan Migration

The 1920s brought a number of changes to the state. A population shift meant that the state was becoming slightly more urban than rural. (By the 1970s more than two-thirds of the population lived in the larger cities in the northern part of the state.) The African American population also grew in numbers during these years, at the same time European immigration declined.

Today, Indiana's economy is shifting again, from a manufacturing base to a service base, although both agriculture and manufacturing remain important both in the number of jobs they provide and in their contribution to the state's gross domestic product.

FAMOUS HOOSIERS

Eugene Debs (1855–1926), railroad labor leader, Socialist Party presidential candidate, and activist
John Dillinger (1903–34), bank robber named Public Enemy Number One by the FBI
Virgil "Gus" Grissom (1926–67), one of the original seven Mercury astronauts
Robert Indiana (b. 1928), Pop artist
Tavis Smiley (b. 1964), journalist, author, political commentator
Kurt Vonnegut (1922–2007), author of novels including *Slaughterhouse-Five* and *Breakfast of Champions*
John Wooden (b. 1910), college basketball's most successful coach with 10 NCAA championships—7 of them consecutive—while he was at UCLA from 1966 to 1973

The Indiana State House has been the center of political life in the state since 1888.

The Historic Central Canal was designed in the early 19th century to promote commerce in Indianapolis. Today, the Canal Walk is the spot in the city to enjoy an afternoon stroll.

Illinois

Land of Lincoln

ILLINOIS

State Sovereignty, National Union

"Hog Butcher for the World," poet Carl Sandburg wrote of Chicago in 1916, "Tool Maker, Stacker of Wheat, / Player with Railroads and the Nation's Freight Handler; / Stormy, husky, brawling, / City of the Big Shoulders." Nearly a century later, the vigorous picture still measures up. Finance has superseded meatpacking as the backbone of Chicago's economy—the city has the second-largest business district in the United States—but food processing remains a major industry, as do manufacturing, publishing, and printing. Trains still churn along Chicago's rails, freighters cruise Lake Michigan into Chicago's ports, and countless goods change hands to be shipped off again. It is certainly stormy, the Windy City, and husky, and—in the midst of a building boom—it remains the City of the Big Shoulders.

It is a great American hub, Chicago—as is the state it crowns. More primary interstates pass through Illinois than any other state in the Union, making it truly America's crossroads. It also carries a reputation as a cultural junction, a bellwether for the nation—vaudevillians once claimed that an act that raised cheers in Peoria, in central Illinois, would be a universal crowd-pleaser.

Nearly a millennium before Chicago, another great city thrived here—Cahokia, the seat of the Mississippian culture, home to some 40,000 people. Today, artifacts buried amid towering mounds of earth are all that remain of the ancient city and its people, who cultivated corn on a grand scale, a practice that continues in Illinois today. The state is the second-largest corn producer in the nation, and the leader in soybean yields. Wheat is grown, and hogs, cattle, and dairy cows are raised. Illinois' fertile flatlands also conceal rich seams of bituminous coal. With six nuclear power plants, it generates more nuclear energy than any other state and exports its electricity throughout the nation. Wind power and biofuels are emerging industries; Illinois corn is used for 40 percent of American ethanol.

It is the fifth-most populous state, with the Chicago metro area accounting for 65 percent of Illinois' population. A traditional battleground between the Democratic and Republican parties, the Land of Lincoln has lately become the Midwest's Democratic bulwark. A historic home to some of the nation's most influential politicians, it has elected more black senators than any other state. Once the edge of the frontier, later a destination for the Great Migration of rural southern blacks, site of one of the world's great cities, and home to seas of cornfields, Illinois plays a prominent role in American culture, from its Big Shoulders on down.

The Loop, as downtown Chicago is known, birthed skyscrapers. Today, it is topped by the Willis Tower, formerly known as the Sears Tower.

Illinois State Facts

Full Name: State of Illinois
Meaning of Name: The French configuration of the Algonquian word *ilenweewa*, meaning "he (or she) speaks normally"
Admitted to the Union: December 3, 1818 (21st state)

Inhabitant: Illinoisan
Capital City: Springfield
Flower: Purple violet
Tree: White oak
Bird: Cardinal

Geography and Ecology

Its arrowhead shape is the result of three rivers. The Mississippi River establishes the state's western border, separating Illinois from Iowa and Missouri and absorbing the Ohio River at the state's southern tip. The Ohio River flows between Illinois and Kentucky, imbibing the southern flow of the Wabash River, which delineates the southern border of Illinois and Indiana. Northeast Illinois is Lake Michigan coastline; the state of Michigan sits eastward, across the lake. To the north is Wisconsin, fitting flush against Illinois. Formed by the confluence of the Des Plaines and Kankakee rivers, and connected to the Chicago River, the Illinois River flows southwest across the state, into the Mississippi River. It is a major link between the Great Lakes and the Mississippi River. Before the advent of trains and automobiles, it was part of a great trade waterway extending from the Atlantic Ocean, up the Hudson River, along the Erie Canal into the Great Lakes, then down the Illinois River to the Mississippi. It was also once a major commercial freshwater fishery.

Three Regions

The Land of Lincoln has three separate geographic regions. Northern Illinois is economically dominated by the Chicago Metropolitan Area, or "Chicagoland," which arcs north into lower Wisconsin and east into Indiana,

Pere Marquette State Park sits on bluffs at the mouth of the Illinois River. Recent conservation efforts have helped the park's dwindled bald eagle population return to strength.

and extends, as suburbs, south and west into Illinois. It is heavily populated, developed, and industrialized terrain. West of Chicagoland are smaller towns amid a countryside of farms and orchards. Central Illinois is flat prairie, more sparsely populated and planted with vast fields of corn and soybeans. The state capital, Springfield, sits along the Illinois River in Central Illinois. South of US Route 50 is Southern Illinois. Distinctly warmer, and composed of more rugged terrain, Southern Illinois aligns itself more with regions in Kentucky, Tennessee, and Missouri than it does with northern regions of the state. Large reserves of coal are mined in "downstate Illinois," as it is called, and the area is more heavily forested than the rest of the state.

Wicked Weather

Northern and Central Illinois experience a continental climate, characterized by four distinct seasons, with hot summers, cold winters, and cool transitional seasons. Its flat terrain and central placement within the contiguous states, and beneath the Great Lakes, leave it vulnerable to extreme weather. Northern and Central Illinois have endured their share of meteorological abuse. In 1936 the deadliest heat wave in U.S. history killed 2,656 people in Illinois, and as recently as 1995 a heat wave broiled Chicago, killing 525 people. Adding insult to injury, Illinois winters are equally brutal, with heavy snowstorms and frigid temperatures, particularly in Chicago, where wind from Lake Michigan rakes the city. One notable incident during the winter of 1830–31 highlighted the difference between the climates of North-Central and Southern Illinois, which has a warmer, slightly subtropical climate: winter ran long, preventing northern regions from planting grain until June. The late-growing harvest was subsequently killed by a September frost. Southern Illinois, with its milder climate, was spared the blight of its grain, and in empathy shipped corn north, earning itself the moniker "Little Egypt," in biblical reference to Joseph's providing Egyptian grain to his famished Israelite brothers.

Land of Lincoln

Paleo-Indians inhabited Illinois at least 10,000 years ago. By the year 800 the Mississippian culture had settled the region; by 1500 the culture had vanished due to disease and political strife. A confederation of tribes called the Illiniwek emerged—the Kaskaskia, Cahokia, Peoria, Michigamea, and Tamaroa among them. Hunter-gatherers and farmers, the Illiniwek tribes lived in semi-permanent villages, where the women planted corn, beans, squash, melon, and sunflowers every spring. To supplement farming, tribal women gathered wild walnuts, pecans, acorns, and hazelnuts, as well as wild strawberries, grapes, and plums. Tubers, such as wild lotus and yellow pond lily, were also staples, and plants, wintergreen and sassafrass, among others, were gathered. In June the tribes migrated west of the Mississippi River to hunt buffalo, returning in late July to harvest their crops. Woodland game was hunted in the fall, and trade with nearby tribes supplied other necessities. It was the Illiniwek that French missionary Jacques Marquette and Quebecois explorer Louis Jolliet met when traveling the Mississippi and Illinois rivers in 1673. By this time the Illiniwek were fighting expansion by the powerful Iroquois Confederacy into their eastern lands. The Illiniwek later battled the Iroquois, and their allies, the British, while aiding the French in the French and Indian War. After losing the war the French vacated the territory, and the diminished Illiniwek were at the mercy of the powerful tribes around them, who sought land to compensate for encroaching British settlement.

CAHOKIA

More than a millennium ago, the Mississippian culture rose to prominence in the midwestern, eastern, and southern United States. The Mississippians were mound builders, dwelling in cities and towns dominated by giant flat-topped, pyramidal earthworks. The greatest of Mississippian cities was Cahokia, on the eastern banks of the Mississippi, near what is today East St. Louis, Illinois. By roughly the year 1000, Cahokia had become a metropolis, and as home to perhaps 40,000 people it was the largest city north of Mexico, until Philadelphia reached such a population in the year 1800. The heart of the city was a palisaded expanse, covering some 200 acres, and home to upper-class dwellings overshadowed by a series of mounds, with Monk's Mound highest among them. The largest earthwork in the world, Monk's Mound housed the paramount chief, or Great Sun, of the region; his palace/temple would have sat atop the mound. From such a height, the Great Sun, generally a man, would view the full reach of the city—outside the central walls, thousands of peasant families dwelled in huts and worked vast cornfields. Fleets of canoes plied the Mississippi River and its tributaries. Archaeologists have also excavated a large circle of wooden posts presumably used to mark solstices and equinoxes, not unlike Stonehenge, thus dubbed Woodhenge. By the year 1200 Cahokia had declined, perhaps due to war, disease, or environmental mismanagement. Though Mississippian culture persisted until the 1500s, by the time European explorers marveled at the Cahokian mounds they were only grand ruins, as they remain.

In 1673 a team led by Jacques Marquette and Louis Jolliet canoed the Mississippi River, opening the waterway to French colonization.

The terraced soil of Monk's Mound rises to more than 100 feet from a base larger than that of the Great Pyramid of Giza.

Massika, at left, a Sauk Indian, and Wakuasse, a Fox Indian, as painted by Karl Bodmer in April of 1833 at St. Louis. Massika had journeyed to St. Louis amid a Sauk and Fox delegation to request the release of chief Black Hawk, who was held as a prisoner of war by the U.S. government.

United States takes Possession

During the Revolutionary War in 1778, George Rogers Clark, commanding a division of the Continental Army, captured the British-held village of Kaskaskia after a difficult six-day march through the forest and prairie of southern Illinois. He declared the Illinois Country part of Virginia; after the 1783 Treaty of Paris, the land was incorporated into the Northwest Territory, accompanying most of the Midwest region east of the Mississippi River. After the British were again defeated in the War of 1812, the federal government issued Illinois land to settlers. In 1818, upon becoming the 21st state, Illinois outlawed slavery within its borders, yet simultaneously took steps to limit settlement by blacks.

Violent Conflicts

As a young state, Illinois weathered conflict. In 1832 Black Hawk, a chief of the Sauk, Fox, and Kickapoo tribes, disputed treaties made with the U.S. government and returned, with a band of roughly 1,500 members, to the tribes' traditional lands east of the Mississippi River. The Illinois militia mustered against the group. Defeated consistently in early skirmishes, the militia became more numerous, organized, and dominant in battle as the year progressed. In July of that year, Black Hawk and his withered forces declared they would stop fighting and return west of the Mississippi River. On August 1, while attempting to surrender, Black Hawk's band was massacred by the militia; the next day, any remaining Indians were also slaughtered, effectively ending the Black Hawk War. In 1839 the Mormons were also expelled from Illinois, after having transformed swamplands on the Mississippi River into Nauvoo, one of the state's largest and most prosperous cities. Mormon dominance over the region's commerce, politics, and press caused unease among non-Mormons, sparking mob violence. The conflict, which caused the death of spiritual leader Joseph Smith, propelled the Mormons on their exodus to Utah.

State History

Illinois

The Midwest

Mr. Lincoln Goes to Washington

Born in Kentucky and raised in Indiana, Abraham Lincoln came of age in New Salem, Illinois, where he worked as a shopkeeper, soldier, postmaster, land surveyor, handyman, and—skilled with an ax—a rail splitter. He also owned his own general store, and was well known around town for his towering physique and his wrestling ability. His political ambitions started early; he was elected to the state legislature in 1834, at age 25. In 1837 he became a self-taught lawyer and earned a reputation as a skilled cross-examiner and rhetorician. Married in 1842, Lincoln became a U.S. congressman in 1846, a position he vacated after one term, due to his anti-Mexican War stance rendering him unpopular. In the late 1850s he gained national fame for opposing slavery during a series of fiery debates with Senator Stephen A. Douglas. In 1860 Lincoln's prestige catapulted him to the presidency, where he faced the immediate secession of southern states and the outbreak of Civil War. His home state served him faithfully during the brutal four-year

The first known photograph of Abraham Lincoln, probably taken in 1848 during his single, controversial term in the U.S. Congress.

Chicago began as a trading post founded in the 1770s by Jean Baptiste Pointe du Sable, a Haitian immigrant who married a Potawatomi woman. A little more than a century later, the Windy City was growing rapidly. By 1892, as seen here, it had sprouted steel-framed skyscrapers.

conflict, sending more men into the Union ranks than any other state but New York, Pennsylvania, and Ohio.

Reaching for the Sky

Between 1870 and 1900 Chicago grew faster than any known city had ever grown—increasing from 299,000 people to roughly 1.7 million. The period began amid conflagration—the great Chicago fire, which having destroyed roughly 18,000 wooden buildings, enabled the city to be rebuilt on a grand scale. The marshy lakeshore would not tolerate heavy masonry structures, so a new kind of steel-framed architecture was practiced, leading to modern building styles subsequently followed world-wide, and enabling the construction of towering but light and sturdy buildings—skyscrapers. As a modern, 20th-century city, Chicago faced numerous problems—rampant pollution by sewage, gangland strife during Prohibition in the 1920s, and racial and political violence in the 1950s and '60s. Today, the city is committed to becoming environmentally cleaner; simultaneously, it is reconfiguring its skyline with new skyscrapers. As Carl Sandburg wrote, "Shoveling, / Wrecking, / Planning, / Building, breaking, rebuilding"—so Chicago goes, ever in motion and renewal, taking Illinois along with it.

Lawmen brandish confiscated beer seized en route to Chicago. The city was infamous for bootlegging during Prohibition, 1920–33.

Constructed 1970–73, the 110-story Sears Tower was once the world's tallest building—1,451 feet of angular steel and tinted glass.

MIGRATION BLUES

Beginning in roughly 1915 and continuing until approximately 1970, southern blacks migrated north and west, seeking new lives free from the oppressive and violent racism of southern society. The peace they sought was elusive. The sudden influx of blacks into predominantly white communities unearthed white northerners' latent racism, and the expansion of the labor force triggered working-class resentment. Violent strife plagued northern cities undergoing racial transition, and ethnically separate societies emerged, with blacks often confined to crowded, rundown neighborhoods. Southern traits and habits brought north only exacerbated the migrants' otherness, but as time passed, migrant culture developed unique avenues of expression, none perhaps more important than music, particularly electric blues. Originally innovated in the Mississippi Delta region, the blues was a spare, stark music, consisting generally of rhythmically played acoustic guitar, harmonica, and singing that named, lamented, and attempted to transcend problems through sheer soulful expression and humor. Carried north with the Great Migration, its sonic austerity exploded in Chicago with electrical force; guitar pickers, singers, and harmonica players of the Delta, like Muddy Waters, Howlin' Wolf, Willie Dixon, Sonny Boy Williamson, and Little Walter, among countless others, became stars in Chicago's black clubs, playing a new, loud, frenzied electric blues. Chicago blues, flanked by Memphis and Texas blues, initiated a revolution in music that led directly to rock and roll, and decades later, hip-hop. Formed within the crucible of migration and discrimination in the urban North, the Chicago blues helped to elevate black American culture to worldwide prominence.

Wisconsin

The Badger State

Forward

This upper Midwestern state is perhaps best known for the dairy products it produces; and in fact, a quarter of the cheese sold within the U.S. does come from Wisconsin. But the economy, the people, and the land of Wisconsin are more varied than that statistic might suggest. More than half the state is forested, but gently rolling pastureland is also abundant. The state is known as America's Dairyland; however, the manufacture of transportation equipment is also vital to the economy. Much of the state is rural, but its largest city, Milwaukee, is one of the Midwest's most important financial centers. And although traditionally conservative, Wisconsin was the birthplace of the Progressive movement and was the first state to outlaw the death penalty, require the use of seatbelts, and pass minimum-wage legislation.

Most of the state's 5.3 million residents live in and around the largest cities: Milwaukee (a manufacturing hub, and home to companies including Harley-Davidson) and Madison (the state's capital, second-largest city, and home of the University of Wisconsin).

Wisconsin's economy is also heavily dependent on the two Great Lakes by which it is bordered: Lake Superior to the north and Lake Michigan to the east. In addition to providing access for domestic and international shipping, these important bodies of water are vital to tourism and manufacturing.

In the 18th century more than 5 million Germans immigrated to the Midwest, many of them settling in Wisconsin. Today, more than half of Wisconsin's population is of German descent, and nowhere is that more evident than in the local cuisine. German and Bavarian restaurants and specialty shops abound, selling bratwurst, Wienerschnitzel, spaetzle, and sauerkraut, along with the state's leading beverage product, beer. Oktoberfest, a traditional Bavarian festival, is celebrated in hundreds of communities across the state, with beer gardens, parades, polka dancing, and traditional food.

Visitors to Wisconsin are drawn by an array of cultural and recreational opportunities. Professional football, baseball, and basketball teams all play here. Cities offer museums, theater, and all kinds of music. The Great Lakes are popular for fishing, boating, and swimming in the summer and ice fishing, skating, and festivals in winter. The state's plentiful wilderness and parklands provide tourists with year-round opportunities to partake of hunting and fishing, hiking, camping, snowmobiling, and dogsledding.

Wisconsin's urban areas are Democratic strongholds in the state, while more rural areas tend to vote Republican. Traditionally, the state supports Republican candidates in presidential elections.

The Wisconson State Capitol, in Madison.

Wisconsin State Facts

Full Name: State of Wisconsin
Meaning of Name: From the Ojibwa meaning "gathering of the waters."
Admitted to the Union: May 29, 1848 (30th state)
Inhabitant: Wisconsinite

Capital City: Madison
Flower: Wood violet
Tree: Sugar maple
Bird: Robin

Geography and Ecology

The area that is now Wisconsin was once covered by Ice Age glaciers. As they retreated around 10,000 years ago, those glaciers left behind a landscape of lakes and valleys, hills and plains. Today, the state comprises five distinct land regions: the Lake Superior Lowland, the Northern Highland, the Central Plain, the Western Upland, and the Eastern Ridges and Lowlands.

The Lake Superior Lowland region is a small, flat area along the shores of Lake Superior.

A Landscape Cut by Glaciers

The Northern Highland region, which includes most of the northern part of the state, is hilly and heavily forested with second-growth hardwoods and evergreens. The

THE BADGER STATE

Wisconsin takes its nickname, the Badger State, *not* because of its large badger population. In fact, very few of the small mammals inhabit the state. That name actually comes from a nickname given to miners of the 1830s who worked in the lead mines of Illinois. They lived not in houses, but rather in shallow holes or caves carved out of the hillsides. Those dwellings were called badger dens, and thus the miners, badgers.

area also has a large concentration of "kettle" lakes, which formed when massive blocks of ice left by retreating glaciers melted. Timms Hill (1,951 ft.), the state's highest point, is in this region.

The Central Plain region cuts a V-shaped swath across the state. It is here that the Wisconsin River created a deep gorge in the landscape, now known as the Dells region. The Dells have been a popular tourist destination since the mid-1800s for both their natural beauty and the resorts that have grown up there.

The Western Upland, a region of rolling green hills and water-etched sandstone bluffs, lies to the west of the Central Plain. The only area of the state untouched by glacial activity is in this region.

Lake Winnebago, in eastern Wisconsin, is the state's largest. The lake's 85 miles of coastline is dotted with harbors and lighthouses. The lake is popular with boaters and fishermen. In winter there can be as many as 10,000 cars and trucks parked at the lake.

Finally, the Eastern Ridges and Lowlands region, which lies east of the Western Upland, is characterized by its green, rolling landscape. A large portion of the state's population resides in this area, which is also the heart of the state's farm country.

The Long and Short of It

Wisconsin's climate is characterized by long, cold, and snowy winters and short summers. Average high temperatures range in the 70s in summer and in the teens in winter. Average annual precipitation is 31 inches.

TOURISM IN WISCONSIN

With more than 115,000 acres of parkland, 15,000 lakes carved by Ice Age glaciers, and 16 million forested acres, Wisconsin supports a tourism industry that is a vital source of income for the state, providing 250,000 full-time jobs. The Wisconsin Dells—a 5-mile-long gorge carved by the 430-mile-long Wisconsin River—attracts more than 3 million visitors alone. The state boasts that a park can be reached within an hour of any town.

State History

Wisconsin

The Midwest

The Badger State

Among Wisconsin's earliest inhabitants were the Paleo-Indian hunting tribes who arrived around the end of the Ice Age, approximately 14,000 years ago.

When the first Europeans arrived, in the early 17th century, the area was populated by at least a dozen groups, including the Fox, Kickapoo, Miami, Ojibwa or Chippewa, and the Winnebagos. Frenchman Jean Nicolet was the first to arrive, in 1634, seeking to extend France's fur trade in the region. The area was controlled by France until 1763, when the British gained control after the French and Indian War. After the Revolutionary War ended in 1783, the area became a territory of the United States.

Population by Americans in those early years was sparse but growing. And the nature of the population was having a great impact on the land. The French and British who had come earlier were interested primarily in trade, Americans were interested in agriculture, building homes in place of trading posts, and clearing land for farms.

Statehood and Economic Growth

By 1836 the area that is now Wisconsin was home to 22,000 people, 16,000 of whom were in the lead-rich region in the southwest part of the state. Another wave of immigration in the 1840s brought millions to the United States, among them Germans and Irish; a great many of them settled in the Wisconsin territory, and the population surged. In 1848 Wisconsin became the 30th state. As the white population increased, native Indians were displaced by force and treaty.

Agriculture and timber were the state's primary sources of income in those years. The Civil War stalled the state's economy; but soon after, farming spread quickly.

Frank Lloyd Wright, one of the world's best-known architects, was born in Wisconsin. Many of his buildings still stand there.

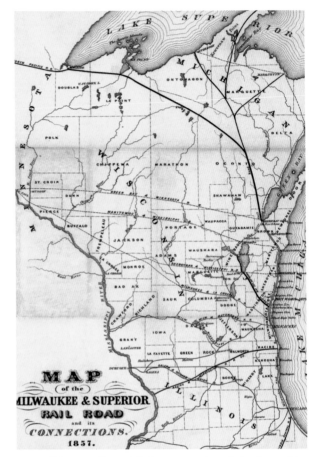

Map of Wisconsin from 1857 shows county boundaries, larger cities, and the railroad network.

The years after the Civil War were marked by the growth of big business—such as the railroads. At the same time, a very few highly placed Republicans in the

THE RISE OF TRIBAL CASINOS

In 1988 Congress passed legislation that allowed American Indians to open and run casinos. Today, over a dozen casinos are in operation in Wisconsin by tribes including the Chippewa, Potawatomi, Menominee, Oneida, and Mohican.

The casinos generate proceeds for important programs and services. However, they continue to be controversial by those who point to the increased crime, including drug trafficking, that has been associated with those businesses.

Milwaukee, Wisconsin, in 1854. The city experienced a huge growth in immigration in the early 19th century. By 1910 Milwaukee was one of two cities (the other was New York) with the largest number of foreign-born residents.

state tightly controlled the government. Many of the same men traveled in both circles, leading to influence peddling in the government.

The Progressive Movement

Distrust of the relationship between business and government in Wisconsin led to the birth, in 1900, of the Progressive movement, which championed social reform in the state. Among the goals of the movement were the elimination of corruption and influence peddling from government; the greater involvement of citizens in the political process by allowing them to initiate and review potential legislation; and the intervention of the government in social problems and injustices.

The 20th Century and Beyond

Over the course of the 1900s, agriculture continued to form the backbone of the state's economy. Dairy farming became a popular alternative to wheat production, which severely depleted the soil of nutrients. In northern areas of the state not suitable for dairy farming, logging and timber-related industries took hold. However, the overenthusiastic harvesting of trees from the late 19th through the early 20th century left the northern forests of the state nearly decimated; only now are they recovering. The lead and zinc mines that once flourished became depleted in the 20th century, and over time they closed, the last one in 1979. Meanwhile, tourism, agriculture, and manufacturing emerged as the driving forces in Wisconsin's economy—as they are today.

Wisconsin Republican senator Joseph Mc-Carthy was the architect of an intense anti-Communist period, which was inspired by the Cold War.

Minnesota

Land of 10,000 Lakes

L'Étoile du Nord (The North Star)

The largest of all the midwestern states, Minnesota is known for its prairies, its moderately liberal citizenry, and its bracingly cold winters. Located on the border with Canada, Minnesota is home to the only part of the United States (outside of Alaska) that is north of the 49th parallel. Here, in Lake of the Woods County, the aurora borealis is a common sight on clear evenings.

Most of Minnesota's 5.1 million residents live in the Minneapolis–St. Paul metropolitan area. The Twin Cities, as they are known, were built around the Minnesota, Mississippi, and St. Croix rivers and are the first and second most populous cities in Minnesota. St. Paul is also the state's capital. The area is also known as the state's cultural center. Here, the arts thrive. The Twin Cities boast more theater seats per capita than any other city in the United States except New York. Minneapolis–St. Paul is also the state's leading trade and industrial center.

Duluth, Minnesota's third largest city, lies in the northwestern part of the state on the western shore of Lake Superior. The busiest of the Great Lakes ports, Duluth is connected by the St. Lawrence Seaway to the Atlantic Ocean.

Rochester, Minnesota, is home to the Mayo Clinic, which is one of the world's largest and most prestigious medical facilities and has catapulted the state to the forefront of medical care and research.

Minnesota's economy is diverse; approximately 75 percent of the working population is employed in one of the service industries. Here, those include education, finance, and retail trade. Manufacturing is also vital to the state's financial health. In addition to computers and office machines, foods processing—butter and cheese production, meatpacking and sugar refining—are leading products.

Agriculture was once a mainstay of the Minnesotan economy. In the late 19th and early 20th centuries, the state led the country in production of milled flour. Today, beef cattle, hogs, dairy products, corn, and soybeans reign.

Minnesota is known as the Land of 10,000 Lakes. In fact, the state may have more than twice that number. Outdoor recreation is important to Minnesotans, who enjoy canoeing, fishing, skiing, skating, hiking, and all manner of outdoor sports. Minnesotans are also passionate about their college and professional sports teams. Whether they're pulling for the University of Minnesota hockey team or the NFL's Minnesota Vikings, fans around the state expect the same rugged determination from their sports stars as they do of themselves.

The Boundary Waters Canoe Area Wilderness has more than 1,200 miles of canoe routes.

Minnesota State Facts

Full Name: State of Minnesota
Meaning of Name: from Dakota Indian word *minisota* ("sky tinted waters")
Admitted to the Union: May 11, 1858 (32nd state)
Inhabitant: Minnesotan

Capital City: St. Paul
Flower: Lady slipper
Tree: Norway pine
Bird: Common loon

Geography and Ecology

Minnesota's topography is divided into two major areas: The Superior Upland and the Central Lowland.

The Superior Upland region is located in the far northeastern portion of the state. This area is characterized by its many low, rounded hills. Minnesota's highest point—Eagle Mountain, at 2,301 feet—is located in this region. The land in this area was gouged by glacial activity; as a result, the landscape is dotted with many rock-bottomed lakes.

The Central Lowland region covers most of the state, and the landscape is highly variable. Prairie alternates with deciduous forest; gently rolling plains are common, but some areas are almost completely flat.

Lakes and Waterways

Minnesota's major rivers include the Minnesota, Mississippi, Rainy, the Red River of the North, and the St. Croix. In addition to Lake Superior, on the state's northeast border, thousands of smaller lakes dot the landscape. These, along with streams and forest, lure millions of visitors to Minnesota each year.

Canoeing, boating, and kayaking are favorite activities in the state. In Voyageurs National Park, located in northern Minnesota, the lakes are the primary means of transportation; it is the only water-based national park in the United States. In northeastern Minnesota, the Boundary Waters Canoe Area Wilderness draws visitors for its 1,200 miles of canoe routes, more than 1 million acres of wilderness, and over 1,000 lakes.

Harsh Winters

Minnesota's weather is notable for its extremes. Winters are long and cold; summers are short but can be extremely hot. In January, temperatures range between 2° F to 15° F. In July the range is 68° F to 74° F. The state's record low temperature, -60° F, occurred in Tower on February 2, 1996.

Annual precipitation in Minnesota ranges from 19 to 32 inches, depending on location. Statewide, average snowfall is 53 inches annually, but occasional blizzards can dump as much as 2 feet of snow in a single storm.

Resources

Timber has been an important natural resource throughout Minnesota's history. Forests cover about a third of the land. Common species are balsam fir, black spruce, jack pine, and eastern white pine. Forests in the state are used primarily in the paper industry.

The state is also rich in iron ore; in fact, the state contributes about 70 percent of the nation's supply. Granite, limestone, sand, and gravel are also mined or quarried in Minnesota.

WINTER CARNIVAL

In 1885 a newspaper reporter from the East Coast described St. Paul as "another Siberia, unfit for human habitation in the winter." The comparison was not entirely inaccurate, at least where weather is concerned. Cold winters are common in Minnesota; the coldest day on record in the Twin Cities registered a *high* temperature of -17° F.

In part to defend itself and to celebrate the fact that St. Paul was now the country's third-largest railway center, St. Paul threw its first Winter Carnival in 1886. Today, it is the oldest such event in the country.

Popular events in the annual 17-day celebration, which occurs in late January through early February, include ice-skating, educational events, and snow and ice carving. In some years, the carnival features an ice palace—an enormous structure constructed of tens of thousands of blocks of ice.

Lake of the Woods
Roseau
Warroad
oseau
Baudette
International Falls
CANADA
Rainy River
Chief Lake
Lake of the Woods
at Lake
Falls
Upper Red Lake
Koochiching
Missquah Hills
Cook
on
Lower Red Lake
Red Lake
Grand Marais
Clearwater
Beltrami
Bagley
Itasca
Ely
Babbitt
Lake
nomen
Bemidji
Mountain Iron
Biwabik
nomen
Cass Lake
Chisholm
Eveleth
Aurora
Hibbing
Gilbert
Keewatin
Silver Bay
Hubbard
Coleraine
Lake Superior
Becker
Grand Rapids
St. Louis
Walker
Cass
Two Harbors
Detroit Lakes
MINNESOTA
Pine River
Cross Lake
Park Rapids
Frazee
Menahga
Hermantown
Perham
Wadena
Aitkin
Carlton
Cloquet
Duluth
New York Mills
Nisswa
Aitkin
Proctor
Wadena
Crosby
Otter Tail
Staples
Brainerd
Moose Lake
Parkers Prairie
Baxter
Mille Lacs Lake
Pine
Todd
Crow Wing
Sandstone
Long Prairie
Little Falls
Pierz
Mille Lacs
Hinckley
Douglas
Kanabec
Alexandria
Osakis
Morrison
Mora
Pine City
Starbuck
Glenwood
Sauk Centre
Benton
Milaca
Rock Creek
Melrose
Sartell
Foley
Braham
Rush City
Stearns
Albany
Sauk Rapids
Princeton
Harris
Pope
Richmond
Waite Park
Saint Cloud
Cambridge
North Branch
Benson
Paynesville
Cold Spring
Sherburne
Isanti
Isanti
Chisago
Kandiyohi
Big Lake
Elk River
Stacy
Spicer
Annandale
Monticello
Wyoming
Meeker
Dayton
Anoka
Forest Lake
Swift
Atwater
Willmar
Litchfield
Buffalo
Hanover
Andover
Chippewa
Dassel
Cokato
Wright
Delano
Rockford
Hennepin
Ramsey
WISCONSIN
Montevideo
Clara City
Howard Lake
Minneapolis
Stillwater
Washington
Hutchinson
Winsted
Carver
Saint Paul
Bayport
Granite Falls
Renville
Olivia Bird Island
Waconia
Shakopee
Richfield
Cottage Grove
Glencoe
Chaska
Jordan
Medicine
McLeod
Norwood
Arbor Lake
Apple Valley
Hastings
Hector
Sibley
Belle
Lakeville
Cottonwood
Renville
Redwood Falls
Fairfax
Winthrop
Gaylord
Plaine
Le Sueur
Montgomery
Jordan
Lonsdale
Northfield
Red Wing
arshall
Scott
Dakota
Lake City
yon
Redwood
Sleepy Eye
New Ulm
Saint Peter
Le Center
Farmington
Cannon Falls
Wabasha
Tracy
Springfield
Mankato
Le Sueur
Rice
Faribault
Kenyon
Zumbrota
Wabasha
Murray
Brown
Madelia
Lake Crystal
Eagle Lake
Waterville
Pine Island
Plainview
Cottonwood
Saint James
Janesville
Owatonna
Kasson
Olmsted
Mountain Lake
Waseca
Waseca
Dodge
Rochester
Eyota
Saint Charles
Wino
Slayton
Fulda
Windom
Mapleton
New Richland
Blooming Prairie
Dodge Center
Hayfield
Stewartville
Watonwan
Blue Earth
Steele
Mower
Chatfield
Nobles
Jackson
Truman
Winnebago
Wells
Freeborn
Spring Valley
Fillmore
Preston
Worthington
Lakefield
Sherburn
Fairmont
Blue Earth
Albert Lea
Austin
Spring Valley
Caledonia
ian
Jackson
Harmony
Spring Grove
Martin
Faribault
IOWA

Minnehaha Falls was made famous by Longfellow's poem The Song of Hiawatha, written in 1855.

Paddlers in Minnesota flock to parks like Boundary Waters Canoe area, a million-acre park.

Land of 10,000 Lakes

The land that is now Minnesota has been inhabited for thousands of years. When the first Europeans came to the area in the mid-1600s, the Dakota, or Minnesota Sioux lived in the area. About 100 years later, the Ojibway, or Chippewa, drove the Dakota from the land, and the two tribes became bitter enemies.

The first Europeans to explore the area were French fur traders, probably in the 1650s. Later, in 1679,

France claimed the land. For the next 133 years the land changed hands several times. It was not until the end of the War of 1812 that the land became part of the United States as the Northwest Territory. In 1849 the Minnesota Territory was established. By 1850 this new territory was home to about 4,000. But as forced treaties with Indians freed up land to Europeans and lumbering increased, immigration into the territory exploded.

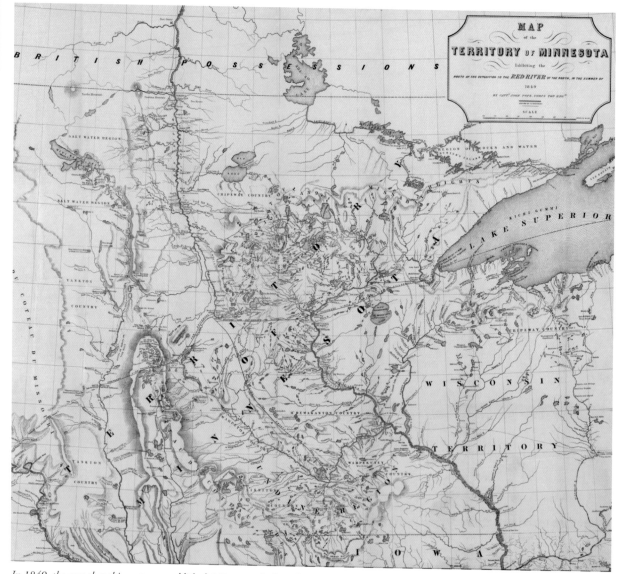

In 1849, the year that this map was published, Minnesota had just been established a territory. The area was technically closed to settlement at the time, having been set aside as Indian Territory.

Many of the first settlers to Minnesota lived in houses built with bricks that were cut from sod. They houses were simple but sturdy.

Statehood

Minnesota became the 32nd state on May 11, 1858. Soon after, the country entered the Civil War, but it was a war closer to home that concerned many in the state. In 1862 conflicts broke out between the government and the Dakota, who had been forced onto a reservation and had too little food. The Dakota Conflict ended with 39 Dakota being hanged for the murder of white settlers. At the same time the Ojibwa were also moved onto reservations.

Despite the conflicts with the Indians, the state began to thrive. Rail lines crossed the state and wheat fields covered the land. Immigrants came from Germany, Norway, and Sweden. By the late 1800s the mining of ore had become an important industry.

World War and Beyond

As was common in other agricultural and manufacturing states, the Depression devastated the Minnesotan

Fort Snelling, near Minneapolis, was built to prevent foreign encroachment on U.S. territories by Canada and Britain.

economy. Demands for lumber and ore during World War II boosted the economy for a time, but it wasn't until the mid 1900s that the economy truly diversified beyond lumber, mining, and agriculture. New industries, including food processing and production of computers, business machines, and electronics, developed in the state. Soon, manufacturing income exceeded that of agriculture.

Minnesota Today

Throughout the last decade of the 20th century, Minnesota continued to diversify its economy. Service industries—including health care, finance, insurance, and real estate—came to the fore, although manufacturing remains important. Today, as tourism dollars become increasingly important to the state's economy, Minnesotans are focusing attention on the state's natural resources, its lakes and streams, wetlands and forests. The health and conservation of these resources is vital both to the state's economic health and the quality of life of its residents.

PROGRESSIVE POLITICS

In 1944 the Democratic-Farmer-Labor-Party (DFL) was formed in Minnesota. A merger of the Democratic Party and the Farmer-Labor Party, the DFL became prominent under U.S. Senator Hubert Humphrey, who later served as vice president under Lyndon Johnson. The formation of the DFL is just one example of Minnesota's fairly strong third-party, populist tradition. As recently as 1998 the state elected as governor Jesse Ventura, a former professional wrestler and Reform Party candidate.

North Dakota

Peace Garden State

Liberty and Union, One and Inseparable, Now and Forever

In the geographic center of the North American continent sits North Dakota, a sea of prairie grass, bizarrely weathered Badlands, rivers, lakes, and hills. It is large and empty, home to a little more than 640,000 people. Once this was the domain of nomadic Plains Indians—the Sioux, Mandan, and Ojibwa, among others. The laying of the Great Northern Railroad, in the 1880s, flooded the area with settlers; between 1870 and 1930 North Dakota's population increased by more than 675,000 people. There, the influx ceased, and throughout the 20th century the state rolls fluctuated. By 1970 some 50,000 people had left the state. By 2000 a little more than 20,000 citizens had been gained, but within the last 8 years North Dakota has again lost population.

It is a pattern seen across much of the Great Plains—depopulation of rural communities, and immigration of young adults to other states and cultural centers. The consequences, if these trends continue, would be dire for the state. Young adults are necessary as workers and citizens—economic, civic, and medical infrastructures require their vitality. For North Dakotan culture to perpetuate itself, young people are needed, especially in the rural towns and farming communities that are rapidly fading.

How the state adjusts its position in a changing nation has been a matter for debate. In 2007 Senator Byron Dorgan proposed the New Homestead Act, which would provide money to individuals willing to settle in rural communities for at least 5 years. The award given would allow settlers enough to buy a house, pay for college, or start a business. Though Senator Dorgan has proposed the bill for the past 5 years, it has not yet been passed.

North Dakotan culture is primarily informed by the state's history of Northern European immigrants. The majority of North Dakotans have German or Norwegian roots, and these influences are seen in state delicacies such as *knoephla* soup—a chicken stew with dumplings—and *Fleischkuekle*, ground beef in dough, deep fried. Pies, pastries and dumplings are apt dishes for the largest producer of spring and durum wheat in the United States. The state also leads the nation in cultivation of barley and sunflower seeds. Food processing is a major industry as well—North Dakota raises more turkeys than any other state. Coal and oil power the state's grid and its finances; vast oil reserves in the west of the state have sent the economy booming. Wind power is also emerging as a major industry—it is estimated that the state could supply 25 percent of the nation's energy by harnessing the mighty gusts that sweep its vast prairie.

Native to the Americas, sunflowers are a major crop in North Dakota, where farmers grow huge fields of the festive plants, mainly for seed.

North Dakota State Facts

Full Name: State of North Dakota
Meaning of Name: From the Santee Sioux's name for themselves, Dakota
Admitted to the Union: November 2, 1889 (39th state)
Inhabitant: North Dakotan

Capital City: Bismarck
Flower: Wild prairie rose
Tree: American elm
Bird: Western meadowlark

Geography and Ecology

It sits high in the central United States, nearly a rectangle but for its meandering border with Minnesota, delineated by the Red River of the North, which starting in the south of the state, flows north through Fargo and Grand Forks, into Lake Winnipeg, Canada. North of the state are the Canadian provinces of Saskatchewan and Manitoba. To the west is Montana; to the south is South Dakota, divided from its northern brother by a once-contentious line of longitude. At 70,762 square miles, North Dakota is roughly 6,000 square miles smaller than its southern twin.

Rich Red River Farmland

Northeastern North Dakota is part of the Red River Valley, a fertile drainage basin that extends far into the Canadian prairie. The valley itself, and the silts that line it, were the byproducts of the enormous ancient Lake Agassiz, which drained away some 8,000 years ago. Flat farm country, the Red River Valley is planted with wheat, corn, barley, oats, sugar beets, and potatoes, among other crops. Livestock is also ranched.

Turtle Mountains

West of the Red River Valley, North Dakota rises into higher plains, called Drift Prairie. These extend north to the Turtle Mountains on the Canadian border, a low, timbered range home to North Dakota's International

Peace Garden. Established in 1932, the Peace Garden straddles the U.S.-Canadian border, is jointly run by the two nations, and is emblazoned with more than 150,000 newly planted flowers every year.

As a rancher living amid the Badlands in the 1880s, Theodore Roosevelt admired the strange landscape, describing it as "desolate, grim beauty."

THE BADLANDS

They gained their name through frustration—French trappers called these strange stretches of terrain "les mauvaises terres à traverser"—the bad lands to cross. To view them, though, is to feel awe and wonder—the eroded twists and humps of rock are sublime sculpture. The Badlands of the Dakotas extend across the western plains of both North and South Dakota. In North Dakota they predominate in Theodore Roosevelt National Park, 110 square miles of wilderness commanded by the beautifully bizarre multicolor rock formations. It is arid land, home to prairie dogs, coyotes, wild horses, and rattlesnakes, among other fauna. Come winter, snow turns the rocks into spectral mounds.

Grasslands

The Missouri River hooks south from northeast North Dakota through the heart of the state, dividing the western Great Plains. North and east of the Missouri River is the Missouri Plateau, hilly prairie marked by kettle ponds.

Wild mustard lights up the North Dakota prairie. A beautiful but aggressive weed, wild mustard can undermine domestic mustard crops.

Southwest of the river the prairie rises to higher elevations. Indian, grama, blue, and buffalo grasses grow on the plains, as do the western prairie fringed orchid, a threatened species, and the wild prairie rose, the state flower. White-tailed and mule deer and pronghorn antelopes also roam the prairie. Wild, free-roaming bison, which once moved in great herds across North Dakota's plains, no longer populate the state, though they are kept privately, on ranches, and in Theodore Roosevelt National Park.

Seasons of Change

The state witnesses a profound variety in its seasons. Rainy, windy springs commonly see flooding in the Red River Valley, sometimes with devastating consequences for towns in the region. Summers are humid in the east, slightly drier in the west, punctuated by turbulent thunderstorms. Tornadoes, peaking in the summer months, can ravage the countryside. Autumn is gusty and cool, segueing to snowbound, frigid winters.

Peace Garden State

Long before Europeans explored the rivers and plains of North Dakota, paleo-Indians settled the area, hunting mammoths and giant bison. Millennia later North Dakota's well-known tribes emerged. The Mandan lived in villages of domelike earth and wood lodges along the banks of the Missouri, Heart, and Knife rivers. They were expert flint-workers, quarrying the rock from nearby deposits and trading it, as blocks or blades, to numerous tribes. The trade networks were so wide-ranging that Knife River flint has been found thousands of miles away, in Maine and Florida. The Hidatsa Tribe also built riverside villages. Dwindling tribal numbers, due to disease and strife, compelled the Mandan, Hidatsa, and Arikara tribes to band together as one nation. To this day the three tribes live together, on the Fort Berthold Reservation, on the eastern edge of North Dakota. The Ojibwa lived in the north of the state, in and around the Turtle Mountains, where they still reside. The powerful Lakota Sioux lived as nomads on the southwestern plains, hunting buffalo, gathering plants, and trading with the nearby Mandan.

Sacagawea eased Lewis and Clark's diplomacy. As Lewis wrote, "She reconciles all the Indians, as to our friendly intentions."

Exploration Upriver

Quebecois explorer Sieur de La Vérendrye, the first white man to see North Dakota, explored the Missouri River in 1738. Four years later, his sons repeated the trek, heading farther upriver. These incursions opened the area for limited trade; the Mandan became middlemen for the region, dealing with the French and British traders. In 1804 Lewis and Clark traveled the Missouri River through North Dakota—which was now purchased American territory—trading for safe passage with the region's tribes.

The Lakota Sioux were hostile to the party as it passed through their region. Demanding more practical items than the trinkets Lewis and Clark offered, they threatened the Corps of Discovery, but a shaky diplomacy prevailed. Hurrying from Lakota territory, Lewis and Clark were welcomed by the Mandan. Thus, the Corps of Discovery spent the winter of 1804–5 as guests of the Mandan, having built a small fort alongside their village. It was here that Sacagawea, a Shoshone woman raised by the Hidatsa, was recruited to translate with tribes farther west.

The Mandan built their villages near riverbanks, where gardens of corn, beans, and squash cultivated along the shore would benefit from annual flooding. Their domed earthen lodges, seen on the bluff, held 40 people. Built by the women, they passed from one maternal generation to the next.

Shuffling Statehood

An epidemic of smallpox plagued North Dakota's tribes in the 1820s. Meanwhile, white settlement in the area increased. By midcentury, steamboats were regularly chugging up the Missouri and Red River, initiating the development of ports like Bismarck, in the center of the state, and Williston, in the far west. In 1861 the federal government established the Dakota Territory, comprising what is now North and South Dakota. The Great Northern Railway, laid across the state in the 1880s, brought a massive influx of settlers, who lobbied for statehood. In 1889 North and South Dakota became separate states. It is not known which state gained statehood first. The animus between the two regions at the time compelled President Benjamin Harrison not to display favoritism. Covering the top half of the proclamations, he shuffled them until he could not be sure which was which, and then signed them. North Dakota has top billing only because it precedes South Dakota in alphabetical order.

Progressives and Population Decline

The 20th century in North Dakota saw political fluctuations. In the 1910s the Non-Partisan League, a group of progressive politicians, challenged the dominance of the Republican Party and established some socialist institutions, including both the state-owned Bank of North Dakota and the North Dakota Mill and Elevator, the largest flour mill in the United States. Today, though its economy is flush, the state seeks ways to attract and retain young adults in its population. As North Dakotans collectively grow older, and prairie communities empty out, some worry that the state's rural culture and infrastructure is irrevocably slipping away.

"Not do I believe that there is in the universe a similar extent of country, equally fertile, well watered, and intersected by such a number of navigable streams."

—Meriwether Lewis, writing from Fort Mandan in North Dakota

In 1872 a village emerged in North Dakota at the place where the Northern Pacific Railroad crossed the Missouri River. Hoping to attract German immigrants to settle in the burgeoning town, seen here in 1883, the railroad named it after Otto von Bismarck, the unifier of Germany.

South Dakota

The Mount Rushmore State

Under God the People Rule

Once, the masses flocked to South Dakota for gold; now they just come for rocks. The Badlands, particularly—more than a million people sojourn to South Dakota each year to marvel at these strange sculptures of wind and time. Still more drive into the Black Hills to gape at Mount Rushmore, the largest sculpture on earth. The four enormous busts are as controversial as they are colossal. The hills they occupy are sacred ground of the Lakota Sioux and were granted to them in perpetuity by an 1868 treaty—eventually broken, like so many others. In the end, Mount Rushmore grandly sums up the pitiless march of Manifest Destiny, and that was precisely what sculptor Gutzon Borglum had in mind when he carved it—a parade of presidents gazing proudly across the conquered West.

Perhaps pride is not all their faces show. They are solemn, and circumspect, as if in eternal meditation on what their efforts have wrought. South Dakota is a good place to gaze across the nation—it is central, rolling prairie pocked with lakes and wrinkled by streams—one can see for miles. It is sparsely settled—populated by a little more than 770,000 people. As with its fellow Great Plains states, rural flight has become a concern; people are abandoning South Dakota's country towns for its cities, and many—young adults in particular—are emigrating from the state entirely, leaving behind an aging population.

But the Black Hills area is gaining people, and Sioux Falls, the state's largest city—with a metropolitan area accounting for nearly a third of the state—has also been growing. In recent years major financial corporations have settled in Sioux Falls, adding thousands of jobs and overhauling the state economy. Though agriculture—particularly the raising of cattle and hogs, and the cultivation of corn, soybeans, and wheat—continues to fortify the state economy, the service sector has become the state's financial backbone. Tourism is also a major moneymaker. Besides those journeying to the Black Hills and the state's national parks, nearly 500,000 people attend the Sturgis Motorcycle Rally, in the west of the state, every August.

The great majority of South Dakotans have German ancestry, and another significant portion are Sioux Indians, living on nine reservations statewide. Politically, the Republican Party dominates, especially in state and presidential elections. All three of the state's congressional representatives are Republicans. As for those four titans on a Black Hills mountainside, each pioneered a different political party in his lifetime, but their affiliations were not carved in stone.

Sculpted over 14 years by 400 workers, Mount Rushmore was deemed complete in 1941. Sculptor Gutzon Borglum had died months earlier.

South Dakota State Facts

Full Name: State of South Dakota
Meaning of Name: From the Santee Sioux's name for themselves, Dakota
Admitted to the Union: November 2, 1889 (40th state)
Inhabitant: South Dakotan

Capital City: Pierre
Flower: Pasqueflower
Tree: Black Hills spruce
Bird: Chinese ring-necked pheasant

South Dakota Geography and Ecology

The Midwest

Geography and Ecology

Like its northern twin, South Dakota is nearly a rectangle, but for the coursing of rivers and the presence of lakes along its edges. It shares a neat northern border with North Dakota and a straight western border with Montana and Wyoming. Nebraska sits flush to the south, except for the curling Missouri River, which forms South Dakota's sinuous southeastern border. Iowa lies east, separated by the Big Sioux River; Minnesota notches South Dakota at the sites of Lake Traverse and Big Stone Lake. Plenty of water flows through the center of the state, as well. The Missouri River snakes south

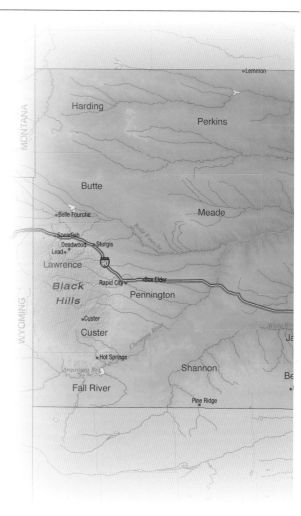

THE BLACK HILLS

They are an anomaly amid the southwestern prairie of South Dakota—sudden mountains, so heavily forested they appear black from a distance. For centuries the Arikara, Cheyenne, Crow, Kiowa, and Pawnee tribes occupied the region, until the Lakota Sioux arrived in the 1700s and forced the other tribes from the hills. The sedimentary shell and granite core of the mountains have hidden great lodes of gold. Prospectors swarmed the area in the 1870s; from 1878 until 2002 the Homestake Mine unearthed more than a billion dollars worth of gold. The gray jags of the Black Hills hide other spectacular sights—an extensive network of caves undermines the region. Chief among these is Wind Cave, the sixth-longest cave in the world and the impetus for the creation of Wind Cave National Park, which preserves the cave, as well as the environment on the surface, where bison, elk, and pronghorn antelope roam.

Called "Paha Sapa" by the Lakota, meaning "hills that are black," these peaks are home to great stands of ponderosa pine.

through the heart of the state, swelling four dammed reservoirs—Lake Oahe, Lake Sharpe, Lake Francis Case, and Lewis and Clark Lake. The Belle Fourche and Cheyenne rivers flow along the northern and southern edges of the Black Hills, respectively, before joining and draining into Lake Oahe. The Big Sioux River pushes south through the eastern half of the state, tumbling into waterfalls at Sioux Falls, where it is harnessed for hydroelectric power.

Grass and Hills

East of the Missouri River, which slices the state in half, South Dakota is gently undulating prairie, decorated with numerous lakes. The James River Basin creates a north-south arc of flat land along the course of the James River. West of the Missouri River lies more rugged terrain—hills and prairie are broken by canyons and studded by buttes. Land use differs east and west of the wide Missouri. The rolling plains in the east are suited

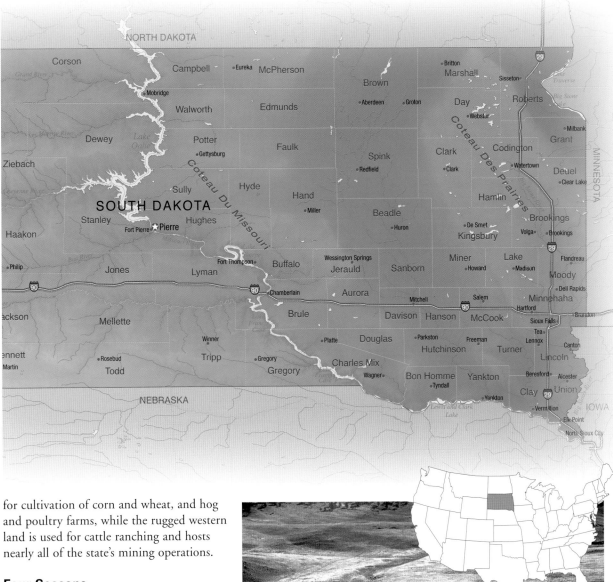

for cultivation of corn and wheat, and hog and poultry farms, while the rugged western land is used for cattle ranching and hosts nearly all of the state's mining operations.

Four Seasons

Residents of South Dakota experience four distinct seasons. Summers are hot, winters are very cold; in transition, spring and autumn are cool. Humidity varies by region—the northwest is drier, while the southeast is wetter and rainier. Hectic thunderstorms punctuate South Dakota summers, dropping hail and whipping strong winds across the plains. Tornadoes also churn through the eastern half of the state; on average some 23 twisters occur yearly. Snow can also fall heavily, generally during late autumn and early spring.

Bison thunder across the plains of Wind Cave National Park. The park's bison population is one of four genetically pure, free-roaming herds on North American public land.

The Mount Rushmore State

At least 11,000 years ago, hunter-gatherer paleo-Indians dwelled in South Dakota; by the 1700s the Arikara, Omaha, Ponca, and Cheyenne tribes occupied the region. Artifacts of the Arikara, including arrowheads, have been found in Badlands National Park. The Cheyenne lived in the Black Hills, and the Omaha lived along the Missouri River. In the late 1700s the Sioux arrived from the Minnesota region and, as fearsome fighters, pushed most other tribes from the land. By the start of the 20th century, the Sioux, after decades spent battling the U.S. Army, had been confined to reservations throughout South Dakota.

A Territory Settled

In 1743 the La Vérendrye brothers boated up the Missouri River, claiming what is now South Dakota for France. In 1803 the region became part of the United States, due to the Louisiana Purchase. Shortly after, Lewis and Clark headed up the Missouri River, through South Dakota, en route to the Pacific Ocean. By 1856 increasing settlement had led to the creation of the city of Sioux Falls, and in 1861 the government established the Dakota Territory. The 1872 connection of the railroad to the eastern city of Yankton initiated a rush of settlement by European immigrants. In 1874 the 7th Cavalry, led by Lieutenant Colonel George Armstrong Custer, discovered gold in the Black Hills, triggering a rush of prospectors to the region.

Deadwood

The rush of gold-hunters and settlers into the Black Hills created the infamous mining camp of Deadwood, a place now emblematic of the vanished Wild West. Its formation was swift—in roughly a year it was home

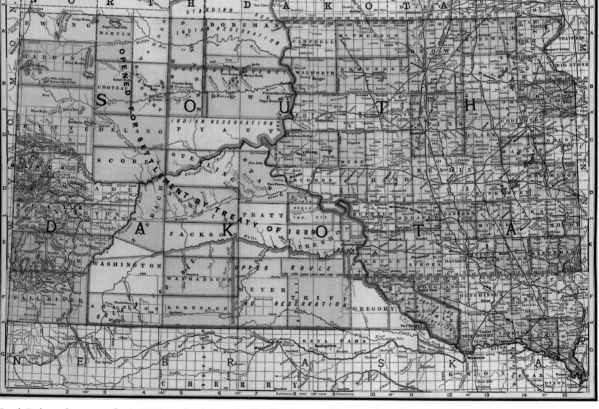

South Dakota, three years after its 1889 statehood. A swath of land in the west of the state, formerly given to the Sioux as a reservation, is shown to be open to homesteaders after an 1889 treaty disenfranchised the Sioux. A network of dark lines indicates railroads spreading across the state.

The rude mining camp of Deadwood in 1876, as prospectors and merchants poured in to try their luck. Prostitution, gambling, and the sale of alcohol and opium thrived in the lawless boomtown.

to 5,000 people, with no government to speak of, and lawlessness reigning amid the gold fever. Bona fide characters of the Old West passed through, among them frontierswoman Calamity Jane and lawman and gun-fighter Wild Bill Hickock, who was shot to death in the back of the head while playing poker in a Deadwood saloon. As a corporate mining industry developed, the town calmed. In 1879 a fire nearly destroyed Deadwood, and many settlers moved on.

Fighting Blight and Rural Flight

During the 1930s South Dakota fell prey to the dust storms that plagued the other Dust Bowl states, ruining harvests and exacerbating the preexisting economic depression. The agricultural necessities of World War II reinvigorated the economy, and agriculture has supported the state until the recent rise of service industries. As the 21st century unfolds, the state hopes to continue its prosperity and to repopulate the vanishing communities in its heartland.

THE WOUNDED KNEE MASSACRE

The Wounded Knee Massacre effectively ended the Indian Wars. By 1890 the midunderstood Ghost Dance movement, which prophesied the renewal of Indian sovereignty, had spread to the Lakota Sioux. After a skirmish in which the great chief Sitting Bull was killed, the U.S. government dispatched additional soldiers to the region to suppress Ghost Dancing. In December of that year, a regiment of soldiers from the 7th Cavalry intercepted a group of Lakota Sioux under the ailing chief Spotted Elk traveling to seek shelter with another chief, Red Cloud, at the Pine Ridge Indian Reservation. The band of Sioux was led to Wounded Knee Creek and told to make camp. Later that evening, the rest of the 7th Cavalry regiment arrived, bringing the total to 500 soldiers. Early the next morning, the Lakota were ordered to surrender their weapons, but one man, who was deaf and didn't understand the order, refused to give up his firearm without compensation. Amid the struggle, the gun fired, prompting a hail of bullets from both sides, at close range, with the cavalry's weaponry greatly outnumbering the Lakota's. In the chaos, Lakota men, women, and children began fleeing across the snowy plain but were chased and gunned down by the cavalry. In less than an hour, nearly 200 Lakota were killed and 50 wounded, while the cavalry lost 25 men and saw 39 wounded. After the massacre a snowstorm swept across the Badlands. Arriving after the storm to bury the Lakota dead, gravediggers found a field of contorted and frozen corpses, which were shoveled into a mass grave.

Spotted Elk's band of Miniconjou Sioux in costume at a dance, Cheyenne River, South Dakota.

Iowa

The Hawkeye State

Our Liberties We Prize and Our Rights We Will Maintain

Named for the Iowa (also known as Ioway) North American Indian people who lived in the area prior to European settlement, Iowa is known as America's breadbasket, and rightly so. This upper midwestern state, bounded on the west by the Missouri River and on the east by the Mississippi, provides the United States with 7 percent of its total food supply. In addition to corn (the state's chief crop), Iowa also leads the country in production of soybeans, eggs, and pork. More than 90 percent of Iowa's total land area is dedicated to farming; that's the highest percentage of land devoted to agriculture in any state.

Although Iowa is known as an agricultural state, its economy is driven primarily by other industries. Production of farm machinery, food processing (primarily of corn and pork products), and service industries are the most important contributors to the state's gross domestic product (GDP). The production of ethanol (or grain alcohol) is now a $12.7 billion industry, making up roughly 10 percent of Iowa's GDP.

Prior to the 1960s most of Iowa's population lived in rural areas. However, since then the state has become more urbanized. Today, a majority of the state's 3.1 million residents live in one of the larger cities. Des Moines (pop. 207,510) is the state's capital and largest city, and home to insurance, printing, and finance industries. Other major urban areas include Cedar Rapids (pop. 128,429) and Davenport (pop. 99,685). One federally recognized American Indian tribe makes its home in Iowa: approximately 13,000 members of the Meskwaki Indians today live on land in central Iowa purchased from the federal government in the 1850s.

Education and educational institutions play an important role in the life of the state. The University of Iowa is the state's oldest public institution of higher learning; founded in 1847, it was also the first public university to admit men and women on an equal basis. The university's Iowa Writers' Workshop is known worldwide, and alumni include novelists John Irving, Flannery O'Connor, and W. P. Kinsella. Iowa State University, established in 1858, routinely ranks among the top public universities in the country.

Since the 1850s Iowa has been a Republican stronghold. Herbert Hoover, the 31st president, was born in West Branch, Iowa. The Herbert Hoover Presidential Library and Museum in West Branch is a popular tourist attraction.

The gilt dome of Iowa's State Capitol can be seen from miles around Des Moines.

Iowa State Facts

Full Name: State of Iowa
Meaning of Name: Probably from an Indian word meaning "this is the place" or "the beautiful land"
Admitted to the Union: December 28, 1846 (29th state)
Inhabitant: Iowan

Capital City: Des Moines
Flower: Wild rose
Tree: Oak
Bird: Eastern goldfinch

Geography and Ecology

Iowa's landscape was formed by glacial movement over thousands of years that eroded much of the land. Four distinct glaciers left their mark on the land here, creating three distinct land regions: the Young Drift Plains, the Dissected Till Plains, and the Driftless Area.

Most of northern and central Iowa make up the Young Drift Plains region. Retreating glaciers in the last ice age deposited the deep, rich topsoil in this mostly flat area. It is where the best farming land in the state is found.

Forming a swath that stretches across the southern part of the state, the land of the Dissected Till Plains region is low and rolling.

In northeast Iowa, the landscape of the Driftless Area—sometimes called the little Switzerland of America—is far different from the rest of the state's terrain. Here, the land was not eroded by glaciers; it is ruggedly hilly and marked by cliffs and rocky outcrops.

Wildlife

Settlement of Iowa has had an enormous impact on the state's wildlife. What was once native prairie—and habitat for animals—became farmland. That transition forced out many native species. Beaver, bison, elk, wolves, and wild turkey were once plentiful, but by 1900 all of those species had disappeared. Some, such as the wild turkey, were reintroduced; others, such as the passenger pigeon and Carolina parakeet, are now extinct.

The largest mammal found in the state today is the white-tailed deer. Among the most common mammals that make their homes in Iowa are coyote, fox, raccoon, and a variety of rodents.

Iowa is home to nearly 400 species of bird, including the official state bird, the eastern goldfinch. Also plentiful are the northern cardinal, blue jay, Eastern screech owl, and the red-tailed hawk.

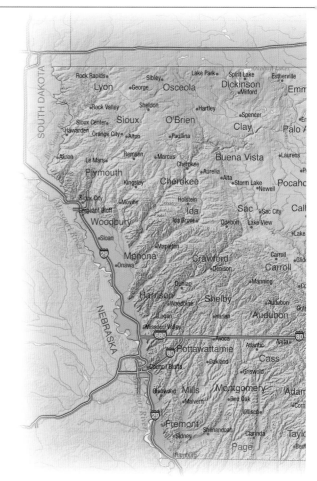

Climate

Iowa's climate is well suited to agriculture. Springtime is wet, summers are warm, and the growing season is relatively long. Winters in Iowa are cold, with temperatures ranging from 14° F to 24° F—although lower temperatures are not uncommon. In summer, highs range from 80° F to more than 100° F.

A CHECKERED LANDSCAPE

Flying over Iowa, one notices the gridlike divisions of its gently rolling landscape. That's because original settlements were laid out in 160-acre parcels, which led to towns and farms also being laid out in the characteristic grid patterns of the countryside.

EFFIGY MOUNDS

One of the most striking features of the Iowan landscape lies at the confluence of the Mississippi and Yellow rivers in the northeastern part of the state, known as the Little Switzerland of America. It is here that approximately 200 earthen mounds were built by Eastern Woodland Indians between 500 BCE and 1300 CE. Some of the mounds are shaped like bears, birds, and other animals; others are conical. These structures are not burial mounds; rather, it is believed that the mounds here were ceremonial sites. Effigy Mounds National Monument was established in 1949 to protect the mounds and their surrounding land.

MINNESOTA

WISCONSIN

Kossuth
Winnebago
Worth
Mitchell
Howard
Winneshiek
Allamakee

Buffalo Center
Northwood
Saint Ansgar
Cresco
Decorah
Lansing
Waukon

Forest City
Manly
Osage
Calmar
Postville

Emmetsburg
Algona
Clear Lake
Nora Springs
Charles City
New Hampton
West Union
Fredericksburg
Clayton
Elkader
Guttenberg

Alto
Britt
Garner
Hancock
Cerro Gordo
Mason City
Sheffield
Floyd
Nashua
Fayette
Sumner
Oelwein
Strawberry Point

Humboldt
Belmond
Butler
Clarksville
Bremer
Tripoli
Fayette

Pocahontas
Humboldt
Eagle Grove
Clarion
Hampton
Shell Rock
Waverly
Denver
Buchanan
Delaware
Dubuque

ontas
Webster
Wright
Franklin
Parkersburg
Black Hawk
Cedar Falls
Waterloo
Independence
Manchester
Farley
Dubuque

Manson
Fort Dodge
Webster City
Iowa Falls
Ackley
Grundy
Evansdale
Jesup
Central City
Monticello
Gascade

Rockwell City
Hamilton
Jewell
Eldora
Grundy Center
Hudson
La Porte City
Vinton
Linn
Anamosa
Springville
Bellevue

City
Story City
Roland
Hardin
Conrad
Reinbeck
Traer
380
Marion
Jackson
Maquoketa

Greene
Jefferson
Ogden
Boone
IOWA
Marshall
Tama
Benton
Cedar Rapids
Mount Vernon
Mechanicsville
Clinton

Boone
Woodward
Madrid
Ames
Nevada
State Center
Marshalltown
Toledo
Tama
Belle Plaine
Solon
North Liberty
Cedar
Tipton
De Witt
Clinton

Guthrie
Dallas
Perry
Huxley
Story
Jasper
Poweshiek
Marengo
Brooklyn
Iowa
Williamsburg
Coralville
Iowa City
West Branch
Scott

ng Center
Panora
Dallas Center
Grimes
Polk City
Ankeny
Polk
Bondurant
Grinnell
Newton
Montezuma
Johnson
West Liberty
Eldridge
Davenport

Adel
Waukee
Urbandale
Altoona
Colfax
Prairie City
Buffalo

Stuart
West Des Moines
Clive
Des Moines
Carlisle
Monroe
New Sharon
Wellman
Kalona
Muscatine

Adair
Madison
Norwalk
Indianola
Pleasantville
Pella
Mahaska
Keokuk
Washington
Columbus Junction
ILLINOIS

Greenfield
Winterset
Warren
Knoxville
Marion
Oskaloosa
Sigourney
Washington
Louisa
Wapello

Creston
Clarke
Osceola
Lucas
Chariton
Monroe
Albia
Eddyville
Ottumwa
Jefferson
Fairfield
Henry
Mount Pleasant
Mediapolis
Winfield

Lenox
Union
Decatur
Wayne
Wapello
Davis
Van Buren
New London
Des Moines
Burlington

Ringgold
Mount Ayr
Leon
Corydon
Centerville
Bloomfield
Keosauqua
West Point
Fort Madison

Lamoni
Appanoose
Lee

MISSOURI
Keokuk

Lake Red Rock, Iowa's largest lake, is a reservoir that was built by the Army Corps of Engineers. Completed in 1969, the lake is a popular spot for boating and fishing.

The Hawkeye State

The area that is now Iowa came to be American territory as part of the 1803 Louisiana Purchase. But from 1804 until 1829 the land was Indian territory, closed to legal settlement by Americans. It wasn't until 1830—when the U.S. government purchased what is now eastern Iowa from the Sac and Fox Indians—that settlers came to the area in large numbers. By 1846, when Iowa became the 28th state, nearly 200,000 called the state home, farming more than a million acres of land.

Population Growth

Just 10 years later Iowa's population had tripled. Germans and Irish came in the greatest numbers, but immigrants also came from the United Kingdom, Scandinavia, the Netherlands, Sweden, and France. Stories of the state's fertile soil had also come east, attracting these newcomers, as did the fact that the state was relatively free of Indian hostilities.

During the Civil War Iowa sided with the Union and sent a higher percentage of its population to fight than any other state. However, no fighting actually occurred on its soil. After the war ended, the expansion of the railroad brought a new wave of immigration, as thousands came to farm the land.

Black Hawk

Agriculture

By 1900 Iowa had become a major agricultural state, producing corn, hay, hogs, and cattle. Corn remains the state's leading crop—and in fact Iowa produces 20 percent of the country's corn supply.

Iowa's rich soil has always been a blessing. Farmers in the state often produce surpluses, which leads to depressed crop prices. To help counter the problem, Iowa now sends a quarter of its food products to international markets.

This picture of Chariton, Iowa, illustrates the checkerboard layout of a typical Iowan town.

Iowa's Economy Today

After about 1950, new, nonagricultural industries came to Iowa. Urban areas grew in population as Iowans left rural areas and small towns. And although agriculture remains vital to the state's economy, manufacturing (primarily of agricultural machinery and food processing) and service industries now contribute more income to the GDP. Today, about 65 percent of working Iowans are employed by a service industry, and that number is expected to grow.

Featuring a wide variety of attractions, the Hawkeye State brings in its share of tourist dollars too. One such spot is the *Field of Dreams* baseball field in Dyersville. The actual field from the popular 1989 motion picture of the same name, this site attracts legions of loyal fans every year. When they ask the film's famous question, "Is this heaven?", the answer still remains, "No, it's Iowa."

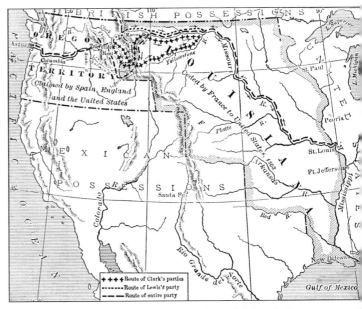

In 1804 Meriwether Lewis and William Clark traveled through the area that would become the state of Iowa.

CULTURE AND EDUCATION IN IOWA

No state's rural areas have a higher standard of living than Iowa's. Education and culture have long been of great importance to residents. The state consistently ranks high in its spending on education and enjoys one of the highest literacy rates in the country—nearly 100 percent of the population over the age of 15 can read and write.

FAMOUS IOWANS

Leon "Bix" Beiderbecke (1903–31), jazz cornetist

George Washington Carver (1861–1943), agricultural chemist and agronomist

Carrie Chapman Catt (1859–1947), feminist leader and suffragist

William F. "Buffalo Bill" Cody (1846–1917), buffalo hunter and U.S. Army scout

Herbert Hoover (1874–1964), 31st president of the United States

Glenn Miller (1904–44), big band leader and composer

Jane Smiley (b. 1949), pulitzer Prize-winning novelist

Grant Wood (1891–1942), painter

Legendary American actor John Wayne was born in this small house in Winterset, Iowa, in 1907. Today, the home is a popular tourist attraction.

Thirty-first president Herbert Hoover was born in this West Branch cottage on August 10, 1874.

Nebraska

The Cornhusker State

Equality Before the Law

Ranches and farmland cover more than 95 percent of Nebraska's landscape; that's more than any other state. And yet, Nebraska is part of an area that was once known as the Great American Desert. Between 1806 and 1820, two Americans—Zebulon M. Pike in 1806–7 and Stephen H. Long in 1820—explored the area east of the Rockies to the Missouri and Mississippi rivers and described the region as Saharan, a vast prairie incapable of supporting agriculture.

Despite the erroneous assumptions about the land, Nebraska did come to be settled and today is a leading agricultural state. Some of its chief products include cattle, hogs, corn, and soybeans. Service industries such as finance and insurance are also important to the Nebraskan economy. Finally, manufacturing—led by the processing of beef—also makes a substantial contribution to the state's gross domestic product.

Nebraska's central location and the topography of the Platte River valley made it a natural thoroughfare for fur traders and the wagon trains of settlers that fueled westward expansion. Later, the Pony Express—the private postal service established in 1860—and the country's first transcontinental railway cut through Nebraska.

Nebraska is a state of small towns: only 13 have a population of more than 10,000. A little more than half the state's population lives in one of the state's two big cities: Omaha (pop. 434,353) and Lincoln (pop. 268,738), both of which are in the eastern part of the state.

Omaha is the state's largest city. It is also a center of food processing, insurance, and health care. Several large corporations, including Berkshire Hathaway, ConAgra, and Union Pacific Railroad, are headquartered there. Boys Town—the famed home for homeless and abused children—is located near Omaha. The Old Market area is a popular destination for visitors to the city for its restaurants, hotels, and shopping.

Lincoln, the state's capital and second-largest city, is home to the headquarters of several large corporations, including the Burlington Northern Santa Fe Railway Corporation and Goodyear Tire and Rubber. The city—originally called Lancaster but renamed Lincoln in honor of the assassinated president in 1867—is also a major educational center in the state: Nebraska Wesleyan University, Union College, and the University of Nebraska-Lincoln are all located in the city. The University of Nebraska State Museum is a popular attraction; its collection of fossils is an important national resource, with more than 1 million items. Lincoln has an extensive system of 114 parks, with more than 99 miles of trails, outdoor pools, gardens, and plazas.

Nebraska's State Capitol, in Lincoln.

Nebraska State Facts

Full Name: State of Nebraska
Meaning of Name: from the Oto Indian word *nebratka*, meaning "flat water."
Admitted to the Union: March 1, 1867 (37th state)
Inhabitant: Nebraskan

Capital City: Lincoln
Flower: Goldenrod
Tree: Cottonwood
Bird: Western meadowlark

Geography and Ecology

Nebraska's topography is made up of two landform regions: the Dissected Till Plains, which cover the eastern fifth of the state, and the Great Plains, which cover the remainder of the state.

The Dissected Till Plains is an area of gently rolling hills. The soil here is rich, well suited to farming. The Great Plains, a generally level area, is made up of several smaller land regions, the most notable of which is perhaps the Sand Hills.

The Sand Hills and Badlands

Covering about a quarter of the state, the Sand Hills area was formed over the last 8,000 years by sediment that eroded and washed out from the Rocky Mountains by Pleistocene-era glaciers. The sandy soil here is unlike any other in the Great Plains. Left unplowed by European settlers who found it unsuitable for farming, the area today is a surviving remnant of the native prairie grasses that used to make up the Great Plains.

Today, the Sand Hills is used by ranchers as grazing land. The soil in the region traps and holds rainfall,

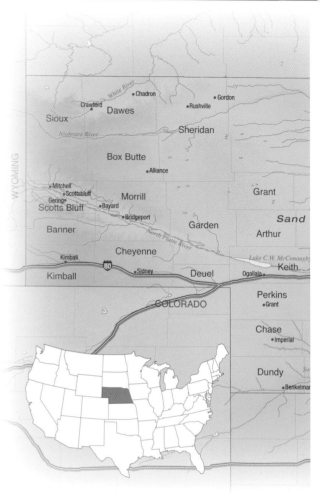

ARBOR DAY

Today, only about 2 percent of the land in Nebraska is forested. But when the land was settled, there were even fewer trees. That all changed with the establishment, in the 1800s, of Arbor Day.

When J. Sterling Morton and his wife came to the Nebraska Territory in 1854, they missed the trees and shrubs of their native Michigan, so they planted trees around their new home. Later Morton became a member of the Nebraska Board of Agriculture. In that capacity he spread information about how trees could serve as windbreaks, keeping soil in place, as well as providing lumber, fuel, and shade.

In 1872 Morton began to advocate for the creation of a statewide tree-planting festival. In 1885 Arbor Day was named a legal holiday in Nebraska; April 22 (Morton's birthday) was the date chosen for its observance. Millions of trees were planted in Nebraska because of Morton and his idea.

Over time more and more states began to celebrate Arbor Day, although its date is often moved to coincide with optimal planting season. Today, Arbor Day is celebrated around the world.

---

creating large reservoirs of groundwater. This makes irrigation easier than in areas without plentiful groundwater. But the area is also an important staging and stopover area for sandhill cranes during migration. Environmentalists are concerned that continued development, ranching, and grazing will result in the loss of this historic region.

Northwestern Nebraska is home to a small area of Badlands. These areas, formed when flash-flooding eroded weak bedrock, are known for their odd and dramatic rock formations.

Weather and Climate

Nebraska's climate is marked by extreme heat in summer and extreme cold in winter. Average January temperature is about 23° F; in July the average is around 76° F. Violent weather—in the form of blizzards, thunderstorms, and tornadoes—is not uncommon in the state.

The topography in Toadstool National Park is unlike what most people expect of Nebraska. This area of badlands in the northwestern part of the state is a landscape of severely eroded sandstone. The park is a treasure trove of fossils.

State History

Nebraska

The Midwest

The Cornhusker State

The land that is now Nebraska was first explored by Europeans—French and Spanish fur trappers—in the early 18th century. But the land came to the United States as part of the Louisiana Purchase, in 1803.

Settlement and Statehood

The 1854 Kansas-Nebraska Act opened the area to settlement—and increased tensions with the Indians. Despite that fact the area was settled rapidly. The Homestead Act of 1864 helped to further accelerate settlement.

Many pioneers in the area built their homes from sod, cutting bricks from areas of grass with densely packed roots that would hold the soil together. Roofs were sometimes made of more durable materials, such as wood, but more often of sod and native grasses.

When Nebraska became the 37th state on March 1, 1867, ranching and farming were the backbones of the state's economy. Both of these industries remain important today.

This iconic land formation, called Chimney Rock, was the most recognizable landmark on the California, Mormon, and Oregon trails leading to the West.

A Changing Economy

The years between the late 1800s and World War II were filled with upheaval for the Nebraskan economy. In the 1890s farmers were hurt by a drought, high railroad shipping charges, and depressed farm prices. These issues led to the rise of the pro-agrarian movement in politics.

World War I helped boost agriculture for a time, but after the war, continued farming of marginal lands once again depressed the economy. By the time of the dust storms in the 1930s, many farm families left for the West Coast. Others dumped milk rather than selling it at lowered prices. Federal aid finally saved many of the farms.

WESTWARD TRAILS

The Indian Intercourse Act of 1834 prevented whites from settling in the area that is now Nebraska, but it did not forbid travel *through* the area. Between 1840 and 1866 more than 350,000 pioneers made their way west across Nebraska on the California, Mormon, and Oregon trails, which followed the Platte River Valley. In 1854 the Kansas-Nebraska Act opened the territory to settlement.

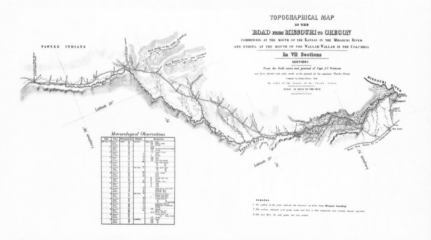

In the early 19th century, Nebraska was a major thoroughfare for westward travelers. In 1854 the area was opened to settlement.

On March 1, 1867, Nebraska gained statehood and the capital was moved from Omaha to Lancaster, which was then renamed Lincoln, after the assassinated president. This map of Lincoln was published in 1889.

World War II benefited the Nebraskan economy: farms produced millions of tons of crops and increased beef production to help ameliorate food shortages. The production of agricultural equipment also became an important source of income. And the Missouri River Basin Project of 1944 brought hydroelectric plants, dams, and reservoirs to the state.

By 1970 more than half of Nebraska's population lived in urban areas. During the 1960s and 1970s, employment in the manufacturing segment grew by almost 50 percent.

Nebraska Today

The years since the 1970s saw the birth of large, more mechanized farms. Service industries—finance, government, and insurance, among them—now contribute the largest portion to the state's economy. And tourism dollars have become more important than ever.

The state faces challenges, of course; among them are concerns about the impact of agriculture on water supplies. With drought a constant concern, more resources are being directed toward conservation of what may be Nebraska's most valuable natural resource.

Nebraska is a leading state in the use of wind energy. These turbines generate electricity.

Missouri

The Show Me State

Salus Populi Suprema Lex Esto (The welfare of the people shall be the supreme law)

In an 1899 speech Missouri congressman Willard Vandiver declared, "I come from a country that raises corn and cotton, cockleburs and Democrats, and frothy eloquence neither convinces nor satisfies me. I'm from Missouri, and you have got to show me." Though it presumably wasn't the first time a Missourian had proudly expressed his state's stubborn character, Vandiver's declaration popularized the notion of Missouri as a land of skeptical stalwarts.

Today, Missouri is still the Show Me State; it still cultivates corn and cotton, and cockleburs still grow, but Democrats don't abound as they used to. Both political parties now fight strenuously to secure the state's blessing, because Missouri has a reputation as a political bellwether for the rest of the nation. The state has voted for the victorious presidential candidate in every election since 1904, excepting only 1956. Microcosmic of the United States, Missouri's urban eastern and western edges, the sites of St. Louis and Kansas City, tend to vote Democratic, while the more rural interior of the state votes Republican.

Missouri's demographic similarity to the greater United States follows the state's history of playing a variety of roles. At one time the edge of the frontier, Missouri is considered the "Gateway to the West." St. Charles, Missouri, was the outpost from which Lewis and Clark launched the Corps of Discovery up the Missouri River and into unknown coun-

try. Linking East and West, Missouri also binds North and South. The Mississippi River meanders down the state's east coast. Once a portal to French explorers, the river became a highway of steamboats and flatboats in the 19th century, trafficking goods and people north and south—a world immortalized in the stories of a onetime Hannibal, Missouri, boy, Samuel Clemens, best known as Mark Twain.

The migration of southern slaveholding planters to the region divided the state politically; during the Civil War Missourians battled each other. By the end of the conflict slavery was unlawful, but the fertile fields of Missouri went on producing. Today, more than 100,000 farms statewide provide for much of the state's finances. Cows, poultry, and hogs are raised, and the state has a burgeoning wine industry. Limestone, coal, lead, and the components of Portland cement are mined, and manufacturing is also crucial to the economy. And then, of course, there's beer, brewed and innovated upon in St. Louis since at least the early 19th century. By the mid-1800s countless breweries were alchemizing water, barley, hops, and yeast into distinctive lagers—a century later, one brewery had become known worldwide. But enough of this frothy eloquence; let's show you Missouri.

The Gateway Arch, finished in 1968, is as tall as it is wide, spanning 630 feet in both directions. It stands over the original plot of St. Louis.

Missouri State Facts

Full Name: State of Missouri
Meaning of Name: From the Miami-Illinois language name of the Missouri tribe, *wimihsoorita*, meaning "those who have dugout canoes"
Admitted to the Union: August 10, 1821 (24th state)

Inhabitant: Missourian
Capital City: Jefferson City
Flower: Hawthorne
Tree: Flowering dogwood
Bird: Bluebird

Geography and Ecology

It sits nearly in the center of the contiguous United States, east of Nebraska, Kansas, and Oklahoma, south of Iowa, and north of Arkansas. The twists and turns of the Mississippi River demarcate most of the state's eastern border, separating Missouri from Illinois, Kentucky, and Tennessee. The Missouri River cuts the state's northwestern border before turning to bisect the state from Kansas City to St. Louis. Northern and western Missouri is prairie, veined with numerous streams and rising in elevation from east to west. The muddy Missouri River, draining water gathered from the Great Plains and Rocky Mountain states, forms the southern boundary of much of Missouri's prairie, before rushing into the Mississippi River at St. Louis.

The Ozark Plateau

South of Missouri's plains lies the Ozark Plateau, a region of highlands stretching from the banks of the Mississippi west into Oklahoma and south into Arkansas. A land of rolling hills, the Ozark Plateau reaches its apex in the St. Francois Mountains, near the Mississippi River. Among the oldest exposed igneous rock in North America—formed over 1.4 billion years ago as islands in prehistoric seas—the St. Francois Mountains range from 500 to a little over 1,500 feet high, with Taum Sauk

Mountain crowning Missouri at 1,772 feet. Mining, ranching, logging, and hunting have been traditional uses of the land. During the 20th century vigorous conservation of the region restored two-thirds of the region's forest cover, which had been denuded by logging and farming. Rivers and streams course through the area; the Ozarks' waters are the habitat of bass and darter, muskrats, otters, and great blue herons. Bobcats prowl the hickory-pine forests hunting rabbits and rodents. Deer, wild turkey, and the occasional armadillo also call the Ozarks home.

Winds from the North and South

In the southeast the Missouri Bootheel juts south against Arkansas. Sitting in the floodplain of the Mississippi and St. Francis rivers, the Bootheel and its surrounding region are rich farmland. Southeastern Missouri, unlike the majority of the state, verges on the subtropical climate of the South, with hot, sticky summers and plenty of precipitation year-round. The rest of the state tolerates colder winters and slightly cooler, drier summers. Extreme shifts in the weather are not uncommon—with few natural barriers to prevailing winds, Missouri must endure collisions of cold Arctic air sweeping south and humid winds from the Gulf of Mexico pushing north. Tornadoes also threaten the state, especially during spring.

CAVING COUNTRY

Missouri's gently rolling Ozark Plateau conceals hundreds of caverns, some small, others enormous. Marvel Cave, in Branson, Missouri, features one of the largest entrance rooms of any cave in North America. Called the Cathedral Room, the giant underground chamber measures 204 feet high, 225 feet wide, and 411 feet long. The Osage Indians considered it a supernaturally sinister place, named it the "Devil's Den," and steered clear. Spanish explorers later attempted to spelunk the cave, seeking minerals or the fabled Fountain of Youth. Today, Marvel Cave is a tourist attraction, like many of the caves beneath the Ozark Plateau. Missouri's northern plains also hide some significant caverns, including Mark Twain Cave, near Hannibal, Missouri, which young Samuel Clemens regularly explored, and where Tom Sawyer and Becky Thatcher presumably got lost in *The Adventures of Tom Sawyer*.

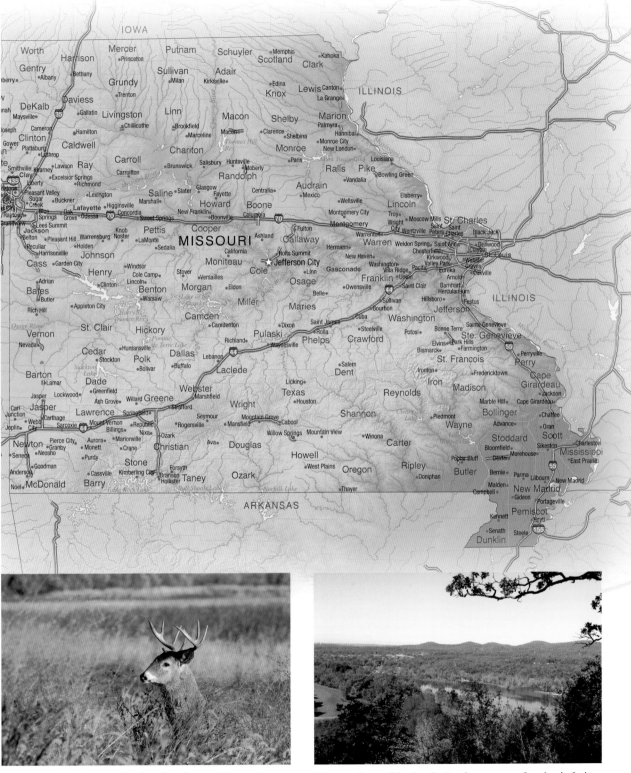

A white-tailed buck, camouflaged in the tall grass of Missouri's northern plains, rolling country formed long ago by glacial activity.

The round tops of the Ozarks rise above autumn forestland of white oak, shortleaf pine, sycamore, cottonwood, sweetgum, and maple.

The Show Me State

Paleo-Indians were the original inhabitants of Missouri, having settled the area roughly 10,000 years ago. By around 800, the Mississippian culture had taken dominion over much of what are now the midwestern and southeastern states. Referred to as the Mound Builders, they lived in hierarchical communities situated among giant earthworks. The 16th century saw the Mississippian people collapse due to disease, strife, and the accelerating push of European exploration. Different tribes emerged in the Missouri region—the Osage lived in southern Missouri, hunting both the western plains and the forests of the Ozark Plateau; the Illini occupied eastern Missouri, along the Mississippi River; the Missouri people called the north of the state home; and the Quepaw and Chickasaw lived on the state's southeastern floodplains. In the 1830s President Andrew Jackson's Indian Removal Act sent the U.S. Army to violently drive the tribes westward from Missouri and clear the state for white settlement.

Missouri slave Dred Scott sued for his freedom in 1846, arguing that time lived in free states had emancipated him. In 1857 the U.S. Supreme Court ruled against Scott, declaring that African Americans had no legal rights. The decision pushed the nation closer to civil war.

Exploration and Immigration

In 1673 French missionary Jacques Marquette and Quebecois explorer Louis Jolliet traveled the Mississippi River from modern-day Wisconsin to Arkansas, canoeing past Missouri. They were the first white men to explore and map the big river. Nine years later, Robert de La Salle, with a force of Frenchmen and American Indians, repeated the journey—traveling this time all the way to the river's mouth and claiming the territory he passed through, including Missouri, for France. In the early 1700s immigrants began settling Missouri, and boat traffic increased on the region's rivers. In 1764 the city of St. Louis was founded.

A little over 40 years later, the Louisiana Purchase had made Missouri, and great swaths of land to the south and west, territory of the United States, and St. Louis was declared the government seat. In 1811 the region's first steamboat passed through, initiating the famed riverboat culture that would last until the early 20th century.

Missouri Divided

The 1820 Missouri Compromise established the state as a slave state, but in 1824 the Missouri Supreme Court ruled that freed black slaves could not be reenslaved. Thus, both freed blacks and enslaved blacks lived under the law in the state, a dichotomy that would divide the state against itself during the Civil War. Though Missourians voted against secession, allegiance to both Union and Confederacy ran high, and the population split into competing camps. Secessionists established a

Situated on the border of slaveholding Missouri and free Kansas, Kansas City saw fierce Civil War combat. After the war the city grew rapidly. Its stockyards, seen here in 1895, served the nation.

By 1859, nearly a century after its founding by the French fur trader Pierre Laclède, St. Louis had been transformed into a bustling hub by massive European immigration and migration by southern blacks. Today, the Gateway City's metropolitan area houses more than 300,000 people.

new state capital in Neosho and joined the Confederate Army, eventually supplying 40,000 troops to the gray ranks. The Union Army, on the other hand, fielded some 110,000 Missourians. Fighting was bitter and brutal, and guerrilla warfare plagued the countryside, with bushwhackers attacking both soldiers and civilians. In 1865 Missouri abolished slavery, prior to the 13th Amendment officially doing so. After the war, the state drafted a new constitution that penalized former supporters of the Confederacy. This constitution was replaced in 1875.

A Commentary on the Nation

Missouri's conflagrations had cooled by the 20th century, but division and

Author Mark Twain, three years before his death in 1910. Twain's years as a Mississippi River steamboat pilot informed his most famous novel, Adventures of Huckleberry Finn.

injustice remained a problem. Blacks endured discrimination in nearly all aspects of public life, as well as racial violence and oppression by police and racist groups like the Ku Klux Klan. After World War II the tide began to turn. Missouri's own Harry Truman, president from 1945 to 1953, introduced a Civil Rights bill to Congress in 1948, and desegregated the armed forces, setting the stage for further breakthroughs. The national Civil Rights upheavals of the 1950s and '60s roiled Missouri, and passing years have seen more, albeit slow, change. As the United States shifts in time, so will Missouri.

A frontier state, a slave state wrestling itself, a battlefield for Civil Rights, a rolling countryside with urban borders and a rural heart, Missouri is, and will remain, a commentary on the nation.

Kansas

The Sunflower State

Ad Astra Per Aspera (To the stars through difficulties)

Kansas lies in America's heartland (in fact, the town of Lebanon is the geographic center of the lower 48 states). The state takes its name from the Kansa tribe of Native Americans that inhabited the area until around 1800.

In addition to being home to the geographic center of the lower 48 states, Kansas is also the location of the "geodetic" center of North America. The Meades Ranch Triangulation Station in Osborne County is the point of origin for all government mapping in the United States.

Almost 90 percent of the land in Kansas is dedicated to agriculture. The state leads the nation in wheat production. It also ranks high in the production of beef, pork, sorghum, and hay.

Despite the fact that most of Kansas is farmland, agriculture employs only about 20 percent of working Kansans. The state's economy has been successful due in part to its diversity. Wichita, the state's largest city, is known as the Air Capital of the World. The city's three largest employers—Cessna Aircraft, Spirit Aerosystems, and Raytheon Aircraft—are all aircraft manufacturers. The production of other transportation equipment—missiles, locomotive parts, snowplows, trailers, and truck parts—also contributes significantly to the economy.

Kansas entered the Union as a free state in 1861 and over the years garnered a reputation as the most Republican state in the United States. A fair share of notable Republican politicians have come from Kansas, including former senators Robert Dole and Nancy Landon Kassebaum. Another notable Republican, President Dwight D. Eisenhower, grew up in the city of Abilene. Indicators of the state's conservatism are readily found throughout history; Kansas was the first state to enact and the last to repeal Prohibition. It has also adopted the stance that marriage is "constituted by a man and a woman only."

Kansas is also known for its Wild West history. Dodge City—where millions of head of cattle were driven from Texas to Kansas's rail yards—had a reputation as a lawless frontier town. Although not as violent as the legend suggests, Dodge City was home for a time to gunfighters John Henry "Doc" Holliday and Bartholomew "Bat" Masterson. (Wyatt Earp is known to have killed only one man while a policeman in the town.)

Arguably, the most famous resident of the state is Dorothy from the motion picture *The Wizard of Oz*. Her fantastic journey back to Kansas is beloved by generations of film fans. In the end Dorothy figured out what most native Kansans already knew: there's no place like home.

Most of the land in Kansas is dedicated to agriculture, and bucolic scenes like these are common.

Kansas State Facts

Full Name: State of Kansas
Meaning of Name: From a Sioux word meaning "people of the south wind"
Admitted to the Union: January 29, 1861 (34th state)
Inhabitant: Kansan

Capital City: Topeka
Flower: Sunflower
Tree: Cottonwood
Bird: Western meadowlark

Geography and Ecology

Kansas can be divided into two major regions: the Central Lowland region and the Great Plains region. The eastern third of the state is the Central Lowland; this area is quite hilly in spots, despite Kansas's reputation as one flat, unbroken plain. The Great Plains, consisting of treeless prairie, covers the rest of the state.

As in other states where farmland now dominates the landscape, plant and animal life have been dramatically altered by man. When Europeans first arrived, prairie grasses would have covered the plains; stands of cottonwood,

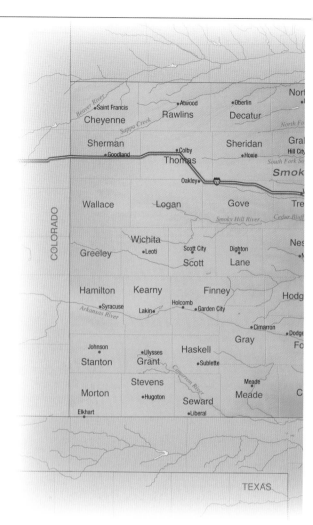

THE GRASSHOPPER PLAGUE OF 1874

Homesteaders encountered hardship as they settled and then farmed the prairies of Kansas. But 1874 brought with it an unexpected calamity: massive swarms of grasshoppers that destroyed their crops.

The habitat of the Rocky Mountain locust was usually in the mountain range of its name. But between 1873 and 1877, a spike in the insect's population caused it to expand its range into the Great Plains, just as the area was also experiencing a population boom. According to contemporary reports, the insects blotted out the sun, and the largest swarms covered an area equal in size to the states of Connecticut, Delaware, Maine, Maryland, Massachusetts, New Hampshire, New Jersey, New York, Pennsylvania, Rhode Island and Vermont—*combined*.

Crops were devastated—along with the wool from some live sheep, fabrics, and even wood. Some settlers fled the area, never to return. But over time the locusts departed and never returned. In fact, shortly thereafter, agriculture destroyed the last of the insect's habitat, and they became extinct.

Kansas was afflicted by the worst Rocky Mountain locust plague in our nation's history.

---

sycamore, and walnut trees could be found along rivers. And although most of Kansas is covered by farms, each year fields and plains burst forth with color as the state flower, the sunflower, comes into bloom.

Native mammals common in the state include foxes, bobcat, coyote, and white-tailed deer. American bison, black bear, beavers, and elk were once common in the state but have since become extirpated. Bison can be seen today only in wildlife refuges.

Precious Resources

Kansas is rich in mineral deposits and is one of the chief mineral producers in the United States. Almost all the 105 counties in the state produce at least one kind of mineral. Coal, crude petroleum, gravel, salt, and sand are just a few of the materials plentiful in the state.

Water is a precious resource in Kansas, especially in the western part of the state, where streams are rare. There, extensive irrigation is depleting the groundwater.

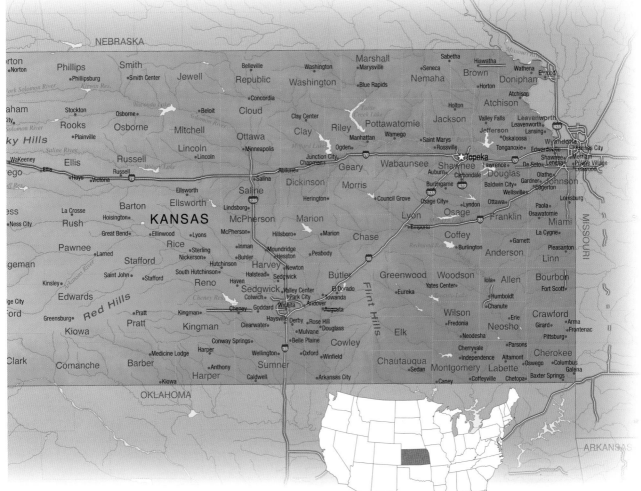

Most of the lakes in the state are manmade and are used for irrigation as well as for recreation, municipal water supplies, and flood control.

Parkland

Kansas is home to several National Historic Sites, including portions of the Lewis & Clark National Historic Trail and the Tallgrass Prairie National Preserve. More than 20 state parks, dotted across the landscape, attract visitors year-round for hiking and camping, fishing and swimming, and wildlife viewing.

Climate

The Kansas climate is known for the temperature extremes it experiences in summer and winter. Average temperatures range from around 32° F. in winter and about 80° F in summer. As happened during the 1930s, droughts do occur. Flooding can also be a problem in the region.

The chalk pyramids of western Kansas were on the floor of a vast inland sea 80 million years ago.

The Sunflower State

When, in 1541, Spanish conquistador Francisco Vásquez de Coronado arrived in the area that is now Kansas, several American Indian tribes, including the Kansa, the Osage, and the Pawnee, inhabited the land. Other tribes—including the Arapaho, Cheyenne, Comanche, and Kiowa—also came into the region in later years, after obtaining horses from the Spanish.

Between 1541 and 1802 the region changed hands between Spain and France several times. Eventually, France came to possess the area but sold it to the United States as part of the Louisiana Purchase in 1803.

Over the next 50 years, the government classified the area as Indian Territory—forcing tribes that had been displaced from eastern regions to relocate there.

THE DUST BOWL

In the 1930s great dust storms blew across the Great Plains states. The planting of shallow-rooted crops such as wheat, a severe drought, poor soil conservation practices, and punishing winds combined to create dust storms that blew dried-out soil like snow. The eroded soil filled the air, causing poor visibility. It swept into homes, where residents tried to stem the tide by sealing windows and doors.

The government stepped in to aid farmers and residents of the region. Over time, the introduction of contour plowing and other soil conservation techniques—along with increased rainfall, brought the disaster to a close in the late 1930s.

The dust storms and erosion of the 1930s were caused by a combination of poor agricultural practices and years of drought.

Statehood and War

Kansas became the 34th state on January 29, 1861, just a few weeks before the Civil War. Despite a tumultuous pre-statehood period, Kansas entered the Union as a free state.

Before, during, and after the Civil War, Kansas was the site of numerous conflicts over land with Indians, who had been continually displaced. Not until 1878 did the sporadic fighting cease.

A Growing Population

As railways made their way westward after the Civil War, so did immigrants—from eastern states as well as European countries, including Germany, Sweden, and Russia. These new arrivals began farming, and established an agricultural tradition that remains vital to the state today.

At the Forefront of Change

Throughout its history Kansas has been the scene of epochal events, from the displacement of American Indians to the conflicts leading up to the Civil War.

In 1954 the United States Supreme Court handed a landmark decision in the *Brown v. Board of Education of Topeka* case. Kansas state laws had established separate schools for blacks and whites, and in its decision the court declared, "separate educational facilities are inherently unequal," leading to the end of segregated schools there and in 20 other states.

Famed aviatrix Amelia Earhart is honored by a bronze statue in her hometown of Atchison, Kansas.

Kansas City, Kansas, in 1869. The city had been offically founded just a year before this map was published.

BLEEDING KANSAS

Between 1854 and 1859 pro- and anti-slavery factions in Kansas fought each other in an effort to control whether the territory would enter the Union as a slave or free state. Because the issue was to be decided by popular vote within the territory, proponents for each side of the debate worked feverishly to promote immigration to the area. Clashes between the groups turned violent and convinced many that the slavery debate would not be settled by peaceful means. Dubbed "Bleeding Kansas" by newspaper editor Horace Greeley, the events of the time played a part in the build-up to the Civil War.

Cowboys in the 19th century drove their cattle to cities like Dodge City, which was a major rail hub. It was once known as Queen of the Cow Towns.

Montana

The Treasure State

Oro y Plata (Gold and silver)

It is called Big Sky Country, because above Montana's vast, unsettled prairie and from the ridges and peaks of its towering mountains, the sky seems to swallow the land. For those who live there, Montana is "the last best place," a huge state with few people—thus an Eden of wilderness and open terrain.

Before Lewis and Clark crossed the state in the early 1800s, the Montana region was the sovereign territory of numerous Plains Indian tribes. Today, Montana is home to 11 Indian nations on 7 reservations scattered throughout the state. It also contains the largest population of grizzly bears in the contiguous 48 states and numerous national parks and forests. What Montana does not possess are great metropolises—none of the state's urban areas have more than 110,00 inhabitants. In fact, as of 2016 the entire state was home to a little more than a million people. Billings, on the state's south-central plains, is Montana's most populous city, with roughly 157,000 people.

Montana's population has been rising in recent years, however, and its economy is growing. Agriculture is the state's financial foundation. Wheat, barley, oats, rye, sugar beets, potatoes, and cherries grow on Montana's prairies, and cattle and sheep are pastured on the plains. Also, Montanans have long been making a living by going underground—significant mineral deposits exist in the Treasure State's mountainous west: gold, silver, coal, and talc, among others. Lumber is a major industry as well, though both logging and mining must be balanced against conservation, since Montana's national parks are its most beautiful and profitable assets, attracting tourists from around the world.

Politically, Montana fluctuates—traditionally it has elected conservatives to its state offices and promoted liberals to federal positions. It was the first state to elect a woman to Congress: Jeanette Rankin, who joined the U.S. House of Representatives in 1916—four years before women were finally given the national right to vote. In the last two decades Montana aligned itself with the Republican Party, but today the governor is a Democrat, as is one of Montana's two U.S. senators and the Lieutenant Governor. However, Montana's U.S. representative is Republican, as is the bulk of the state House of Representatives.

Such political swings indicate a population of varied histories and ideals. A vast, wild land, Montana has plenty of room for outcasts and sojourners, progressives and traditionalists. It is one of America's bastions of the sublime: miles and miles of unbroken plains shadowed in the west by soaring peaks and primeval forest, all under the Big Sky.

Majestic wilderness: called the "Crown of the Continent" by naturalist George Bird Grinnell, Glacier National Park was established in 1910.

Montana State Facts

Full Name: State of Montana
Meaning of Name: Derived from the Spanish word *montaña*, meaning "mountain"
Admitted to the Union: November 8, 1889 (41st state)
Inhabitant: Montanan

Capital City: Helena
Flower: Bitterroot
Tree: Ponderosa pine
Bird: Western meadowlark

Geography and Ecology

It is the fourth-largest state in the Union, a huge trapezoid stretching 630 miles from the Dakotas to Idaho, situated above Wyoming and below three Canadian provinces. The majority of Montana is grassland, ranging from the state's eastern border to the Rocky Mountains, where the Continental Divide splits the state. West of the divide Montana is alpine country, ridged by numerous high mountain ranges and fertile valleys. The Bitterroot Range establishes the state border with Idaho. The Cabinet Mountains sit farther north, while in the Rocky Mountain Front, where the mountains meet the prairie, the Lewis Range constitutes many of Glacier National Park's towering peaks. Montana's southern Rockies rise in parallel ranges, including the Gallatin Range, the Absaroka Mountains, and the Beartooth Mountains, home to Montana's highest point, 12,799-foot Granite Peak.

Rivers Run Through It

No other state's rivers drain to three different watersheds, but at Triple Divide Peak, in Glacier National Park, the meeting of the Continental and Laurentian divides compels Montana's water to flow in three separate directions: northeast to the Hudson Bay in Canada, southeast to the Gulf of Mexico, and west to the Pacific Ocean. These divided waters feed mighty rivers. Water flowing

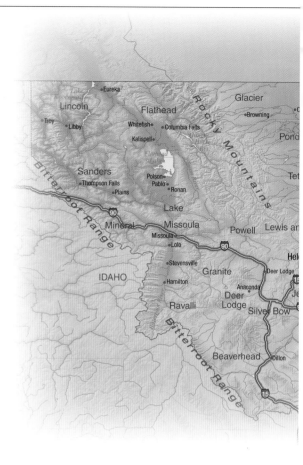

A tributary of the Yellowstone River, the Bighorn River flows north from Wyoming into Montana, draining the state's eastern prairie.

down the western slope of Triple Divide Peak enters the Flathead River, which empties into the Columbia River watershed. The southeastern side of the peak drains into Atlantic Creek, which feeds the Marias River before it enters the Missouri River near Loma, Montana. The northeastern side of the mountain drains into St. Mary Lake, which sends the St. Mary River north to Alberta, Canada.

Divided Weather

Just as the Continental Divide influences Montana's rivers, it also influences the state's weather. Warm Pacific air blowing from the west has difficulty surmounting the Rockies; likewise, cooler prairie air tends to stay east of the mountains. In the high country west of the divide, summers are cool and moist, and winters are mild. On the plains, summers are warm and occasionally hot, with cool evenings. Prairie winters can be quite cold, with moderate snowfall, though at high elevations east and west, especially in the mountains, snow buries the Montana landscape.

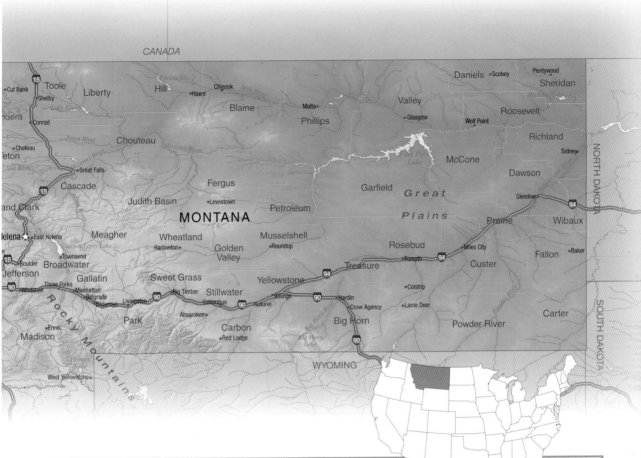

Glacier National Park

It is one of the most pristine places on the planet—more than a million acres of mirrored lakes, skyscraping mountains, waterfalls, tundra, and dense forests of spruce, fir, pine, and aspen. Of course, what earned the park its name are the glaciers glazing its high mountain valleys. These glaciers have garnered considerable scientific attention recently, since they are melting at a rapid pace, due—most experts assert—to global warming. It is not certain what effect on the park's environment the continued melting of glaciers will have. As it stands now, more than 1,000 species of plants and hundreds of different animals populate Glacier. Mountain goats are easy to spot scaling craggy slopes. Bighorn sheep, moose, elk, and deer also call the park home. Predators include coyotes, wolves, black bears, and the elusive mountain lion. Raptors fly the big sky, and 23 species of fish live in the park's lakes, rivers, and streams. Any hiker through the park must be especially wary of grizzly bears. Ironically, this unspoiled wilderness is one of the nation's great drives—most visitors view the park by negotiating the rises, falls, twists, and hairpin turns of the Going-to-the-Sun Road, which crosses the park from east to west.

Come winter, the cold, alpine water of St. Mary Lake, on the east side of Glacier National Park, can freeze into ice 4 feet thick.

The Treasure State

More than 10,000 years ago, hunter-gatherer paleo-Indians populated the Montana region, diversifying over millennia. South of Billings, Pictograph Cave contains thousands of artifacts indicative of Indian presence, including pictographs that date to 2,100 years ago. By the time of European contact, distinct tribes occupied various sections of Montana. Expert riders, the Crow people lived as nomads on the plains in the southern part of the state, dwelling in tepees, hunting buffalo, and moving with the seasons. The Crow kept enormous herds of horses—as late as 1914, Crow horse populations numbered nearly 40,000. The Cheyenne lived a nomadic lifestyle on the eastern Montana prairie after having made a series of historical migrations from the Great Lakes region. The Lakota occupied portions of southeastern Montana. The Blackfeet, Assiniboine, and Gros Ventres moved around the northwestern Montana plains, near the base of the Rockies. West of the Rockies lived the Kootenai and Salish people, as well as the Pend d'Oreilles, who built winter lodges from woven mats of cattails. These three tribes united to form the Confederated Salish and Kootenai Tribes of the Flathead Nation and today occupy the Flathead Reservation in northwestern Montana, on the Flathead River.

William Clark cut his name into Pompeys Pillar during the Corps of Discovery's return trek. Clark named the huge rock for the infant son of Sacagawea, whom he called "Pomp."

European Exploration

During the mid 1700s the Vérendrye family, Frenchmen from Quebec, explored the upper Missouri River. Entering what is now eastern Montana, they were the first Europeans to document sighting the Rocky Mountains. In 1803 the Louisiana Purchase placed the majority of Montana under the dominion of the United States, and in 1805 and 1806 Lewis and Clark crossed and recrossed the state, traveling the Missouri River west to its headwaters in the Rocky Mountains and exploring the Marias River. Etched into Pompeys Pillar, north of Billings, is the only physical evidence of Lewis and Clark's journey to be found along their route—William Clark's signature, dated July 25, 1806.

SITTING BULL

He was born in South Dakota and died in North Dakota, but the event that made Tatanka Iyotake, or Sitting Bull, famous across the United States was the Battle of the Little Bighorn on the southern Montana plains. As a Hunkpapa Lakota boy, he had been given the nickname Hunkesni, meaning "slow," because he was deliberate and careful in his actions. Not that he wasn't a swift and fearless warrior—by his teenage years he was a fast runner, skilled on horseback, and expert with the bow and arrow. In battle against rival tribes, Sitting Bull distinguished himself as a leader and was elected a war chief. He also possessed a deeply spiritual mind and became a holy man, participating in religious rituals and meditating on the world and beliefs of his people.

Sitting Bull

During the mid-1800s Sitting Bull emerged as a Lakota political leader, guiding his people through continual conflict with

A Piegan Blackfeet village on the plains of north-central Montana, as seen in the early 1830s, not long before smallpox, brought west by explorers, killed 6,000 tribal members. At one time nomadic bison hunters, today the Blackfeet live on a reservation at the eastern foot of the Lewis Range.

rival tribes and encroaching white settlers. In 1875 Sitting Bull nego-tiated an alliance between the Sioux, Cheyenne, and Arapaho tribes, creating the mass of warriors that would overwhelm the forces of Lieutenant Colonel Custer at the Battle of the Little Bighorn. Prior to the victorious battle, Sitting Bull had a vision of soldiers falling upside down from the sky, foretelling the U.S. defeat. After his vision was proven, Sitting Bull and the Lakota became prime targets of the U.S. Army and fled to Canada. Cold and starvation forced the tribe back over the border, and Sitting Bull surrendered to the authorities.

His story was far from finished, though—in his later years he became a major player in Buffalo Bill's Wild West, touring the nation for the significant fee of $50 a week. The coda of Sitting Bull's life occurred on the Standing Rock Reservation, where conditions had deteriorated to squalor. A messianic movement had emerged, the Ghost Dance, which the Lakota Sioux believed would return their sovereignty over the land. Though ambivalent about the movement, Sitting Bull was arrested; during a scuffle, Indian agents assassinat-ed him. The year was 1890, the frontier was closed, and Sitting Bull, who grew up following the old ways, who led his people against the invasion of an unfamiliar world, was gone.

Sitting Bull, photographed with Buffalo Bill Cody in 1885.

The chimneys of smelters, mines, and mills belch plumes of smoke over Butte, which by 1884 was booming due to copper extraction. Famous for its many elegant brothels, Butte is also important for its resolute labor unions, which rose to counter malign and corrupt mining corporations.

Capitalizing on the Country

Lewis and Clark's revelations about the West's teeming wilderness inspired wealthy fur traders like John Jacob Astor and William Ashley to capitalize on the region. Soon scores of voyageurs were emptying Montana of beaver to sell to European hatmakers. In 1862 gold was discovered near the town of Bannack, and settlers poured into the region; in 1864 Montana became a United States Territory. By the 1870s increasing collisions between settlers and Indians led to U.S. Army campaigns against Montana's tribes. Montana was the scene of great Indian military triumphs—in 1876 a swarm of Sioux, Cheyenne, and Arapaho warriors obliterated forces under George Armstrong Custer at the Battle of the Little Bighorn. There were also devastating defeats—in 1877, after outmaneuvering the U.S. Army for 1,700 miles and fighting 13 battles in a little more than three months, the Nez Perce, under Chief Joseph and Looking Glass, were finally defeated after a grueling five-day battle in Montana's freezing Bear Paw Mountains, 40 miles from the salvation of the Canadian border.

Electrification and Industrialization

The advent of electric technologies in the late 1800s turned Butte, a city rife with copper deposits, into a boomtown. In the early 20th century, the Anaconda Copper Mining Company became a political power-broker, and labor unions struggled against its influence, leading to violent clashes. In 1909 the U.S. government allotted 320 acres in Montana to homesteaders willing to farm the land; the resulting influx of yeoman farmers created the agricultural industry that drives Montana today. Jeanette Rankin, who fought to secure Montana's women the right to vote in 1914, was elected to the U.S. House of Representatives in 1916, becoming the first female member of Congress. She focused her energies on maternal and child health care legislation but was vilified by the press for her pacifist stance in the face of World War I, and did not seek reelection. Today, at the outset of the 21st century, Montana still fluctuates politically, as it moves into a service-based economy, sharing its treasured wild spaces with nearly 10 million visitors per year, streaming in from all over the world.

Jeanette Rankin

CUSTER'S LAST STAND

A practical joker at West Point, George Armstrong Custer graduated last in his class, but the outbreak of the Civil War made him an officer, and he became one of the most distinguished and flamboyant officers in the U.S. Army by war's end. A snappy dresser and daring leader, he was known for his fearlessness and, some thought, foolishness. He was a scrupulous planner, though, and knew all the angles before making a "Custer Dash," followed by a swarm of blue-coated soldiers, upon the Confederate forces. Custer openly attributed his success to "luck." During the Indian Wars, both Lieutenant Colonel Custer's luck and foresight faltered disastrously against the fearsome Sioux.

It took awhile for fortune to frown on Custer. In 1868 his troops destroyed a Cheyenne village during the Battle of Washita River. Among the prisoners taken was a woman named Monaseetah, with whom Custer is alleged to have fathered a child. Meanwhile, his devoted wife, Elizabeth, followed him on his tours of duty; in 1867 Custer had been court-martialed for vacating his post to

George Armstrong Custer

spend time with her, but he was considered too valuable an officer to let languish. In 1874 Custer and the 7th Cavalry discovered gold in the Black Hills of South Dakota, triggering the Black Hills Gold Rush and further angering the Sioux, who considered the hills sacred ground.

On the morning of June 25, 1876, Custer's men encountered a Sioux village on the Little Bighorn River. Worried that there would not be another chance to surprise the Indians, Custer split the cavalry into three divisions and ordered an attack, which commenced that afternoon. By early evening the 7th Cavalry had been routed by the Sioux, Cheyenne, and Arapaho warriors, who outnumbered the U.S. forces by roughly 1,800 to 600. Custer's division was completely obliterated, and Custer, the man the Indians called "Yellow Hair," was killed. Custer's defeat was front-page news, and the flamboyant soldier became more famous in death than he had been in life. As for the U.S. Army, it lost the battle but went on to win the war— by the close of the 19th century, the Plains Indian way of life was destroyed.

This fanciful 1889 illustration captures the chaos of the Battle of the Little Bighorn, when Sioux forces under Crazy Horse, White Bull, and Gall swarmed Custer's cavalry. Custer, seen firing two pistols, was actually wearing buckskin during the battle, rather than army blue.

Idaho

The Gem State

Esto Perpetua (Let it be forever)

Nestled in the far West between six states and the nation of Canada, and long insulated from the incursions of colonists and explorers, Idaho is now one of the fastest growing states in the nation. Since the turn of the 21st century, the Gem State's population has risen by more than 135,000 people, and the Boise Metropolitan Area—the state's commercial heart—has swelled to accommodate the new growth. Not that Idaho is becoming crowded—it remains a land of rugged nature and sublime sights, well preserved in its many national parks and recreation areas.

A historic fork in the pioneers' journey westward—where the California and Oregon trails diverged—Idaho is bisected by a wilderness of mountains and rivers and has traditionally been divided geographically and culturally. The Idaho Panhandle holds Spokane, Washington—20 miles over the border—to be its urban hub. The southern portion of the state, however, is served by the capital city Boise, and its burgeoning metropolitan area, including the cities of Nampa, Caldwell, and Meridian. Northern and southern Idaho are not linked by an interstate highway; to travel from Pocatello, in the south, to Coeur D'Alene, in the north, one would need to drive I-15 into western Montana, and then take I-90 back into Idaho. Despite these divisions, the state is mostly in political agreement. The Republican Party has held Idaho's two House seats for most of the last two decades, and no Idaho Democrat has been elected to the Senate since 1980. The governor is Republican, and the state Legislature is likewise all Republican.

Though named the Gem State, precious stones are not Idaho's economic catalysts. Idaho's truest gems are its famous potatoes. Silver mining is a major industry, and above ground, logging remains vital, but the economy is diversifying—electronic manufacturing has boomed, and Boise is now home to major fabricators of computer chips, as well as a computer printer plant and related industry. The Idaho National Laboratory, a government nuclear energy research lab near Idaho Falls, is also a major employer. Tourism is, of course, a staple in Idaho's economy. In the winter, skiers flood the state's slopes and resorts; in the summer, hikers, campers, and vacationers traverse Idaho's open spaces. It is this wilderness that defines the state and its people, whether one is a farmer or a rancher, a hunter or a hiker, a city-dweller in the south, or an American Indian living on the Coeur D'Alene Reservation in the north.

The Snake River undulates across Idaho's fertile Snake River Plain on its 1,040-mile trek from Yellowstone's peaks to the Columbia River.

Idaho State Facts

Full Name: State of Idaho
Meaning of Name: either from an imaginary American Indian word created by George M. Willing, or from the actual Coeur d'Alene phrase *ah-d'hoo*, meaning "greetings by surprise"
Admitted to the Union: July 3, 1890 (43rd state)

Inhabitant: Idahoan
Capital City: Boise
Flower: Syringa (mock orange)
Tree: Western white pine
Bird: Mountain bluebird

Geography and Ecology

It is an L-shaped state, fitting like a puzzle piece against the mountainous western edge of Montana. Idaho's southern border sits squarely atop the states of Utah and Nevada, and its western side forms nearly another straight line, broken only by the twisting Snake River as it slithers through Hells Canyon, demarcating the border with Oregon. Within these weird dimensions, Idaho is a land of sublime and unforgiving wilderness. The Rocky Mountains stand along the state's eastern flank and send rugged ranges into Idaho's center. The Bitterroot Range rises and falls along the Montana-Idaho border, the Clearwater Mountains loom above the eastern Idaho Panhandle, the Sawtooth Range's jagged triangular peaks soar northwest of Sun Valley, and the Salmon River Mountains occupy central Idaho, birthing the Salmon River, which flows northwest to the state line.

True Wilderness

Such arduous and beautiful landforms have allowed vast tracts of Idaho to stay undeveloped. Multiple national parks protect the state's ranges and rivers. The state's largest managed land area, the Frank Church–River of No Return Wilderness Area, spans 2.3 million acres. Containing the Clearwater and Salmon River mountains, and crisscrossed by the swift and lively Salmon River, it is not only Idaho's most vast protected wilderness, but also the largest contiguous wilderness preserve in the continental United States.

The Sawtooth Range stands above the vast Sawtooth National Forest, reserved in 1905 by President Theodore Roosevelt, and jeweled by myriad rivers and more than 1,000 lakes.

Diverse Fauna

Though hikers and white-water rafters ply its ridges and rapids, the truest denizens of Idaho's primal interior are its wild animals. Bighorn sheep and mountain goats scale rocky slopes; elk, moose, mule deer, and white-tailed deer forage in deep woods of aspen, hemlock, cedar, and pine. Solitary cougars hunt from ledges and stalk the forests and fields. Lynx and red fox prowl for small woodland wildlife. Gray wolves and coyote team in gregarious packs, seeking big game; black bears feast on bugs, berries, nuts, small mammals, and fish. Idaho's rivers teem with salmon, trout, bass, steelhead, and sturgeon. Eagles, hawks, and osprey hunt from the sky, and grouse and partridge gather food on the ground. The Idaho wilds are even home to that most ferocious of fauna, the wolverine.

Meat and Potatoes

Amid such nature, Idaho's citizens adhere to wild traditions. Humans have hunted and fished Idaho for thousands of years; today a large portion of the state's inhabitants still fish and hunt for sport, sustenance, and profit. The arrival of autumn, with its crisp temperatures, signals the start of hunting season. As fall defers to winter, temperatures sink, and deep snow blankets high elevations. As winter turns to spring, the melting of these alpine snows provides irrigation for more than 2 million acres of farmland, primarily in the Snake River Basin in the south. In the early spring potato farmers begin to plant their tubers, which are perfectly suited to the lowlands of southern Idaho and their warm summer days, cool nights, and volcanic soils. Potatoes are harvested from mid-July until November. The farms of southern Idaho also produce a range of fruits, vegetables, and grains. Ranchers put substantial herds of cattle out to pasture on higher ground in the center of the state.

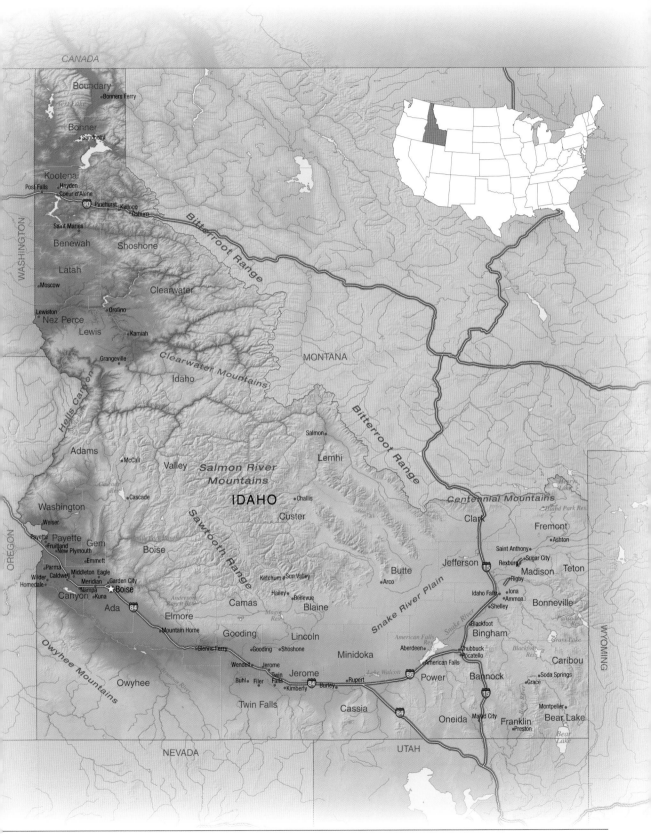

CANADA

Boundary
Bonners Ferry

Bonner
Sandpoint

Kootenai
Post Falls   Hayden
Coeur d'Alene
90 Pinehurst Kellogg
Osburn
Saint Maries

WASHINGTON

Benewah

Latah
Shoshone

Moscow
Clearwater

Lewiston   Orofino
Nez Perce
Lewis   Kamiah

Grangeville

Hells Canyon

Clearwater Mountains

Idaho

MONTANA

Adams

Salmon

McCall

Valley   Salmon River
Mountains

Lemhi

Bitterroot Range

Centennial Mountains

Island Park Res.

Washington

Cascade

IDAHO

Challis

Custer

Clark

Fremont

Ashton

Weiser

Sawtooth Range

Saint Anthony
Jefferson   15   Rexburg   Sugar City

Payette
Fruitland
New Plymouth

Gem

Boise

Butte

Arco

Madison   Teton

Rigby

Emmett

Ketchum Sun Valley

Snake River Plain

Idaho Falls   Iona
Ammon

Bonneville

OREGON

Parma
Caldwell
Middleton Eagle
Wilder   Meridian
Homedale   Nampa   Garden City
Canyon   Kuna   Boise
Ada

Hailey Bellevue

Camas

Blaine

Shelley

Blackfoot   Bingham

Grays Lake

Elmore

Anderson
Ranch Res.

Mountain Home

Gooding

Lincoln

American Falls
Res.

Chubbuck
Pocatello

Caribou

Soda Springs

Owyhee Mountains

Glenns Ferry

Gooding Shoshone

Minidoka

Aberdeen

American Falls

Bruneau River

Owyhee

Wendell   Jerome
Buhl Filer   Twin
Falls
Kimberly

Jerome

84   Rupert
Burley

86   Power

Bannock   Grace

Lake Walcott

15

Montpelier

Twin Falls

Cassia

Oneida   Malad City

Bear River

Bear Lake

84   Franklin
Preston

Bear
Lake

NEVADA

UTAH

WYOMING

The Gem State

On August 12, 1805, the Corps of Discovery, led by Meriwether Lewis and William Clark, rode through Lemhi Pass, high in the Rocky Mountains, becoming the first people of European descent to enter present-day Idaho. While passing through the region, Lewis and Clark traded with the Shoshone and Nez Perce Indians, whose paleo-Indian ancestors had settled uncharted Idaho more than 14,000 years before. The Nez Perce and Coeur d'Alene tribes migrated throughout northern Idaho and its surrounding territories. The Bannock and Shoshone people roamed Idaho's southern regions. These tribes lived hunter-gatherer lifestyles, changing camps from summer to winter. Fish, deer, and bison were staples of the tribes' diets, as well as gathered vegetables, such as camas bulbs.

Fur Traders and Missionaries

For the first half of the 19th century, only missionaries and fur traders saw promise in the wilderness of the Idaho region. English Canadian fur trader David Thompson established the region's first trading post, Kullyspell House, in 1809. In 1836 Presbyterian missionaries Henry H. Spalding and his wife, Eliza, built a mission at Lapwai, in northwestern Idaho. An industrious fellow, Spalding opened Idaho's first school, printed the region's first book, transcribed the Nez Perce langauge, created the first irrigation system in the area, and planted Idaho's first potatoes.

Chief Joseph in 1903. A wartime leader of the Nez Perce, he continued to fight diplomatically for his people after their confinement to an Idaho reservation.

Pioneers in the Territory

The Oregon Treaty of 1846 gave the United States sovereignty over the Oregon Territory, which included present-day Washington, Oregon, and Idaho. By mid-century thousands of yearly emigrants drove their wagons over the Oregon Trail, headed for open land in Oregon or the goldfields of California. In 1860 the discovery of gold in Idaho sparked a gold rush. To establish control over the frenzied area, President Abraham Lincoln declared Idaho a U.S. Territory in 1863. Gold rushes continued

The lead-silver mining town of Hailey, in Idaho's Wood River Valley, three years after its 1881 founding. The first town in Idaho to install electric lights, Hailey is now a ski town, home to roughly 7,900 people.

throughout the second half of the 19th century, and myriad settlers streamed in. Mormon pioneers settled in southeast Idaho, Confederate refugees and free blacks staked claims in the territory after the Civil War, Irish immigrants fleeing the potato famine found a new potato paradise, Basque settlers worked as farmers and ranchers, and scores of Chinese became businesspeople, miners, and railroad workers. Conflict with local Indian tribes intensified amid the larger war waged by the U.S. government to eradicate the American Indian people and confine them to reservations.

Joining the Union

In 1890 Idaho was admitted as the 43rd U.S. state. The gold mines of old gave way to lead-silver mines around Coeur D'Alene, which operated at an enormous scale and became embroiled in labor strife. Years of violent conflict between union workers, mine bosses, and the state and federal government culminated in the 1905 assassination of Idaho governor Frank Steunenberg. The early 20th century saw the Idaho economy shift from a mining basis to agriculture. With the construction of Milner Dam and irrigation canals, the south-central plains of Idaho became Magic Valley, a major agricultural zone. A series of dams and reservoirs initiated farm and civic development statewide.

Esto Perpetua

Political antagonism once divided northern and southern Idaho, nearly sinking its quest for statehood. Today, the state is unified and prospering, though its untamable wilderness remains open to anyone seeking to secede from larger society. The Aryan Nation considered Idaho its home base until 2001, and in the early 1990s U.S. marshals waged a bloody standoff with white separatists in northern Idaho. The average travelers through Idaho's wilderness, though, are hunters and fisherman, or hikers sojourning in nature. Idaho's Indian tribes still inhabit the state. The Coeur d'Alene Reservation in northwestern Idaho is home to more than 6,000 people. Roughly another 6,000 Shoshone and Bannock Indians live on Fort Hall Indian Reservation on the Snake River Plain. The old Idaho Territory—rugged home to the Nez Perce and Coeur d'Alene, a byway for pioneers, a gold haven, and a potato paradise—continues on, into the 21st century. As the motto says, let it be forever.

The capital of Idaho, the Boise metropolis is home to more than 200,000 people. Named for the Boise River, the city originated as a fort established by the U.S. Army in 1863. The site of significant growth in recent years, Boise houses the headquarters of several major corporations.

Wyoming

The Equality State

Equal Rights

There are more cattle than people in Wyoming. This is symbolic not only of Wyoming's Wild West past as a habitat for ranchers and cattlemen, cowboys, and rustlers—it also indicates the inhospitality of the land. Though well suited to gargantuan herds of cattle, and home to myriad wildlife, Wyoming resists human settlement like no other state in the Union. It is the 10th largest state, but the least populous—a little more than 584,000 people live within its rectangular borders.

Once, the great American Indian Horse culture ranged across its vast plains. Later, the pioneers beat rough wagon trails across the Rocky Mountains, and then the Union Pacific Railroad sculpted its unbroken road to the west. Now, roughly half of Wyoming is federal land, preserved as national forests and grasslands. The state's numerous natural wonders, from the boiling ground of Yellowstone National Park in the northwest, to the monolithic Devils Tower in the northeast, are major tourist attractions, garnering more than $2 billion annually. It is Wyoming's underground landforms, though, that account for the majority of the state's yearly purse. Coal, natural gas, coal bed methane, oil, uranium, and trona are all extracted from subterranean Wyoming. The state employs the most miners in the United States, produces more coal than any other state, and contains the largest known troves of trona—a valuable evaporite mineral used to make glass, soaps, paper, and pharmaceuticals—in the world.

Due to its prosperous tourism industry and vast mineral commodities, Wyoming has an unemployment rate below the national average. Historically, it is a place of political firsts. Preservation of the American wilderness began in Wyoming with the establishment of Yellowstone as the world's first national park in 1872. Three years prior, Wyomingites had pioneered in gender politics, granting suffrage to women more than 60 years before the 19th amendment made it national law. Today, Wyoming—like much of the American West—is a land of conservative and predominately Republican politics. However, though the state has not supported a Democratic president since 1964, Democratic governors have prevailed in Wyoming throughout the last few decades. Wyoming's politicians have made the state's mining and energy industries a top priority, but the state's well-preserved wilderness is perhaps Wyoming's truest gift to its own citizens and to the nation. Long a beautiful and difficult land, Wyoming remains a rugged jewel of the American West. It is still a place for ranchers and cowboys, explorers and pioneers.

In Lakota legend, Mato, the giant bear, scarred Devils Tower with his claws while trying to capture two Sioux boys atop the huge rock.

Wyoming State Facts

Full Name: State of Wyoming
Meaning of Name: From the Delaware Indian phrase *mecheweami-ing*, meaning "on the great plain"
Admitted to the Union: July 10, 1890 (44th state)
Inhabitant: Wyomingite

Capital City: Cheyenne
Flower: Indian paintbrush
Tree: Plains cottonwood
Bird: Meadowlark

Geography and Ecology

It is a giant rectangle sitting in the heart of the American West, its borders fitting cleanly against Idaho, Montana, Colorado, and Utah. The Great Plains climb west from South Dakota and Nebraska across the plateau of Wyoming, terminating at the dramatic wall of the Rocky Mountains. Wyoming's greatest heights occur in the pointed Tetons and the craggy and towering Wind River Mountains, both of which run north to south in western Wyoming. The smaller Bighorn Mountains loom above north-central Wyoming, and the Black Hills sit on the Wyoming–South Dakota border, an isolated range amid leagues of prairie grass.

Rivers Run Wild

The Continental Divide slants from northwest to southern Wyoming, affecting the drainage of the state's various rivers. The Green River flows from the Wind River Mountains into Utah and eventually Colorado, where it drains into the Colorado River. Also flowing west, the Snake River drains into the Columbia River, whereas the Yellowstone River—the longest undammed river in the contiguous United States—flows northeast into Montana and supplies the mighty Missouri River. In south-central Wyoming the Great Divide Basin terminates the flow of any watercourses in the area—rivers must flow around the basin or else disappear into its arid soil.

Semiarid with a Chance of Severe Storms

Summer days in Wyoming are hot; summer nights are cool. Generally dry and windy, Wyoming's weather varies according to latitude and altitude. The cold season is punctuated by great Arctic gusts. However, Chinooks can sweep off the mountains and cause warm winter days. Mountainous elevations are typically cold and snowbound in winter, though statewide, precipitation falls sparingly, especially in northern Wyoming's Bighorn Basin, which averages only 5 to 8 inches per year. The state's southern and eastern plains often host torrential thunderstorms. Tornadoes occasionally twist through the southeastern corner of the state.

The jagged Tetons loom above the Grand Teton River. Yellow aspens on the riverbank indicate that autumn has come to northwest Wyoming.

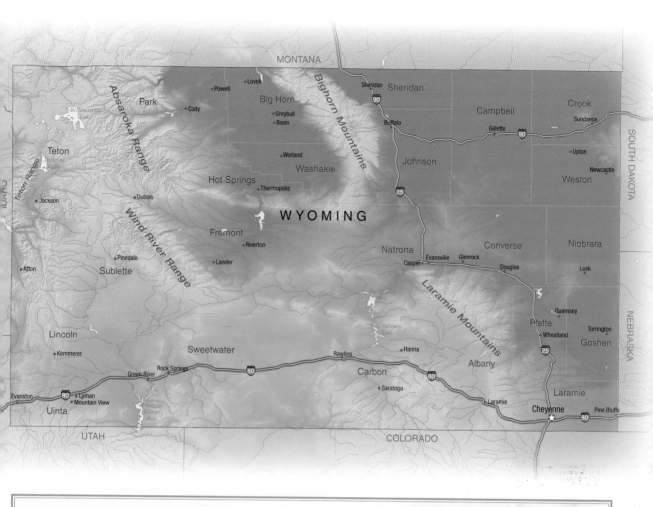

Yellowstone National Park

The world's first national park, Yellowstone sits amid the Greater Yellowstone Ecosystem, one of the last large, nearly fully preserved ecosystems in the Earth's northern temperate zone. In other words, it is a pristine wilderness, albeit a turbulent one. The underbelly of Yellowstone is a hive of volcanic activity. The Yellowstone Caldera, beneath the center of the park, is the largest supervolcano in North America. Its prehistoric eruptions were literally Earth-shaking events; it is still active, though not expected to erupt anytime soon. Indications of Yellowstone's boiling basements abound. Numerous geysers regularly erupt into towers of water. Steaming lakes and hot springs dot the landscape. Yet, amid such hellish habitats, myriad flora and fauna thrive. Cougars, lynx, black bears, grizzly bears, and gray wolves (which were successfully reintroduced to the park in 1995) hunt and scavenge on Yellowstone's flowering riverbanks and amid forests of pine, fir, and aspen. Great herds of bison are a stirring site in Yellowstone's valleys; other large herbivores include moose, elk, deer, pronghorn antelope, mountain goat, and bighorn sheep. Unique wildlife exists even at the microscopic level—Yellowstone's warm waters host a range of bacteria, some of which could be used to cure diseases. Rounding out the ecological picture are the park's human visitors, who hike, fish, and camp in the backcountry. Hunting is not permitted.

A 1938 poster advertising Yellowstone.

The Equality State

The paleo-Indians were here first—the Clovis, Plano, and Folsom cultures among them. Millennia passed and more distinct tribes emerged—the Arapaho, Bannock, Blackfeet, Cheyenne, Crow, Gros Ventre, Kiowa, Nez Perce, Shoshone, and Ute—who traveled the Great Plains and western forests, hunting bison and gathering wild plants. The introduction of Spanish horses in the 1500s transformed the Plains Indians into a horse culture; hunting and battle were performed on horseback, and Plains Indian warriors developed into some of the finest horsemen in the world.

Wagons and Trains

The Lewis and Clark expedition passed north of the Wyoming region, but in 1806 John Colter left the party on its return journey to explore and trap in the Wyoming wilderness. Perhaps the first white American in Wyoming, Colter described the volcanic Yellowstone region, though few believed his tales of bubbling pools and geysers. Mountain man Jim Bridger also trekked through the Wyoming wilderness; in 1850 he located

Famous for his tall tales, Jim Bridger served as an explorer, trapper, scout, and guide in the mountainous western frontier from 1822 until the 1860s.

a pass through the Rockies eventually used by the Union Pacific Railroad and Interstate 80. The trails blazed by Wyoming's early explorers cleared the way for waves of migration. During the mid-19th century the Oregon Trail cut through the heart of the state, ferrying hundreds of thousands of settlers to the far West. The Union Pacific Railroad also pushed westward across the state, meeting the Central Pacific tracks in Utah in 1869 and establishing the first transcontinental railroad in North America.

The Cowboy State

The Homestead Act of 1862 inspired scores of yeoman farmers and ranchers to settle in Wyoming. Meanwhile, wealthy livestock tycoons drove huge herds of cattle across the state's eastern plains. It wasn't so much a land of cowboy versus Indian as it was cowboy versus cowboy—the huge herder and the small rancher competed, often violently, for land and resources. The Indians battled the U.S. Army, who campaigned to destroy Wyoming's tribes and confine them to ever-dwindling plots of land. By 1890

THE HOLE-IN-THE-WALL GANG

Nestled in Wyoming's Bighorn Mountains is a secluded valley, sealed off by a giant wall of red sandstone and accessible only by a gap in the ridge known as the Hole in the Wall. Miles from any town, in rugged high country, a couple of bandits could easily guard Hole in the Wall from the authorities. The outlaws that used Hole in the Wall are mythic figures of the Old West: Robert LeRoy Parker (alias Butch Cassidy), Harry Longabaugh (alias the Sundance Kid), Elzy Lay, News Carver, Laura Bullion, Flat Nose Curry, and Kid Curry, among others. Multiple gangs operated out of Hole in the Wall simultaneously, with stringent ground rules ensuring amicable relations between the outlaws. In the late 1800s Butch Cassidy's Wild Bunch, the most famous of the Hole-in-the-Wall gangs, robbed banks and trains throughout the frontier, garnering hundreds of thousands of dollars and national fame. By the 1910s the Wild West had pacified; bands of outlaws faded from the scene, and their hideouts—the Hole in the Wall among them—became relics of a bygone age.

Butch Cassidy's Wild Bunch, circa early 1901, in Fort Worth, Texas. The Sundance Kid sits at the left, Cassidy sits at the right.

the Indian wars were over, and Wyoming had become the 44th state. The livestock wars continued, with rustlers fighting sheriffs and ruthless range detectives.

Still Wild

Wyoming's picaresque narratives waned after the turn of the 20th century. Modern times have seen the state become stable and, due to its numerous mineral resources, rather prosperous. However, it is still a wild place, and many of the old sights seen by explorers and trappers are visible today. Surely, nobody doubts John Colter's tall tales about Yellowstone now that roughly 3 million people experience it every year. But the state's droves of tourists and thriving mining industry must be properly managed. Wyoming is a land that puts people in touch with deep and wild roots—and with careful preservation, it should stay that way.

The Union Pacific Railroad crossed Wyoming's Laramie Mountains via Malloy's Cut, one of numerous earthworks accomplished by Chinese or Irish immigrant workers, often under excruciating conditions.

Cheyenne, Wyoming's capital, sits on the state's southeastern plains. Here it is seen as a burgeoning sprawl, in 1882. The city had seemingly sprung from the ground 15 years before, with nearly 4,000 people settling there in four months, earning it the title "Magic City of the Plains."

Colorado

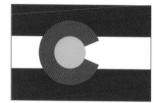

Nil Sine Numine (Nothing without providence)

In the summer of 1893, a Wellesley English professor, Katherine Lee Bates, stood atop Pikes Peak and heard a poem unfurl in her head, a paean to the grandeur of the American landscape. Schoolchildren nationwide now sing her praises to Colorado's—and, by extension America's—"purple mountain majesties / Above the fruited plain!" Beautiful as it was, late-19th-century Colorado was also a land of dangerous mining operations, labor conflict, and lawless infrastructure. Time has smoothed some of history's scars, but Colorado remains a place of beauty and turmoil.

Containing nearly 650,000 people, Colorado's capital, Denver, is the metropolis of the central Mountain States. Sitting on the High Plains, east of the Rocky Mountains, Denver is a hive of economic activity; the city's thriving finance industry has earned the moniker "Wall Street of the West." The federal government has also been one of the area's major employers since the Denver Mint opened in 1863. The National Oceanographic and Atmospheric Association and the National Institute of Standards and Technology are situated in Boulder. Major military-industrial contractors manufacture missiles, satellites, and spacecraft at factories in Denver and Boulder. The U.S. Air Force Academy and Peterson Air Force Base occupy Colorado Springs; and NORAD, the North American Aerospace Defense Command, is headquartered deep inside Cheyenne Mountain in the center of the state.

Mining and energy companies also ply subterranean Colorado, extracting gold, oil, and natural gas from beneath the state's mountainous crust. Major telecommunications companies utilize Denver's high elevation and central location for easy worldwide signal transmissions. Colorado is also a prominent locale for the food processing industry, and much of its eastern grasslands are used for ranching and agriculture. Rounding out the state's economy are the more than 20 million annual visitors touring Colorado's state and national parks.

Tourists are not the only consistent influx across Colorado's borders; immigration from Mexico and Central American countries has increased the state's Hispanic population to unprecedented levels. Today, Colorado has the sixth-largest proportion of Hispanic residents among the 50 states. The state's ethnic diversity is mirrored by its political complexity—it voted predominantly Republican just after the turn of the century, but since 2011 political power has been almost evenly split at the state and federal levels. A beautiful land, home to both military and conservationist branches of the U.S. government, home to the descendants of both German emigrants and Spanish colonists—Colorado is a complex state.

Sunrise in Denver. Founded in 1858 by prospectors, later a corrupt center of the Wild West, Denver is now a cosmopolitan capital.

Colorado State Facts

Full Name: State of Colorado
Meaning of Name: From the Spanish word *colorado*, meaning reddish-brown
Admitted to the Union: August 1, 1876 (38th state)
Inhabitant: Coloradan

Capital City: Denver
Flower: Mountain columbine
Tree: Colorado or blue spruce
Bird: Lark bunting

Geography and Ecology

Like its northern neighbor, Wyoming, Colorado has borders that follow lines of longitude and latitude, giving it a rectangular stature. Its southern border runs cleanly along a portion of the Oklahoma panhandle and atop the northern edge of New Mexico until it meets the Four Corners, where Arizona, Utah, Colorado, and New Mexico touch at a single survey point. Eastern Colorado is prairie, which ascends westward from Nebraska and Kansas and defers to the rugged Rocky Mountains in the center of the state. West of the Rockies is the Colorado Plateau, a high, arid region studded by mesas and jagged rock formations and cut by canyons.

Rocky Mountain High

Towering summits abound in Colorado's ranges—Mt. Elbert, a picturesque 14,440-foot-high peak, is the tallest mountain in the Rockies, and the second-tallest in the contiguous 48 states. The rounded summit of Pikes Peak rises to 14,115 feet; sitting in the Front Range, at the eastern edge of the Rockies, it is visible far across the Colorado plains. All in all, 54 mountains in the Colorado Rockies soar above 14,000 feet. The entire state looms above its surroundings—it is the only state in the nation to sit completely above 1,000 meters (3,281 feet). The capital, Denver, touts itself as the "Mile-High City" because its elevation is exactly 5,280 feet above sea level. The South Platte River flows through Denver—having originated in the Rockies west of the city, it winds across

Colorado National Monument, a high, arid, rugged wilderness in the west of the state, is home to juniper trees, rattlesnakes, and coyotes.

the prairie and flows into the Platte River in Nebraska. The Colorado River begins in north-central Colorado at La Poudre Pass Lake, high in Rocky Mountain National Park, and flows west into Utah and south into Arizona. The Rio Grande also has its source in the southern Colorado Rockies, before it slices south through New Mexico and demarcates the sinuous Texas-Mexico border.

Wild Denizens

Colorado's varied habitats host a range of wildlife. The state's eastern grasslands support scores of small animals. Prairie chickens and sharp-tailed grouse range the plains, eating bugs and seeds. The ferruginous hawk hunts from the air, as does the burrowing owl, which nests on the ground, in the burrows of abandoned prairie dog towns. The swift fox roams the grasslands, hunting prairie dogs and rabbits. The Massasauga rattlesnake feasts on rodents. Bison and pronghorn antelope are among the larger prairie herbivores, and coyotes exist statewide. The Colorado Rockies are home to woodland wildlife, large and small—cougar, lynx, black bears, and grizzly bears are the region's largest predators; deer, elk, mountain goat, and bighorn sheep are the largest herbivores. Bald eagles fish for trout and scavenge carrion. Great horned owls snare rodents in their swooping claws.

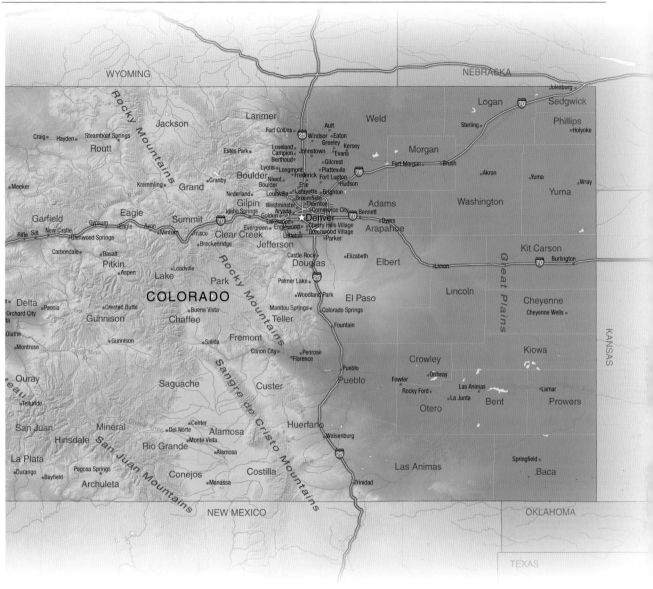

Dry Grasslands, Snowy Mountains

Colorado's climate varies according to its landforms. The eastern grasslands are semi-arid, relatively hot and dry, with precipitation falling sparingly but turbulently, often as thunderstorms. Enough rain falls on the plains to support the cultivation of corn, wheat, and hay. Tornadoes also occur on the plains, causing some significant damage over the years. Snow can fall heavily on the plains in the winter, and it blankets the Rockies, attracting skiers from across the nation to resort towns like Aspen and Steamboat Springs in the western Rockies.

Named after explorer Zebulon Pike, who first documented the mountain and made a futile attempt at climbing it in 1806, Pikes Peak is composed of singular pink granite.

The Centennial State

Tens of thousands of years ago, paleo-Indians settled the Colorado region. Over millennia, distinct tribes formed. The Apache lived a nomadic lifestyle on the Colorado plains, before emigrating south to Texas, New Mexico, and Arizona. The Arapaho and Cheyenne tribes lived on the grasslands at the base of the Rocky Mountains. The Shoshone lived in northwestern Colorado, and the Ute tribe dominated Colorado west of the Rockies.

Cliff Palace, at Mesa Verde National Park in southwestern Colorado, was constructed slightly less than a millenium ago by the Ancient Pueblo people. Built of adobe masonry beneath a sandstone cliff, the ancient village presumably housed some 100–150 people before being abandoned by the year 1300.

Disputed Territory

In the late 16th century Spanish explorers began traveling through the Colorado region. By the 19th century Colorado had become a complicatedly disputed territory. In 1803 the United States acquired what is now roughly the eastern half of the state from France as part of the Louisiana Purchase. Land west of the Continental Divide belonged to Mexico, which disputed U.S. dominion over the land to the east. The United States's victory in the Mexican-American War simplified the situation somewhat—the U.S. officially acquired the entire Colorado region. In 1851 Colorado's first town, San Luis, was created by Mexican migrants who had moved to the area when it was still part of Mexico. Settlers also emigrated from the eastern United States, creating a polyglot society amid the traditional claimants to the land, the American Indian tribes, whom the U.S. government subsequently dispossessed of the territory.

A soldier, bison hunter, and global celebrity, William F. "Buffalo Bill" Cody visited Europe and toured North America for decades with his show "Buffalo Bill's Wild West" before dying in 1917 in Colorado.

Centennial Statehood

On August 1, 1876, after more than a decade of gold rushes and population growth, the former Colorado Territory was declared the 38th state. At the close of the 19th century, Colorado was still the Wild West—dangerous mining operations created princes and prisoners of American capitalism, and in the mining boomtowns, law and order were defined by corrupt and callous mining companies, or by outlaws like Robert Ford and Soapy Smith.

A Complicated State

During the 20th century Colorado's political divisions quaked against each other. In the 1920s the Ku Klux Klan became a powerful political group in the state. By the 1940s trends had shifted—Colorado's Republican governor, Ralph Carr, denounced racism and the wartime internment of Japanese Americans. He was quickly disowned by his own party and voted from office. Denver, as immortalized in Jack Kerouac's book *On the Road*, was a destination for members of the Beat Generation in the late

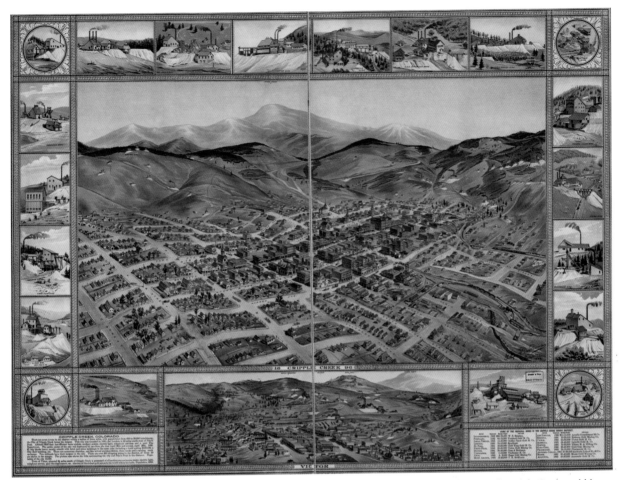

Cripple Creek in 1896, five years after gold was struck in the alpine valley. Many believe that the ample ore around Cripple Creek could have been found sooner had not the 1884 Mount Pisgah Hoax, in which gold was planted amid worthless rocks, soured prospectors on the region.

1940s and '50s, but changing times also brought cultural crisis, as race riots erupted in the city in the 1960s. Skyrocketing oil prices during the energy crisis of the 1970s and '80s made Denver's oil companies very wealthy; when the prices dropped in the mid-'80s, however, severe unemployment followed. The bleakest day in Colorado in recent memory was the Columbine High School massacre of 1999, when two teenage students shot and killed 12 classmates and a teacher and wounded 23 other people. Today, at the outset of the 21st century, Colorado's economy is prosperous, but if history is any indication, it will always be a complicated state, known for both its wild beauty and fractious politics.

OPPRESSING LABOR

Colorado's mining industry originated with the 1959 Pikes Peak Gold Rush, considered the largest gold rush in American history. By the 1890s miners had established labor unions to fight for safer and fairer working conditions. The Western Federation of Miners organized the Cripple Creek strike of 1894, and won, due to the Colorado government's mustering of the state militia on behalf of the workers. However, during the Colorado Labor Wars of 1903–5, the government sided with the mine bosses. The National Guard was called in, joining an oppressive force of Pinkerton detectives and hired guns that violently expelled unionized miners from the area. The brutality continued: in 1914, the National Guard killed 45 people, many of them women and children, during an attack on a camp of striking coal miners; in 1927, in the town of Columbine, state police with machine guns killed a group of miners during a skirmish. These bloody trends finally began to abate in 1933, when the federal government declared it the right of all Colorado coal miners to join a union without retaliation from their employers.

Utah

The Beehive State

Industry

One wonders, why the Beehive State? Utah is not a more prominent beekeeping locale than anywhere else in the Union. Truth be told, the beehive represents Utah's past and the goals of Utah's founders, the Mormons, who traveled more than 1,300 miles, on wagon, horse, and foot, to live in a place nobody else wanted to settle. The beehive symbolizes their group ethic of obedience, industriousness, and resourcefulness—the traits they believed would ensure their success as a society and a faith. Utah's main hive, then, is Salt Lake City, the state's capital and the worldwide seat of the Mormon religion. More than 191,000 people live in the Salt Lake City metropolitan area, on the shores of the Great Salt Lake, in the shadows of the Wasatch Mountains, beneath the castled spires of the Salt Lake Temple.

Because more than 80 percent of Utahns live in urban areas concentrated in the north of the state, most of the state remains wild and depopulated. The federal government owns the majority of Utah's land as national parks, forests, and recreation areas. Tourism is an economic staple for Utah, with droves of visitors exploring the state's beautiful and often desolate backcountry. Come wintertime, hordes of skiers converge upon Utah's slopes. The landscape supports Utah in other ways: fossil fuel and mineral mining are strong industries—the state possesses ample seams of coal, as well as natural gas and oil. Deposits of gold, copper,

silver, zinc, and lead are mined in northern Utah. Salt is also produced on Utah's numerous salt flats.

Though the Mormon Church still dominates Utah's culture and politics, roughly 40 percent of the population is not Mormon, and some speculate that the non-Mormon population will become the majority within the next few years. Long a political battleground, Utah has seen relative political stability in recent times, at least when compared to its long history of wrestling with the federal government over its religious rights. The state remains a haven of Republican Party politics; the more conservative positions of the Republican Party have allied well with the more conservative doctrines of the Mormon Church, making it difficult for liberal Democrats to gain a foothold among Mormon voters.

The promised land of America's homegrown religious pioneers, Utah has seemingly poised itself well in today's world. The economy is robust, and the state's beautiful and mysterious wilderness attracts visitors from around the globe. Also, in 2002, the world's greatest athletes converged on the state for the Winter Olympics—marking the fourth time that the United States has hosted the winter games. Hark, the Beehive State is buzzing.

The angel Moroni, clad in gold, sounds his heraldic trumpet from the east-central spire of the Salt Lake Temple, which took 40 years to build.

Utah State Facts

Full Name: State of Utah
Meaning of Name: From the Ute phrase meaning "people of the mountains"
Admitted to the Union: January 4, 1896 (45th state)
Inhabitant: Utahn

Capital City: Salt Lake City
Flower: Sego lily
Tree: Blue spruce
Bird: California gull

Geography and Ecology

It is a notched rectangle, its squared borders delineated by lines of longitude and latitude. Wyoming and Idaho neighbor Utah to the north, Nevada flanks it to the west, and Arizona, New Mexico, and Colorado meet Utah at the Four Corners. Eastern Utah is part of the Colorado Plateau, high, arid country spreading west to the Wasatch Range, which bisects Utah north to south and constitutes the western edge of the Rocky Mountains. Where the mountains end, the Great Basin begins—a vast, deserted expanse stretching from western Utah across Nevada and into southeastern California. The Great Basin is endorheic, meaning that it contains no outlet to the sea—any water that flows into the Great Basin stays there.

Big Rivers

Big rivers do traverse western Utah—the Sevier River flows 280 miles south to north, emptying into the Sevier Lake. The Virgin River, a tributary of the mighty Colorado River, winds through the southwestern corner of the state, into Arizona and Nevada. As for the Colorado River, it slices across southeastern Utah, flowing through Lake Powell on its way to the Grand Canyon in Arizona, and the Gulf of California. Other large rivers drain the

Eroded over eras by the wind, into what seems a colossal pair of sand-stone legs, Delicate Arch towers 52 feet above Arches National Park.

eastern portion of the state, the Green River chief among them, having snaked south from Wyoming, around Utah's towering Uinta Mountains into Colorado, and then south again, before merging with the Colorado River.

Veering among Extremes

It is a land of hot, dry weather. Most of western Utah is baked desert in the summer; eastern California's Sierra Nevada impedes Pacific rainstorms from reaching much of the region. The Wasatch Mountains similarly shield eastern Utah from most rainfall. But storms do break through, generally in the winter months. The summer can see occasional monsoon rains sweep up from the Gulf of California, flash flooding the desert. Utah's mountains wear deep snow in the winter, considered by resident skiers to be the "greatest snow on Earth." Winters are generally quite cold, and Utah's overall temperature pattern veers among extremes: cold winters give way to hot summers that are likewise characterized by broiling days and cool nights.

National Treasures

Utah is home to five national parks; all are situated in the south of the state, but each is characterized by distinct and spectacular landforms. Arches National Park spans some 119 miles north of the city of Moab; its rocky landscape is decorated with numerous towering arches and columns. Bryce Canyon National Park occupies remote heights in south-central Utah where centuries of erosion have created countless shafts of rock called hoodoos, which can reach 200 feet in height. Canyonlands National Park, located south of Moab, is a maze of slot canyons, box canyons, mesas, rivers, and buttes. Capitol Reef National Park, located near the town of Torrey, features numerous sandstone domes and monoliths. Finally, Zion National Park, located in Utah's southwest corner, straddles four different ecological zones. Its desert terrain is home to cactus and sagebrush. High elevations allow forests of piñon pine and juniper to grow, and even higher mesas see stands of aspen and ponderosa pine. Cottonwoods, willows, and maples grow alongside Zion's rivers. All in all, more than 75 species of mammals, 32 species of reptiles and amphibians, and roughly 289 species of birds coexist in Zion's diverse wilderness.

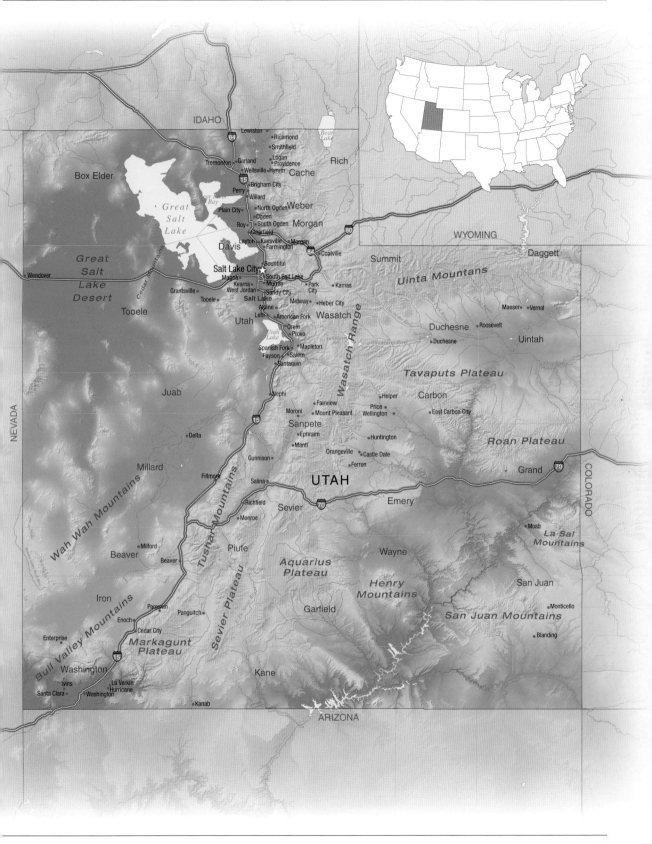

IDAHO

Lewiston
Richmond
Smithfield
Logan
Providence
Tremonton
Garland
Wellsville Hyrum
Brigham City
Perry
Willard
Plain City
North Ogden
Ogden
Roy
South Ogden
Clearfield
Layton
Kaysville
Morgan
Farmington
Bountiful
Coalville
Salt Lake City
Magna
South Salt Lake
Kearns
Murray
Park
West Jordan
Sandy City
City
Salt Lake
Kamas
Midway
Heber City
Alpine
Lehi
American Fork
Orem
Provo
Spanish Fork
Mapleton
Payson
Salem
Santaquin
Nephi
Fairview
Moroni
Mount Pleasant
Price
Wellington
East Carbon City
Ephraim
Manti
Huntington
Orangeville
Castle Dale
Gunnison
Ferron
Fillmore
Salina
Richfield
Monroe
Milford
Beaver
Beaver
Parowan
Panguitch
Enoch
Cedar City
Enterprise
Ivins
La Verkin
Santa Clara
Washington
Hurricane
Kanab

Box Elder
Bear Lake
Rich
Cache
Weber
Morgan
Davis
Summit
Daggett
Great Salt Lake
Bear River Bay
Wendover
Grantsville
Tooele
Great Salt Lake Desert
Tooele
Utah
Utah Lake
Wasatch
Uinta Mountans
Maeser Vernal
Duchesne
Roosevelt
Uintah
Duchesne
Tavaputs Plateau
Carbon
Roan Plateau
Juab
Delta
Sanpete
Wasatch Range
Emery
Grand
Millard
UTAH
Sevier
Moab
La Sal Mountains
Piute
Wayne
San Juan
Aquarius Plateau
Henry Mountains
Iron
Garfield
San Juan Mountains
Monticello
Sevier Plateau
Tushar Mountains
Blanding
Wah Wah Mountains
Bull Valley Mountains
Markagunt Plateau
Washington
Kane

Cedar Mountains

NEVADA

WYOMING

COLORADO

ARIZONA

The Beehive State

The Great Hunt Panel, carved by Fremont artisans in Nine Mile Canyon, depicts the myriad beasts hunted on Utah's eastern plateaus. Home to the highest concentration of ancient rock art in North America, Nine Mile Canyon is threatened today by encroaching natural gas prospectors.

For many years Utah was a nation within a nation, a world apart from the rest of the United States, a place where the Mormons could finally, after years of persecution and exodus, practice their faith and be left alone. The wasteland that Brigham Young led his flock to settle was not without earlier occupants, though. Paleo-Indians hunted and gathered in the region as far back as 12,000 years ago. Pictographs and petroglyphs throughout Utah record the existence of the Fremont culture, who lived in the region more than 1,000 years ago, alongside the ancient Puebloan culture, occupying adobe dwellings, hunting and farming the land, and skillfully crafting pottery. By the time the Spanish explored the region, the Diné (Navajo), Apache, and Paiute people occupied arid southern Utah, the Ute tribe lived in the forests and plateaus of central and eastern Utah, and the Shoshone occupied the mountainous northeast of the region.

Brigham Young

crossing the Wasatch Mountains. They proceeded to create a city from scratch in the desert, digging irrigation canals, plowing fields, logging mountain timber for churches, houses, and schools, and laying out a grid of wide streets and expansive family plots, with a great temple planned at its center. One month after the Mormons' arrival, nearly 30 cabins had been built; within a year, Great Salt Lake City, as it was then called, housed 4,000 people.

In 1849 the Treaty of Guadalupe Hidalgo made the land officially American territory. In this new context, Brigham Young had even greater aspirations. He proposed a vast state governed by the Mormons, called Deseret—a word originally devised by Mormon prophet Joseph Smith to mean "honeybee." The federal government did not honor the proposal—they instead created the smaller Utah Territory and installed Brigham Young as its governor. From here on out, though, the relationship between the Mormons and the U.S. government became decidedly testy.

The Deseret Empire

On July 24, 1847, the first wave of Mormon pioneers, led by Brigham Young, entered the Salt Lake Valley after

Clashes and Statehood

By the mid-1850s the Mormons had officially become a problem for the U.S. government; chief among the grievances was the Mormon practice of polygamy, considered immoral and un-American. A chess match of diplomacy and lukewarm warfare ensued—U.S. troops marched into the state in 1857 to quell the supposed Mormon rebels. Brigham Young surrendered his governorship to the army, though he never truly relinquished his power over state affairs. The destruction of the Mormon society had been averted and the 1861 outbreak of the Civil War ensured that the government would focus its armies elsewhere. But unease in the region continued for the rest of the century, between the Mormons and the government, between Mormon settlers and rushes of non-Mormon settlers drawn to the region by mineral mining, and between the Indians and the government. The Mormons had chosen to live in a degree of harmony with Utah's tribes, but the continued incursion of non-Mormon settlers enabled the government to pursue their policy of destroying the American Indians. In 1890 the Mormon Church officially banned polygamy; at long last, in 1896, Utah was granted statehood.

Busy as Bees

Tensions cooled in Utah during the 20th century, and the nation within a nation was folded into the American fabric, though it still seems, in many ways, a sovereign place. In the 1950s uranium mining boomed in southeastern Utah. The establishment of Utah's National Parks also made tourism a major moneymaker, as did the creation of ski resorts in the Wasatch Mountains. In 2016, Utah's economy was rated number one in the nation, but it must be careful to balance its aspirations with the limitations of its beautiful land. The hive cannot exist without the bees—and vice versa.

"This is the right place, drive on."

—Brigham Young, viewing the Salt Lake Valley ahead of his wagon,
after the Mormons' 1,300-mile exodus

Salt Lake City, seen here 44 years after its founding, was a triumph of urban planning. By 1891 the grid was sprawling ever outward and a non-Mormon party governed the city. With the soaring Salt Lake Temple nearly finished, though, the Mormon Church dominated the skyline.

New Mexico

Land of Enchantment (Tierra del Encanto)

Crescit Eundo (It grows as it goes)

The name gives it away—New Mexico was once Spanish land—a province of Nueva España, or New Spain. Today, the land claimed in 1598 by "the Last Conquistador," Juan de Oñate, is one of the most culturally Hispanic states in the Union. Age-old ancestral ties and waves of recent immigration have given New Mexico the most predominantly Hispanic population among the United States. Also, a significant number of New Mexicans are Ute, Apache, Pueblo, or Navajo people.

Atop a 367-foot mesa in the state's western desert is the Acoma Pueblo, where people have lived since at least the 1100s, making it the oldest continuously inhabited village in the United States. Here, the Puebloans adhere to old traditions, but even at Acoma Pueblo, the thrust of European influence could not be avoided. The 1641 construction of the Spanish Mission of San Esteban Rey in the village has led many Acoma Puebloans to practice Catholicism alongside the ancient Puebloan religion.

One of America's most Catholic states, New Mexico is also home to many freethinkers. The Land of Enchantment has attracted myriad pilgrims over the years. In the late 1800s the Santa Fe Railroad brought hordes of cattlemen and outlaws, like Billy the Kid. By the early 20th century, the area around Taos had become a destination for artists, who established a creative community that continues today.

The state's diverse narratives are mirrored by its varied landforms—deep forests and rugged mountains accompany vast pink deserts and stark plateaus studded by buttes and mesas. Ranching and dairy farming are prominent agricultural practices, alongside scientifically controlled dryland farming, which coaxes large yields of hay and sorghum, as well as chile peppers, pecans, and pinto beans from the arid earth. Pine nuts are harvested from the piñon pine, and the trees themselves contribute to a sizable lumber industry. Subterranean New Mexico is rich in minerals such as uranium, manganese, and copper. Tourism to the state's open spaces and historic spots is also a major moneymaker.

New Mexico has a history of voting for the victorious presidential candidate—since its 1912 statehood, it has supported only three failed campaigns. These days, the Democratic Party dominates politics, although the governor is Republican. As the old Nuevo México evolves into a 21st-century state, ancient ways accompany innovation to push New Mexico forward. The city of Santa Fe is one of the great artistic centers of the United States, Albuquerque is booming financially, and on the pueblos, ancient traditions preserve the history of those who were here first.

The clustered houses of Taos Pueblo, now home to roughly 150 Pueblo people, are occupied traditionally, without electricity or running water.

New Mexico State Facts

Full Name: State of New Mexico
Meaning of Name: Named after Mexico City, which had been named after the Aztec city, Mexico-Tenochtitlan
Admitted to the Union: January 6, 1912 (47th state)
Inhabitant: New Mexican

Capital City: Santa Fe
Flower: Yucca flower
Tree: Two-needle piñon pine
Bird: Greater roadrunner

Geography and Ecology

It is a big boxy state with a boot heel, its borders running mostly along lines of longitude and latitude. In the east, it sits flush against the Oklahoma panhandle. Texas pushes three miles west of that boundary to form a long, straight eastern border, and also spans hundreds of miles along southern New Mexico. The Land of Enchantment's southwestern boundary and its jutting bootheel border the Mexican states of Chihuahua and Sonora. New Mexico's western and northern borders meet Arizona, Utah, and Colorado at the Four Corners, which also conjoins two tracts of Indian land—the Navajo Indian Reservation and the Ute Mountain Indian Reservation.

Rios Importantes

The Rio Grande meanders south through the heart of the state before turning southeast to define the Texas-Mexico border. Shallow and slow moving, it cannot support commercial shipping, though the river is siphoned for irrigation and drinking water by Colorado, New Mexico, and Texas, seriously overburdening its resources. In 1938 the three states signed the Rio Grande Compact, which equitably apportioned the river. For the first 30 years of the compact, Colorado effectively ignored the restrictions, causing it to owe an enormous debt of water to New Mexico, which in turn owed a substantial amount to Texas. Today, water deficits are still a concern—droughts in recent years have again placed New Mexico in Texas's debt. Another major watercourse, the Pecos River, begins north of Santa Fe and flows southeast into Texas, where it joins the Rio Grande. It is dammed in the southeast corner of the state to irrigate cropland. The Canadian River, curling through northeastern New Mexico, is also repeatedly dammed.

Pied Beauty

The landscape itself is blessed with variation. In the north the towering Sangre de Cristo Mountains, the southernmost spur of the Rocky Mountains, follow the Rio Grande south and flatten out below Santa Fe. Numerous peaks above 13,000 feet, including Wheeler Peak, the state's highest point, at 13,161 feet, dominate the mountains, which often bear a reddish tint at sunrise and sunset. Great swaths of forest also cover northern New Mexico, composed of piñon pine, juniper, and spruce, home to bears, cougars, mule deer, and wild

The Rio Grande Gorge, near Taos, plunges to a depth of 800 feet. Part of the Taos Plateau volcanic field, it houses numerous hot springs.

Not sand, but rather rolling dunes of cool-to-the-touch gypsum crystals form the splendid desolation of White Sands National Monument.

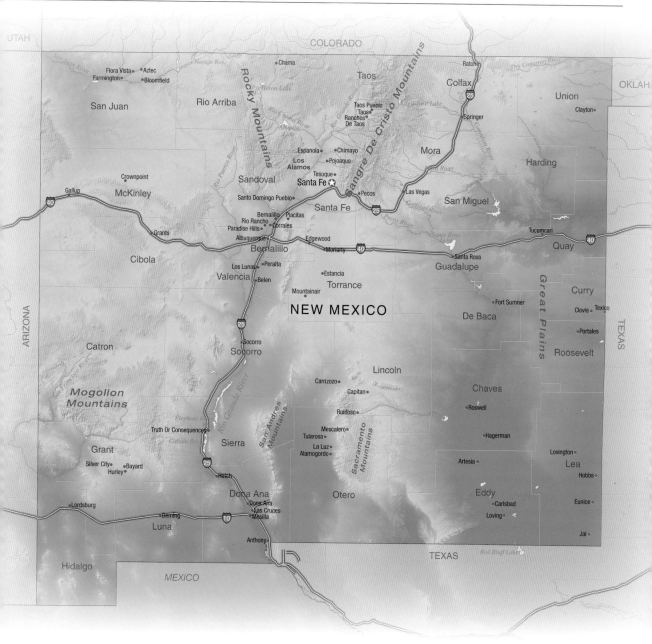

turkeys, among other fauna. Large grasslands accompany these forests, home to prairie dogs and pronghorn antelope. Northeastern New Mexico, as part of the Colorado Plateau, is arid and severe—reddish rocky country shadowed by buttes and mesas. Southern New Mexico is mostly dry, deserted terrain, ranging from the richly inhabited Gila Wilderness—home to bobcats, black bears, Mexican wolves, pronghorns, peccaries, coral snakes, and aptly named Gila monsters—to the stunning gypsum wastes of White Sands National Monument.

Dry Country

A high state, with a mean elevation of 5,700 feet, New Mexico is overwhelmingly dry, averaging only 15 inches of precipitation per year. Summers are scorching at lower elevations but cooler on higher land, and punctuated by brief and torrential thunderstorms that flash flood dry low country and provide the majority of the year's precipitation. Winters are especially dry and can plunge below freezing. Snow occasionally falls at high elevations and blankets New Mexico's tallest peaks.

Land of Enchantment (Tierra del Encanto)

Stone tools and ancient campsites record the presence of the prehistoric Clovis culture, which occupied the southwest some 10,000 years ago. By the year 700 the Ancient Pueblo people had become dominant in the region, living in adobe houses, crafting clay pottery, and cultivating crops by redirecting water for irrigation. After experiencing a golden age from roughly 900 to 1130, the Ancient Pueblo culture fragmented due to climate change and political strife. By 1400 the Ancient Puebloans had merged with the modern Pueblo people, who lived in adobe villages, including the Acoma, Taos, and Zuni pueblos, which are still occupied today. The semi-nomadic Apache and Navajo (Diné) tribes also occupied the New Mexico region.

The Spanish Arrive

In 1541 an army of Spaniards under the command of Francisco Vásquez de Coronado journeyed into New Mexico seeking the famed Seven Golden Cities of Cibola. The group failed spectacularly, but during

Ancient Pueblo people presumably used the great kiva at Chetro Ketl for religious and communal functions. The site dates back nearly a millenium.

Santa Fe has been the capital of New Mexico for nearly 400 years, dating back to the state's years as a Spanish colony. Originally planned by the Spanish to radiate from a central plaza, Santa Fe's grid had begun to arrange into more conventional blocks by 1882—the time of this map.

the journey some horses escaped; the descendants of these horses later transformed western American Indian culture. In 1598 Juan de Oñate established the New Spanish province of Nuevo México. Oñate attempted to subjugate the Pueblo Indians, who resisted assimilation. In the 1670s the uneasy peace between the Spaniards and Puebloans degenerated, and in 1680 the spiritual leader Popé led the Pueblo Revolt, driving the Spaniards from New Mexico. In 1692 the Spanish returned and reconquered the region, albeit with more caution: they no longer aggressively Catholicized the Pueblos.

American Conquest

In 1821 Mexico won its independence from Spain and assumed control of New Mexico. By this time American mountain men had begun exploring the region—

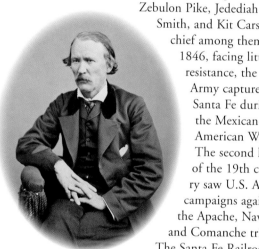

Kit Carson

Zebulon Pike, Jedediah Smith, and Kit Carson chief among them. In 1846, facing little resistance, the U.S. Army captured Santa Fe during the Mexican-American War. The second half of the 19th century saw U.S. Army campaigns against the Apache, Navajo, and Comanche tribes. The Santa Fe Railroad brought a surge of settlers and droves of cattlemen and cattle, not to mention outlaws, one of whom was William H. Bonney, better known as Billy the Kid. A participant in the Lincoln County War of 1878, which pitted ranchers against local merchants, Billy the Kid was a rustler, a gambler, and a gunman. In 1881 Sheriff Pat Garrett shot him to death at the ripe old age of 21.

Crescit Eundo

Finally granted statehood in 1912, New Mexico hosted significant scientific controversy in the 20th-century. U.S. government physicists developed the first atomic bomb at Los Alamos Research Center in northern New Mexico, successfully detonating it at White Sands Proving Grounds in 1945. In 1947, near the city of Roswell, the U.S. Air Force recovered debris that is believed by some to be pieces of an alien spacecraft. Controversy and conspiracy aside, New Mexico is flourishing in the 21st century. The private sector in Albuquerque is booming, attracting scores of new residents and accompanying industries. As the motto says, it grows as it goes.

GEORGIA O'KEEFFE

American artists had been making pilgrimages to New Mexico for many years by the time Georgia O'Keeffe traveled there in 1928, but today, no artist's work is considered so emblematic of the region. She came seeking new inspiration, something beyond the concrete canyons and steel skyscrapers of New York City. In the Southwest she found natural analogues to those manmade structures—buttes and mesas, desert plains, and deep, dramatic skies. She also discovered the shapely adobe walls of buildings like Ranchos de Taos church, and the minute mysteries of bleached bones. In 1940 she purchased a house on Ghost Ranch, in the north of the state. A few years after her husband Alfred Stieglitz's death, in 1946 she moved to New Mexico permanently. A solitary person, she lived in relative isolation in the barren country, painting abstract desertscapes and capturing the minutiae of architecture, skulls, and flowers.

In 1997, 11 years after her death, much of Georgia O'Keeffe's work was given to the Georgia O'Keeffe Museum, in Santa Fe.

Arizona

The Grand Canyon State

Ditat Deus (God enriches)

Of all the sublime sights of the American West, none is perhaps as revelatory as a gaze into the Grand Canyon, where millions of years of erosion have exposed the prehistoric innards of the earth. It is a veritable novel of geologic formation, as if the Colorado River and its tributaries, in epic cursive, have inscribed the narratives of our planetary history. The exposed stratum at the bottom of the canyon is nearly 2 billion years old; other layers contain fossils of 500-million-year-old trilobites. For a young nation the Grand Canyon is an instructive glimpse at the colossal history that preceded the American experiment. Though it is but a gash on the map, we are but specks to the eons of stories it tells.

Long the homeland of the Havasupai people, the Grand Canyon went mostly unexplored by white Americans until a team led by John Wesley Powell traversed its entirety in 1869. By this time Arizona was already a territory of the United States, though it would not become a state for nearly another 50 years. The last of the contiguous 48 states to achieve statehood, Arizona finalized the general geographic shape of the nation and solidified the border with Mexico.

Today, that border is considered by many to be not solid enough. In 2005 Arizona governor Janet Napolitano declared the state's border counties to be in a state of emergency, due to masses of illegal immigrants, and the reputation of the state as a drug-smuggling portal. However, Arizona's history and customs are durably tied to Mexico. The region was Mexican land before it became a U.S. territory, and the southern portions of Arizona are profoundly Mexican-American. In 2003 there were more Hispanic births in Arizona than those of any other demographic.

Arizona is a land of change and fluctuation, where farms flourish in the desert, where prosperity seems at odds with the starkness of nature. In 1911 the completion of the Theodore Roosevelt Dam on the Salt River initiated an irrigation system that revolutionized the arid landscape. Once the top producer of cotton in the United States, Arizona still fields huge yields of the fluffy crop, as well as lettuce, hay, melons, and spinach, among other vegetables. Copper mining has long packed the state's purse, though today the service sector dominates the economy. The fastest-growing state in the Union, Arizona seems bound for continued abundance, but it must conserve its resources and adapt to its changing demographics. As the Grand Canyon shows, time transforms even the oldest and hardest of rocks.

At the base of that reddish strata, the Colorado River slowly continues to carve. Some 5 million people visit the Grand Canyon yearly.

Arizona State Facts

Full Name: State of Arizona
Meaning of Name: Disputed; either from the Basque phrase, *aritz onak*, meaning "good oaks," or from the O'odham phrase, *ali shonak*, meaning "small spring"
Admitted to the Union: February 14, 1912 (48th state)

Inhabitant: Arizonan
Capital City: Phoenix
Flower: Saguaro blossom
Tree: Palo verde
Bird: Cactus wren

Geography and Ecology

It is the heart of the American Southwest—a large, relatively deserted state sharing a long border with Mexico. East and north it sits flush against New Mexico and Utah, and touches Colorado at the Four Corners, on the Navajo Indian Reservation. Its western boundary with Nevada and California is

This plaque marks the conjunction of the Four Corners states.

mostly delineated by the twisting Colorado River, which, snaking south from the Grand Canyon, empties into the Gulf of California. The myriad rivers coursing through Arizona's arid terrain are instrumental in irrigating crops and hydrating the population. The Gila River spans southern Arizona, originating in western New Mexico, flowing along the Gila Mountains, and then down into the valley, where the Coolidge Dam stifles its water for irrigation. By the time it passes through the Gila River Indian Reservation, south of Phoenix, it is more of a stream than a river, but it eventually trickles into the Colorado River in the far west of the state. The Salt River, a tributary of the Gila River, is also extensively dammed, and passes through Phoenix. The Verde River, which flows southeast through the center of the state, before joining the Salt River, is similarly dammed and reserved for irrigation and drinking water.

Land of the Ponderosa and Saguaro

Known for its great swaths of desert terrain, Arizona also possesses large expanses of forested high country. Along and above the Mogollon Rim, which extends from central Arizona eastward to the New Mexico border, great stands of ponderosa pine cover the landscape. The Coconino National Forest, located at the northern edge of the Mogollon Rim, is the site of the San Francisco Peaks, tall mountains crowned by 12,637-foot Humphreys Peak, the highest point in Arizona. The majority of Arizona is basin and range topography, however—desert country of low valleys crossed by rocky ranges. The Sonoran Desert in southwestern Arizona is perhaps the state's most emblematic terrain and the only place in the world that supports the huge saguaro cactus. It also houses desert toads and sidewinders, rattlesnakes, and king snakes. Roadrunners sprint about, catching tarantulas and scorpions. Gila woodpeckers burrow nests in saguaro cacti, and elf owls utilize abandoned woodpecker holes for their own nests. Coyotes stalk jackrabbits, scavenge carrion, and gulp down the fruit of the prickly pear cactus.

Bipolar Weather

Arizona rises thousands of feet from its desert basins to its plateaus and forested mountains, which leads to a varied climate. The state is famous for warm winters and springs and scorching hot, dry summer days, which fade to cool summer nights. Such weather has attracted droves

West Mitten, East Mitten, and Merrick Butte loom hundreds of feet above the floor of Monument Valley, within the Navajo Reservation.

The saguaro cactus can grow to 40 feet and live for 150 years. Bats pollinate the cactus by drinking the nightly nectar of its blossoms.

of retirees in recent years, seeking to escape cold north-ern winters. This desert climate is common in southern Arizona, but in the north of the state, which is at a higher elevation, temperatures drop significantly—summers are mild, and winters are cold. Reflecting the bipolarity of the state's climate, the Phoenix metro area endures more days over 100° F than any other American city, while Flagstaff weathers more days below freezing than any other city in the contiguous 48 states. Precipitation is sparing, falling during winter cold fronts and as summer monsoons, which are punctuated by torrential thunderstorms.

The Grand Canyon State

Projectile points discovered in the American Southwest indicate the presence of the Clovis culture, migratory paleo-Indians who lived some 11,000 years ago. The Clovis culture gave way to the Archaic culture, who, it is believed, were engaging in rudimentary corn cultivation some 3,000 years ago. By the year 200 three distinct ancient cultures occupied the Arizona region simultaneously. The Ancient Pueblo people lived in adobe dwellings in the north of the state. The Mogollon culture occupied southeastern Arizona, amid a great swath of territory extending south into Mexico. The Hohokam people lived in central Arizona. All three cultures cultivated various crops utilizing irrigation canals and were distinctive craftspeople. Trade among these cultures and with Mesoamerican people is evident. By the 15th century all three groups had diminished; it is presumed that they were absorbed into more recent Indian cultures, including the Pueblo and the Pima. During this time the Navajo (Diné) and Apache tribes moved into northern Arizona.

Enter the Spaniards

In 1535 explorer Alvar Nuñez Cabeza de Vaca presumably passed through Arizona on his odyssey across the Southwest. In 1540 Francisco Vásquez de Coronado, leading a sizable group, traveled through Arizona, into New Mexico, and northwest to Kansas, searching for the Seven Cities of Gold. A lieutenant of the group became the first European to see the Grand Canyon. During the 1600s numerous Catholic missions were established—most prominent among the missionaries was Father Eusebio Kino, who successfully converted numerous Indians and explored and mapped the Southwest. The Spanish established Arizona's first white village at Tubac in 1772 and raised a fort at Tucson in 1776.

Mexican Victory and Defeat

In 1821 Arizona became Mexican land after the Mexican War of Independence. The Mexican government awarded land grants to their citizens to settle the region, but

In 1885 Phoenix housed roughly 3,500 people. Laid out on a north-south grid in the fertile Salt River Valley, the town utilized ancient irrigation canals dug by the Hohokam people. After the turn of the century, Phoenix's population boomed; today it is the fifth-largest city in the nation.

In 1540 a huge force of soldiers, Indians, monks, and African slaves followed Coronado deep into America on a fruitless search for gold.

"We are peopled from all states, as well as from Mexico, Spain, China, Japan, and many other countries. Since ancient times Indians have lived on our lands, or maybe I should say we have lived on theirs, but the important thing is that we share the land."

—Barry Goldwater (1909–98), five-term U.S. senator from Arizona and 1964 presidential candidate

Mexican sovereignty there was short-lived. Enduring persistent attacks from the Apaches, Mexican settlers also witnessed the arrival of American trappers and mountain men, who sought beavers in Arizona's rivers. In 1846 the United States and Mexico went to war. The Mormon Battalion held a bloodless standoff with Mexican forces at Tucson. The Treaty of Guadalupe-Hidalgo, signed in 1848, gave America the Arizona region north of the Gila River. In 1854 the United States paid $10 million for the remaining southern portion of Arizona.

The Apache leader Geronimo, in 1898, 12 years after his surrender to the U.S. Army. Legendary for his elusiveness and courage, he battled against Mexican and American conquest for nearly 30 years.

American Land

Southern Arizona and New Mexico seceded from the Union in 1861 to form the Arizona Territory of the Confederate States of America. The region witnessed the westernmost battle of the Civil War, at Picacho Pass, north of Tucson, where Union and Confederate forces fought to a draw. In 1864 the U.S. Army, led by Colonel Kit Carson, conquered the Navajo people at Canyon de Chelly, in the northwest of the state, brutally herding them on a 300-mile walk to the squalid reservation of Fort Sumner, New Mexico. Gold rushes led to Arizona boomtowns later in the 19th century. In 1877 the U.S. government created the Desert Land Act, which guaranteed immigrants 640 acres of land and caused a wave of new settlement in Arizona.

Still Growing

New Deal programs were instrumental in rescuing the state's agricultural areas during the Depression, and World War II placed a continuous demand on Arizona's copper, zinc, and lead mines. Numerous manufacturing businesses and military bases were also established to help the war effort, as the state was considered well-insulated from possible coastal attacks. Arizona was also the site of Japanese internment camps. After World War II the development of air-conditioning tamed Arizona's brutal summers, and the region's population soared. Today, Arizona continues to grow, though as the majority of state land is federally owned, the beautifully deserted spaces the state is known for should survive for many years to come.

Nevada

The Silver State

All For Our Country

It's a safe bet that when one hears the name Nevada, one thinks first of the florid neon of Las Vegas, of rattling roulette wheels and rows of slot machines, of crafty cardsharps and hapless losers. Or perhaps one thinks of burlesque and bawd—of sequined showgirls, grinning magicians, and easygoing entertainers. A place where intimations of money and sex glitter in gold and pink against the desert sky; where lovers can buy an easy wedding or a quick divorce; where one can win a princely ransom, or leave toting pauper's pockets.

Long before Sin City emerged like a shimmering oasis from the Las Vegas Valley, Nevada was a state for gamblers. In the 1800s migrants heading west to California had to push across the wastelands of the Great Basin before traversing the forbidding Sierra Nevada into the land of milk and honey. Where Nevada's Humboldt River ended, the Forty-Mile Desert began—a waterless stretch of scorched earth littered with discarded wagons, dead and bloated oxen, and the decaying corpses of unfortunate migrants. The Forty-Mile Desert was a dangerous bet, and though many travelers survived, plenty lost it all.

Years later, it was not what lay beyond Nevada that drew the masses, but what lay beneath it. Between 1859 and 1878, roughly $400 million worth of silver and gold was mined from the Comstock Lode in western Nevada. Today, mining remains prosperous, but it yields nothing close to the relative values of the 1800s. Now, it is the gleam of golden marquees and the rush of silver from slot machines that fill the state's coffers. Tourism is the backbone of the state economy—the casinos and resorts of Las Vegas, Reno, and Lake Tahoe entice travelers from all over the world.

The libertarian state government assesses no personal or corporate income tax and has taken lenient stances on marriage, divorce, and prostitution. Many counties in Nevada allow prostitution in the form of brothels. Though sex work is legal in neither Reno nor Las Vegas, escort services are ubiquitous and rarely prosecuted. Nevada's political preferences fluctuate—though the current governor is Republican, the Democratic Party is powerful in the state legislature, and one U.S. senator hails from each party. Despite being perhaps the most barren state in the Union, Nevada is growing in population, particularly in the Las Vegas area, where new neighborhoods consistently sprout from the sand. Odds are, new settlers will keep coming, but they must take heed—Nevada's always been a gamble.

Bright lights, big city: the Las Vegas Strip, home to many of the largest hotels and casinos in the world, is technically south of the city limits.

Nevada State Facts

Full Name: State of Nevada
Meaning of Name: Spanish for "snow-covered"; taken from the so-named Sierra Nevada mountains
Admitted to the Union: October 31, 1864 (36th state)
Inhabitant: Nevadan

Capital City: Carson City
Flower: Sagebrush
Tree: Piñon pine
Bird: Mountain bluebird

Geography and Ecology

It is a large, wedge-shaped state, its entire western and southern border obtusely angled against California. In the north it shares a straight boundary with Oregon and Idaho; in the east its flush border with Utah and Arizona is perplexed by the twisting Colorado River. The towering Sierra Nevada, from which the state takes its name, sits mostly west of Nevada, in California, but some ranges veer into west-central Nevada, near Lake Tahoe. The White Mountains of California also push ever so slightly into Nevada and contain the state's highest point, 13,146-foot Boundary Peak. The richly forested Spring Mountains rise west of Las Vegas. Called a sky island, the range is biologically diverse, containing isolated ecosystems that do not exist in the stark land below the mountains. The range's forests are composed of 37 species of trees, piñon pine, juniper, and mountain mahogany among them, as well as creosote bush and white bursage at lower elevations. In eastern Nevada the Snake Range looms above Great Basin National Park. Topped by Wheeler Peak, the Snake Range is home to stands of 3,000-year-old bristlecone pine. Cougars, bobcats, ermine, and ringtail cats live in this alpine country, as well as mule deer, marmots, and shrews. Northern goshawks glide through the sky and dive for rabbits and ground squirrels.

The Great Basin

The majority of Nevada lies within the Great Basin, a large, arid plateau alternately studded by mountain ranges and channeled by valleys. It is an endorheic region, meaning that any rivers flowing into the region are absorbed and will not flow out. Numerous lakes and sinks are the watersheds for Nevada's rivers. Pyramid Lake, in northwest Nevada, imbibes the Truckee River, which flows from Lake Tahoe. Slightly east lies the Carson Sink, a large dry lakebed into which flow irrigation canals and the Carson River. To the north of the Carson Sink lies the Humboldt Sink, which absorbs the Humboldt River. The longest river in the Great Basin, the Humboldt provided a route for the California Trail, which ferried 250,000 migrants to California. In southeastern Nevada the Colorado River demarcates the Nevada-Arizona border. In 1935 the completion of the Hoover Dam on the Colorado River created Lake Mead, the largest artificial lake and reservoir in the United States.

Hot and Dry

Cattle and sheep ranching and the cultivation of hay constitute Nevada's agricultural industry. Potatoes, onions, garlic, barley, and wheat are also cultivated. Adapting to the state's arid climate and barren terrain, Nevada's farms are situated in river valleys and intensely irrigated. Nevada's desert climate is apt for growing alfalfa hay, which the state ships to dairy farms in nearby states and exports to other countries. By and large, the Silver State experiences hot summers, though they vary in length. Northeast Nevada experiences short, hot summers and long, cold winters. In the west of the state, winters are lengthy but less cold, while summers are still brief and hot. Southern Nevada, on the other hand, has long, hot summers and short, mild winters. Lying in the rain shadow of the Sierra Nevada, the state experiences little rainfall, though snow falls liberally on the state's northern mountains during the winter.

Looking north at the Spring Mountains, named for their numerous springs—many of which seep below the sandstone crags of Red Rock, at right.

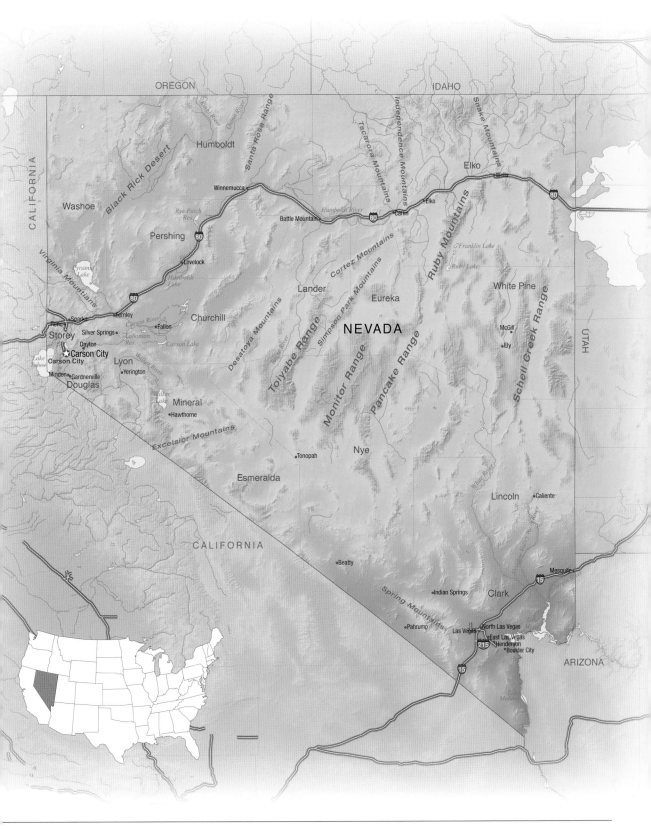

OREGON

IDAHO

CALIFORNIA

Owyhee River

Quinn River

Santa Rosa Range

Humboldt

Black Rock Desert

Washoe

Independence Mountains

Tscarora Mountains

Snake Mountains

Elko

Wells

Winnemucca

80

Rye Patch Res.

Battle Mountain

Humboldt River

Carlin

Elko

Pershing

80

Ruby Mountains

Franklin Lake

Lovelock

Humboldt Lake

Cortez Mountains

Ruby Lake

Virginia Mountains

Pyramid Lake

Lander

Eureka

White Pine

Simpson Park Mountains

NEVADA

Sparks

Fernley

Reno

Storey

Silver Springs

Carson River

Churchill

Fallon

Lahontan Res.

Desatoya Mountains

Reese River

McGill

Ely

Dayton

Carson City

Carson Lake

Toiyabe Range

Monitor Range

Pancake Range

Schell Creek Range

UTAH

Lake Tahoe

Lyon

Minden

Gardnerville

Walker River

Yerington

Douglas

Silver Lake

Mineral

Hawthorne

Excelsior Mountains

Nye

Tonopah

Lincoln

Caliente

Esmeralda

White River

CALIFORNIA

Beatty

Spring Mountains

Mesquite

15

Indian Springs

Clark

Pahrump

North Las Vegas

Las Vegas

East Las Vegas

215

Henderson

Boulder City

ARIZONA

15

Virgin River

Muddy

311

State History

Nevada

The Mountain States

The Silver State

Some 12,000 years ago paleo-Indians inhabited the Nevada area, eventually giving way to hunter-gatherer Archaic peoples. By the year 100 the Ancient Pueblos occupied the Pueblo Grande de Nevada—also known as the Lost City—which existed in southern Nevada until roughly 1150. An Ancient Pueblo population center, the Lost City stretched as far as 5 miles through the Moapa Valley, incorporating farms and villages of adobe houses. As the Ancient Pueblo declined, the Northern and Southern Paiute tribes settled in Nevada. The Northern Paiute occupied northwestern Nevada, living around desert wetlands, hunting rabbits and antelope, and

Jedediah Smith

gathering pine nuts and roots. The Northern Paiute battled the Washoe people and, utilizing horses, eventually subjugated them. The Southern Paiute lived in the Mojave Desert, in southern Nevada, and fought the nearby Navajo and Ute tribes.

Crossing the Wasteland

The solitary missionary Fray Francisco Garcés explored the southern Nevada region in 1775, blazing a trail on foot from the Colorado River to the Spanish missions on the California coast. In 1827, after having become the first Americans to traverse the Sierra Nevada, famed mountain man Jedediah Smith and a party of explorers continued

Virginia City, in 1875, when mining in the Comstock Lode began to decline. The 1858 discovery of silver in these hills attracted swarms of prospectors and miners, including a young Samuel Clemens, who first used his pen name, Mark Twain, in 1863 while writing for the local newspaper.

east across the bleak center of Nevada. Fourteen years later, the Bartleson-Bidwell Party—the first wagon team on the California Trail—trudged on foot across Nevada and into California. A handful of pioneers followed suit during the 1840s, including the ill-fated Donner Party, whose members became stranded in the Sierra Nevada during an autumn snowstorm and resorted to cannibalism to survive. The 1849 discovery of gold in California turned the trail across Nevada into a rugged highway for prospectors and migrants.

Silver and Statehood

In 1858 silver was discovered in Nevada, leading to the boomtown of Virginia City and initiating a multimillion-dollar mining industry. In order to unearth the unprecedented quantities of gold and silver, the mines dug into the Comstock Lode employed new techniques in nearly all facets of the mining and amalgamation process. Nevada became a U.S. territory in 1861, and on October 31, 1864, the federal government declared Nevada a state, just in time to provide a bounce in votes for President Abraham Lincoln during the tight 1864 election.

Growth in the Desert

Gambling, which was rife in mining towns, was outlawed in 1909. Its relegalization in 1931 transformed the state's economy. The expansion of Las Vegas made Nevada the fastest-growing state in the nation during the last half-century. Today, the state's population is still rising, but the growth is stretching the state's resources thin. Water shortages loom on the horizon, and Nevada is scrambling to establish sustainable water technology that will conserve the environment and serve the population. As Nevadans are aware, one cannot overcome the desert, one can only adapt. Just as any gambler knows—you can't beat the house.

The Hoover Dam generates more than 4 billion kilowatt hours of electricity annually and distributes it to Nevada, Arizona, and Southern California.

FROM OASIS TO SIN CITY

In the 1800s Mexicans journeying along the Old Spanish Trail would drink from the springs that bubbled up in the Las Vegas Valley. The natural aquifers fertilized greenery on the desert plain—thus, the area was dubbed Las Vegas, or "the meadows." The glimmering Las Vegas of today can be traced to the 1931–36 construction of the Hoover Dam, which brought an influx of workers into the area. In 1941 mobster Bugsy Siegel came to Las Vegas, enticed by the city's legal gambling. Siegel bought a stake in the construction of a luxury hotel and casino south of the Las Vegas city limits, on what would become the Las Vegas Strip. Taking control of the project, Siegel christened the building "The Flamingo," after his long-legged girlfriend. The hotel opened in 1946; Siegel was shot to death a year later. Struggling initially, by 1947 the casino had become a success, mounting lavish stage shows and luring droves of tourists. Soon, more casinos and megaresorts rose on the Las Vegas strip—Sin City was born. Today, nearly 37 million annual travelers seek to fill their cups with gold from the oasis of Las Vegas.

Washington

The Evergreen State

Alki (By and by)

There are rain forests in Washington that are among the most biodiverse ecosystems on the planet—deep, dark, wet timberlands of sitka spruce and western hemlock reaching hundreds of feet into the silvery sky, where rain clouds gather and shower down constant moisture. In these forests, mosses clothe trunks, rocks, and anything that doesn't move. Fallen, decaying trees become nurse logs—spongy stages for the drama of small growth, where seedlings root and imbibe water and nutrients, before growing to replace their fallen guardians. So these evergreen ecosystems replenish themselves—the old clearing a path for the new.

Drive the highways of Washington, and you will also see plenty of huge downed trunks hauled on flatbeds—logging and lumber have long been prime industries of the Cascade region. In the early 1900s Washington was considered a wild west of lumberjacks—hardworking and even harder drinking men who felled trees by day and caroused in skid-row towns by night. Mythology aside, it was grueling, dangerous work, and early 20th-century lumber camps were the sites of many violent labor disputes. Whether among loggers in the state's interior, or dockworkers on the coast, Washington developed a powerful labor movement—one that often raised the ire of both the local and federal government.

The Evergreen State is still a progressive enclave, especially in the communities west of the Cascade Range. The metropolis of Seattle, home to some 3.2 million people, is a national cultural center—theater and performance poetry thrive in the city, and the Seattle music scene became prominent worldwide in the 1990s. Politically, the Democratic Party dominates the state—the legislature has a Democratic majority, and the governor is a Democrat, as are both U.S. senators, and the majority of the state's federal representatives. Also, Washington's two U.S. senators are women—it is the only state so distinguished.

Logging remains an important industry, and the fertile plains of eastern Washington have made it one of the chief agricultural states in the Union. It is a top producer of potatoes, cherries, pears, carrots, and lentils, among other crops. Washington is also a technological center—its computer software industry is important worldwide. Committed to the concerns of its billion-dollar corporations, Washington has lately focused on the needs of its environment as well, and is trying to preserve its natural wealth for future generations. Thus, like the seedling from the nurse log, a new Washington state continually grows from the old.

The rain forests of the Olympic Wilderness, in western Washington, host epic growth and decay and house numerous rare plants and animals.

Washington State Facts

Full Name: State of Washington
Meaning of Name: Named after George Washington, the first president of the United States
Admitted to the Union: November 11, 1889 (42nd state)
Inhabitant: Washingtonian

Capital City: Olympia
Flower: Coast rhododendron
Tree: Western hemlock
Bird: Willow goldfinch

Geography and Ecology

It is the northwest cornerstone of the contiguous United States, bordering Canada along the historically controversial 49th parallel. The Snake River, in the southeast, interrupts the flush eastern boundary with Idaho. In the south the twisting Columbia River demarcates much of the border with Oregon. In the west the Pacific Ocean washes upon the rugged Washington coast and, at Puget Sound, plunges deep into the state's northwestern interior. A vast bay formed by glaciers tens of thousands of years ago, Puget Sound is a complex series of channels and harbors amid numerous green islands. Together, its major cities—Seattle and Tacoma—constitute one of the largest container ports in North America, and the largest ferry fleet in the United States serves its myriad islands.

Rain Forests and Volcanoes

The rugged Cascade Range divides the state, rising in great peaks from Canada to California. The major mountains of the Washington portion of the range—Mt. Baker, Glacier Peak, Mt. Rainier, Mt. St. Helens, and Mt. Adams—are active volcanoes, though only Mt. St. Helens has been actively erupting, and with disastrous results in 1980. Mt. Rainier, at 14,410 feet, is the highest peak in the Cascade Range. Dominating the Washington landscape, it can be seen from hundreds of miles away. The Cascades divide the state geographically, ecologically, and climatically—west of the range, mild, humid sea air

Mount Rainier, looming southeast of Seattle, wears 35 square miles of glaciers and snowfields, which feed many of Washington's rivers.

supports great expanses of temperate rain forest. Richly diverse, these dense woodlands sustain more biomass per acre than any terrestrial habitat worldwide. Composed of huge conifers, as well as maples, alders, and cottonwoods, the rain forests are home to elk, black-tailed deer, Pacific tree frogs, northern spotted owls, and raccoons. Black bears feast on herbs, berries, bark, bugs, and salmon, and cougars and bobcats slink through the mossy undergrowth. Many of Washington's rain forests are federal land and protected as national forests, though large portions are privately owned by logging companies.

East of the Mountains

East of the Cascades much of Washington is semiarid, short-grass prairie, as well as arid desert. The Yakima River flows southeast through the center of the state—it irrigates the dry country around it, creating rich farmland. The mighty Columbia River imbibes the Yakima River in southeast Washington. An immense river, ferrying more water into the Pacific than any other North American

watercourse, the Columbia is dammed at multiple locations for hydroelectric power and irrigation—its water fertilizes hundreds of thousands of acres of farmland in central Washington. These dams—the colossal Grand Coulee Dam among them— are essential to the state's economic infrastructure but also interrupt the traffic of fish in the river. Numerous species of fish swim the Columbia River, including salmon and rainbow trout, which travel upriver to their natal streams to spawn.

A Climate Divided

The Cascades throw a rain shadow across eastern Washington, stifling Pacific air masses and containing precipitation within the western portion of the state. Thus, eastern Washington is significantly drier, with hotter summers and colder winters, and less precipitation year-round. West of the mountains summers are cool and winters are mild, albeit wet and constantly foggy and cloudy. High elevations west of the Cascades experience considerable winter snowfall.

An irrgation canal delivers water to apple and pear orchards in the Yakima River valley. Washington's tree fruit is eaten nationwide.

The Evergreen State

Archaeologists estimate that Washington was among the first populated zones in North America—human remains in the state date back 13,000 years. As thousands of years passed, hunter-gatherer paleo-Indian cultures gave way to numerous tribes along the Pacific coast and throughout inland Washington. The coastal tribes lived off the sea and the land, catching fish and shellfish and using large cedar canoes to hunt seals and whales. Deer, elk, and bear were also hunted. These tribes lived in cedar longhouses and practiced ornate carving, including the crafting of totem poles. Many of the coastal tribes still occupy traditional lands—the Makah live on the northwest corner of the Olympic Peninsula, and the Quileute, Hoh, and Quinault occupy reservations on Washington's west coast. The Lumm, Swinomish, and Puyallup live along Puget Sound. Inland, powerful tribes occupied the state's

eastern plains—the Yakama lived on the Columbia River plateau and fished the rich stocks of salmon swimming upriver. The Colville occupied the banks of the northern Columbia River. Today, both tribes occupy large reservations in eastern Washington.

Mariners Offshore

In 1592, while sailing for Spain, the Greek captain Juan de Fuca entered the narrow outlet of the Puget Sound. No European set foot in Washington, however, until Bruno de Heceta rowed ashore at what is now Grenville Bay in 1775. He claimed the land for Spain, but the British were angling after the territories as well. In 1778 British explorer James Cook extensively mapped the Pacific Northwest coast. Four years later American captain Robert Gray sailed 13 miles up the Columbia River,

Named after the local Suquamish and Duwamish chief, Seattle saw its first white settlers—the Denny party—in 1851. This 1891 map shows a sprawling city, only 18 months after the Great Seattle Fire. The extensive post-fire reconstruction transformed Seattle into Washington's metropolis.

Makah whalers in the early 1900s, towing a harpooned whale to shore, where it will be harvested for its meat, oil, bones, and sinew.

claiming the surrounding land for the newly formed United States of America.

Pioneers Roll In

In 1805 Lewis and Clark canoed the Columbia River to the Oregon coast. The Adams-Onís Treaty of 1819 saw Spain cede the Northwest to the United States. Great Britain still claimed the land, but in 1846 the Treaty of Oregon settled the dispute, partitioning the region and establishing the northern border of the United States, and what is now Canada, at the 49th parallel. As pioneers streamed into Oregon along the Oregon Trail, many journeyed north and settled around Puget Sound. In 1855 the Yakama Indians battled miners, settlers, and eventually the U.S. Army before being confined to a reservation.

Lumberjacks in 1902, skidding logs using a steam train. Logging has long been a profitable, albeit dangerous, industry in Washington.

MT. ST. HELENS ERUPTS

On the morning of May 18, 1980, Mt. St. Helens, a 9,677-foot peak in Washington's Cascade Range, erupted catastrophically, killing 57 people and roughly 7,000 big game animals. It destroyed everything within a 250-square-mile area, including 250 homes, 47 bridges, 15 miles of railroad tracks, and 185 miles of highway. It is the largest eruption in recorded American history—the energy released was tens of thousands times that of an atomic bomb. Within a few days ash from the eruption had spread as far away as Oklahoma and Minnesota. Volcanologists had been strenuously monitoring the peak for months—several small eruptions and a giant bulge in the mountain caused by surging magma preceded the disaster. Volcanologist David A. Johnston, stationed 6 miles from the volcano, was the first to report the eruption, radioing, "Vancouver! Vancouver! This is it!" moments before being engulfed in the blast. His unfound remains were presumably buried beneath the 23-square-mile avalanche. Though horrifically destructive, the blast of Mt. St. Helens has enabled scientists to more accurately predict, and suitably prepare for, future volcanic eruptions.

Mt. St. Helens sent ash plumes 60,000 feet into the sky.

Evergreen

Washington gained statehood in 1889; loggers were already harvesting the rain forests, and the ports of Puget Sound swarmed with trade. As the 20th century progressed, shipbuilding and aircraft construction emerged as major industries. In 1941 the Grand Coulee Dam, the largest dam in the world at the time, was erected on the Columbia River. The 21st century finds Washington both prosperous and stable, home to some of America's wealthiest corporations, most progressive politics, and richest biodiversity. If it continues to balance the weight of both economic and environmental necessities, it will surely remain Evergreen.

Oregon

The Beaver State

Alis Volat Propriis (She flies with her own wings)

"Great joy in camp," explorer William Clark wrote in his journal on the evening of November 7, 1805, "we are in View of the Ocian [*sic*]." In reality, Lewis and Clark's Corps of Discovery had seen the estuary of the Columbia River, but they were near enough to the ocean to celebrate heartily—their 2-year voyage from Pittsburgh to the Pacific coast had almost come to fruition. A little over a month later, the crew was encamped at Fort Clatsop, on foggy headlands south of the mouth of the Columbia River and east of the wintry ocean. They spent a brutal winter there, weathering cold rain and wet sea wind and trading with the local Clatsop Indians before embarking back upriver, across the mountains and the plains, to the United States of America.

A little more than a half-century later, that damp and dreamed-of destination was itself one of the United States. In the intervening years it had become a promised land for American pioneers, who traveled on wagon wheels and foot for the same great distance followed by Lewis and Clark, seeking new lives in the American West. Before that, it had been an Eden for wealthy fur traders, who dispatched hordes of trappers into the Oregon wilderness to gather pelts from the musky, industrious animal that gives the state its nickname.

Today, the Beaver State is home to some 3.7 million people. The agricultural bounty of the Willamette Valley, which sustained the migrants of the mid-1900s, still supports the state today. The fertile floodplains yield untold bushels of raspberries, blackberries, blueberries, strawberries, and cherries, as well as beans, broccoli, and cauliflower. Brewers nationwide use Willamette Valley hops, and wine-making has blossomed in the region, with local vineyards earning worldwide acclaim. The valley is also a top producer of Christmas trees, grass seed, hazelnuts, and flowers.

Logging, a longtime industry in Oregon's rain forests, has diminished in recent years, due to overharvesting and environmental protection. High-technology industries have bolstered the state economy. Politically, the state generally allies with the Democratic Party—the current governor is a Democrat, as are the majority of the state's U.S. representatives. A prosperous area of diverse landforms, progressive politics, and cutting-edge technology, the Beaver State is as busy as its namesake.

Once a travelers' way station on the banks of the Willamette River, Portland is now a diverse, progressive metropolis of more than 600,000 people.

Oregon State Facts

Full Name: State of Oregon
Meaning of Name: Unknown; may be derived from the misspelled phrase *ouaricon-sint*, indicating the "Ouisiconsink" (Wisconsin) River on an 18th-century French map
Admitted to the Union: February 14, 1859 (33rd state)

Inhabitant: Oregonian
Capital City: Salem
Flower: Oregon grape
Tree: Douglas fir
Bird: Western meadowlark

Geography and Ecology

It possesses one of the most picturesque coastlines in the world—362 miles of evergreen promontories overlooking the roaring Pacific, where towering stacks of rock project from the coastal floor. To the north of Oregon, the powerful Columbia River defines much of the border with Washington. In the east, the sinuous Snake River demarcates roughly half the boundary with Idaho. In the south, California and Nevada border Oregon along the 42nd parallel. Oregon's beaches are entirely public land, and 320 miles of the coastline are preserved as the Oregon Coast National Wildlife Refuge Complex. The area is rich in wildlife. Northern elephant and harbor seals and California and Steller sea lions live along the coast. Gray, humpback, and killer whales are seen often; sperm, minke, and blue whales occasionally appear. Harbor and Dall's porpoises swim along the coast, and bottlenose dolphins cavort far offshore. Tide pools shelter numerous invertebrates, including sea stars, sea anemones, sponges, mussels, limpets, crabs, and sea urchins.

Mountains and Craters

The rolling and heavily forested mountains of Oregon's Coast Range flank the seashore, stifling the turbulent, rainy marine weather and enabling the Willamette Valley, east of the mountains, to enjoy a pleasant growing season. East of the Willamette Valley, the Cascade Range rises in great volcanic peaks, including Mt. Hood, at 11,239 feet, Mt. Jefferson, at 10,497 feet, and the Three Sisters— three adjacent summits that all rise above 10,000 feet. In southern Oregon Mt. Mazama rises to 8,159 feet but it has no peak to speak of—it blew off during a tumultuous eruption some 7,000 years ago. Today the caldera atop Mt. Mazama holds Crater Lake, the deepest lake in the United States. Bottoming out at 1,949 feet, Crater Lake attracts droves of tourists and is protected as Oregon's only national park.

Watercourses and Barren Land

The mighty Columbia River carries sea traffic upriver to Oregon's ports, and salmon to their spawning grounds.

Near Portland it absorbs the Willamette River, which begins in the Cascades and flows north, irrigating the Willamette Valley before winding through Portland and into the Columbia. East of the Cascades the Deschutes River also flows north into the Columbia, irrigating the arid country of central Oregon. A rapid river, the Deschutes is home to a unique type of rainbow trout and is a fly-fishing mecca. The Owyhee River curls through southeastern Oregon and drains into the Snake River. It is dammed to irrigate potato farms in the region. South-central Oregon is part of the Great Basin, and thus arid desert. Rivers flowing through this barren region have no outlet to the sea—they drain into the area's alkali lakes.

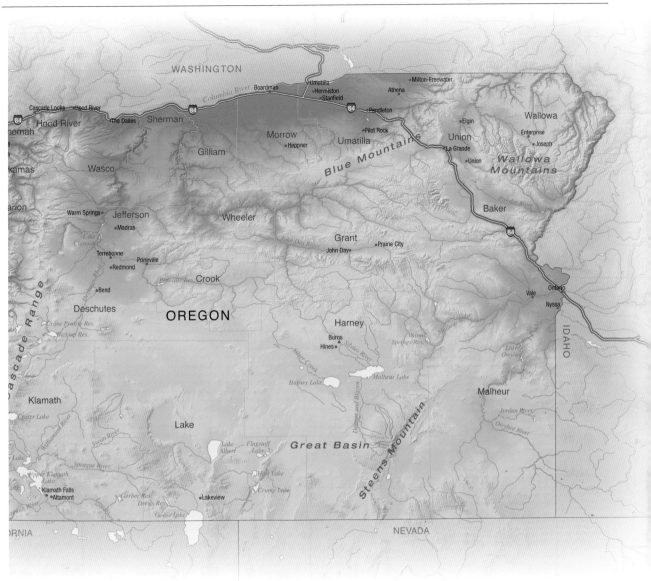

Wet and Dry

Western Oregon is predominantly wet year-round, though the Coast Range creates a rain shadow for the Willamette Valley, allowing it drier, more pleasant weather. East of the Cascades precipitation is sparing, in some cases to the extreme, with parts of the Harney Basin receiving only 6 inches of rain per year. Temperatures are moderate in the wet western regions, with cool summers and generally mild, rainy, foggy winters with snow at high elevations. East of the Cascades winters are cold and summers are hot and dry.

Filled mostly by snowfall, Crater Lake is one of the clearest, purest lakes in the world.

The Beaver State

In 1938, at Fort Rock Cave in barren central Oregon, anthropologist Luther Cressman found dozens of 10,000-year-old sage-bark sandals. The paleo-Indians who had worn this ancient footwear gave way, over millenia, to numerous tribes occupying diverse settlements. The Bannock were a horse culture of the southeastern Oregon basin. The Klamath lived around the Upper Klamath Lake and were skilled fishermen. The Nez Perce occupied large villages in northeast Oregon, on the Columbia River Plateau, migrating east and west to hunt and fish. The Chinook lived along the lower and middle Columbia River, in communities of cedar plank houses. They were skilled at fishing and whale hunting. The Kalapuya lived inland, along the rivers that coursed between the Cascades and the Coast Range. Today, Oregon's tribes live on seven reservations, scattered throughout the state.

Celilo Falls was an ancient fishing and trading site for Oregon's Indians, who netted countless salmon from scaffolds above the roaring water. The Dalles Dam, completed in 1957, permanently submerged the falls.

Looking northeast at bustling Portland, 1890. Mt. Hood looms due east. To the north is Mt. St. Helens, 90 years before it blew its top.

By Sea and by Land

Spanish galleons visited the region as far back as the late 16th century, and some may have landed or wrecked on the Oregon shore. In 1778 the British captain James Cook landed at Cape Foulweather on the central coast, and in 1792 American captain Robert Gray sailed his ship, *Columbia*, up the river that now bears its name. A little over a decade later, the Corps of Discovery boated down the Columbia and passed a rough Oregon winter. Lewis and Clark hoped a trading ship could be chartered to ferry the party back east, but none arrived.

At the End of the Oregon Trail

Following on the heels of Lewis and Clark were fur traders sent by John Jacob Astor, who established Fort Astoria, the first permanent American settlement on the Pacific Ocean. In the 1840s migrants traveling the Oregon Trail settled the Columbia River plateau and the Willamette Valley. In 1850 the U.S. Congress enacted the Donation Land Claim Act, granting 160 acres to every unmarried adult white male citizen, and 320 acres to every couple that arrived in Oregon before December of the year. This act coincided with efforts to push Oregon's tribes onto reservations.

Politically Polarized

Admitted as a state in 1859, Oregon sent troops to the Union side during the Civil War. In the 1880s the Northern Pacific Railroad linked to Portland, conveying droves of settlers to the region. The early 1900s saw increased immigration to the area, and also backlashes of anti-immigration sentiment. Simultaneously, the Progressive movement initiated populist, anti-corporate politics. Still progressive, the Beaver State is also politically polarized—its liberal, urban population often vies against conservative rural communities. Oregon's divisions are aptly summed up by the state's competing mottos. "She flies with her own wings" has long been the official motto, but in 1861 and 1957, the state's watchwords became "the Union." A proposal to make that change again was struck down in 1999.

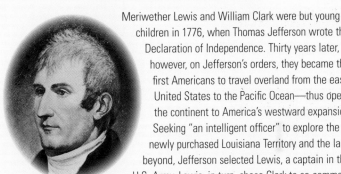

THE CORPS OF DISCOVERY

Meriwether Lewis and William Clark were but young children in 1776, when Thomas Jefferson wrote the Declaration of Independence. Thirty years later, however, on Jefferson's orders, they became the first Americans to travel overland from the eastern United States to the Pacific Ocean—thus opening the continent to America's westward expansion. Seeking "an intelligent officer" to explore the newly purchased Louisiana Territory and the lands beyond, Jefferson selected Lewis, a captain in the U.S. Army. Lewis, in turn, chose Clark to co-command the expedition. The first departure point was Pittsburgh, on August 31, 1803, and only one of the 33-member Corps of Discovery perished during the next 3 years of hard travel, on land and water, with no aid from the government or anyone back east. Their relationships with the various Indian tribes of the interior were alternately tense and gracious, and came to violence only once, when two Blackfeet were killed during a midnight skirmish. The mission documented myriad new animals and plants, samples of which were liberally gathered for the curious Jefferson. On one occasion the president delightedly opened a recently delivered box to find a live prairie dog scurrying around inside.

Meriwether Lewis

William Clark

California

The Golden State

Eureka

"California is a garden of Eden," Woody Guthrie sang in the 1930s, "a paradise to live in or see. But believe it or not, you won't find it so hot, if you ain't got the do re mi." It was the time of the Dust Bowl migration, when 200,000 refugees from the blighting dust storms of the Great Plains streamed into California, seeking work, shelter, and a new start. They hoped California held salvation—it had been the promised land before, back in the mid-1800s, when pioneers braved the hazards of the California Trail to reach the goldfields and fertile valleys of the Pacific seaboard. But Depression-era California was no longer the frontier—in less than a century, it had become home to more than 5 million people, all in need of work. More often than not the Dust Bowl migrants found unemployment, rude shelter, poverty, and more depression. What jobs existed were harsh and meagerly paid. Still, the migrants poured in, as they do today. The Golden State remains a promised land.

The most populous state in the Union, California is home to more than 38.8 million people. Soaring immigration in recent years has given the state nearly as many Hispanics as non-Hispanics. Its population is remarkably diverse—more than 200 languages are spoken in California, and it has more Latinos, Asian Americans, and American Indians than any other state. Historically home to numerous Indian tribes, California was a Spanish and then Mexican province before it joined the United States, and varied narratives are evident in its population, architecture, and culture. Much of Southern California is built in the Spanish Mission style. California cuisine is strongly influenced by Asian and Mexican flavors, and the state is the birthplace of fast food as it is known today.

The land is as diverse as its people—volcanic mountains and temperate rain forest in the north give way to fertile valleys in the center of the state and desert in the south. California's agricultural industry is the largest in the United States, and the state possesses one of the 10 largest economies in the world. Politically, California leans Democratic, but it has elected prominent Republican governors. Through all its migrations and fluctuations, the Golden State remains the object and subject of innumerable quests. Some come for a job and a home, others for fortune and fame. If you ain't got the do re mi, well, many still believe it can be found in California.

The world's longest bridge upon its completion in 1937, the Golden Gate Bridge spans 8,981 feet across the mouth of the San Francisco Bay.

California State Facts

Full Name: State of California
Meaning of Name: Derived from the name of a mythical paradise inhabited by black Amazons, as recounted by Spanish writer García Ordóñez Rodríguez de Montalvo
Admitted to the Union: September 9, 1850 (31st state)

Inhabitant: Californian
Capital City: Sacramento
Flower: California poppy
Tree: California redwood
Bird: California quail

Geography and Ecology

The third-largest state in the Union, California occupies roughly 840 miles of the Pacific coast of the United States. In the north Oregon sits squarely atop the Golden State; in the east, beyond the Sierra Nevada, the state of Nevada nestles into California's crook. Arizona lies across the Colorado River in the southeast. Mexico's Baja California sits to the south, across the national border. In the west is the wild blue Pacific, teeming with rare and beautiful sea life. Along the California coast and veering inland, the San Andreas Fault seams the state—its transforming plates have caused numerous destructive earthquakes, and geologists speculate that another big one is nigh.

Plentiful Peaks

Towering mountains loom above the state. The Klamath Mountains range from southern Oregon into northwest California and support unique flora, including Lawson's cypress, foxtail pine, and kalmiopsis. The volcanic Cascades form the spine of north-central California, crowned by the picturesque Mt. Shasta, a dormant volcano that touches the sky at 14,179 feet. The Coast Ranges loom above the Pacific Ocean all the way to Southern California and are home to the tallest trees in the world, the California redwood, which can grow to heights of nearly 400 feet and live for more than 2,000 years. The base can be as thick as 30 feet. A popular tourist attraction, one of the last "tunnel trees," with a tunnel carved through the base, fell during a storm in late 2016. Rising along the eastern border of California, down into the center of the state, is the Sierra Nevada, the historical obstacle for migrants and gold rushers. Jagged, snowy peaks, the Sierra Nevada is home to Mt. Whitney, the highest point in the contiguous United States, at 14,505 feet.

Desert Lands

Less than 80 miles east of the highest point in the lower 48 United States is the lowest point in North America, Death Valley. Sunken, scorching, and deserted, it is the site of a prehistoric inland sea and bottoms out at 282 feet below sea level. It lies within the Mojave Desert, which stretches across southeastern California, into Nevada, Utah, and Arizona. The rare Joshua tree, a species of yucca with an acrobatically twisted trunk and spheres of spiny leaves, thrives in the Mojave Desert.

Agricultural Paradise

Plunging south, from the Cascades to Southern California, between the Coast Ranges and the Sierra Nevada, is California's Central Valley. Its northern section is called the Sacramento Valley; its southern portion is the San Joaquin Valley. Linking the two regions is the delta created by the San Joaquin and Sacramento rivers, which irrigate their respective portions of the Central Valley. Referred to as the "fruit basket of the world," the Central Valley is the most profitable agricultural center in the United States, and the nation's top producer of tomatoes, grapes, almonds, cotton, asparagus, and apricots.

Picturesque on the surface, Monterey Bay is home to diverse and abundant sea life and is the site of the 11,800-foot-deep Monterey Canyon, where bizarre creatures thrive in the cold, black depths.

OREGON
IDAHO

Yreka • Montague
Siskiyou
Weed
Mount Shasta
Dunsmuir • McCloud
Burney
Lassen
Lewiston
Redding
Anderson
Cottonwood
Shasta
Red Bluff
Los Molinos
Corning
Orland
Hamilton City • Magalia
Chico • Paradise
Glenn
Willows
Butte
Biggs • Palermo
Oroville
Colusa
Colusa • Live Oak
Gridley • Yuba
Sutter
Williams
Lucerne
Clearlake Oaks
Lower Lake
Lake
Calistoga
Windsor
Santa Rosa
Napa
Vallejo
San Rafael
San Francisco
Berkeley
Oakland
Alameda
Hayward
San Mateo
Redwood City
San Mateo
Boulder Creek
Santa Cruz
Marina
Monterey
Soledad

Modoc
Alturas
Pit River

Tule Lake
Clear Lake
Goose Lake

NEVADA

Susanville
Westwood
Chester
Greenville
Plumas
Portola
Sierra
Nevada
Placer
Nevada City
Colfax
Foresthill
Auburn

El Dorado
Pollock Pines
Alpine
Amador
Sutter Creek
Jackson
Ione
Calaveras
San Andreas
Tuolumne
Angels Camp
Twain Harte
Linden
Jamestown
Sonora

CALIFORNIA

Mariposa
Mono
Mammoth Lakes

Madera
Bishop
Big Pine

Lone Pine
Inyo

Giant sequoias rule the Giant Forest in Sequoia National Park. The bark of the giant sequoia can reach 3 feet thick at the base of the tree.

Pacific Ocean

NEVADA

ARIZONA

MEXICO

Cool, Hot, and Dry

The climate of California varies widely, according to its landforms and latitude. In the northwest a temperate climate prevails, with warm summers and cool, rainy winters. Much of the state is blessed with a Mediterranean climate of hot, dry summers and cool winters, spattered with occasional rain. The state's mountains gather snow in the winter. In recent years dry conditions have led to numerous, damaging wildfires in Southern California.

The Golden State

Anthropologists have determined that the Arlington Springs Man, excavated in 1959–60 on Santa Rosa Island, off the coast of Santa Barbara, lived roughly 13,000 years ago. The location of the remains on one of the Channel Islands indicates that California's earliest settlers could negotiate the Pacific Ocean; indeed, many of the myriad tribes that evolved in California over millennia were skilled seafarers. The population of California, by the time of European contact, was perhaps the most diverse of any region in the United States. Numerous tribes occupied coastal and inland California, adapting to the array of landforms in the region. The Chumash lived in Southern California, from what is now Los Angeles north to San Luis Obispo, and settled three of the Channel Islands. Talented fishermen and mariners, they also hunted and gathered for food. They were skilled basketmakers and craftspeople and developed a unique cosmology, which they recorded in rock paintings. Some speculate that at some point, the Polynesians may have visited the Chumash and perhaps inspired their uniquely designed canoes. The Tongva people lived south of the Chumash and were also seafarers. The Mohave people occupied the arid desert that bears their name. The Ohlone people called the San Francisco and Monterey Bay areas home, fishing the sea and hunting elk, antelope, and deer. They constructed villages of domed huts made with woven rushes, and redwood houses. The territory of the Pomo was coastal northern California and inland. They lived in associated bands, fishing, hunting, and gathering for food. Their mythology is particularly well known today, especially tales involving the wily trickster and creator god Coyote.

San Francisco in 1847, less than a year after it was occupied and renamed by the United States during the Mexican-American War. Previously dubbed Yerba Buena, after an aromatic herb abundant in the region, the city would soon explode in population due to the California Gold Rush.

A Pomo woman cooks acorns outside her woven-cane hut in the early 1900s. Today, some 5,000 Pomo occupy northwestern California.

European Exploration

Beginning in the early 16th century, Spanish and English vessels explored the California coast. In the 1530s Spanish expeditions—some joined by Hernán Cortés, conqueror of the Aztecs—journeyed into the state seeking the fabled Seven Cities of Cibola, which were supposedly paved in gold and silver. Legends also recounted tales of a land called California, peopled exclusively by black Amazons and ruled by a queen named Califia. These storied locales were never found. In September of 1542 Juan Rodríguez Cabrillo landed at San Diego Bay and claimed the land for Spain. The English navigator Sir Francis Drake also apparently claimed California for England after sailing into one of its harbors, but no record exists of exactly which harbor he navigated into. Over the coming years numerous Spanish vessels explored and mapped the California shore. The British captain James Cook mapped the entirety of the West Coast in 1778.

The Mission System

In 1697 the Spanish, having long settled the colony of New Spain in what is now Mexico, established the Misión de Nuestra Señora de Loreto Conchó in Baja California. Missions were soon planted farther north,

EUREKA!

The Mexican-American War had not officially ended when, in January of 1848, gold was discovered at Sutter's Mill in the hills east of Sacramento. The news of gold in California spread around the world like a fever. First, Californians statewide hastened toward the California goldfields, but as the news spread in the early days of 1849, hordes of Americans, as well as Oregonians, Hawaiians, Mexicans, Peruvians, New Zealanders, Australians, and Chinese sensed destiny and set off for California. They came by sea and by land, risking injury, disease, and death, for the dream of the riches California held. For many of these earliest rushers—the roughly 90,000 "Forty-niners"—the dreams would be realized. Six months of gold panning could yield the equivalent of six years worth of ordinary wages. Many migrants also became wealthy as businesspeople serving the boomtowns. However, for most gold rushers, the risk was not worth the reward. As the years went on, and the gold decreased, the individual miner lost out to large corporations capable of extracting hard-to-find ore. By 1855 the California Gold Rush was over. It had completely transformed the region. Some 300,000 people had moved to the state, turning hamlets into cities and transforming California from a frontier wilderness into a place of worldwide renown. In 1850, only two years after it was taken away from Mexico, California became the 31st state in the Union.

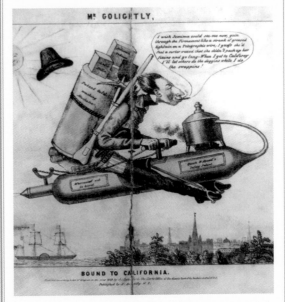

An 1849 cartoon satirizing the fervor of the Forty-niners—this ecstatic salesman rides a rocket west to hardware store heaven.

In 1891, 110 years after its founding by the Spanish, Los Angeles was sprawling. The discovery of oil in the region a year later pushed the population to 100,000 by 1900. Today, the metropolis of Los Angeles is home to nearly 3.9 million people.

and by the mid-1700s, 21 Spanish missions existed in Alta California, as California was then known. In 1768, in the wake of the Seven Years War, King Carlos III expelled Jesuit missionaries from New Spain and installed Franciscans instead, led by Fray Junípero Serra. Responsible for seven missions on the California coast, Fray Serra was a zealous, fiery preacher and a hardy explorer who made it his life's work to convert California's Indians to Christianity. Though he did what he thought was best for the Indians, the mission system subjected them to brutal slave labor and violent punishment for disobedience of mission laws. Few Indians within the mission system lived long, healthy lives.

Mexican Territory

To secure their presence in Alta California against the incursions of English and Russian navies, the Spanish built numerous forts, called presidios. They also awarded land grants to citizens of New Spain willing to ranch livestock in Alta California. These prosperous ranches became keystones of the Alta Californian economy. In 1821 Mexico won its

THE 1906 SAN FRANCISCO EARTHQUAKE

In less than a year, gold-seeking Forty-niners transformed San Francisco from a port village into a burgeoning city; in roughly four days, the 1906 San Francisco earthquake and its attendant inferno turned it all to rubble. It occurred at 5:12 in the morning of April 18, when the San Andreas Fault ruptured for 296 miles north and south of the city. The epicenter of the earthquake was just south of San Francisco, and the effect was catastrophic—the structurally fragile buildings of the city crumbled amid the shaking. Even more destructive was the infrastructure that was crippled—gas mains broke, inciting fires that ripped through the rubble as if it were kindling. Water mains also fractured, impeding firefighters' ability to battle the blazes. Other fires were sparked by the firefighters' attempts to quell the flames by using dynamite to create firebreaks, and many blazes were caused by arson, as property insurance at the time promised restitution only for fire, not for earthquake damage. All in all, it was chaos and inferno—roughly 80 percent of the city was obliterated, 20,000 people displaced, and a reported 700 people killed, though it is believed that the figure underestimates the death toll considerably. The aftermath of the earthquake was no better—soldiers sent to secure the town shot and killed an estimated 500 people for the crime of looting, although many of them may have only been seeking their own possessions. The city was rebuilt hurriedly and poorly, though in coming years the scientific lessons gleaned from the earthquake enabled numerous innovations in earthquake modeling and structural engineering. Today, San Francisco is one of the most earthquake-safe cities in the world.

independence from Spain and assumed control of Alta California, initiating sweeping changes. The missions were secularized and the clergy expelled; any Mexican born in Spain was considered illegal and deported. In 1826 Jedediah Smith and his team of mountain men became the first Americans to enter California overland, after crossing the stark Mojave Desert. On later journeys Smith and his crew traveled throughout northern California, paving the way for droves of American pioneers. The American presence in northern California, which the Spanish had not settled, steadily increased as migrants braved the California Trail in the 1840s.

California Attacked

On May 13, 1846, the United States declared war on Mexico, and the U.S. Army and Navy converged on California. In June of that year, a group of American Californians successfully revolted against the Mexican garrison in Sonoma and raised the flag of the sovereign California Republic. A week later the U.S. Army occupied the fort, and the short-lived California Republic

was disbanded. In the south, Mexican officials fled the onslaught of the Americans, but small forces of Mexican citizens took up arms and bravely but futilely battled the U.S. Army, finally surrendering in 1847. On February 2, 1848, Mexico gave California to the United States upon the signing of the Treaty of Guadalupe Hidalgo.

All that Glitters

By the early 20th century, California was an industrial and agricultural power. It went on to become the motion picture capital of the world, as well as a center of progressive politics and philosophy. The most populous and diverse state in the nation, home to the myriad races, cultures, and languages furnished by historical and modern migrations, California has developed a unique, multicultural character, though not without significant strife. Harrowing race riots in 1965 and 1992 exposed continuing trends of social struggle and economic inequality. Long a fabled destination for explorers, the Golden State remains a place where dreams are realized and dashed in equal measure, and constantly born anew.

HOLLYWOOD

Well before Hollywood became the motion picture capital of the world, it was a small farming community 7 miles from the burgeoning city of Los Angeles. In the 1880s developer and entrepreneur Hobart Johnstone Whitley settled the area and called it Hollywood, for reasons that cannot be confirmed (though many believe that the Toyon holly that flourishes in the region inspired its name). By 1900 Hollywood was a quaint village, home to 500 people and connected to Los Angeles by streetcar. In 1910 the town was annexed to Los Angeles proper to secure access to the metropolitan water supply. That same year filmmaker D. W. Griffith traveled to Los Angeles to shoot a movie. While exploring the region, he and his troupe happened upon Hollywood and stayed in the town for months, filming. Upon returning to New York, Griffith spread the word about Hollywood's hospitality toward his moviemaking, and soon scores of filmmakers traveled to the town, turning it into the movie capital of the world within the decade. Movie studios built gigantic lots in the region, small worlds in which sets could be constructed and filmed on a grand scale. Television and music studios also migrated to the city, as did droves of dreamers, seeking fame in film. Though the movie business has spread to myriad locations around the world, Hollywood remains its center, the place where starry-eyed searchers chase celluloid celebrity.

North Hollywood, in full swing in 1929. By this time Tinseltown was movie mecca, and the film industry was dominated by the Hollywood studio system, in which actors and directors were employed by only one studio and worked according to their studio's regulations.

Alaska

North to the Future

In the wee morning hours of March 30, 1867, after a full night of haggling, Russian minister Eduard de Stoeckl sold 586,412 square miles of Russian land to the United States for a little over 7 million dollars. Secretary of State William Seward, who negotiated the deal, had bought, for roughly 2 cents an acre, the northwestern corner of North America. A vast, frozen territory unconnected to the United States, smothered by glaciers, and impossible to farm, it was home to a handful of Russian villages, the Arctic-dwelling Inupiat, bears, and impassable mountains that dwarfed those on the rest of the continent. In short, it was utter wilderness and, many thought, a complete waste of money. "Seward's folly," the pundits called it, or "Seward's icebox."

Ten days later the U.S. Congress ratified the controversial sale, reasoning that Alaska would be a bulwark in the nation's dominion over North America. Great Britain and the United States were still uneasy about sharing the continent; owning the northwestern hinterlands would prevent Britain from consolidating their control over the area above the 49th parallel. Roughly 30 years later the sparsely settled District of Alaska became valuable for another reason—gold was discovered in the adjacent Yukon Territory, and prospectors and miners streamed into Alaska, settling the state.

Mining sustained Alaska well into the 20th century, with copper joining gold as a major resource. Today, both of these are still excavated, along with zinc and other metals, but it is petroleum extraction that makes Alaska one of the richest states in the nation. The 1968 discovery of vast oil reserves beneath the state's North Slope was a new bonanza in the Last Frontier. Hoping to preserve the petroleum windfall, the state wisely established the Alaska Permanent Fund, which invests 25 percent of annual oil revenues on the citizens' behalf and pays a yearly stipend to every Alaskan. Initially worth $734,000 in 1977, the fund now contains some 40 billion dollars; in 2007 it paid $1,654 to every law-abiding adult citizen.

Tourism has emerged as another pillar in Alaska's economy—the rugged splendor of the state's wilderness draws droves of yearly visitors and inspires an environmental movement that dedicatedly fights for preservation of Alaska's ecosystems. In recent years environmentalists and oil corporations have disagreed over increased drilling in Alaska's Arctic National Wildlife Refuge, a wild Eden sitting atop huge fields of oil. Hopefully, Alaska will come to both an ecological and economical solution—the largest state in the Union should be big enough for both development and conservation.

Buffeted by frigid, especially thin air due to its height and latitude, Denali (Mt. McKinley) is among the world's most treacherous climbs.

Alaska State Facts

Full Name: State of Alaska
Meaning of Name: Derived from the Aleut word *alyeska*, meaning "great land"
Admitted to the Union: January 3, 1959 (49th state)
Inhabitant: Alaskan

Capital City: Juneau
Flower: Forget-me-not
Tree: Sitka spruce
Bird: Willow ptarmigan

Geography and Ecology

It is a vast state—the largest in the nation by far. Texas, the second-largest state, is barely half the size of Alaska. In the east Alaska borders Canada's Yukon Territory; in the southeast the state's rugged panhandle lies west of the province of British Columbia. Isolated from the lower United States, Alaska is nearly surrounded by water and possesses 6,640 miles of coastline—the most of any of the fifty states. The Aleutian Islands stretch 1,200 miles from the Alaska Peninsula toward Russia; crossing the international date line, they extend farther west than the Hawaiian Islands in the mid-Pacific.

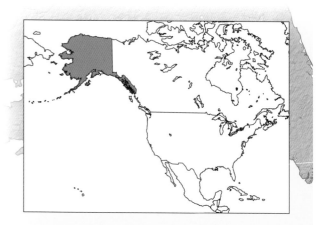

Among Great Mountains

The tallest mountain in North America, Denali (Mt. McKinley) scrapes the sky at 20,320 feet. Fanned out around it are the numerous behemoth peaks of the Alaska Range, including Mt. Foraker, at 17,400 feet, and Mt. Hunter, at 14,573 feet. Southeastern Alaska also possesses colossal, snowy summits, many above 14,000 feet. Alaska has numerous active volcanoes, including the Chigmit Mountains of southwestern Alaska and the Aleutian Range, extending from the Alaska Peninsula along the Aleutian Islands. At the base of Denali lies the Denali National Park and Preserve, nearly 10,000 miles of wilderness. At its lower elevations the park is taiga forest. Its higher ground is tundra, and at its mountainous eleva-

tions, glaciers blanket the rocky terrain. Diverse wildlife populates the park: Great herds of caribou ramble about the tundra and the taiga, solitary moose occupy forest and swamplands, and Dall sheep clamber along mountain slopes. Smaller fauna includes ground squirrels, marmots, pikas, beavers, and snowshoe hares. Gray wolves, foxes, martens, lynx, and wolverines hunt and scavenge in the Denali wilderness, as do large populations of black and grizzly bears.

Where No Roads Go

Most of Alaska's people live in south-central Alaska, in and around the largest city, Anchorage. The state's second-largest city, Fairbanks, sits alongside the Chena

A caribou forages in the autumn tundra, lit red by turning fireweed and wild blueberry. Soon snow will blanket this glowing terrain.

River, in the Alaska interior, and is flanked by small towns. The majority of the state is sparsely populated wilderness called the Alaskan bush, which, disconnected from Alaska's network of roads, can be reached only by airplane. Locally, Alaskans living in far-flung bush towns like Nome, Kotzebue, Aniak, or Barrow travel by snowmobile, snow cat, boat, or dogsled. Most of the Alaska bush is permafrost, meaning that the ground is perennially frozen. Land above the Arctic Circle is consistently snow-covered and mostly treeless.

Land of the Midnight Sun

Due to its high latitude, Alaska experiences polar nights in the winter and polar days in the summer. In the depth of winter, the sun never rises above the horizon, causing minuscule daylight in southern Alaska and two months of total darkness in northern Alaska. Likewise, at the height of summer, the sun never falls below the horizon, providing 24 hours of sunlight around the summer solstice. Such long summer days allow the few agricultural regions of the state to grow colossal produce, including 35-pound broccoli, 20-pound carrots, and 45-pound cabbages. Summers in southern Alaska are mild, and winters are cold and snowy. In the Alaska interior, weather varies to extremes—summers are hot, and winters are brutally cold. In the Alaskan bush, above the Arctic Circle, it is cold year-round, barely rising above freezing in high summer.

State History

Alaska

The Pacific States

The Last Frontier

There is no consensus as to when the first humans crossed the Bering Land Bridge from Asia to Alaska. Some place the migration as far back as 25,000 years ago; others assert that it was only 12,000 years ago. There is slightly more agreement on the fact that these first Alaskans eventually dispersed south and east, developing diverse cultures and populating the Americas. In Alaska itself, over millennia, these prehistoric migrants evolved into numerous societies occupying various landscapes. The Tlingit, Haida, and Tsimshian lived in the Alaska panhandle region and along the coast of what is now British Columbia. Skilled seafarers and fishermen all, these groups competed for land and resources and shared cultural traits, particularly the carving of elaborate totem poles. The Aleuts populated the weather-beaten, volcanic Aleutian Islands and were fishermen, gatherers, and expert basketmakers. The seminomadic Athabascans occupied the Alaska interior. The Inupiat settled in the Arctic north, and the Yup'ik occupied western Alaska. These Eskimo people mastered the extremities of their region—hunting game in more temperate areas, and large ocean life, like seals, walruses, and whales, on the frozen sea, and utilizing all parts of their prey for practical purposes.

Russia Goes East

In 1741 Danish mariner Vitus Bering and Russian Alexei Chirikov explored western North America for Russia. They returned toting lavish otter pelts, inspiring Russian fur traders to head east and capitalize on Alaska's wilderness. By 1790 Russia had established permanent settlements on the Aleutian Islands and Kodiak Island. Their occupation of the land was ensured through conflict with the local natives,

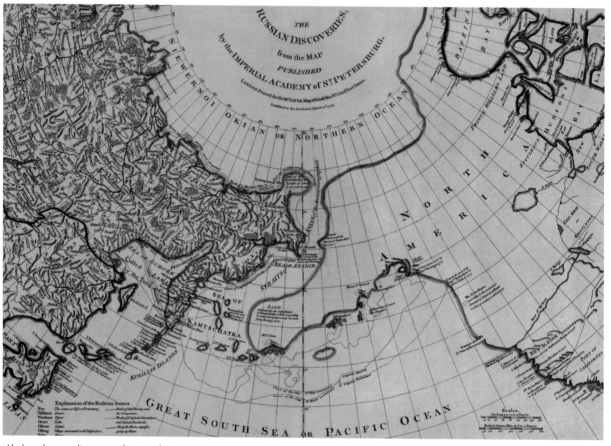

Alaska takes a rudimentary shape in this 1775 Russian map, which incorporates the findings of Bering and Chirikov and traces their routes. A number of prominent mountains are mapped, as is Bering Island, where Vitus Bering and 28 of his men died of scurvy in December of 1741.

An Inupiat family in 1899, outside their tent of skin. A young malamute sits alongside the man—it will help with hauling and hunting.

A city of tents in 1915, Anchorage developed during midcentury into a metropolis that now contains roughly 300,000 people.

who were brutally pushed from their homes. By the early 1800s American fur traders were competitively trapping the region. When the fur trade bottomed out, Russian profits from Alaska dwindled. To Russian politicians the unprofitable Alaskan territory, still riddled by strife with the Alaskan natives, seemed more valuable to sell than to keep.

Seward's Folly

The American purchase of Alaska was initially derided, but paid off by the 1890s when gold was discovered in the nearby Yukon Territory, sparking the Klondike Gold Rush. Numerous towns formed in the District of Alaska, as it was then known, including Skagway, which was ruled by con man and crime boss Soapy Smith. In 1899 prospectors found gold in the far west town of Nome, initiating more settlement of the Alaska interior. In 1914 the U.S. government purchased the Alaska Northern Railroad, arduously built over a period of 12 years, and expanded it to connect the coastal town of Seward with the interior city of Fairbanks. President Warren G. Harding journeyed to Alaska in 1923 to drive the golden spike. The Alaska Railroad is still profitably used today.

North to the Future

In 1925 a diphtheria outbreak in Nome required 20 mushers and 150 sled dogs to relay a 20-pound capsule of antitoxin 674 miles in just over five days, weathering blizzards, gales, and subzero temperatures. The Iditarod Trail Sled Dog Race, run every March, commemorates the event. During World War II the Aleutian Islands of Kisku and Attu were occupied by the Japanese and then wrested away by the United States after two weeks of brutal fighting. Alaska's strategic importance and the discovery of oil in the region inspired the federal government to finally declare Alaska a state in 1958. In the latter half of the 20th century, Alaska endured two major disasters—a catastrophic 9.2 magnitude earthquake that crippled the state's infrastructure, and the 1989 Exxon-Valdez oil spill, which dumped 11 million gallons of crude oil into Prince William Sound, killing hundreds of thousands of animals. Today, that ecosystem is still recuperating, representing the dark side of the conflict between preserving the diverse wilderness that makes Alaska unique and extracting the prized resources that make it wealthy.

"To the lover of pure wildness Alaska is one of the most wonderful countries in the world . . . Tracing shining ways through fjord and sound, past forests and waterfalls, islands and mountains and far azure headlands, it seems as if surely we must at length reach the very paradise of the poets, the abode of the blessed."

—John Muir, American naturalist (1838–1914)

Hawaii

The Aloha State

Ua Mau ke Ea o ka 'Aina i ka Pono (The life of the land is perpetuated in righteousness)

The crimson lava of Kilauea flows constantly these days, continuing the long history of creation and destruction that formed the Hawaiian archipelago. Over epochs, it was red-hot, liquid rock that built these green isles, as undersea volcanoes extruded layer upon layer of magma until their summits poked through the ocean veil and became islands. Measured from the sea floor to its high point on Mauna Kea, the big island of Hawaii is the tallest mountain in the world. It is still transforming, with new lava seeping and cooling—thus, the eighth-smallest state in the Union slowly grows larger. No matter how much it grows though, Hawaii will stay an ocean away from its counterparts. Isolated 2,100 miles from the continental United States, in the center of the North Pacific Ocean, the 50th state possesses some of the most unusual flora and fauna in the world, species that are constantly under threat as its population increases.

Since its annexation by the United States in 1898, Hawaii has gained citizens every decade—today more than 1.42 million people call the islands home, with the majority residing on the island of Oahu, in the Honolulu metropolitan area. It is one of the few states in which whites do not constitute the majority of the population. Most Hawaiians are Asian American, with roots in Japan, the Philippines, or China; another significant portion is native Hawaiian, with ancestry traced to the Polynesians who settled the archipelago well over a millennium ago. Hawaii is the only state with two official state languages, English and Hawaiian, though a pidgin known as Hawaii Creole English linguistically connects the diverse population, interweaving English with Hawaiian, Chinese, Japanese, and Tagalog words.

For many years agriculture dominated the Hawaiian economy, including sandalwood logging, sugarcane farming, and pineapple cultivation. Pineapples and sugarcane remain major crops, but tourism revenue has assumed dominance over the state's finances. More than 7 million people visit the islands annually, pouring billions of dollars into Hawaii's coffers. Politically, the state has leaned Democratic throughout its history. Today, its four congressional members are Democratic, as well as the majority in the state legislature. Hawaii possesses one of the most progressive health-care systems in the United States, publicly insuring more than 95 percent of its residents and emphasizing preventive care. Hawaiians consequently require less treatment than American mainlanders, though many observers believe that this is not due to their health-care system, but is rather a side effect of living in an island paradise.

These red rivers, 1,300° F or hotter, built Hawaii from the bottom of the ocean. Today, Hawaii's Kilauea is the world's most active volcano.

Hawaii State Facts

Full Name: State of Hawaii
Meaning of Name: May refer to the original homeland of the Polynesians, Hawaiki, or to the legendary fisherman Hawai'iloa, who discovered the islands
Admitted to the Union: August 21, 1959 (50th state)

Inhabitant: Hawaiian
Capital City: Honolulu
Flower: Hawaiian hibiscus
Tree: Kukui nut tree
Bird: Hawaiian goose

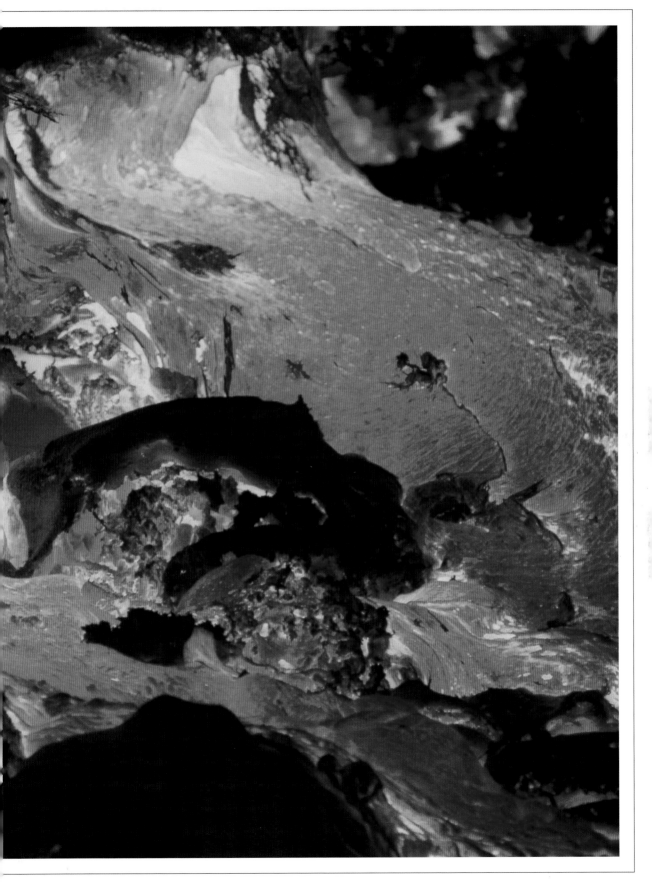

Geography and Ecology

In all, Hawaii is a chain of 137 islands, atolls, islets and seamounts, extending some 1,500 miles southeast to northwest across the Pacific Ocean. Of these, seven islands constitute the inhabited State of Hawaii: Niihau, Kauai, Oahu, Molokai, Lanai, Maui, and the big island, Hawaii. An eighth, Kahoolawe, is considered a main island, though it has no permanent residents. The only state in the nation completely surrounded by water, Hawaii is not part of North America. It is considered to be within Oceania, the region of islands in the Pacific Ocean including Tonga, French Polynesia, and the Marshall Islands, as well as Australia and Indonesia, among others.

Among the Volcanoes

The landscape of the Hawaiian Islands is rugged and wild. Formed by epochs of volcanic activity, the islands now represent the peaks of the volcanoes that formed them. On the big island of Hawaii, the five separate volcanoes responsible for the island—Kohala, Mauna Kea, Hualalai, Mauna Loa, and Kilauea—still loom above it. Three of these volcanoes are now dormant, but Kilauea and Mauna Loa are spectacularly active. At 13,679 feet high, Mauna Loa is the world's largest shield volcano; it was formed by swift lava that, instead of erupting, flowed down the sides of the mountain, creating shallow slopes. It last erupted in 1984, spilling scorching lava down its flanks; the heavy flows nearly reached the city of Hilo before the eruption

ceased. Kilauea, the newest Hawaiian volcano, is only 4,091 feet high but is the most active volcano on the planet, emitting lava flows both inland and out to sea. It can be a turbulent, destructive monster—in 1990 its lava destroyed the towns of Kalapana and Kaimu, and in 2008 an explosion from the volcano threw debris across 74 acres of Hawaii.

Rare Birds

The dormant volcano Mauna Kea towers 13,796 feet above Hawaii. On the island of Kauai, the Waimea Canyon plunges 3,000 feet from high cliffs. Initially formed by the collapse of the volcano that created the island, the canyon has also been slowly carved by the

Honolulu, which means "sheltered bay," in the Hawaiian language, is home to Waikiki Beach and the green expanse of Kapiolani Park.

The red basalt cliffs of Waimea Canyon are clothed by numerous endemic plants, including iliau, lehua trees and 'uki'uki grass.

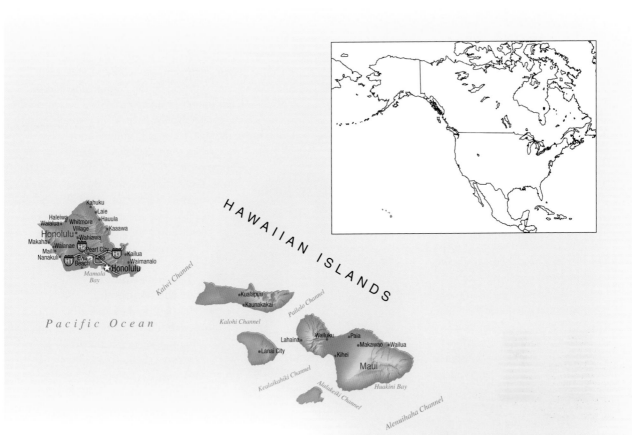

Waimea River. It is among the many state and national parks instituted to protect Hawaii's rare wilderness, which includes many endemic species, transported over the millennia to the world's most isolated islands by wind, water, and wings. Many of these unique species have vanished over years of human occupation—fossils indicate a range of extinct bird species once native to Hawaii, including an eagle, two kinds of crows, huge ducks called moa-nalos, and several owls.

Two Seasons

It is the only tropical state in the Union, possessing a pleasant but varied climate, due to each island having separate landscapes and unique exposure to trade winds. Native Hawaiians traditionally recognized only two seasons: Kau, the warm season, when the sun was high and the wind was consistent; and Hoo-ilo, the cool season, when the sun was lower, to the south, and the winds were changeable. This pattern is accurate, the only exceptions being at Hawaii's highest elevations, where it is consistently cooler. Precipitation varies from region to region, according to a land's elevation and position in relation to trade winds.

The Aloha State

Hawaiian legend states that ages ago, the fisherman Hawai'iloa settled the Hawaiian Islands after accidentally discovering them. Historians, however, believe that the first settlers of Hawaii were Polynesians from the Marquesas, who sailed across the Pacific Ocean in double-hulled canoes, possibly as early as the year 300. From here the history is complicated—Hawaiian lore recounts the tale of Pa'ao, a high priest and skilled navigator, who sailed from Tahiti with a crew of men, conquering the Hawaiian Islands and introducing Tahitian customs. Historians dispute whether this happened—in recent years archaeological evidence has indicated that only the Marquesan population, gradually developing, peopled the islands. Most historians believe that the story of Pa'ao is simply an important myth that traces Hawaiian customs to the divinity of the high priesthood. Conversely, many Hawaiians now see Pa'ao as not a hero, but as the beginning in a line of invaders who undermined traditional Hawaiian culture.

Captain Cook Arrives

Skilled fishermen and farmers, Hawaiians lived in communal villages, according to a caste system. The four levels of society were Ali'i (royalty), Kahuna (priesthood), Maka'ainana (commoners), and Kauwa (outcasts or

slaves). Human sacrifice was practiced to appease the gods. Laws were outlined by the Hawaiian religious system of kapu (taboo), which determined socially and personally acceptable behavior. In 1778 Captain James Cook made the first European landing on the shores of Hawaii. Returning to the Sandwich Islands—as he called them—in 1779, Cook and his crew became embroiled in violence with the Hawaiians, and the legendary navigator was killed. He had mapped Hawaii's coordinates, however; soon European and American ships were regular visitors to the islands.

Captain James Cook

The Rise and Fall of the Monarchy

In 1810 Kamehameha the Great established a monarchy that ruled Hawaii for nearly the entire 19th century. Missionary and colonial intrusion was constant, however, and Hawaii transformed under European influence. Foreign governments were determined to overthrow the islands. In 1843 a British warship captured Honolulu, demanding the cession of Hawaii to the British Empire. The situation was diplomatically defused. In 1887 King David Kalakaua's advisers forced him to sign a new constitution that favored Hawaiian, European, and American businessmen and plantation owners. Six years later a force of U.S. Marines deployed

---

Kamehameha the Great, painted in 1817.

KAMEHAMEHA THE GREAT

Lore states that Kamehameha the Great entered the world in 1758, when Halley's Comet split the sky—a sign that he was born to unite the Hawaiian Islands. As a boy learning about warfare and politics, he showed a glum disposition, earning him his name, which means "loneliness of a god." An ambitious young chief and warrior, Kamehameha defeated his ruling cousin Kiwala'o in battle in 1782; after killing two more chiefs, he took control of the entire big island of Hawaii. Next he set his sights on conquering the archipelago. In brutal combat from 1795 until 1810, Kamehameha built up an enormous military and subsequently broke down the armies of each island, becoming the first king of united Hawaii. Codifying the legal system and initiating trade with the United States and Europe, he urged Hawaiians to resist colonization and remain united. After his death in 1819, Kamehameha's favorite wife, Ka'ahumanu, became the de facto ruler of Hawaii, guiding the young sons of Kamehameha into ruling positions. The first king's royal line ruled for several generations.

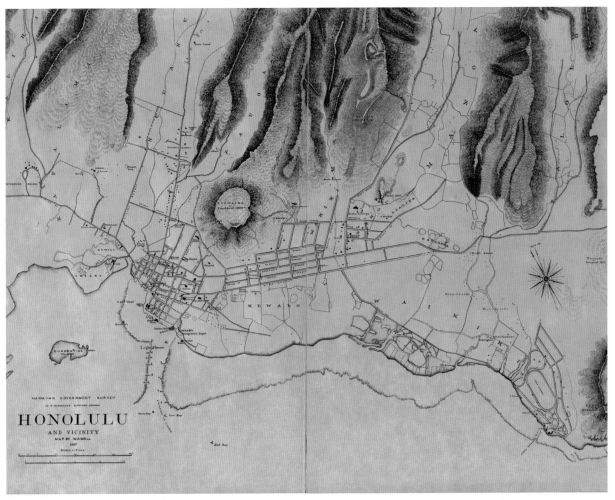

In 1804, after conquering Oahu, Kamehameha the Great moved his royal court from Hawaii to Waikiki. Honolulu became the permanent capital in 1845. Here it is 1887, the year King Kalakaua signed the Bayonet Constitution, undermining both the monarchy and the poor.

to Hawaii under the pretense of guarding American installations; instead they overthrew the monarchy. In 1898 the United States annexed Hawaii.

The 50th State

Already a tourism destination, as an American territory Hawaii became an especially popular spot for wealthy travelers. It also became a Pacific outpost for the U.S. military and witnessed catastrophe in 1941 when the Japanese navy attacked the U.S. naval base at Pearl Harbor, killing 2,388. In 1959 the archipelago became America's 50th state. Created ages ago by lava seeping from the bottom of the sea, Hawaii continues to grow in size and in numbers, as more Americans flock every year to settle on its green shores.

The USS Arizona *sinks with 1,177 aboard after being obliterated by a bomb during the Japanese attack on Pearl Harbor on December 7, 1941.*

ALABAMA

DEMOGRAPHY

Population (2016): 4,863,300
Population (2006): 4,599,030
Under 18: 24%
65 or older: 15%
Density in p/sq mile (2015): 95.9
Persons per household: 2.57
Population by race % (2015):
   White: 69.5%
   Black: 26.8%
   American Indian/Aleut/Eskimo:
   0.7%
   Asian: 1.4%
   Hispanic: 4.2%
   White/Non-Hispanic: 66.0%
   Native Hawaiian and Other Pacific
   Islander: 0.1%
   Persons reporting two or more
   races: 1.6%

POPULATION CHARACTERISTICS

Marriage rate (per 1,000): 7.4
Birth rate (per 1,000)(2014): 12.0
Infant mortality rate (2015): 8.7
Percent of population with bachelor's
   degree: 23.5%
Average household income (2015):
   $44,509
Median home value: $125,500
Poverty rate: 19.2%
Average life expectancy: 75.4
Crime rate per 100,000:
   Violent: 427.4
   Property: 3,177.6
Federal and state prisoners (2014):
   32,381

ECONOMY

Chief industries: pulp and paper,
   chemicals, electronics, apparel,
   textiles, primary metals, lumber
   and wood products, food
   processing, fabricated metals,
   automotive tires, oil and gas
   exploration
Chief manufactured goods:
   electronics, cast iron and plastic
pipes, fabricated steel products,
   ships, paper products, chemicals,
   steel, mobile homes, fabrics,
   poultry processing, soft drinks,
   furniture, tires
Chief crops: cotton, greenhouse and
   nursery, peanuts, sweet potatoes
Nonfuel minerals: cement, stone,
   lime, sand, and gravel
Sales tax (2016): 8.97%
Gross state product: $199.7 bil

GOVERNMENT AND POLITICS

US representatives: 7
Electoral votes: 9
State governors:
   Robert J. Bentley, R: 2011–
   Bob Riley, R: 2003–2011
   Donald Eugene Siegelman, D:
   1999–2003
   Forrest Hood James Jr., D, R:
   1995–1999
   James Elisha Folsom Jr., D: 1993–
   1995
   Harold Guy Hunt, R: 1987–1993

DESTINATIONS

Major cities (2015 population):
   Birmingham: 212,461
   Montgomery: 200,602
   Mobile: 194,288
   Huntsville: 190,582
   Tuscaloosa: 90,468
International airports:
   Birmingham and Huntsville
National monuments, landmarks,
   and parks: First Whitehouse of the
   Confederacy, Civil Rights Museum,
   Helen Keller's Birthplace, Carver
   Museum, Alabama Space and
   Rocket Center, Moundville State
   Monument, Pike Pioneer Museum,
   USS *Alabama* Memorial Park,
   Russell Cave National Monument
Web site: www.alabama.gov

ALASKA

DEMOGRAPHY

Population (2016): 741,894
Population (2006): 670,053
Under 18: 28%
65 or older: 11%
Density in p/sq mile (2015): 1.3
Persons per household: 2.84
Population by race % (2015):
   White: 69.5%
   Black: 26.8%
   American Indian/Aleut/Eskimo:
   0.7%
   Asian: 1.4%
   Hispanic: 4.2%
   White/Non-Hispanic: 66.0%
   Native Hawaiian and Other Pacific
   Islander: 0.1%
   Persons reporting two or more
   races: 1.6%

POPULATION CHARACTERISTICS

Marriage rate (per 1,000): 7.4
Birth rate (per 1,000)(2014): 15.6
Infant mortality rate (2015): 5.4
Percent of population with bachelor's
   degree: 28%
Average household income (2015):
   $75,112
Median home value: $250,000
Poverty rate: 11.4%
Average life expectancy: 78.3
Crime rate per 100,000:
   Violent: 635.8
   Property: 2,760.0
Federal and state prisoners (2014):
   5216

ECONOMY

Chief industries: petroleum,
   tourism, fishing, mining, forestry,
   transportation, aerospace
Chief manufactured goods: fish
   products, lumber and pulp, furs
Chief crops: greenhouse products,
   barley, oats, hay, potatoes, lettuce,
   aquaculture
Nonfuel minerals: zinc, gold, lead,
   sand and gravel
Sales tax (2016): 1.78%
Gross state product: $52.7 bil

---

* Sales tax: City, county, and municipal rates vary. Rates shown are weighted by population to compute an average local tax rate.

GOVERNMENT AND POLITICS

US representatives: 1

Electoral votes: 3

State governors:

Bill Walker, I: 2014–

Sean Parnell, R: 2009–2014

Sarah Palin, R: 2006–2009

Frank H. Murkowski, R: 2002–2006

Tony Knowles, D: 1994–2002

Walter J. Hickel, AIP: 1990–1994

Steve Cowper, R: 1986–1990

DESTINATIONS

Major cities (2015 population):

Anchorage: 298,695

Juneau: 32,756

Fairbanks: 32,469

Ketchikan: 13,758

Sitka: 8,920

International airports:

Anchorage, Fairbanks, Juneau

National monuments, landmarks, and parks: Inside Passage, Portage Glacier, Ketchikan Totems, Glacier Bay National Park and Preserve, Denali National Park, Mt. Roberts Tramway, White Pass and Yukon Route railroad, Katmai National Park

Web site: www.state.ak.us

ARIZONA

DEMOGRAPHY

Population (2016): 6,931,071

Population (2006): 6,166,318

Under 18: 25%

65 or older: 15%

Density in p/sq mile (2015): 45.2

Persons per household: 2.71

Population by race % (2015):

White: 83.5%

Black: 4.8%

American Indian/Aleut/Eskimo: 5.3%

Asian: 3.4%

Hispanic: 30.7%

White/Non-Hispanic: 55.8%

Native Hawaiian and Other Pacific Islander: 0.3%

Persons reporting two or more races: 2.7%

POPULATION CHARACTERISTICS

Marriage rate (per 1,000): 5.9

Birth rate (per 1,000)(2015): 12.9

Infant mortality rate (2015): 5.5

Percent of population with bachelor's degree: 27.50%

Average household income (2015): $52,248

Median home value: $167,500

Poverty rate: 17.4%

Average life expectancy: 79.6

Crime rate per 100,000

Violent: 635.8

Property: 3,197.5

Federal and state prisoners (2014): 42,259

ECONOMY

Chief industries: manufacturing, construction, tourism, mining, agriculture

Chief manufactured goods: electronics, printing and publishing, foods, metals, aircraft and missiles, apparel

Chief crops: cotton, lettuce, cauliflower, broccoli, sorghum, barley, corn, wheat, citrus fruits

Nonfuel minerals: copper, sand and gravel

Sales tax (2016): 8.25%

Gross state product: $290.9 bil

GOVERNMENT AND POLITICS

US representatives: 9

Electoral votes: 11

State governors:

Doug Ducey, R: 2015–

Jan Brewer, R: 2009–2015

Janet Napolitano, D: 2003–2009

Jane Dee Hull, R: 1997–2003

J. Fife Symington III, R: 1991–1997

Rose Mofford, D: 1988–1991

Evan Mecham, R: 1987–1988

DESTINATIONS

Major cities (2015 population):

Phoenix: 1,563,025

Tucson: 531,641

Mesa: 471,825

Chandler: 260,828

Gilbert: 247,542

International airports:

Phoenix, Tucson

National monuments, landmarks, and parks: Grand Canyon, the Painted Desert, Petrified Forest National Park, Canyon de Chelly, Meteor Crater, Sedona, Biosphere 2, Navajo Nation National Monument

Web site: www.az.gov

ARKANSAS

DEMOGRAPHY

Population (2016): 2,988,248

Population (2006): 2,810,872

Under 18: 26%

65 or older: 15%

Density in p/sq mile (2015): 51.3

Persons per household: 2.53

Population by race % (2015):

White: 79.5%

Black: 15.7%

American Indian/Aleut/Eskimo: 1.0%

Asian: 1.6%

Hispanic: 7.2%

White/Non-Hispanic: 73.1%

Native Hawaiian and Other Pacific Islander: 0.3%

Persons reporting two or more races: 2.0%

POPULATION CHARACTERISTICS

Marriage rate (per 1,000): 10.0

Birth rate (per 1,000)(2015): 12.7

Infant mortality rate (2015): 7.5

Percent of population with bachelor's degree: 21.1%

Average household income (2015): $42,798

Median home value: $72,800

Poverty rate: 19.1%

Average life expectancy: 76

Crime rate per 100,000:
  Violent: 480.1
  Property: 3,338.0

Federal and state prisoners (2014): 17,874

ECONOMY

Chief industries: manufacturing, agriculture, tourism, forestry

Chief manufactured goods: food products, chemicals, lumber, paper, plastics, electric motors, furniture, auto components, airplane parts, apparel, machinery, steel

Chief crops: rice, soybeans, cotton, tomatoes, grapes, apples, commercial vegetables, peaches, wheat

Nonfuel minerals: bromine, stone, cement, sand and gravel

Sales tax (2016): 9.30%

Gross state product: $119 bil

GOVERNMENT AND POLITICS

US representatives: 4

Electoral votes: 6

State governors:
  Asa Hutchinson, R: 2015–
  Mike Beebe, D: 2007–2015
  Mike Huckabee, R: 1996–2007
  Jim Guy Tucker, D: 1992–96
  Bill Clinton, D: 1983–92, 1979–1981
  Frank D. White, R: 1981–83

DESTINATIONS

Major cities (2015 population):
  Little Rock: 197,992
  Fort Smith: 88,194
  North Little Rock: 66,504
  Fayetteville: 82,830
  Jonesboro: 73,907

International airports:
  Blytheville

National monuments, landmarks, and parks: Hot Springs National Park, Eureka Springs, Ozark Folk Center, Blanchard Caverns, Crater of Diamonds, Archeological State Park, Buffalo National River, Mid-America Museum, Pea Ridge National Military Park, Tanyard Springs, Wiederkehr Wine Village

Web site: www.state.ar.us

CALIFORNIA

DEMOGRAPHY

Population (2016): 39,250,017

Population (2006): 36,457,549

Under 18: 25%

65 or older: 13%

Density in p/sq mile (2015): 251.3

Persons per household: 2.97

Population by race % (2015):
  White: 72.9%
  Black: 6.5%
  American Indian/Aleut/Eskimo: 1.7%
  Asian: 14.8%
  Hispanic: 38.8%
  White/Non-Hispanic: 38%
  Native Hawaiian and Other Pacific Islander: 0.4%
  Persons reporting two or more races: 3.8%

POPULATION CHARACTERISTICS

Marriage rate (per 1,000): 6.2

Birth rate (per 1,000)(2015): 12.9

Infant mortality rate (2015): 4.6

Percent of population with bachelor's degree: 26.60%

Average household income (2015): $63,636

Median home value: $385,500

Poverty rate: 15.3%

Average life expectancy: 80.8

Crime rate per 100,000
  Violent: 396.1
  Property: 2,441.1

Federal and state prisoners (2014): 136,088

ECONOMY

Chief industries: agriculture, tourism, apparel, electronics, telecommunications, entertainment

Chief manufactured goods: electronic and electronic equipment, computers, industrial machinery, transportation equipment and instruments, food

Chief crops: milk and cream, grapes, cotton, flowers, oranges, rice, nursery products, hay, tomatoes, lettuce, strawberries, almonds, asparagus

Nonfuel minerals: gravel, sand, cement, stone, boron minerals, soda ash

Sales tax (2016): 8.48%

Gross state product: $2,481.3 bil

GOVERNMENT AND POLITICS

US representatives: 53

Electoral votes: 55

State governors
  Jerry Brown, D: 2011–
  Arnold Schwarzenegger, R: 2003–2011
  Gray Davis, D: 1999–2003
  Pete Wilson, R: 1991–1999
  George Deukmejian, R: 1983–1991
  Edmund Gerald Brown Jr., D: 1975–1983

DESTINATIONS

Major cities (2015 population):
  Los Angeles: 3,971,883
  San Diego: 1,394,928
  San Jose: 1,026,908
  San Francisco: 864,816
  Fresno: 520,052

International airports:
  Fresno, Los Angeles, Oakland, Ontario, Sacramento, San Diego, San Francisco, San Jose

National monuments, landmarks, and parks: The *Queen Mary*, Palomar Mountain, Disneyland, Getty Center, Tournament of Roses

---

* Sales tax: City, county, and municipal rates vary. Rates shown are weighted by population to compute an average local tax rate.

and the Rose Bowl, Universal Studios, Long Beach Aquarium of the Pacific, Golden State Museum, San Diego Zoo, Yosemite Valley, Lassen and Sequoia-Kings Canyon National Parks, Mojave and Colorado Deserts, Monterey Peninsula, Inyo National Forest, Humboldt Redwoods State Park
Web site: www.ca.gov

COLORADO

DEMOGRAPHY
Population (2016): 5,540,545
Population (2006): 4,753,377
Under 18: 24%
65 or older: 14%
Density in p/sq mile (2015): 41.5
Persons per household: 2.57
Population by race % (2015):
   White: 87.5%
   Black: 4.5%
   American Indian/Aleut/Eskimo: 1.6%
   Asian: 2.6%
   Hispanic: 21.3%
   White/Non-Hispanic: 68.7%
   Native Hawaiian and Other Pacific Islander: 0.2%
   Persons reporting two or more races: 2.9%

POPULATION CHARACTERISTICS
Marriage rate (per 1,000): 6.8
Birth rate (per 1,000)(2015): 12.4
Infant mortality rate (2015): 4.8
Percent of population with bachelor's degree: 32.70%
Average household income (2015): $66,596
Median home value: $247,800
Poverty rate: 11.5%
Average life expectancy: 80
Crime rate per 100,000
   Violent: 309.1
   Property: 2,530.1
Federal and state prisoners (2014): 20,646

ECONOMY
Chief industries: manufacturing, construction, government, tourism, agriculture, aerospace, electronics equipment
Chief manufactured goods: computer equipment and instruments, foods, machinery, aerospace products
Chief crops: corn, wheat, hay, sugar beets, barley, potatoes, apples, peaches, pears, dry edible beans, sorghum, onions, oats, sunflowers, vegetables
Nonfuel minerals: sand and gravel, cement, molybdenum concentrates, gold stone
Sales tax (2016): 7.52%
Gross state product: $313.7 bil

GOVERNMENT AND POLITICS
US representatives: 7
Electoral votes: 9
State governors:
   John Hickenlooper, D: 2011–
   Bill Ritter, D: 2007–2011
   Bill Owens, R: 1999–2007
   Roy Romer, D: 1987–1999
   Richard D. Lamm, D: 1975–1987
   John D. Vanderhoof, R: 1973–1975

DESTINATIONS
Major cities (2015 population):
   Denver: 682,485
   Colorado Springs: 456,568
   Aurora: 359,407
   Fort Collins: 161,175
   Lakewood: 152,597
International airports:
   Denver
National monuments, landmarks, and parks: Rocky Mountain, Black Mountain, Gunnison National Parks, Aspen Ski Resort, Garden of the Gods, Great Sand Dunes, Pikes Peak and Mt. Evans highways, Mesa Verde National Park, Grand Mesa National Forest, Burlington's Old Town, Bent's Fort,

Georgetown Loop Historic Mining Railroad Park
Web site: www.colorado.gov

CONNECTICUT

DEMOGRAPHY
Population (2016): 3,576,452
Population (2006): 3,504,809
Under 18: 23%
65 or older: 16%
Density in p/per sq mile (2015): 741.6
Persons per household: 2.59
Population by race: % (2015):
   White: 80.8%
   Black: 11.6%
   American Indian/Aleut/Eskimo: 0.5%
   Asian: 4.6%
   Hispanic: 15.4%
   White/Non-Hispanic: 68.2%
   Native Hawaiian and Other Pacific Islander: 0.1%
   Persons reporting two or more races: 2.2%

POPULATION CHARACTERISTICS
Marriage rate (per 1,000): 5.3
Birth rate (per 1,000)(2015): 10.1
Infant mortality rate (2015): 5.0
Percent of population with bachelor's degree: 37.6%
Average household income (2015): $72,889
Median home value: $270,500
Poverty rate: 10.5%
Average life expectancy: 80.8
Crime rate per 100,000:
   Violent: 236.9
   Property: 1,920.4
Federal and state prisoners (2014): 16,636

ECONOMY
Chief industries: manufacturing, retail trade, government, services, finances, insurance, real estate
Chief manufactured goods: aircraft

engines and parts, submarines, helicopters, machinery and computer equipment, electronics and electrical equipment, medical instruments, pharmaceuticals
Chief crops: nursery stock, Christmas trees, mushrooms, vegetables, sweet corn, tobacco, apples
Nonfuel minerals: stone, sand and gravel, clays, gemstones
Sales tax (2016): 6.35%
Gross state product: $252.9 bil

GOVERNMENT AND POLITICS
US representatives: 5
Electoral votes: 7
State governors:
Dannel Malloy, D: 2011–
M. Jodi Rell, R: 2004–2011
John G. Rowland, R: 1995–2004
Lowell P. Weicker Jr., I: 1991–1995
William A. O'Neill, D: 1980–1991
Ella T. Grasso, D: 1975–1980

DESTINATIONS
Major cities (2015 population):
Bridgeport: 147,629
New Haven: 130,322
Stamford: 128,874
Hartford: 124,006
Waterbury: 108,802
International airports:
Windsor Locks
National monuments, landmarks, and parks: Mark Twain House, Yale University, Peabody Museum, Mystic Seaport, Mystic Marine Life Aquarium, P. T. Barnum Museum, Gillette Castle, USS Mashantucket Pequot Museum and Research Center, Foxwoods Resort and Casino, Mohegan Sun, Lake Compounce
Web site: www.state.ct.us

DELAWARE

DEMOGRAPHY
Population (2016): 952,065

Population (2006): 853,476
Under 18: 22
65 or older: 16
Density in p/per sq mile (2015): 485.3
Persons per household: 2.61
Population by race % (2015):
White: 70.4%
Black: 22.4%
American Indian/Aleut/Eskimo: 0.7%
Asian: 3.9%
Hispanic: 9.0%
White/Non-Hispanic: 63.2%
Native Hawaiian and Other Pacific Islander: 0.1%
Persons reporting two or more races: 2.5%

POPULATION CHARACTERISTICS
Marriage rate (per 1,000): 5.7
Birth rate (per 1,000)(2015): 11.7
Infant mortality rate (2015): 7.0
Percent of population with bachelor's degree: 30.0%
Average household income (2015): $57,756
Median home value: $231,500
Poverty rate: 12.4%
Average life expectancy: 78.4
Crime rate per 100,000
Violent: 489.1
Property: 2,982.0
Federal and state prisoners (2014): 6,995

ECONOMY
Chief industries: chemicals, agriculture, finance, poultry, shellfish, tourism, auto assembly, food processing, transportation equipment
Chief manufactured goods: nylon, apparel, luggage, foods, autos, processed meats and vegetables, railroad and aircraft equipment
Chief crops: soybeans, potatoes, corn, mushrooms, lima beans, green peas, barley, cucumbers, wheat,

grain, sorghum, greenhouse and nursery
Nonfuel minerals: sand and gravel, magnesium compounds, gemstones
Sales tax (2016): none
Gross state product: $68.7 bil

GOVERNMENT AND POLITICS
US representatives: 1
Electoral votes: 3
State governors:
John Carney, D: 2017–
Jack Markell, D: 2009–2017
Ruth Ann Minner, D: 2001–2009
Thomas R. Carper, D: 1993–2001
Dale Edward Wolf, R: 1992–1993
Michael Newbold Castle, R: 1985–1992
Pierre Samuel du Pont, R: 1977–1985

DESTINATIONS
Major cities (2015 population):
Wilmington: 71,948
Dover: 37,522
Newark: 33,817
Middletown: 20,372
Milford: 10,252
International airports:
Philadelphia/Wilmington
National monuments, landmarks, and parks: Ft. Christina Monument, Hagley Museum, Winterthur Museum and Gardens, John Dickenson Home, Rehoboth Beach, Dover Downs International Speedway
Web site: www.delaware.gov

FLORIDA

DEMOGRAPHY
Population (2016): 20,612,439
Population (2006): 18,089,888
Under 18: 22%
65 or older: 19%
Density in p/sq mile (2015): 378.0
Persons per household: 2.66
Population by race % (2015):

---

* Sales tax: City, county, and municipal rates vary. Rates shown are weighted by population to compute an average local tax rate.

White: 77.7%

Black: 16.8%

American Indian/Aleut/Eskimo: 0.5%

Asian: 2.8%

Hispanic: 24.5%

White/Non-Hispanic: 55.3%

Native Hawaiian and Other Pacific Islander: 0.1%

Persons reporting two or more races: 2.5%

POPULATION CHARACTERISTICS

Marriage rate (per 1,000): 8.2

Birth rate (per 1,000)(2015): 11

Infant mortality rate (2015): 6.1

Percent of population with bachelor's degree: 27%

Average household income (2015): $48,825

Median home value: $159,000

Poverty rate: 15.7%

Average life expectancy: 79.4

Crime rate per 100,000

Violent: 540.5

Property: 3,415.5

Federal and state prisoners (2014): 102,870

ECONOMY

Chief industries: tourism, agriculture, manufacturing, construction, services, international trade

Chief manufactured goods: electrical and electronic equipment, transportation equipment, food, printing and publishing, chemicals, instruments, industrial machinery

Chief crops: citrus fruits, vegetables, melons, greenhouse and nursery products, potatoes, sugarcane, strawberries

Nonfuel minerals: phosphate rock, stone, cement, sand and gravel

Sales tax (2016): 6.66%

Gross state product: $888.1 bil

GOVERNMENT AND POLITICS

US representatives: 27

Electoral votes: 29

State governors:

Rick Scott, R: 2011–

Charlie Crist, R: 2007–2011

Jeb Bush, R: 1999–2007

Kenneth Hood Mackay Jr., D: 1998–1999

Lawton Chiles, D: 1991–1998

Robert Martinez, D, R: 1987–1991

DESTINATIONS

Major cities (2015 population):

Jacksonville: 868,031

Miami: 441,003

Tampa: 369,075

Orlando: 270,934

St. Petersburg: 257,083

International airports

Daytona Beach, Ft. Lauderdale/Hollywood, Ft. Meyers, Jacksonville, Key West, Miami, Orlando, St. Petersburg/Clearwater, Sarasota/Bradenton, Tampa, West Palm Beach

National monuments, landmarks, and parks: Miami Beach, St. Augustine, Castillo de San Marcos, Walt Disney World, Sea World, Universal Studios, Spaceport USA, Kennedy Space Center, Everglades National Park, Ringling Museum of Art, Ringling Museum of the Circus, Cypress Gardens, Busch Gardens, U.S. Astronaut Hall of Fame, Mariana Caverns, Silver Springs

Web site: www.myflorida.com

GEORGIA

DEMOGRAPHY

Population (2016): 10,310,371

Population (2006): 9,363,941

Under 18: 26%

65 or older: 13%

Density in p/sq mile (2015): 177.6

Persons per household: 2.72

Population by race % (2015):

White: 77.1%

Black: 13.3%

American Indian/Aleut/Eskimo: 0.9%

Asian: 5.6%

Hispanic: 17.6%

White/Non-Hispanic: 61.6%

Native Hawaiian and Other Pacific Islander: 0.2%

Persons reporting two or more races: 2.6%

POPULATION CHARACTERISTICS

Marriage rate (per 1,000): 6.2

Birth rate (per 1,000)(2015): 12.9

Infant mortality rate (2015): 6.6

Percent of population with bachelor's degree: 29.8%

Average household income (2015): $50,768

Median home value: $178,600

Poverty rate: 13.5%

Average life expectancy: 75.3

Crime rate per 100,000:

Violent: 377.3

Property: 3,281.2

Federal and state prisoners (2014): 52,949

ECONOMY

Chief industries: services, manufacturing, retail trade

Chief manufactured goods: textiles, apparel, food, pulp and paper products

Chief crops: peanuts, corn, cotton, tobacco, hay, soybeans

Nonfuel minerals: clay, stone, cement, sand and gravel

Sales tax (2016): 7.01%

Gross state product: $497.9 bil

GOVERNMENT AND POLITICS

US representatives: 14

Electoral votes: 16

State governors:

Nathan Deal, R: 2011–

Sonny Perdue, R: 2003–2011

Roy E. Barnes, D: 1999–2003

Zell Miller, D: 1991–1999
Joe Frank Harris, D: 1983–1991
George Dekle Busbee, D: 1975–
1983

DESTINATIONS
Major cities (2015 population):
    Atlanta: 463,878
    Augusta: 197,182
    Columbus: 200,579
    Macon: 153,515
    Savannah: 145,674
International airports:
    Atlanta, Savannah
National monuments, landmarks,
    and parks: State Capitol, Stone
    Mtn. Park, Six Flags over Georgia,
    Kennesaw Mountain National
    Battlefield Park, Martin Luther
    King Jr. National Historic Site,
    Underground Atlanta, Jimmy
    Carter Library and Museum,
    Chickamauga and Chattanooga
    National Military Park, Dahlonega,
    Chattahoochee National Forest,
    Brasstown Bald Mountain,
    Franklin D. Roosevelt's Little
    White House, Warm Springs,
    Pine Mtn., Andersonville National
    Historic Site, Okefenokee Swamp,
    Jekyll Island, Cumberland Island
    National Seashore, historic
    riverfront district of Savannah
Web site: www.georgia.gov

HAWAII

DEMOGRAPHY
Population (2016): 1,428,557
Population (2006): 1,285,498
Under 18: 24%
65 or older: 17.0%
Density in p/sq mile (2015): 222.9
Persons per household: 3.11
Population by race % (2015):
    White: 26.7%
    Black: 2.6%
    American Indian/Aleut/Eskimo:
    0.5%

Asian: 37.3%
Hispanic: 10.4%
White/Non-Hispanic: 22.9%
Native Hawaiian and Other Pacific
    Islander: 9.9%
Persons reporting two or more
    races: 23%

POPULATION CHARACTERISTICS
Marriage rate (per 1,000): 15.9
Birth rate (per 1,000)(2015): 13.5
Infant mortality rate (2015): 5.6
Percent of population with bachelor's
    degree: 30.8%
Average household income (2015):
    $64,514
Median home value: $515,300
Poverty rate: 10.6%
Average life expectancy: 81.3
Crime rate per 100,000:
    Violent: 259.2
    Property: 3,050.0
Federal and state prisoners (2014):
    5,866

ECONOMY
Chief industries: tourism, defense,
    sugar, pineapples
Chief manufactured goods: processed
    sugar, canned pineapple, clothing,
    foods, printing and publishing
Chief crops: sugar, pineapple,
    macadamia nuts, fruits, coffee,
    vegetables, floriculture
Nonfuel minerals: stone, sand and
    gravel
Sales tax (2016): 4.35%
Gross state product: $80.4 bil

GOVERNMENT AND POLITICS
US representatives: 2
Electoral votes: 4
State governors:
    David Ige, D: 2014–
    Neil Abercrombie, D: 2010–2014
    Linda Lingle, R: 2002–2010
    Benjamin J. Cayetano, D: 1994–
    2002
    John Waihee, D: 1986–1994

George Ryoichi Ariyoshi, D:
    1974–1986
John Anthony Burns, D: 1962–
    1974
William Francis Quinn, R: 1957–
    1962

DESTINATIONS
Major cities (2015 population):
    Honolulu: 352,769
    Pearl City: 47,698
    Hilo: 43,263
    Kailua: 38,635
    Waipahu: 38,216
International airports:
    Hilo, Honolulu, Kailua, Kahului
National monuments, landmarks,
    and parks: Hawaiian Volcanoes,
    Haleakala National Parks, National
    Memorial Cemetery of the Pacific,
    Diamond Head, USS *Arizona*
    Memorial, Pearl Harbor, Polynesian
    Cultural Center, Nu'uanu Pali,
    Waimea Canyon, Wailoa and
    Wailuku River State Parks
Web site: www.hawaii.gov

IDAHO

DEMOGRAPHY
Population (2016): 1,683,140
Population (2006): 1,466,465
Under 18: 27%
65 or older: 15%
Density in p/sq mile (2015): 20.0
Persons per household: 2.72
Population by race % (2015):
    White: 93.4%
    Black: 0.8%
    American Indian/Aleut/Eskimo:
    1.7%
    Asian: 1.5%
    Hispanic: 12.2%
    White/Non-Hispanic: 82.5%
    Native Hawaiian and Other Pacific
    Islander: 0.2%
    Persons reporting two or more
    races:
    2.3%

---

*   Sales tax: City, county, and municipal rates vary. Rates shown are weighted by population to compute an average local tax rate.

POPULATION CHARACTERISTICS

Marriage rate (per 1,000): 8.2
Birth rate (per 1,000)(2015): 13.8
Infant mortality rate (2015): 5.5
Percent of population with bachelor's
    degree: 25.9%
Average household income (2015):
    $51,624
Median home value: $162,900
Poverty rate: 15.1%
Average life expectancy: 79.5
Crime rate per 100,000
    Violent: 212.2
    Property: 1,854.8
Federal and state prisoners (2014):
    8,117

ECONOMY

Chief industries: manufacturing,
    agriculture, tourism, lumber,
    mining, electronics
Chief manufactured goods: electronic
    components, computer equipment,
    processed, foods, lumber and
    wood products, chemical products,
    machinery
Chief crops: potatoes, peas, dry
    beans, sugarbeets, alfalfa seeds,
    lentils, wheat, hops, barley, plums,
    and prunes
Nonfuel minerals: phosphate rock,
    sand and gravel, molybdenum
    concentrates, silver, cement
Sales tax (2016): 6.03%
Gross state product: $65.5 bil

GOVERNMENT AND POLITICS

US representatives: 2
Electoral votes: 4
State governors:
    C. L. Butch Otter, R: 2007–
    James E. Risch, R: 2006–2007
    Dirk Kempthorne, R: 1999–2006
    Philip E. Batt, R: 1995–1999
    Cecil Dale Andrus, D: 1987–1995,
    1971–1977

DESTINATIONS

Major cities (2015 population):

Boise: 218,281
Meridian: 90,739
Nampa: 89,839
Idaho Falls: 59,184
Pocatello: 54,441
International airports:
none
National monuments, landmarks,
    and parks: Hells Canyon, World
    Center for Birds of Prey, Craters of
    the Moon, Sun Valley, Crystal Falls
    Cave, Shoshone d'Alene, Sawtooth
    National Recreation Area, River
    of No Return Wilderness Area,
    Redfish Lake
Web site: www.state.id.us

ILLINOIS

DEMOGRAPHY

Population (2016): 12,801,539
Population (2006): 12,831,970
Under 18: 25%
65 or older: 15%
Density in p/sq mile (2015): 231.6
Persons per household: 2.62
Population by race % (2015):
    White: 77.3%
    Black: 14.7%
    American Indian/Aleut/Eskimo:
    0.3%
    Asian: 5.5%
    Hispanic: 16.9%
    White/Non-Hispanic: 61.9%
    Native Hawaiian and Other Pacific
    Islander: 0.1%
    Persons reporting two or more
    races: 1.9%

POPULATION CHARACTERISTICS

Marriage rate (per 1,000): 5.9
Birth rate (per 1,000)(2015): 12.2
Infant mortality rate (2015): 6.2
Percent of population with bachelor's
    degree: 32.3%
Average household income (2015):
    $60,413
Median home value: $173,800
Poverty rate: 13.6%

Average life expectancy: 79
Crime rate per 100,000
    Violent: 370.0
    Property: 2,075.9
Federal and state prisoners (2014):
    48,278

ECONOMY

Chief industries: services,
    manufacturing, travel, wholesale
    and retail trade, finance, insurance,
    real estate, construction, health
    care, agriculture
Chief manufactured goods:
    machinery, electrical and electronic
    equipment, primary and fabricated
    metals, chemical products, printing
    and publishing, food, and kindred
    products
Chief crops: corn, soybeans, wheat,
    sorghum, hay
Nonfuel minerals: stone, cement,
    sand and gravel, lime
Sales tax (2016): 8.64%
Gross state product: $776.9 bil

GOVERNMENT AND POLITICS

US representatives: 18
Electoral votes: 20
State governors:
    Pat Quinn, D: 2009–
    Rod R. Blagojevich, D: 2003–2009
    George H. Ryan, R: 1999–2003
    Jim Edgar, R: 1991–1999
    James Robert Thompson, R:
    1977–1991
    Daniel Walker, D: 1973–1977

DESTINATIONS

Major cities (2015 population):
    Chicago: 2,720,546
    Rockford: 148,278
    Joliet: 147,861
    Naperville: 147,100
    Aurora: 142,990
    Springfield: 116,565
    Peoria: 115,070
International airports:
    O'Hare, Chicago Midway, Gary-
    Chicago

National monuments, landmarks, and parks: Lincoln shrines at Springfield, Cahokia Mounds, Starved Rock State Park, Crab Orchard Wildlife Refuge, Mormon Settlement at Nauvoo, Illinois State Museum, Shawnee National Forest, Sears Tower, Wrigley Field, Millennium Park
Web site: www.illinois.gov

INDIANA

DEMOGRAPHY
Population (2016): 6,633,053
Population (2006): 6,313,520
Under 18: 26.0%
65 or older: 16%
Density in p/sq mile (2015): 184.8
Persons per household: 2.56
Population by race % (2015):
   White: 85.8%
   Black: 9.6%
   American Indian/Aleut/Eskimo: 0.4%
   Asian: 1.3%
   Hispanic: 6.7%
   White/Non-Hispanic: 80.0%
   Native Hawaiian and Other Pacific Islander: 0.1%
   Persons reporting two or more races: 1.9%

POPULATION CHARACTERISTICS
Marriage rate (per 1,000): 6.9
Birth rate (per 1,000)(2015): 12.7
Infant mortality rate (2015): 7.0
Percent of population with bachelor's degree: 24.1%
Average household income (2015): $51,983
Median home value: $124,200
Poverty rate: 14.5%
Average life expectancy: 77.6
Crime rate per 100,000
   Violent: 365.3
   Property: 2,649.4
Federal and state prisoners (2014): 29,271

ECONOMY
Chief industries: manufacturing, services, agriculture, government, wholesale and retail trade, transportation and public utilities
Chief manufactured goods: primary metals, transportation equipment, motor vehicles and equipment, industrial machinery and equipment, electrical and electronic equipment
Chief crops: corn, soybeans, wheat, nursery and greenhouse products, vegetables, popcorn, hay, fruit, tobacco, mint
Nonfuel minerals: stone, cement, sand and gravel, lime
Sales tax (2016): 9.64%
Gross state product: $227.3 bil

GOVERNMENT AND POLITICS
US representatives: 9
Electoral votes: 11
State governors:
   Eric Holcomb, R: 2017–
   Mike Pence, R: 2013–2017
   Mitch Daniels, R: 2005–2013
   Joseph E. Kernan, D: 2003–2005
   Frank O'Bannon, D: 1997–2003
   Evan Bayh, D: 1989–1997
   Robert D. Orr, R: 1981–1989

DESTINATIONS
Major cities (2015 population):
   Indianapolis: 853,173
   Fort Wayne: 260,326
   Evansville: 119,943
   South Bend: 101,576
   Carmel: 88,713
International airports:
   Indianapolis, Fort Wayne
National monuments, landmarks, and parks: Lincoln Log Cabin Historic Site, George Rogers Clark Park, Wyandotte Cave, Tippecanoe Battlefield Memorial Park, Benjamin Harrison home, Indianapolis 500 raceway and museum, Indiana Dunes, National

College Football Hall of Fame, Hoosier National Forest
Web site: www.in.gov

IOWA

DEMOGRAPHY
Population (2016): 3,134,693
Population (2006): 2,982,085
Under 18: 25%
65 or older: 16%
Density in p/sq mile (2015): 52.4
Persons per household: 2.42
Population by race % (2015):
   White: 91.8%
   Black: 3.5%
   American Indian/Aleut/Eskimo: 0.5%
   Asian: 1.6%
   Hispanic: 5.7%
   White/Non-Hispanic: 86.7%
   Native Hawaiian and Other Pacific Islander: 0.1%
   Persons reporting two or more races: 1.8%

POPULATION CHARACTERISTICS
Marriage rate (per 1,000): 6.3
Birth rate (per 1,000)(2015): 12.7
Infant mortality rate (2015): 4.8
Percent of population with bachelor's degree: 21.2%
Average household income (2015): $60,855
Median home value: $82,500
Poverty rate: 10.5%
Average life expectancy: 79.7
Crime rate per 100,000
   Violent: 273.5
   Property: 2,093.8
Federal and state prisoners (2014): 8,838

ECONOMY
Chief industries: agriculture, communications, construction, finance, insurance, trade, services, manufacturing
Chief manufactured goods: processed food products, tires, farm

---

* Sales tax: City, county, and municipal rates vary. Rates shown are weighted by population to compute an average local tax rate.

machinery, electronic products, appliances, household furniture, chemicals, fertilizers, auto accessories

Chief crops: silage, grain, corn, soybeans, oats, hay

Nonfuel minerals: cement, stone, sand and gravel, gypsum, lime

Sales tax (2016): 6.79%

Gross state product: $174 bil

GOVERNMENT AND POLITICS

US representatives: 4

Electoral votes: 6

State governors:
Terry E. Branstad, R: 2011–
Chet Culver, D: 2007–2011
Thomas J. Vilsack, D: 1999–2007
Terry E. Branstad, R: 1983–1999
Robert D. Ray, R: 1969–1983
Robert David Fulton, D: 1969–1969

DESTINATIONS

Major cities (2015 population):
Des Moines: 210,330
Cedar Rapids: 128,429
Davenport: 99,685
Sioux City: 82,684
Waterloo: 68,747

International airports:
Des Moines

National monuments, landmarks, and parks: Herbert Hoover Birthplace and Library, Effigy Mounds National Park, Grant Wood's paintings and memorabilia, Davenport Municipal Art Gallery, Living History Farms, Adventureland, Boone and Scenic Valley Railroad, Greyhound Parks, Prairie Meadows horse racing, Mississippi and Missouri Rivers, Iowa Great Lakes

Web site: www.iowa.gov

KANSAS

DEMOGRAPHY

Population (2016): 2,907,289

Population (2006): 2,764,075

Under 18: 28%

65 or older: 14%

Density in p/sq mile (2015): 35.6

Persons per household: 2.55

Population by race % (2015):
White: 86.7%
Black: 6.3%
American Indian/Aleut/Eskimo: 1.0%
Asian: 2.9%
Hispanic: 11.6%
White/Non-Hispanic: 76.4%
Native Hawaiian and Other Pacific Islander: 0.1%
Persons reporting two or more races: 2.9%

POPULATION CHARACTERISTICS

Marriage rate (per 1,000): 5.9

Birth rate (per 1,000)(2015): 13.4

Infant mortality rate (2015): 6.4

Percent of population with bachelor's degree: 31.0%

Average household income (2015): $54,865

Median home value: $132,000

Poverty rate: 13.0%

Average life expectancy: 78.7

Crime rate per 100,000
Violent: 348.6
Property: 2,735.2

Federal and state prisoners (2014): 9,663

ECONOMY

Chief industries: manufacturing, finance, insurance, real estate, services

Chief manufactured goods: transportation equipment, machinery and computer equipment, food and spirits, printing and publishing

Chief crops: wheat, sorghum, corn, hay, soybeans, sunflowers

Nonfuel minerals: cement, helium, salt, stone

Sales tax (2016): 8.60%

Gross state product: $149.6 bil

GOVERNMENT AND POLITICS

US representatives: 4

Electoral votes: 6

State governors:
Sam Brownback, R: 2011–
Mark Parkinson, D: 2009–2011
Kathleen Sebelius, D: 2003–2009
Bill Graves, R: 1995–2003
Joan Finney, D: 1991–1995
John Michael Hayden, R: 1987–1991
John Carlin, D: 1979–1987

DESTINATIONS

Major cities (2015 population):
Wichita: 389,965
Overland Park: 186,515
Kansas City: 151,306
Olathe: 134,305
Topeka: 127,265

International airports:
Kansas City

National monuments, landmarks, and parks: Eisenhower Center, Agriculture Hall of Fame and National Center, Bonner Springs, Dodge City/Boot Hill and Frontier Town, Old Cowtown Museum, Fort Scott and Fort Larned, Kansas Cosmosphere and Space Center, Woodlands Racetrack, U.S. Calvary Museum, Fort Riley, NCAA Visitors Center, Heartland Park Raceway

Web site: www.travelks.com

KENTUCKY

DEMOGRAPHY

Population (2016): 4,436,974

Population (2006): 4,206,074

Under 18: 25%

65 or older: 16%

Density in p/sq mile (2015): 112.0

Persons per household: 2.5

Population by race % (2015):
White: 88.1%
Black: 8.3%

American Indian/Aleut/Eskimo: 0.2%
Asian: 1.0%
Hispanic: 3.4%
White/Non-Hispanic: 85.1%
Native Hawaiian and Other Pacific Islander: 0%
Persons reporting two or more races: 1.8%

POPULATION CHARACTERISTICS

Marriage rate (per 1,000): 7.2
Birth rate (per 1,000)(2015): 12.6
Infant mortality rate (2015): 6.8
Percent of population with bachelor's degree: 22.3%
Average household income (2015): $42,387
Median home value: $123,200
Poverty rate: 18.5%
Average life expectancy: 76
Crime rate per 100,000
    Violent: 211.6
    Property: 2,246.9
Federal and state prisoners (2014): 21,657

ECONOMY

Chief industries: manufacturing, services, finance, insurance, real estate, retail trade, public utilities
Chief manufactured goods: transportation and industrial machinery, apparel, printing and publishing, food products, electrical and electronic equipment
Chief crops: tobacco, corn, soybeans
Nonfuel minerals: stone, lime, cement, sand and gravel
Sales tax (2016): 6.0%
Gross state product: $193.3 bil

GOVERNMENT AND POLITICS

US representatives: 6
Electoral votes: 8
State governors:
    Matt Bevin, R: 2015–
    Steven L. Beshear, D: 2007–2015
    Ernie Fletcher, R: 2003–2007

Paul E. Patton, D: 1995–2003
Brereton C. Jones, D: 1991–1995
Wallace G. Wilkinson, D: 1987–1991

DESTINATIONS

Major cities (2015 population):
    Louisville: 615,366
    Lexington: 314,488
    Bowling Green: 63,616
    Owensboro: 59,042
    Covington: 49,997
International airports:
    Covington/Cincinnati, Louisville
National monuments, landmarks, and parks: Kentucky Derby, Land Between Lakes National Recreation Area, Kentucky Lake and Lake Barkley, Mammoth Cave National Park, Echo River, Lake Cumberland, Lincoln's Birthplace, My Old Kentucky Home State Park, Cumberland Gap Historical Park, Kentucky Horse Park, Shaker Village
www.kentuckytourism.com

LOUISIANA

DEMOGRAPHY

Population (2016): 4,681,666
Population (2006): 4,468,976
Under 18: 26%
65 or older: 13%
Density in p/sq mile (2015): 108.1
Persons per household: 2.61
Population by race % (2015):
    White: 63.2%
    Black: 32.5%
    American Indian/Aleut/Eskimo: 0.7%
    Asian: 1.4%
    Hispanic: 5.0%
    White/Non-Hispanic: 59.1%
    Native Hawaiian and Other Pacific Islander: 0%
    Persons reporting two or more races: 1.6%

POPULATION CHARACTERISTICS

Marriage rate (per 1,000): 6.8
Birth rate (per 1,000)(2015): 13.6
Infant mortality rate (2015): 8.4
Percent of population with bachelor's degree: 22.5%
Average household income (2015): $45,922
Median home value: $144,100
Poverty rate: 19.6%
Average life expectancy: 75.7
Crime rate per 100,000
    Violent: 514.7
    Property: 3,458.8
Federal and state prisoners (2014): 38,030

ECONOMY

Chief industries: wholesale and retail trade, tourism, manufacturing, construction, transportation, communication, public utilities, finance, insurance, real estate, mining
Chief manufactured goods: chemical products, foods, transportation equipment, electronic equipment, petroleum products, lumber, wood, and paper
Chief crops: soybeans, sugarcane, rice, corn, cotton, sweet potatoes, pecans, sorghum, aquaculture
Nonfuel minerals: salt, sand and gravel, stone, lime
Sales tax (2016): 9.0%
Gross state product: $239.3 bil

GOVERNMENT AND POLITICS

US representatives: 6
Electoral votes: 8
State governors:
    John Bel Edwards, D: 2016–
    Bobby Jindal, R: 2008–2016
    Kathleen Babineaux Blanco, D: 2004–2008
    Mike Foster Jr., R: 1996–2004
    Buddy Elson Roemer III, D, R: 1992–1996
    Edwin Washington Edwards, D: 1988–1992

*   Sales tax: City, county, and municipal rates vary. Rates shown are weighted by population to compute an average local tax rate.

DESTINATIONS
Major cities (2015 population):
New Orleans: 389,617
Baton Rouge: 228,590
Shreveport: 197,204
Lafayette: 127,657
Lake Charles: 76,070
International airports:
New Orleans
National monuments, landmarks,
and parks: French Quarter, Battle
of New Orleans site, Longfellow-
Evangeline Memorial Park, Kent
House Museum, Hodges Gardens,
Natchitoches, USS *Kidd* Memorial
Web site: www.louisiana.gov

MAINE

DEMOGRAPHY
Population (2016): 1,331,479
Population (2006): 1,321,574
Under 18: 20%
65 or older: 21%
Density in p/sq mile (2015): 43.1
Persons per household: 2.37
Population by race % (2015):
White: 94.9%
Black: 1.4%
American Indian/Aleut/Eskimo:
0.6%
Asian: 1.2%
Hispanic: 1.6%
White/Non-Hispanic: 93.6%
Native Hawaiian and Other Pacific
Islander: 0%
Persons reporting two or more
races: 1.7%

POPULATION CHARACTERISTICS
Marriage rate (per 1,000): 7.6
Birth rate (per 1,000)(2015): 9.7
Infant mortality rate (2015): 7.0
Percent of population with bachelor's
degree: 29.0%
Average household income (2015):
$50,756
Median home value: $173,800
Poverty rate: 13.4%

Average life expectancy: 79.2
Crime rate per 100,000
Violent: 127.8
Property: 1,986.4
Federal and state prisoners (2014):
2,242

ECONOMY
Chief industries: manufacturing,
agriculture, estate construction
Chief manufactured goods: paper
and wood products, transportation
equipment
Chief crops: potatoes, aquaculture
products
Nonfuel minerals: sand and gravel,
cement, stone, peat
Sales tax (2016): 5.50%
Gross state product: $57.3 bil

GOVERNMENT AND POLITICS
US representatives: 2
Electoral votes: 4
State governors
Paul LePage, R: 2011–
John E. Baldacci, D: 2003– 2011
Angus S. King Jr., I: 1995–2003
John Rettie McKernan Jr., R:
1987–1995
Joseph Edward Brennan, D:
1979–1987
James Bernard Longley, I: 1975–
1979

DESTINATIONS
Major cities (2015 population):
Portland: 66,881
Lewiston: 36,202
Bangor: 32,391
South Portland: 25,556
Auburn: 22,871
International airports:
Bangor, Portland
National monuments, landmarks,
and parks: Acadia National Park,
Old Orchard Beach, Portland Head
Light, Baxter State Park
Web site: www.state.me.us

MARYLAND

DEMOGRAPHY
Population (2016): 6,016,447
Population (2006): 5,615,727
Under 18: 24%
65 or older: 13%
Density in p/sq mile (2015): 618.7
Persons per household: 2.69
Population by race % (2015):
White: 59.6%
Black: 30.5%
American Indian/Aleut/Eskimo:
0.6%
Asian: 4.9%
Hispanic: 9.5%
White/Non-Hispanic: 52.0%
Native Hawaiian and Other Pacific
Islander: 0.1%
Persons reporting two or more
races: 2.7%

POPULATION CHARACTERISTICS
Marriage rate (per 1,000): 6.2
Birth rate (per 1,000)(2015): 12.5
Infant mortality rate (2015): 6.5
Percent of population with bachelor's
degree: 37.9%
Average household income (2015):
$73,594
Median home value: $286,900
Poverty rate: 9.7%
Average life expectancy: 80.5
Crime rate per 100,000
Violent: 446.1
Property: 2,507.5
Federal and state prisoners (2014):
21,011

ECONOMY
Chief industries: manufacturing,
services, biotechnology and
information technology, tourism
Chief manufactured goods: electrical
and electronic equipment, food and
kindred products, chemicals and
allied products, printed materials
Chief crops: greenhouse and nursery
products, soybeans, corn

Nonfuel minerals: cement, stone, sand and gravel
Sales tax (2016): 6.0%
Gross state product: $365.4 bil

GOVERNMENT AND POLITICS
US representatives: 8
Electoral votes: 10
State governors:
Larry Hogan, R: 2015–
Martin O'Malley, D: 2007–2015
Robert Leroy Ehrlich Jr., R: 2003–2007
Parris N. Glendening, D: 1995–2003
William Donald Schaefer, D: 1987–1995
Harry Roe Hughes, D: 1979–1987

DESTINATIONS
Major cities (2015 population):
Baltimore: 621,849
Frederick: 69,479
Waldorf: 67,752
Gaithersburg: 67,456
Rockville: 66,980
International airports:
Baltimore
National monuments, landmarks, and parks: The Preakness at Pimlico track, The Maryland Million at Laurel Race Course, Ocean City, restored Ft. McHenry, Edgar Allan Poe house, Ravens Football at Memorial Stadium, Camden Yards, Harborplace, Antietam Battlefield, South Mountain Battlefield, U.S. Naval Academy, Maryland State House
Web site: www.maryland.gov

MASSACHUSETTS

DEMOGRAPHY
Population (2016): 6,811,779
Population (2006): 6,349,097
Under 18: 21%
65 or older: 15%
Density in p/sq mile (2015): 871.1

Persons per household: 2.56
Population by race % (2015):
White: 82.1%
Black: 8.4%
American Indian/Aleut/Eskimo: 0.5%
Asian: 6.6%
Hispanic: 11.2%
White/Non-Hispanic: 73.5%
Native Hawaiian and Other Pacific Islander: 0.1%
Persons reporting two or more races: 2.3%

POPULATION CHARACTERISTICS
Marriage rate (per 1,000): 5.5
Birth rate (per 1,000)(2015): 10.8
Infant mortality rate (2015): 4.2
Percent of population with bachelor's degree: 40.5%
Average household income (2015): $67,861
Median home value: $333,100
Poverty rate: 11.5%
Average life expectancy: 80.5
Crime rate per 100,000
Violent: 391.4
Property: 1,857.1
Federal and state prisoners (2014): 10,713

ECONOMY
Chief industries: services, trade, manufacturing
Chief manufactured goods: electrical and electronic equipment, instruments, industrial machinery and equipment, printing and publishing, fabricated metal products
Chief crops: cranberries, greenhouse, nursery, vegetables
Nonfuel minerals: stone, sand and gravel, lime, clays
Sales tax (2016): 6.25%
Gross state product: $484.9 bil

GOVERNMENT AND POLITICS
US representatives: 9

Electoral votes: 11
State governors:
Charlie Barker, R: 2015–
Deval Patrick, D: 2007–2015
Mitt Romney, R: 2003–2007
Jane Maria Swift, R: 2001–2003
Argeo Paul Cellucci, R: 1997–2001
William Floyd Weld, R: 1991–1997

DESTINATIONS
Major cities (2015 population):
Boston: 667,137
Worcester: 184,815
Springfield: 154,341
Lowell: 110,699
Cambridge: 110,402
International airports:
Boston
National monuments, landmarks, and parks: Provincetown artists' colony, Cape Cod, Plymouth Rock, Plimoth Plantation, *Mayflower II*, Freedom Trail, Isabella Stewart Gardner Museum, Museum of Fine Arts, Children's Museum, Museum of Science, New England Aquarium, JFK Library, Boston Ballet, Boston Pops, Boston Symphony Orchestra, Tanglewood, Jacob's Pillow Dance Festival, Hancock Shaker Village, Berkshire Scenic Railway Museum, Norman Rockwell Museum, Edith Wharton and Herman Melville homes, Salem, Old Sturbridge Village, Deerfield Historical District, Walden Pond, Naismith Memorial Basketball Hall of Fame
Web site: www.mass.gov

MICHIGAN

DEMOGRAPHY
Population (2016): 9,928,300
Population (2006): 10,095,643
Under 18: 23%
65 or older: 17%
Density in p/sq mile (2015): 175.5

---

* Sales tax: City, county, and municipal rates vary. Rates shown are weighted by population to compute an average local tax rate.

Persons per household: 2.51
Population by race % (2015):
  White: 79.7%
  Black: 14.2%
  American Indian/Aleut/Eskimo: 0.7%
  Asian: 3.0%
  Hispanic: 4.9%
  White/Non-Hispanic: 75.6%
  Native Hawaiian and Other Pacific Islander: 0%
  Persons reporting two or more races: 2.3%

POPULATION CHARACTERISTICS

Marriage rate (per 1,000): 6.0
Birth rate (per 1,000)(2015): 11.5
Infant mortality rate (2015): 7.0
Percent of population with bachelor's degree: 26.9%
Average household income (2015): $54,203
Median home value: 122,400
Poverty rate: 15.8%
Average life expectancy: 78.2
Crime rate per 100,000
  Violent: 427.3
  Property: 2,043.9
Federal and state prisoners (2014): 43,390

ECONOMY

Chief industries: manufacturing, services, tourism, agriculture, forestry/lumber
Chief manufactured goods: automobiles, transportation equipment, machinery, fabricated metals, food products, plastics, office furniture
Chief crops: corn, wheat, soybeans, dry beans, potatoes, hay, sweet corn, apples, cherries, sugar beets, blueberries, cucumbers, Niagra grapes
Nonfuel minerals: cement, sand and gravel, iron ore, stone, salt
Sales tax (2016): 6.0%
Gross state product: $468.3 bil

GOVERNMENT AND POLITICS

US representatives: 14
Electoral votes: 16
State governors
  Rick Snyder, R: 2011
  Jennifer M. Granholm, D: 2003–2011
  John Engler, R: 1991–2003
  James Johnston Blanchard, D: 1983–1991
  William Grawn Milliken, R: 1969–1983
  George Wilcken Romney, R: 1963–1969

DESTINATIONS

Major cities (2015 population):
  Detroit: 677,116
  Grand Rapids: 195,097
  Warren: 135,358
  Sterling Heights: 132,052
  Ann Arbor: 117,070
International airports:
  Detroit, Flint, Grand Rapids, Kalamazoo, Lansing, Saginaw
National monuments, landmarks, and parks: Henry Ford Museum, Greenfield Village, Fredrick Meijer Gardens and Sculpture Park, Michigan Space Center, Tahquamenon Falls, DeZwaan windmill and Tulip Festival, Soo Locks, St. Mary's Falls Ship Canal, Sault Ste. Marie, Kalamazoo Aviation History Museum, Museum of African American History
Web site: www.michigan.gov

MINNESOTA

DEMOGRAPHY

Population (2016): 5,519,952
Population (2006): 5,167,101
Under 18: 25%
65 or older: 16%
Density in p/sq mile (2015): 68.9
Persons per household: 2.49

Population by race % (2015):
  White: 85.4%
  Black: 6.0%
  American Indian/Aleut/Eskimo: 1.3%
  Asian: 3.5%
  Hispanic: 5.2%
  White/Non-Hispanic: 81%
  Native Hawaiian and Other Pacific Islander: 0%
  Persons reporting two or more races: 2.4%

POPULATION CHARACTERISTICS

Marriage rate (per 1,000): 5.6
Birth rate (per 1,000)(2015): 12.8
Infant mortality rate (2015): 5.1
Percent of population with bachelor's degree: 33.7%
Average household income (2015): $68,730
Median home value: $186,200
Poverty rate: 10.2%
Average life expectancy: 81.1
Crime rate per 100,000
  Violent: 229.1
  Property: 2,297.5
Federal and state prisoners (2014): 10,637

ECONOMY

Chief industries: agribusiness, forest products, mining, manufacturing, tourism
Chief manufactured goods: food, chemical and paper products, industrial machinery, electrical and electronic equipment, computers, printing and publishing, scientific and medical instruments, fabricated metal products, forest products
Chief crops: corn, soybeans, wheat, sugar beets, hay, barley, potatoes, sunflowers
Nonfuel minerals: iron ore, sand and gravel, stone
Sales tax (2016): 7.27%
Gross state product: $328.3 bil

GOVERNMENT AND POLITICS
US representatives: 8
Electoral votes: 10
State governors:
  Mark Dayton, D: 2011–
  Tim Pawlenty, R: 2003–2011
  Jesse Ventura, MIP: 1999–2003
  Arne Helge Carlson, R: 1991–1999
  Rudolph George Perpich,
    D-Farmer-Labor: 1983–1991
  Albert Harold Quie, R: 1979–1983

DESTINATIONS
Major cities (2015 population):
  Minneapolis: 410,939
  St. Paul: 300,851
  Rochester: 112,225
  Bloomington: 86,435
  Duluth: 86,110
International airports:
  Minneapolis-St. Paul
National monuments, landmarks,
  and parks: Minneapolis Institute
  of Arts, Walker Art Center,
  Minneapolis Sculpure Garden,
  Minnehaha Falls, Guthrie Theater,
  Ordway Theater, Voyageurs
  National Park, Mayo Clinic, North
  Shore of Lake Superior
Web site: www.state.mn.us

MISSISSIPPI

DEMOGRAPHY
Population (2016): 2,988,726
Population (2006): 2,910,540
Under 18: 26%
65 or older: 14%
Density in p/sq mile (2015): 60.6
Persons per household: 2.62
Population by race % (2015):
  White: 59.5%
  Black: 37.6%
  American Indian/Aleut/Eskimo:
  0.5%
  Asian: 1.1%
  Hispanic: 3.1%
  White/Non-Hispanic: 57.0%
  Native Hawaiian and Other Pacific

Islander: 0.1%
Persons reporting two or more
  races: 1.2%

POPULATION CHARACTERISTICS
Marriage rate (per 1,000): 7.0
Birth rate (per 1,000)(2015): 12.9
Infant mortality rate (2015): 9.3
Percent of population with bachelor's
  degree: 20.7%
Average household income (2015):
  $40,037
Median home value: $103,100
Poverty rate: 22.0%
Average life expectancy: 75
Crime rate per 100,000
  Violent: 278.5
  Property: 2,921.2
Federal and state prisoners (2014):
  18,793

ECONOMY
Chief industries: warehousing
  and distribution services,
  manufacturing, government,
  wholesale and retail trade
Chief manufactured goods: chemicals
  and plastics, food and kindred
  products, furniture, lumber
  and wood products, electrical
  machinery, transportation
  equipment
Chief crops: cotton, rice, soybeans
Nonfuel minerals: sand and gravel,
  clays, stone, cement
Sales tax (2016): 7.07%
Gross state product: $105.8 bil

GOVERNMENT AND POLITICS
US representatives: 4
Electoral votes: 6
State governors:
  Phil Bryant, R: 2012–
  Haley Barbour, D: 2004–2012
  David Ronald Musgrove, D:
  2000–2004
  Daniel Kirkwood Fordice Jr., D:
  1992–2000

Raymond Edwin Mabus, D:
  1988–1992
William A. Allain, D: 1984–1988

DESTINATIONS
Major cities (2015 population):
  Jackson: 170,674
  Gulfport: 71,856
  Southaven: 52,589
  Hattiesburg: 46,805
  Biloxi: 45,637
International airports:
  Jackson
National monuments, landmarks, and
  parks: Vicksburg National Military
  Park and Cemetery, Natchez
  Trace, Antebellum homes, Smith
  Robertson Museum, Mynelle
  Gardens, Mardi Gras and Shrimp
  Festival, Gulf Islands National
  Seashore
Web site: www.ms.gov

MISSOURI

DEMOGRAPHY
Population (2016): 6,093,000
Population (2006): 5,842,713
Under 18: 25%
65 or older: 15%
Density in p/sq mile (2015): 88.5
Persons per household: 2.49
Population by race % (2015):
  White: 83.3%
  Black: 11.8%
  American Indian/Aleut/Eskimo:
  0.6%
  Asian: 2.0%
  Hispanic: 4.1%
  White/Non-Hispanic: 79.8%
  Native Hawaiian and Other Pacific
  Islander: 0.1%
  Persons reporting two or more
  races: 2.2%

POPULATION CHARACTERISTICS
Marriage rate (per 1,000): 6.2
Birth rate (per 1,000)(2015): 12.4
Infant mortality rate (2015): 6.6

---

* Sales tax: City, county, and municipal rates vary. Rates shown are weighted by population to compute an average local tax rate.

Percent of population with bachelor's degree: 27.1%
Average household income (2015): $59,196
Median home value: $138,400
Poverty rate: 14.8%
Average life expectancy: 77.5
Crime rate per 100,000
  Violent: 442.9
  Property: 2,906.5
Federal and state prisoners (2014): 31,942

ECONOMY
Chief industries: agriculture, manufacturing, aerospace, tourism
Chief manufactured goods: transportation equipment, food and related products, electrical and electronic equipment, chemicals
Chief crops: soybeans, corn, wheat, hay
Nonfuel minerals: stone, cement, lead, lime, sand and gravel
Sales tax (2016): 7.86%
Gross state product: $294.4 bil

GOVERNMENT AND POLITICS
US representatives: 8
Electoral votes: 10
State governors:
  Eric Greitens, R: 2017–
  Jay Nixon, D: 2009–2017
  Matt Blunt, R: 2005–2009
  Robert L. Holden, D: 2001–2005
  Roger B. Wilson, D: 2000–2001
  Mel Eugene Carnahan, D: 1993–2000
  John Ashcroft, R: 1985–1993

DESTINATIONS
Major cities (2015 population):
  Kansas City: 475,378
  St. Louis: 315,685
  Springfield: 166,810
  Columbia: 119,108
  Independence: 117,255
,International airports
  Kansas City, St. Louis

National monuments, landmarks, and parks: Silver Dollar City, Mark Twain Area, Pony Express Museum, Harry S. Truman Library, Gateway Arch, Worlds of Fun, Lake of the Ozarks, Churchill Memorial, State Capitol
Web site: www.state.mo.us

MONTANA

DEMOGRAPHY
Population (2016): 1,042,520
Population (2006): 944,632
Under 18: 24%
65 or older: 18%
Density in p/sq mile (2015): 7.1
Persons per household: 2.42
Population by race % (2015):
  White: 89.2%
  Black: 0.6%
  American Indian/Aleut/Eskimo: 6.3%
  Asian: 0.8%
  Hispanic: 3.6%
  White/Non-Hispanic: 86.5%
  Native Hawaiian and Other Pacific Islander: 0.1%
  Persons reporting two or more races: 2.7%

POPULATION CHARACTERISTICS
Marriage rate (per 1,000): 8.0
Birth rate (per 1,000)(2015): 12.2
Infant mortality rate (2015): 5.8
Percent of population with bachelor's degree: 29.5%
Average household income (2015): $51,395
Median home value: $193,500
Poverty rate: 14.6%
Average life expectancy: 78.5
Crime rate per 100,000
  Violent: 323.7
  Property: 2,472.9
Federal and state prisoners (2014): 3,699

ECONOMY
Chief industries: agriculture, timber, mining, tourism, oil and gas
Chief manufactured goods: food products, wood and paper products, primary metals, printing and publishing, petroleum and coal products
Chief crops: wheat, barley, sugar beets, hay oats
Nonfuel minerals: gold, palladium, platinum, sand and gravel
Sales tax (2016): none
Gross state product: $45.2 bil

GOVERNMENT AND POLITICS
US representatives: 1
Electoral votes: 3
State governors:
  Steve Bullock, D: 2013–
  Brian Schweitzer, D: 2005–2013
  Judy Martz, R: 2001–2005
  Marc Racicot, R: 1993–2001
  Stan Stephens, R: 1989–1993
  Ted Schwinden, D: 1981–1989

DESTINATIONS
Major cities (2015 population):
  Billings: 157,000
  Missoula: 71,022
  Great Falls: 59,638
  Bozeman: 43,405
  Butte-Silver Bow: 33,922
International airports:
  Billings, Missoula
National monuments, landmarks, and parks: Glacier National Park, Yellowstone National Park, Museum of the Rockies, Museum of the Plains Indian, Blackfeet Reservation, Little Bighorn Battlefield National Monument, Custer National Cemetery, Flathead Lake, Lewis and Clark Caverns State Park, Lewis and Clark Interpretive Center
Web site: www.state.mt.us

NEBRASKA

DEMOGRAPHY
Population (2016): 1,907,116
Population (2006): 1,768,331
Under 18: 28%
65 or older: 14%
Density in p/sq mile (2015): 24.7
Persons per household: 2.48
Population by race % (2015):
  White: 89.1%
  Black: 5.0%
  American Indian/Aleut/Eskimo:
  1.4%
  Asian: 2.3%
  Hispanic: 10.4%
  White/Non-Hispanic: 80.0%
  Native Hawaiian and Other Pacific
  Islander: 0.1%
  Persons reporting two or more
  races: 2.1%

POPULATION CHARACTERISTICS
Marriage rate (per 1,000): 6.4
Birth rate (per 1,000)(2015): 13.9
Infant mortality rate (2015): 4.9
Percent of population with bachelor's
  degree: 29.3%
Average household income (2015):
  $60,747
Median home value: $133,200
Poverty rate: 12.6%
Average life expectancy: 79.8
Crime rate per 100,000
  Violent: 280.4
  Property: 2,523.5
Federal and state prisoners (2014):
  5,441

ECONOMY
Chief industries: agriculture and
  manufacturing
Chief manufactured goods: processed
  foods, industrial machinery, printed
  materials, electrical and electronic
  equipment, primary and fabricated
  metal products, transportation
  equipment
Chief crops: corn, sorghum, soybeans,
hay, wheat, dry beans, oats,
  potatoes, sugar beets
Nonfuel minerals: cement, stone,
  sand and gravel, lime
Sales tax (2016): 6.87%
Gross state product: $113.3 bil

GOVERNMENT AND POLITICS
US representatives: 3
Electoral votes: 5
State governors:
  Pete Ricketts, R: 2015–
  Dave Heineman, R: 2005–2015
  Mike Johanns R: 1999–2005
  E. Benjamin Nelson, D: 1991–
  1999
  Kay A. Orr, R: 1987–1991
  Joseph Robert (Bob) Kerrey, D:
  1983–1987

DESTINATIONS
Major cities (2015 population):
  Omaha: 443,885
  Lincoln: 277,348
  Bellevue: 55,510
  Grand Island: 51,440
  Kearney: 33,021
International airports:
  none
National monuments, landmarks,
  and parks: State Museum Elephant
  Hall, State Capitol, Stuhr Museum
  of the Prairie Pioneer, Museum of
  the Fur Trade, Henry Dorley Zoo,
  Joslyn Art Museum, Ashfall Fossil
  Beds, Strategic Air Command
  Museum, Boys Town, Arbor Lodge
  State Park, Buffalo Bill Ranch
  State Historical Park, Pioneer
  Village, Oregon Trail Landmarks,
  Scotts Bluff National Monument,
  Chimney Rock National Historic
  Site, Ft. Robinson, Hastings
  Museum
Web site: www.state.ne.us

NEVADA

DEMOGRAPHY
Population (2016): 2,940,058
Population (2006): 2,495,529
Under 18: 25%
65 or older: 14%
Density in p/sq mile (2015): 26.3
Persons per household: 2.74
Population by race % (2015):
  White: 75.7%
  Black: 9.3%
  American Indian/Aleut/Eskimo:
  1.6%
  Asian: 8.5%
  Hispanic: 28.1%
  White/Non-Hispanic: 50.7%
  Native Hawaiian and Other Pacific
  Islander: 0.6%
  Persons reporting two or more
  races: 2.6%

POPULATION CHARACTERISTICS
Marriage rate (per 1,000): 31.0
Birth rate (per 1,000)(2015): 12.6
Infant mortality rate (2015): 5.1
Percent of population with bachelor's
  degree: 23.0%
Average household income (2015):
  $52,008
Median home value: $173,700
Poverty rate: 14.7%
Average life expectancy: 78.1
Crime rate per 100,000
  Violent: 635.6
  Property: 2,625.4
Federal and state prisoners (2014):
  12,537

ECONOMY
Chief industries: gaming, tourism,
  mining, manufacturing,
  government, retailing, warehousing,
  trucking
Chief manufactured goods: food
  products, plastics, chemicals,
  aerospace products, lawn and
  garden irrigation equipment,
  seismic and machinery-monitoring
  devices
Chief crops: hay, alfalfa seed,
  potatoes, onions, garlic, barley,
  wheat

---

* Sales tax: City, county, and municipal rates vary. Rates shown are weighted by population to compute an average local tax rate.

Nonfuel minerals: gold, sand and
  gravel, lime, stone, diatomite
Sales tax (2016): 7.98%
Gross state product: $139.7 bil

GOVERNMENT AND POLITICS
US representatives: 4
Electoral votes: 6
State governors:
  Brian Sandoval, R: 2011–
  Jim Gibbons, R: 2007–2011
  Kenny Guinn, R: 1999–2007
  Bob Miller, D: 1989–1999
  Richard H. Bryan, D: 1983–1989
  Robert Frank List, R: 1979–1983

DESTINATIONS
Major cities (2015 population):
  Las Vegas: 623,747
  Henderson: 285,667
  Reno: 241,445
  North Las Vegas: 234,807
  Paradise: 232,000
International airports:
  Las Vegas, Reno
National monuments, landmarks,
  and parks: Lake Tahoe, Reno, Las
  Vegas, Lauglin, Elko County (all
  legalized gambling sites), Hoover
  Dam, Lake Mead, Great Basin
  National Park, Valley of Fire State
  Park, Virginia City, Red Rock
  Canyon National Conservation
  Area, Liberace Museum, Las Vegas
  Strip, Guinness World Records
  Museum, Lost City Museum,
  Lamoille Canyon, Pyramid Lake
Web site: www.nv.gov

NEW HAMPSHIRE

DEMOGRAPHY
Population (2016): 1,334,795
Population (2006): 1,314,895
Under 18: 22%
65 or older: 16%
Density in p/sq mile (2015): 148.6
Persons per household: 2.49
Population by race % (2015):

White: 93.9%
Black: 1.5%
American Indian/Aleut/Eskimo:
  0.3%
Asian: 2.6%
Hispanic: 3.4%
White/Non-Hispanic: 91.0%
Native Hawaiian and Other Pacific
  Islander: 0%
Persons reporting two or more
  races: 1.6%

POPULATION CHARACTERISTICS
Marriage rate (per 1,000): 6.9
Birth rate (per 1,000)(2015): 9.5
Infant mortality rate (2015): 4.9
Percent of population with bachelor's
  degree: 34.9%
Average household income (2015):
  $75,675
Median home value: $237,300
Poverty rate: 8.2%
Average life expectancy: 80.3
Crime rate per 100,000
  Violent: 196.1
  Property: 1,962.7
Federal and state prisoners (2014):
  2,963

ECONOMY
Chief industries: tourism,
  manufacturing, agriculture, trade,
  mining
Chief manufactured goods:
  machinery, electrical and electronic
  products, plastics, fabricated metal
  products
Chief crops: dairy products, nursery
  greenhouse products, hay,
  vegetables, fruit, maple syrup, sugar
  products
Sales tax (2016): none
Gross state product: $73.9 bil

GOVERNMENT AND POLITICS
US representatives: 2
Electoral votes: 4
State governors:
  Chris Sununu, R: 2017–

Maggie Hassan, D: 2013–2017
John Lynch, D: 2005– 2013
Craig Benson, R: 2003–2005
Jeanne Shaheen, D: 1997–2003
Stephen Merrill, R: 1995–1999
Judd Gregg, R: 1989–1993

DESTINATIONS
Major cities (2015 population):
  Manchester: 110,229
  Nashua: 87,970
  Concord: 42,620
  Dover: 30,880
  Rochester: 30,038
International airports:
  none
National monuments, landmarks,
  and parks: Mt. Washington, Lake
  Winnipesaukee, White Mountain
  National Forest, Franconia,
  Pinkham notches, the Flume,
  Cannon Mountain aerial tramway,
  Strawberry Banke, Shaker Village,
  Saint-Gaudens National Historic
  Site, Mt. Monadnock
Web site: www.state.nh.us

NEW JERSEY

DEMOGRAPHY
Population (2016): 8,944,469
Population (2006): 8,724,560
Under 18: 24%
65 or older: 15%
Density in p/sq mile (2015): 1,210.1
Persons per household: 2.75
Population by race % (2015):
  White: 72.6%
  Black: 14.8%
  American Indian/Aleut/Eskimo:
    0.6%
  Asian: 9.7%
  Hispanic: 19.7%
  White/Non-Hispanic: 56.2%
  Native Hawaiian and Other Pacific
    Islander: 0.1%
  Persons reporting two or more
    races: 2.1%

POPULATION CHARACTERISTICS

Marriage rate (per 1,000): 5.6
Birth rate (per 1,000)(2015): 11.5
Infant mortality rate (2015): 4.5
Percent of population with bachelor's degree: 36.8%
Average household income (2015): $68,357
Median home value: $315,900
Poverty rate: 10.8%
Average life expectancy: 80.3
Crime rate per 100,000
  Violent: 261.2
  Property: 1,626.5
Federal and state prisoners (2014): 21,590

ECONOMY

Chief industries: pharmaceuticals and drugs, telecommunications, biotechnology, printing and publishing
Chief manufactured goods: chemicals, electronic equipment, food
Chief crops: nursery and greenhouse, tomatoes, blueberries, peaches, peppers, cranberries, soybeans
Nonfuel minerals: stone, sand and gravel, greensand, marl, peat
Sales tax (2015): 6.97%
Gross state product: $567.7 bil

GOVERNMENT AND POLITICS

US representatives: 12
Electoral votes: 14
State governors:
  Chris Christie, R: 2010–
  Jon Corzine, D: 2006–2010
  Richard J. Codey, D: 2002–2006
  James E. McGreevey, D: 2002–2004
  John O. Bennett, R: 2002–2002
  Donald T. DiFrancesco, R: 2001–2002

DESTINATIONS

Major cities (2015 population):
  Newark: 281,944
  Jersey City: 264,290
  Paterson: 147,754
  Elizabeth: 129,007
  Edison: 102,701
International airports:
  Atlantic City and Newark
National monuments, landmarks, and parks: 127 miles of beaches, Atlantic City, Grover Cleveland Birthplace, Cape May Historic District, Edison National Historic Site, Six Flags Great Adventure, Liberty State Park, Meadowlands Sports Complex, Pine Barrens wilderness area, Princeton University, State Aquarium, Long Beach Island
Web site: www.state.nj.us

NEW MEXICO

DEMOGRAPHY

Population (2016): 2,081,015
Population (2006): 1,954,599
Under 18: 26%
65 or older: 17%
Density in p/sq mile (2015): 17.2
Persons per household: 2.68
Population by race % (2015):
  White: 82.5%
  Black: 2.6%
  American Indian/Aleut/Eskimo: 10.5%
  Asian: 1.7%
  Hispanic: 48.0%
  White/Non-Hispanic: 38.4%
  Native Hawaiian and Other Pacific Islander: 0.1%
  Persons reporting two or more races: 2.5%

POPULATION CHARACTERISTICS

Marriage rate (per 1,000): 6.2
Birth rate (per 1,000)(2015): 12.6
Infant mortality rate (2015): 6.1
Percent of population with bachelor's degree: 26.3%
Average household income (2015): $45,119
Median home value: $160,300
Poverty rate: 20.4%
Average life expectancy: 78.4
Crime rate per 100,000
  Violent: 597.4
  Property: 3,697.4
Federal and state prisoners (2014): 7,021

ECONOMY

Chief industries: government, services, trade
Chief manufactured goods: foods, machinery, apparel, lumber, printing, transportation equipment, electronics, semiconductors
Chief crops: hay, onions, chiles, greenhouse and nursery, pecans, cotton
Nonfuel minerals: potash, copper, sand and gravel, cement, stone
Sales tax (2015): 7.54%
Gross state product: $93.3 bil

GOVERNMENT AND POLITICS

US representatives: 3
Electoral votes: 5
State governors:
  Susan Martinez, R: 2011–
  Bill Richardson, D: 2003–2011
  Gary E. Johnson, R: 1995–2003
  Garrey E. Carruthers, R: 1987–1990
  Toney Anaya, D: 1983–1987
  Bruce King, D: 1991–1995, 1979–1983, 1971–1975

DESTINATIONS

Major cities (2015 population):
  Albuquerque: 559,121
  Las Cruces: 101,543
  Rio Rancho: 94,171
  Santa Fe: 84,099
  Roswell: 48,544
International airports:
  Albuquerque
National monuments, landmarks, and parks: Carlsbad Caverns National Park, Santa Fe, White

---

* Sales tax: City, county, and municipal rates vary. Rates shown are weighted by population to compute an average local tax rate.

Sands National Monument, Acoma Pueblo, Taos, Taos Art Colony, Taos Ski Valley, Ute Lake State Park
Web site: www.state.nm.us

NEW YORK

DEMOGRAPHY
Population (2016): 19,745,289
Population (2006): 19,306,183
Under 18: 23%
65 or older: 16%
Density in p/sq mile (2015): 420.1
Persons per household: 2.66
Population by race % (2015):
  White: 70.1%
  Black: 17.6%
  American Indian/Aleut/Eskimo: 1.0%
  Asian: 8.8%
  Hispanic: 18.8%
  White/Non-Hispanic: 56.0%
  Native Hawaiian and Other Pacific Islander: 0.1%
  Persons reporting two or more races: 2.4%

POPULATION CHARACTERISTICS
Marriage rate (per 1,000): 7.1
Birth rate (per 1,000)(2015): 12.1
Infant mortality rate (2015): 5.0
Percent of population with bachelor's degree: 34.2%
Average household income (2015): $58,005
Median home value: $283,400
Poverty rate: 15.4%
Average life expectancy: 80.5
Crime rate per 100,000
  Violent: 381.8
  Property: 1,604
Federal and state prisoners (2014): 52,518

ECONOMY
Chief industries: manufacturing, finance, communications, tourism, transportation, services
Chief manufactured goods: books and periodicals, clothing and apparel, pharmaceuticals, machinery, instruments, toys and sporting goods, electronic equipment, automotive and aircraft components
Chief crops: apples, grapes, strawberries, cherries, pears, onions, potatoes, cabbage, sweet corn, green beans, cauliflower, field corn, hay, wheat, oats, dry beans
Nonfuel minerals: wollastonite, stone, cement, salt, sand and gravel
Sales tax (2016): 8.49%
Gross state product: $1,433.5 bil

GOVERNMENT AND POLITICS
US representatives: 27
Electoral votes: 29
State governors:
  Andrew Cuomo, D: 2011–
  David A. Paterson, D: 2008–2010
  Eliot Spitzer, D: 2007–2008
  George E. Pataki, R: 1995–2007
  Mario Matthew Cuomo, D: 1983–1995
  Hugh Leo Carey, D: 1975–1983

DESTINATIONS
Major cities (2015 population):
  New York: 8,550,405
  Buffalo: 258,071
  Rochester: 209,802
  Yonkers: 201,116
  Syracuse: 144,142
International airports:
  Albany, Buffalo, New York, Newburgh, Rochester, Syracuse
National monuments, landmarks, and parks: New York City, Adirondack and Catskill Mtns., Finger Lakes, Great Lakes, Thousand Islands, Niagra Falls, Saratoga Springs, Philipsburg Manor, Sunnyside (Washington Irving's home), the Dutch Church of Sleepy Hollow
Web site: www.state.ny.us

NORTH CAROLINA

DEMOGRAPHY
Population (2016): 10,146,788
Population (2006): 8,856,505
Under 18: 24%
65 or older: 14%
Density in p/sq mile (2015): 212.3
Persons per household: 2.55
Population by race % (2015):
  White: 71.2%
  Black: 22.1%
  American Indian/Aleut/Eskimo: 1.6%
  Asian: 1.9%
  Hispanic: 9.1%
  White/Non-Hispanic: 63.8%
  Native Hawaiian and Other Pacific Islander: 0.1%
  Persons reporting two or more races: 2.1%

POPULATION CHARACTERISTICS
Marriage rate (per 1,000): 7.0
Birth rate (per 1,000)(2015): 12.1
Infant mortality rate (2015): 7.2
Percent of population with bachelor's degree: 28.4%
Average household income (2015): $50,797
Median home value: $154,900
Poverty rate: 16.4%
Average life expectancy: 77.8
Crime rate per 100,000
  Violent: 329.5
  Property: 2,750.1
Federal and state prisoners (2014): 37,096

ECONOMY
Chief industries: manufacturing, agriculture, tourism
Chief manufactured goods: food products, textiles, industrial machinery and equipment, electrical and electronic equipment, furniture, tobacco products, apparel
Chief crops: tobacco, cotton, soybeans, corn, food grains, peanuts, sweet potatoes

Nonfuel minerals: stone, phosphate rock, sand and gravel, feldspar
Sales tax (2015): 6.9%
Gross state product: $495.4 bil

GOVERNMENT AND POLITICS
US representatives: 13
Electoral votes: 15
State governors:
Roy Cooper, D: 2017–
Pat McCrory, R: 2013–2017
Beverly Perdue, D: 2009–2013
Michael F. Easley, D: 2001–2009
James B. Hunt Jr., D: 1993–2001
James G. Martin, R: 1985–1993
James E. Holshouser Jr., R: 1973–1977
Robert Walter Scott, D: 1969–1973

DESTINATIONS
Major cities (2015 population):
Charlotte: 827,097
Raleigh: 451,066
Greensboro: 285,342
Durham: 257,636
Winston-Salem: 241,218
International airports:
Charlotte, Greensboro, Raleigh/Durham, Wilmington
National monuments, landmarks, and parks: Cape Hatteras National Seashore, Cape Lookout National Seashore, Great Smokey Mountains, Guilford Courthouse Park, Moore's Creek Park, 66 different Revolution battle sites, Bennett Place, Fort Raleigh, Wright Brothers National Memorial at Kitty Hawk, Battleship *North Carolina,* North Carolina Zoo, NC Symphony, NC Museum, Carl Sandburg Home, Biltmore House and Gardens
Web site: www.nc.gov

NORTH DAKOTA

DEMOGRAPHY
Population (2016): 757,952

Population (2006): 635,867
Under 18: 24%
65 or older: 15%
Density in p/sq mile (2015): 11.0
Persons per household: 2.33
Population by race % (2015):
White: 88.6%
Black: 2.4%
American Indian/Aleut/Eskimo: 5.5%
Asian: 1.4%
Hispanic: 3.5%
White/Non-Hispanic: 85.8%
Native Hawaiian and Other Pacific Islander: 0.1%
Persons reporting two or more races: 2.1%

POPULATION CHARACTERISTICS
Marriage rate (per 1,000): 6.2
Birth rate (per 1,000)(2015): 14.9
Infant mortality rate (2015): 6.2
Percent of population with bachelor's degree: 27.7%
Average household income (2015): $57,415
Median home value: $153,800
Poverty rate: 10.8%
Average life expectancy: 79.5
Crime rate per 100,000
Violent: 265.1
Property: 2,116.5
Federal and state prisoners (2014): 1,718

ECONOMY
Chief industries: agriculture, mining, tourism , manufacturing, telecommunications, energy, food processing
Chief manufactured goods: Farm equipment, processed foods, fabricated metal, high-tech electronics
Chief crops: spring wheat, durum, barley, flaxseed, oats, potatoes, dry edible beans, honey, soybeans, sugar beets, sunflowers, hay

Nonfuel minerals: sand and gravel, lime, stone, clays
Sales tax (2016): 6.82%
Gross state product: $55.9 bil

GOVERNMENT AND POLITICS
US representatives: 1
Electoral votes: 3
State governors:
Doug Burgum, R: 2016–
Jack Dalrymple, R: 2010–2016
John Hoeven, R: 2000–2010
Edward Thomas Schafer, R: 1992–2000
George Albert Sinner, D: 1985–1992
Allen Ingvar Olson, R: 1981–1985
Arthur Albert Link, D: 1973–1981

DESTINATIONS
Major cities (2015 population):
Fargo: 118,523
Bismarck: 71,167
Grand Forks: 57,011
Minot: 49,450
Mandan: 21,382
International airports:
Fargo
National monuments, landmarks, and parks: North Dakota Heritage Center, Bonanzaville, Ft. Union Trading Post National Historical Site, Lake Sakakawea, International Peace Garden, Theodore Roosevelt National Park, Ft. Abraham Lincoln State Park and Museum, Dakota Dinosaur Museum, Knife River Indian Villages National Historical Site
Web site: www.discovernd.com

OHIO

DEMOGRAPHY
Population (2016): 11,614,373
Population (2006): 11,478,006
Under 18: 24%
65 or older: 15%
Density in p/sq mile (2015): 284.2

---

*   Sales tax: City, county, and municipal rates vary. Rates shown are weighted by population to compute an average local tax rate.

Persons per household: 2.45
Population by race % (2015):
White: 82.7%
Black: 12.7%
American Indian/Aleut/Eskimo: 0.3%
Asian: 2.1%
Hispanic: 3.6%
White/Non-Hispanic: 79.8%
Native Hawaiian and Other Pacific Islander: 0.1%
Persons reporting two or more races: 2.1%

POPULATION CHARACTERISTICS

Marriage rate (per 1,000): 5.9
Birth rate (per 1,000)(2015): 12.1
Infant mortality rate (2015): 7.4
Percent of population with bachelor's degree: 26.1%
Average household income (2015): $53,301
Median home value: $129,900
Poverty rate: 14.8%
Average life expectancy: 77.8
Crime rate per 100,000
Violent: 284.9
Property: 2,587.7
Federal and state prisoners (2014): 51,519

ECONOMY

Chief industries: manufacturing, trade, services
Chief manufactured goods: transportation equipment, machinery, primary and fabricated metal products
Chief crops: corn, hay, winter wheat, oats, soybeans
Nonfuel minerals: stone, sand and gravel, salt, lime, cement
Sales tax (2016): 7.14%
Gross state product: $610.9 bil

GOVERNMENT AND POLITICS

US representatives: 16
Electoral votes: 18
State governors:
John Kasich, R: 2011–

Ted Strickland, D: 2007–2011
Bob Taft, R: 1999–2007
Nancy P. Hollister, R: 1998–1999
George V. Voinovich, R: 1991–1998
Richard F. Celeste, D: 1983–1991

DESTINATIONS

Major cities (2015 population):
Columbus: 850,106
Cleveland: 388,072
Cincinnati: 298,550
Toledo: 279,789
Akron: 197,542
International airports:
Akron, Cincinnati, Cleveland, Columbus, Dayton
National monuments, landmarks, and parks: Mound City Group, Hopewell Culture National Historical Park, Neil Armstrong Air and Space Museum, Air Force Museum, Pro Football Hall of Fame, Kings Island amusement park, Lake Erie islands, Cedar Point amusement park, homes and memorials for the following US presidents: W. H. Harrison, Grant, Garfield, Hayes, McKinley, Harding, Taft, B. Harrison, Amish Region, Tuscarawas/Holmes counties, German Village, Sea World, Jack Nicklaus Sports Center, Bob Evans Farm, Rio Grande, Rock and Roll Hall of Fame and Museum
Web site: www.ohio.gov

OKLAHOMA

DEMOGRAPHY

Population (2016): 3,923,561
Population (2006): 3,579,212
Under 18: 26%
65 or older: 14%
Density in p/sq mile (2015): 50.3
Persons per household: 2.59
Population by race % (2015):
White: 74.8%

Black: 7.8%
American Indian/Aleut/Eskimo: 8.6%
Asian: 2.2%
Hispanic: 10.1%
White/Non-Hispanic: 66.5%
Native Hawaiian and Other Pacific Islander: 0.2%
Persons reporting two or more races: 6.0%

POPULATION CHARACTERISTICS

Marriage rate (per 1,000): 7.4
Birth rate (per 1,000)(2015): 13.9
Infant mortality rate (2015): 7.1
Percent of population with bachelor's degree: 24.1%
Average household income (2015): $47,077
Median home value: $117,900
Poverty rate: 16.1%
Average life expectancy: 75.9
Crime rate per 100,000
Violent: 406.0
Property: 2,885.9
Federal and state prisoners (2014): 27,650

ECONOMY

Chief industries: manufacturing, mineral and energy exploration and production, agriculture, services
Chief manufactured goods: nonelectrical machinery, transportation equipment, food products, fabricated metal products
Chief crops: soybeans, corn, pecans, cotton, hay, wheat, peanuts, grain sorghum
Nonfuel minerals: stone, cement, sand and gravel, iodine
Sales tax (2016): 8.82%
Gross state product: $185.9 bil

GOVERNMENT AND POLITICS

US representatives: 5
Electoral votes: 7
State governors:
Mary Fallin, R: 2011–

Brad Henry, D: 2003–2011
Francis Anthony Keating, R: 1995–2003
David Lee Walters, D: 1991–1995
Henry Louis Bellmon, R: 1987–1991
George Patterson Nigh, D: 1979–1987

DESTINATIONS
Major cities (2015 population):
Oklahoma City: 631,346
Tulsa: 403,505
Norman: 120,284
Broken Arrow: 106,563
Lawton: 96,655
International airports:
Oklahoma City, Tulsa
National monuments, landmarks, and parks: Cherokee Heritage Center, Oklahoma City National Memorial, White Water Bay and Frontier City theme parks, Will Rogers Memorial, National Cowboy Hall of Fame, Remington Park Race Track, Ft. Gibson Stockade, Ouachita National Forest, Tulsa's art deco district, Wichita Mtns.Wildlife Refuge, Woolaroc Museum and Wildlife Preserve, Sequoyah's Home Site, Philbrook Museum of Art, Gilcrease Museum
Web site: www.ok.gov

OREGON

DEMOGRAPHY
Population (2016): 4,093,465
Population (2006): 3,700,758
Under 18: 23%
65 or older: 15%
Density in p/sq mile (2015): 42.0
Persons per household: 2.54
Population by race % (2015):
White: 87.6%
Black: 2.1%
American Indian/Aleut/Eskimo: 1.4%

Asian: 4.4%
Hispanic: 12.7%
White/Non-Hispanic: 76.6%
Native Hawaiian and Other Pacific Islander: 0.4%
Persons reporting two or more races: 3.7%

POPULATION CHARACTERISTICS
Marriage rate (per 1,000): 6.9
Birth rate (per 1,000)(2015): 11.5
Infant mortality rate (2015): 5.1
Percent of population with bachelor's degree: 30.8%
Average household income (2015): $60,834
Median home value: $237,300
Poverty rate: 15.4%
Average life expectancy: 79.5
Crime rate per 100,000
Violent: 232.3
Property: 2,946.6
Federal and state prisoners (2014): 15,075

ECONOMY
Chief industries: manufacturing, services, trade, finance, insurance, real estate, government, construction
Chief manufactured goods: electronics and semiconductors
Chief crops: greenhouse, hay, wheat, grass seed, potatoes, onions, Christmas trees, pears, mint
Nonfuel minerals: sand and gravel, stone, cement, diatomite, lime
Sales tax (2016): none
Gross state product: $217.6 bil

GOVERNMENT AND POLITICS
US representatives: 5
Electoral votes: 7
State governors:
Kate Brown, D: 2015–
John Kitzhaber, D: 2011–2015
Ted Kulongoski, D: 2003–2011
John A. Kitzhaber M.D., D: 1995–2003

Barbara Roberts, D: 1991–1995
Neil Goldschmidt, D: 1987–1991
Victor G. Atiyeh, R: 1979–1987

DESTINATIONS
Major cities (2015 population):
Portland: 632,309
Salem: 164,549
Eugene: 163,460
Gresham: 110,553
Hillsboro: 102,347
International airports:
Portland, Medford
National monuments, landmarks, and parks: John Day Fossil Beds National Monument, Columbia River Gorge, Timberline Lodge, Mt. Hood National Forest, Crater Lake National Park, Oregon Dunes National Recreation Area, Ft. Clatsop National Memorial, Oregon Caves National Monument, Oregon Museum of Science and Industry, High Desert Museum, Multnomah Falls, Diamond Lake, Evergreen Aviation Museum
Web site: www.oregon.gov

PENNSYLVANIA

DEMOGRAPHY
Population (2016): 12,784,227
Population (2006): 12,440,621
Under 18: 23%
65 or older: 17%
Density in p/sq mile (2015): 286.1
Persons per household: 2.5
Population by race % (2015):
White: 82.6%
Black: 11.7%
American Indian/Aleut/Eskimo: 0.4%
Asian: 3.4%
Hispanic: 6.8%
White/Non-Hispanic: 77.4%
Native Hawaiian and Other Pacific Islander: 0.1%
Persons reporting two or more races: 1.9%

* Sales tax: City, county, and municipal rates vary. Rates shown are weighted by population to compute an average local tax rate.

POPULATION CHARACTERISTICS

Marriage rate (per 1,000): 5.7

Birth rate (per 1,000)(2015): 11.1

Infant mortality rate (2015): 6.9

Percent of population with bachelor's
degree: 28.6%

Average household income (2015):
$60,389

Median home value: $166,000

Poverty rate: 13.2%

Average life expectancy: 78.5

Crime rate per 100,000
Violent: 314.1
Property: 1,812.8

Federal and state prisoners (2014):
50,694

ECONOMY

Chief industries: agribusiness,
advanced manufacturing, health
care, travel and tourism, depository
institutions, biotechnology,
printing and publishing, research
and consulting, trucking and
warehousing, transportation by air,
engineering and management, legal
services

Chief manufactured goods: fabricated
metal products, industrial
machinery and equipment,
transportation equipment,
chemicals and pharmaceuticals,
lumber and wood products, stone,
clay, and glass products

Chief crops: corn, hay, winter wheat,
mushrooms, apples, potatoes, oats,
vegetables, tobacco, grapes, peaches

Nonfuel minerals: stone, cement,
sand and gravel, lime

Sales tax (2016): 6.34%

Gross state product: $709.8 bil

GOVERNMENT AND POLITICS

US representatives: 18

Electoral votes: 20

State governors:
Tom Wolf, D: 2015–
Tom Corbett, R: 2011–2015
Edward G. Rendell, D: 2003–2011

Mark Schweiker, R: 2001–2003
Tom Ridge, R: 1995–2001
Robert P. Casey Sr., D: 1987–1995
Dick Thornburgh, R: 1979–1987

DESTINATIONS

Major cities (2015 population):
Philadelphia: 1,567,442
Pittsburgh: 304,391
Allentown: 120,207
Erie: 99,475
Reading: 87,879

International airports:
Allentown, Harrisburg,
Philadelphia, Pittsburgh, Wilkes-
Barre/Scranton

National monuments, landmarks,
and parks: Independence National
Historical Park, Franklin Institute
Science Museum, Philadelphia
Museum of Art, Valley Forge
National Historic Park, Gettysburg
National Military Park,
Pennsylvania Dutch Country,
Hershey, Duquesne Incline,
Carnegie Institute, Heinz Hall,
Pocono Mtns., Pennsylvania's
Grand Canyon, Allegheny National
Forest, Laurel Highlands, Presque
Isle State Park, Falling Water at
Mill Run, Johnstown, SteamTown
U.S.A., State Flagship *Niagara*, Oil
Heritage Region

Web site: www.state.pa.us

RHODE ISLAND

DEMOGRAPHY

Population (2016): 1,056,426

Population (2006): 1,067,610

Under 18: 22%

65 or older: 16%

Density in p/sq mile (2015): 1,021.6

Persons per household: 2.49

Population by race % (2015):
White: 84.8%
Black: 7.9%
American Indian/Aleut/Eskimo:
1.0%

Asian: 3.6%

Hispanic: 14.4%

White/Non-Hispanic: 73.9%

Native Hawaiian and Other Pacific
Islander: 0.2%

Persons reporting two or more
races: 2.6%

POPULATION CHARACTERISTICS

Marriage rate (per 1,000): 6.4

Birth rate (per 1000)(2005): 10.4

Infant mortality rate (2015): 6.5

Percent of population with bachelor's
degree: 31.9%

Average household income (2015):
$55,701

Median home value: $238,000

Poverty rate: 13.9%

Average life expectancy: 79.9

Crime rate per 100,000
Violent: 219.2
Property: 2,586.9

Federal and state prisoners (2014):
3,359

ECONOMY

Chief industries: agribusiness,
advanced manufacturing, health
care, travel and tourism, depository
institutions, biotechnology,
printing and publishing, research
and consulting, trucking and
warehousing, transportation by air,
engineering and management, legal
services

Chief manufactured goods: fabricated
metal products, industrial
machinery and equipment,
transportation equipment,
chemicals and pharmaceuticals,
lumber and wood products, stone,
clay, and glass products

Chief crops: corn, hay, winter wheat,
mushrooms, apples, potatoes, oats,
vegetables, tobacco, grapes, peaches

Nonfuel minerals: stone, cement,
sand and gravel, lime

Sales tax (2016): 7.0%

Gross state product: $56.1 bil

GOVERNMENT AND POLITICS

US representatives: 2

Electoral votes: 4

State governors:

  Gina Raimondo, D: 2015–

  Lincoln Chafee, D: 2013–2015

  Lincoln Chafee, I: 2011–2013

  Don Carcieri, R: 2003–2011

  Lincoln Almond, R: 1995–2003

  Bruce G. Sundlun, D: 1991–1995

  Edward D. DiPrete, R: 1985–1991

  Joseph Garrahy, D: 1977–1985

DESTINATIONS

Major cities (2015 population):

  Providence: 179,207

  Warwick: 81,699

  Cranston: 81,073

  Pawtucket: 71,591

  East Providence: 47,408

International airports:

National monuments, landmarks, and parks: Newport mansions, yachting races, Block Island, Touro Synagogue, first U.S. Baptist church, Slater Mill Historic Site, Gilbert Stuart Birthplace

Web site: www.state.ri.us

SOUTH CAROLINA

DEMOGRAPHY

Population (2016): 4,961,119

Population (2006): 4,321,249

Under 18: 24%

65 or older: 17%

Density in p/sq mile (2015): 162.9

Persons per household: 2.56

Population by race % (2015):

  White: 68.4%

  Black: 27.6%

  American Indian/Aleut/Eskimo: 0.5%

  Asian: 1.6%

  Hispanic: 5.5%

  White/Non-Hispanic: 63.8%

  Native Hawaiian and Other Pacific Islander: 0.1%

  Persons reporting two or more races: 1.8%

POPULATION CHARACTERISTICS

Marriage rate (per 1,000): 7.5

Birth rate (per 1,000)(2015): 11.9

Infant mortality rate (2015): 7.2

Percent of population with bachelor's degree: 25.8%

Average household income (2015): $46,360

Median home value: $139,900

Poverty rate: 16.6%

Average life expectancy: 77.0

Crime rate per 100,000

  Violent: 497.7

  Property: 1,897.5

Federal and state prisoners (2014): 21,401

ECONOMY

Chief industries: tourism, agriculture, manufacturing

Chief manufactured goods: textiles, chemicals and allied products, machinery and fabricated metal products, apparel

Chief crops: tobacco, cotton, soybeans, corn, wheat, peaches, tomatoes

Nonfuel minerals: cement, stone, sand and gravel, clays

Sales tax (2016): 7.22%

Gross state product: $201.0 bil

GOVERNMENT AND POLITICS

US representatives: 7

Electoral votes: 9

State governors:

  Henry McMaster, R: 2017–

  Nikki Haley, R: 2011–2017

  Mark Sanford, R: 2003–2011

  Jim Hodges, D: 1999–2003

  David M. Beasley, R: 1995–1999

  Carroll A. Campbell Jr., R: 1987–1995

  Richard Wilson Riley, D: 1979–1987

DESTINATIONS

Major cities (2015 population):

  Columbia: 133,803

  Charleston: 136,609

  North Charleston: 108,304

  Mount Pleasant: 81,317

  Rock Hill: 71,548

International airports: Charleston, Greenville/Spartanburg, Myrtle Beach

National monuments, landmarks, and parks: Historic Charleston, Ft. Sumter National Monument, Charleston Museum, Middleton Place, Magnolia Plantation, Cypress Gardens, Drayton Hall, Myrtle Beach, Hilton Head Island, Revolutionary War battle sites, Andrew Jackson State Park and Museum, South Carolina State Museum, Riverbanks Zoo

Web site: www.myscgov.com

SOUTH DAKOTA

DEMOGRAPHY

Population (2016): 865,454

Population (2006): 781,919

Under 18: 26%

65 or older: 16%

Density in p/sq mile (2015): 11.3

Persons per household: 2.43

Population by race % (2015):

  White: 85.5%

  Black: 1.8%

  American Indian/Aleut/Eskimo: 8.9%

  Asian: 1.4%

  Hispanic: 3.6%

  White/Non-Hispanic: 82.9%

  Native Hawaiian and Other Pacific Islander: 0.1%

  Persons reporting two or more races: 2.2%

POPULATION CHARACTERISTICS

Marriage rate (per 1,000): 7.2

Birth rate (per 1,000)(2015): 14.4

Infant mortality rate (2015): 7.7

Percent of population with bachelor's degree: 27.0%

Average household income (2015): $55,065

Median home value: $140,500

---

*   Sales tax: City, county, and municipal rates vary. Rates shown are weighted by population to compute an average local tax rate.

Poverty rate: 13.7%
Average life expectancy: 79.5
Crime rate per 100,000
    Violent: 326.5
    Property: 1943.0
Federal and state prisoners (2014): 3,608

ECONOMY

Chief industries: manufacturing, services, agriculture
Chief manufactured goods: food and kindred products, machinery, electrical and electronic equipment
Chief crops: corn, soybeans, oats, wheat, sunflowers, sorghum
Nonfuel minerals: cement, sand and gravel, stone, gold
Sales tax (2016): 5.84%
Gross state product: $47.2 bil

GOVERNMENT AND POLITICS

US representatives: 1
Electoral votes: 3
State governors:
    Dennis Daugaard, R: 2011–
    Mike Rounds, R: 2003–2011
    William J. Janklow, R: 1995–2003
    Walter D. Miller, R: 1993–1995
    George S. Mickelson, R: 1987–1993
    Harvey Wollman, D: 1978–1979

DESTINATIONS

Major cities (2015 population):
    Sioux Falls: 171,544
    Rapid City: 73,569
    Aberdeen: 28,102
    Watertown: 23,657
    Brookings: 22,073
International airports: none
National monuments, landmarks, and parks: Black Hills, Mt. Rushmore, Needles Highway, Harney Peak, Deadwood, Custer State Park, Jewel Cave National Monument, Badlands National Park, Ft. Sisseton, Great Plains Zoo and Museum, Sioux Falls, Corn Palace, Wind Cave National Park, Crazy Horse Memorial
Web site: www.state.sd.us

TENNESSEE

DEMOGRAPHY

Population (2016): 6,651,194
Population (2006): 6,038,803
Under 18: 24%
65 or older: 16%
Density in p/sq mile (2015): 160.1
Persons per household: 2.55
Population by race % (2015):
    White: 78.8%
    Black: 17.1%
    American Indian/Aleut/Eskimo: 0.4%
    Asian: 1.8%
    Hispanic: 5.2%
    White/Non-Hispanic: 74.4%
    Native Hawaiian and Other Pacific Islander: 0.1%
    Persons reporting two or more races: 1.8%

POPULATION CHARACTERISTICS

Marriage rate (per 1,000): 8.5
Birth rate (per 1,000)(2015): 12.4
Infant mortality rate (2015): 7.0
Percent of population with bachelor's degree: 24.9%
Average household income (2015): $47,330
Median home value: $142,100
Poverty rate: 16.7%
Average life expectancy: 76.3
Crime rate per 100,000
    Violent: 608.4
    Property: 2,936.2
Federal and state prisoners (2014): 28,769

ECONOMY

Chief industries: manufacturing, trade, services, tourism, finance, insurance, real estate
Chief manufactured goods: chemicals, food, transportation equipment, industrial machinery and equipment, fabricated metal products, rubber and plastic products, paper and allied products, printing and publishing
Chief crops: tobacco, cotton, lint, soybeans, grain, corn
Nonfuel minerals: stone, cement, sand and gravel, zinc, clays
Sales tax (2016): 9.46%
Gross state product: $315.9 bil

GOVERNMENT AND POLITICS

US representatives: 9
Electoral votes: 11
State governors:
    Bill Haslam, R: 2011–
    Phil Bredesen, D: 2003–2011
    Don Sundquist, R: 1995–2003
    Ned Ray McWherter, D: 1987–1995
    Lamar Alexander, R: 1979–1987
    Ray Blanton, D: 1975–1979

DESTINATIONS

Major cities (2015 population):
    Memphis: 655,770
    Nashville-Davidson: 654,610
    Knoxville: 185,291
    Chattanooga: 116,588
    Clarksville: 149,176
International airports:
    Memphis and Nashville
National monuments, landmarks, and parks: Reelfoot Lake, Lookout Mountain, Fall Creek Falls, Great Smokey Mountains National Park, Lost Sea, Cherokee National Forest, Cumberland Gap National Park, The Hermitage: Andrew Jackson's home, homes of Presidents Polk and Andrew Johnson, American Museum of Science and Energy, Parthenon, Grand Ole Opry, Opryland, Dollywood theme park, Tennessee Aquarium, Graceland, Alex Haley Home and Museum, Casey Jones Home and Museum
Web site: www.tn.gov

TEXAS

DEMOGRAPHY
Population (2016): 27,862,596
Population (2006): 23,507,783
Under 18: 28%
65 or older: 12%
Density in p/sq mile (2015): 105.2
Persons per household: 2.85
Population by race % (2015):
    White: 79.7%
    Black: 12.5%
    American Indian/Aleut/Eskimo:
    1.0%
    Asian: 4.7%
    Hispanic: 38.8%
    White/Non-Hispanic: 43.0%
    Native Hawaiian and Other Pacific
    Islander: 0.1%
    Persons reporting two or more
    races: 1.2%

POPULATION CHARACTERISTICS
Marriage rate (per 1,000): 7.2
Birth rate (per 1,000)(2015): 14.6
Infant mortality rate (2015): 5.8
Percent of population with bachelor's
    degree: 27.6%
Average household income (2015):
    $56,473
Median home value: $136,000
Poverty rate: 15.9%
Average life expectancy: 78.5
Crime rate per 100,000
    Violent: 405.9
    Property: 2,831.3
Federal and state prisoners (2014):
    166,043

ECONOMY
Chief industries:
    manufacturing, trade, oil and gas
    extraction, services
Chief manufactured goods: industrial
    machinery and equipment, foods,
    electrical and electronic products,
    chemicals and allied products,
    apparel
Chief crops: cotton, grains, sorghum

grain, vegetables, citrus and other
    fruits
Nonfuel minerals:
    cement, stone, sand and gravel, lime,
    salt
Sales tax (2016): 8.17%
Gross state product: $1,630.1 bil

GOVERNMENT AND POLITICS
US representatives: 36
Electoral votes: 38
State governors:
    Greg Abbott, R: 2015–
    Rick Perry, R: 2000–2015
    George W. Bush, R: 1995–2000
    Dorothy Ann Willis Richards, D:
    1991–1995
    William P. Clements Jr., R: 1987–
    1991
    Mark White, D: 1983–1987

DESTINATIONS
Major cities (2015 population):
    Houston: 2,296,224
    San Antonio: 1,469,845
    Dallas: 1,300,092
    Austin: 931,830
    Fort Worth: 833,319
International airports:
    Amarillo, Austin, Corpus Christi,
    Dallas/Ft. Worth, El Paso,
    Houston, San Antonio
National monuments, landmarks,
    and parks: Padre Island National
    Seashore, Guadalupe Mountains
    National Parks, The Alamo, Ft.
    Davis, Six Flags Amusement
    Park, Sea World, Fiesta Texas,
    San Antonio Missions National
    Historical Park, Cowgirl Hall
    of Fame, Lyndon B. Johnson
    Library and Museum, Texas State
    Aquarium, Kimball Art Museum,
    George Bush Library
Web site: www.state.tx.us

UTAH

DEMOGRAPHY
Population (2016): 3,051,217
Population (2006): 2,550,063

Under 18: 32%
65 or older: 11%
Density in p/sq mile (2015): 36.5
Persons per household: 3.17
Population by race % (2015):
    White: 91.2%
    Black: 1.3%
    American Indian/Aleut/Eskimo:
    1.5%
    Asian: 2.5%
    Hispanic: 13.7%
    White/Non-Hispanic: 61.6%
    Native Hawaiian and Other Pacific
    Islander: 1.0%
    Persons reporting two or more
    races: 2.4%

POPULATION CHARACTERISTICS
Marriage rate (per 1,000): 8.1
Birth rate (per 1,000)(2015): 17.3
Infant mortality rate (2015): 5.0
Percent of population with bachelor's
    degree: 31.1%
Average household income (2015):
    $66,258
Median home value: $215,900
Poverty rate: 11.3%
Average life expectancy: 80.2
Crime rate per 100,000
    Violent: 215.6
    Property: 2,980
Federal and state prisoners (2014):
    7,026

ECONOMY
Chief industries: services, trade,
    manufacturing, government,
    transportation, utilities
Chief manufactured goods:
    medical instruments, electronic
    components, food products,
    fabricated metals, transportation
    equipment, steel and copper
Chief crops: hay, corn, wheat, barley,
    apples, potatoes, cherries, onions,
    peaches, pears
Nonfuel minerals: copper, cement,
    salt, gold, sand and gravel
Sales tax (2016): 6.69%
Gross state product: $147.5 bil

---

* Sales tax: City, county, and municipal rates vary. Rates shown are weighted by population to compute an average local tax rate.

GOVERNMENT AND POLITICS

US representatives: 4

Electoral votes: 6

State governors:
Gary Herbert, R: 2009–
Jon Huntsman Jr., R: 2005–2009
Olene S. Walker, R: 2003–2005
Michael O. Leavitt, R: 1993–2003
Norman H. Bangerter, R: 1985–1993
Scott M. Matheson, D: 1977–1985

DESTINATIONS

Major cities (2015 population):
Salt Lake City: 192,672
West Valley City: 136,208
Provo: 115,264
West Jordan: 111,946
Orem: 94,457
International airports:
Salt Lake City
National monuments, landmarks, and parks: Temple Square, Mormon Church headquarters, Great Salt Lake, Canyonlands, Bryce Canyon, Arches, and Capitol Reef National Parks, Rainbow Bridge, Timpanogos Cave, Natural Bridges National Monuments, Lake Powell, Flaming Gorge National Recreation Area
Web site: www.utah.gov

VERMONT

DEMOGRAPHY

Population (2016): 624,594
Population (2006): 623,908
Under 18: 22%
65 or older: 17%
Density in p/sq mile (2015): 65.8
Persons per household: 2.36
Population by race % (2015):
White: 94.8%
Black: 1.3%
American Indian/Aleut/Eskimo: 0.4%
Asian: 1.6%
Hispanic: 1.8%

White/Non-Hispanic: 93.3%
Native Hawaiian and Other Pacific Islander: 0%
Persons reporting two or more races: 1.9%

POPULATION CHARACTERISTICS

Marriage rate (per 1,000): 8.1
Birth rate (per 1,000)(2015): 9.5
Infant mortality rate (2015): 4.3
Percent of population with bachelor's degree: 36%
Average household income (2015): $59,494
Median home value: $217,500
Poverty rate: 10.2%
Average life expectancy: 80.5
Crime rate per 100,000
Violent: 99.3
Property: 1,406.6
Federal and state prisoners (2014): 1,979

ECONOMY

Chief industries: manufacturing, tourism, agriculture, trade, finance, insurance, real estate, government
Chief manufactured goods: machine tools, furniture, scales, books, computer components, specialty foods
Chief crops: dairy products, apples, maple syrup, greenhouse/nursery, vegetables, small fruits
Nonfuel minerals: stone, sand and gravel, gemstones, talc
Sales tax (2016): 6.17%
Gross state product: $30.0 bil

GOVERNMENT AND POLITICS

US representatives: 1
Electoral votes: 3
State governors:
Phil Scott, R: 2017–
Peter Shumlin, D: 2011–2017
Jim Douglas, R: 2003–2011
Howard Dean, M.D., D: 1991–2003
Richard A. Snelling, R: 1991–1991

Madeleine M. Kunin, D: 1985–1991
Thomas P. Salmon, D: 1973–1977

DESTINATIONS

Major cities (2015 population):
Burlington: 42,452
South Burlington: 18,791
Colchester: 16,986
Rutland: 15,824
Essex: 10,111
International airports:
Burlington
National monuments, landmarks, and parks: Shelburne Museum, Rock of Ages Quarry, Vermont Marble Exhibit, Bennington Battle Monument, Calvin Coolidge homestead, Maple Grove Maple Museum, Ben and Jerry's Factory
Web site: www.vermont.gov

VIRGINIA

DEMOGRAPHY

Population (2016): 8,411,808
Population (2006): 7,642,884
Under 18: 24%
65 or older: 14%
Density in p/sq mile (2015): 206.6
Persons per household: 2.62
Population by race % (2015):
White: 70.2%
Black: 19.7%
American Indian/Aleut/Eskimo: 0.5%
Asian: 6.5%
Hispanic: 9.0%
White/Non-Hispanic: 62.7%
Native Hawaiian and Other Pacific Islander: 0.1%
Persons reporting two or more races: 2.9%

POPULATION CHARACTERISTICS

Marriage rate (per 1,000): 7.0
Birth rate (per 1,000)(2015): 12.4
Infant mortality rate (2015): 6.3
Percent of population with bachelor's degree: 36.3%

Average household income (2015): $61,486

Median home value: $245,000

Poverty rate: 11.2%

Average life expectancy: 79.0

Crime rate per 100,000
Violent: 196.2
Property: 1,866.5

Federal and state prisoners (2014): 37,544

ECONOMY

Chief industries: services, trade, government, manufacturing, tourism, agriculture

Chief manufactured goods: food processing, transportation equipment, printing, textiles, electrical and electronic equipment, industrial machinery and equipment, lumber and wood products, chemicals, rubber and plastic, furniture

Chief crops: tobacco, grain, corn, soybeans, winter wheat, peanuts, lint and seed cotton

Nonfuel minerals: stone, cement, sand and gravel, lime, clays

Sales tax (2016): 5.63%

Gross state product: $481.1 bil

GOVERNMENT AND POLITICS

US representatives: 11

Electoral votes: 13

State governors:
Terry McAuliffe, D: 2014–
Bob McDonnell, R: 2010–2014
Tim Kaine, D: 2006–2010
Mark Warner, D: 2002–2006
James S. Gilmore III, R: 1998–2002
George Allen, R: 1994–1998
L. Douglas Wilder, D: 1990–1994

DESTINATIONS

Major cities (2015 population):
Virginia Beach: 452,745
Norfolk: 246,393
Chesapeake: 235,429
Arlington: 229,164

Richmond: 220,289
Newport News: 182,385

International airports:
Arlington, Norfolk, Loudoun County, Richmond, Newport News

National monuments, landmarks, and parks: Colonial Williamsburg, Busch Gardens, Wolf Trap Farm, Arlington National Cemetery, Mt. Vernon, home of George Washington, Jamestown Festival Park, Jefferson's Monticello, Stratford Hall (Robert E. Lee's birthplace), Appomattox, Shenandoah National Park, Blue Ridge Parkway, Virginia Beach, Paramount's King's Dominion

Web site: www.virginia.gov

WASHINGTON

DEMOGRAPHY

Population (2016): 7,288,000

Population (2006): 6,395,798

Under 18: 24%

65 or older: 16%

Density in p/sq mile (2015): 107.9

Persons per household: 2.58

Population by race % (2015):
White: 80.3%
Black: 4.1%
American Indian/Aleut/Eskimo: 1.9%
Asian: 8.4%
Hispanic: 12.4%
White/Non-Hispanic: 69.8%
Native Hawaiian and Other Pacific Islander: 0.7%
Persons reporting two or more races: 4.6%

POPULATION CHARACTERISTICS

Marriage rate (per 1,000): 6.2

Birth rate (per 1,000)(2015): 12.5

Infant mortality rate (2015): 4.9

Percent of population with bachelor's degree: 32.9%

Average household income (2015): $67,243

Median home value: $259,500

Poverty rate: 12.2%

Average life expectancy: 79.0

Crime rate per 100,000
Violent: 285.2
Property: 3,463.8

Federal and state prisoners (2014): 18,120

ECONOMY

Chief industries: advanced technology, aerospace, biotechnology, international trade, forestry, tourism, recycling, agriculture, food processing

Chief manufactured goods: computer software, aircraft, pulp and paper, lumber and plywood, aluminum, processed fruits and vegetables, machinery, electronics

Chief crops: apples, hay, potatoes, farm forest products

Nonfuel minerals: sand and gravel, cement, stone, diatomite, lime

Sales tax (2016): 8.89%

Gross state product: $445.4 bil

GOVERNMENT AND POLITICS

US representatives: 10

Electoral votes: 12

State governors:
Jay Inslee, D: 2013–
Christine Gregoire, D: 2005–2013
Gary Locke, D: 1997–2005
Michael Lowry, D: 1993–1997
Booth Gardner, D: 1985–1993
John Dennis Spellman, R: 1981–1985

DESTINATIONS

Major cities (2015 population):
Seattle: 684,451
Spokane: 213,272
Tacoma: 207,948
Vancouver: 172,860
Bellevue: 139,820

International airports:
Seattle/Tacoma, Spokane, Boeing Field

National monuments, landmarks, and

---

* Sales tax: City, county, and municipal rates vary. Rates shown are weighted by population to compute an average local tax rate.

parks: Seattle Waterfront, Seattle Center and Space Needle, Museum of Flight, Underground Tour, Mt. Rainier, Olympic and Cascades National Parks, Mt. St. Helens, Puget Sound, San Juan Islands, Grand Coulee Dam, Columbia River Gorge National Scenic Area, Spokane Riverfront Park

Web site: www.access.wa.gov

WEST VIRGINIA

DEMOGRAPHY

Population (2016): 1,831,102
Population (2006): 1,818,470
Under 18: 23%
65 or older: 19%
Density in p/sq mile (2015): 76.7
Persons per household: 2.44
Population by race % (2015):
   White: 93.6%
   Black: 3.6%
   American Indian/Aleut/Eskimo:
   0.2%
   Asian: 0.8%
   Hispanic: 1.5%
   White/Non-Hispanic: 92.3%
   Native Hawaiian and Other Pacific
   Islander: 0%
   Persons reporting two or more
   races: 1.6%

POPULATION CHARACTERISTICS

Marriage rate (per 1,000): 6.6
Birth rate (per 1,000)(2015): 11.2
Infant mortality rate (2015): 7.4
Percent of population with bachelor's
   degree:: 19.2%
Average Household Income (2015):
   $42,824
Median home value: $103,800
Poverty rate: 17.9%
Average life expectancy: 75.4
Crime rate per 100,000
   Violent: 302.0
   Property: 2,020
Federal and state prisoners (2014):
   6,896

ECONOMY

Chief industries: manufacturing,
   mining, tourism, services
Chief manufactured goods:
   machinery, plastic and hardwood
   products, fabricated metals,
   chemicals, aluminum, automotive
   parts, steel
Chief crops: apples, peaches, hay,
   tobacco, corn, wheat, oats
Nonfuel minerals: stone, cement,
   sand and gravel, lime, salt
Sales tax (2016): 6.20%
Gross state product: $74.3 bil

GOVERNMENT AND POLITICS

US representatives: 3
Electoral votes: 5
State governors:
   Jim Justice, D: 2017–
   Earl Ray Tomblin, D: 2010–2017
   Joe Manchin III, D: 2005–2010
   Bob Wise, D: 2001–2005
   Cecil H. Underwood, R: 1997–
   2001
   Gaston Caperton, D: 1989–1997
   Arch A. Moore, R: 1985–1989

DESTINATIONS

Major cities (2015 population):
   Charleston: 49,736
   Huntington: 48,638
   Parkersburg: 30,991
   Morgantown: 30,708
   Wheeling: 27,648
International airports:
   none
National monuments, landmarks,
   and parks: Harpers Ferry National
   Historic Park, Science and
   Cultural Center, White Sulphur
   and Berkley Springs mineral water
   spas, New River Gorge, Wubter
   Okacem Exhibition Coal Mine,
   Monongahela National Forest,
   Fenton Glass, Viking Glass,
   Blenko Glass, Sternwheek Regatta,
   Mountain State National Forest
   Festival, Snowshow Ski Resort,

Canaan State Park, Mountain Stage
Arts and Crafts Fair, Ogle Bay

Web site: www.wv.gov

WISCONSIN

DEMOGRAPHY

Population (2016): 5,778,708
Population (2006): 5,556,506
Under 18: 24%
65 or older: 15.0%
Density in p/sq mile (2015): 106.6
Persons per household: 2.42
Population by race % (2015):
   White: 87.6%
   Black: 6.6%
   American Indian/Aleut/Eskimo:
   1.1%
   Asian: 2.8%
   Hispanic: 6.6%
   White/Non-Hispanic: 81.9%
   Native Hawaiian and Other Pacific
   Islander: 0.1%
   Persons reporting two or more
   races: 1.8%

POPULATION CHARACTERISTICS

Marriage rate (per 1,000): 5.6
Birth rate (per 1,000)(2015): 11.6
Infant mortality rate (2015): 6.0
Percent of population with bachelor's
   degree: 27.8%
Average household income (2015):
   $55,425
Median home value: $165,800
Poverty rate: 12.1%
Average life expectancy: 80.0
Crime rate per 100,000
   Violent: 290.3
   Property: 1,974
Federal and state prisoners (2014):
   22,597

ECONOMY

Chief industries: services
   manufacturing, trade, government,
   agriculture, tourism
Chief manufactured goods: food
   products, motor vehicles and

equipment, paper products, medical instruments and supplies, printing, plastics

Chief crops: corn, hay, soybeans, potatoes, cranberries, sweet corn, peas, oats, snap beans

Nonfuel minerals: stone, sand and gravel

Sales tax (2016): 5.41%

Gross state product: $302.1 bil

GOVERNMENT AND POLITICS

US representatives: 8

Electoral votes: 10

State governors:

Scott Walker, R: 2011–

Jim Doyle, D: 2003–2011

Scott McCallum, R: 2001–2003

Tommy G. Thompson, R: 1987–2001

Anthony S. Earl, D: 1983–1987

Lee Sherman Dreyfus Jr., R: 1979–1983

DESTINATIONS

Major cities (2015 population):

Milwaukee: 600,155

Madison: 248,941

Green Bay: 105,207

Kenosha: 99,858

Racine: 77,742

International airports:

Green Bay, Milwaukee

National monuments, landmarks, and parks: Old Wade House and Carnegie Museum, Villa Louis, Prairie du Chien, Circus World Museum, Wisconsin Dells, Old World Wisconsin, Door County Peninsula, Chequamegon National Forest, Nicolet National Forest, Lake Winnebago, House on the Rock, Monona Terrace

Web site: www.wisconsin.gov

WYOMING

DEMOGRAPHY

Population (2016): 585,501

Population (2006): 515,004

Under 18: 27%

65 or older: 15%

Density in p/sq mile (2015): 6.0

Persons per household: 2.5

Population by race % (2015):

White: 92.7%

Black: 1.4%

American Indian/Aleut/Eskimo: 2.7%

Asian: 1.0%

Hispanic: 9.9%

White/Non-Hispanic: 84.0%

Native Hawaiian and Other Pacific Islander: 0.1%

Persons reporting two or more races: 2.1%

POPULATION CHARACTERISTICS

Marriage rate (per 1,000): 7.3

Birth rate (per 1,000)(2015): 13.1

Infant mortality rate (2015): 5.2

Percent of population with bachelor's degree: 25.7%

Average household income (2015): $60,925

Median home value: $194,800

Poverty rate: 11.1%

Average life expectancy: 78.3

Crime rate per 100,000

Violent: 195.5

Property: 1,902.6

Federal and state prisoners (2014): 2,383

ECONOMY

Chief industries: mineral extraction, oil, natural gas, tourism and recreation, agriculture

Chief manufactured goods: refined petroleum, wood, stone, clay products, foods, electronic devices, sporting apparel, aircraft

Chief crops: wheat, beans, barley, oats, sugar beets, hay

Nonfuel minerals: soda ash, clays, helium, sand and gravel

Sales tax (2016): 5.42%

Gross state product: $39.9 bil

GOVERNMENT AND POLITICS

US representatives: 1

Electoral votes: 3

State governors:

Matt Mead, R: 2011–

Dave Freudenthal, D: 2003–2011

Jim Geringer, R: 1995–2003

Michael J. Sullivan, D: 1987–1995

Edward Herschler, D: 1975–1987

Stanley K. Hathaway, R: 1967–1975

DESTINATIONS

Major cities (2015 population):

Cheyenne: 63,335

Casper: 60,285

Gillette: 32,649

Laramie: 32,158

Rock Springs: 23,692

International airports:

Casper

National monuments, landmarks, and parks: Yellowstone National Park, Grand Teton National Park, National Elk Refuge, Devils Tower National Monument, Ft. Laramie National Historical Center, Cheyenne Frontier Days

Web site: www.wyoming.gov

DISTRICT OF COLUMBIA

DEMOGRAPHY

Population (2016): 681,170

Population (2006): 581,530

Under 18: 18%

65 or older: 13%

Density in p/sq mile (2015): 61.4

Persons per household: 2.24

Population by race % (2015):

White: 44.1%

Black: 48.3%

American Indian/Aleut/Eskimo: 0.6%

Asian: 4.2%

Hispanic: 10.6%

White/Non-Hispanic: 36.1%

Native Hawaiian and Other Pacific

---

* Sales tax: City, county, and municipal rates vary. Rates shown are weighted by population to compute an average local tax rate.

Islander: 0.2%
Persons reporting two or more races: 2.7%

POPULATION CHARACTERISTICS
Marriage rate (per 1,000): 8.2
Birth rate (per 1,000)(2015): 14.4
Infant mortality rate (2015): 7.3
Percent of population with bachelor's degree:: 54.6%
Average household income (2015): $70,071
Median home value: $475,800
Poverty rate: 17.3%
Average life expectancy: 76.5
Crime rate per 100,000
   Violent: 1,244.4
   Property: 5,182.5
Federal and state prisoners (2014): 2,448

ECONOMY
Chief industries: government, services, tourism
Sales tax (2016): 5.75%
Gross state product: $122.1 bil

GOVERNMENT AND POLITICS
US representatives: 1
Electoral votes: 3
Mayors:
   Muriel Bowser, D: 2015–
   Vincent C. Gray, D: 2011–2015
   Adrian Fenty, D: 2007–2011
   Anthony A. Williams, D: 199–2007
   Marion Barry, D: 1995–1999
   Sharon Pratt Kelly, D: 1991–1995
   Marion Barry, D: 1979–1991
   Walter Washington, D: 1975–1979

DESTINATIONS
International airports:
   Arlington (VA), Dulles (VA)
National monuments, landmarks, and parks: The Capitol, Federal Bureau of Investigation, Folger Shakespeare Library, Holocaust Memorial Museum, Jefferson Memorial, John F. Kennedy Center, Korean War Veterans Memorial, Library of Congress, Lincoln Memorial, National Archives and Records, National Gallery of Art, Franklin Delano Roosevelt Memorial, Smithsonian Institution, Vietnam Veterans Memorial, Washington Monument, White House, National World War II Memorial
Web site: www.dc.gov

Image Credits

The following abbreviations are used:
IO—Index Open, SS—Shutterstock,
JI—Jupiter Images Corporation,
BSP—BigStockPhoto, IS—iStockphoto,
LOC—Library of Congress, WI—Wikimedia
Commons, NPS—National Parks Service,
USGS— U.S. Geological Survey, FEMA—
Federal Emergency Management Agency,
NOAA—National Oceanic and Atmospheric
Administration, UST—U.S. Department of
the Treasury, DW—Digital Wisdom, Inc.,
BIA—Bureau of Indian Affairs

(t=top; b=bottom; l=left; r=right; c=center;
bg=background)

Out of Many, One

i SS/Beth Van Trees **iii** SS/Beth Van Trees
vc Architect of the Capitol **vb** BSP/Jonathan
Larsen/Diadem Images **vbg** LOC **vi** SS/Mike
Grindley **vi-viib** LOC **viit**r WI/Jdrewes (www.jandrewes.
de) **viib** BSP/Fort Collins Video, LLC/Larry
Chapman **viii** IO/Vstock, LLC **1** LOC **2b**l
WI **2t**r WI **3b**l SS/Gennady Stetsenko **3b**r
SS/Haemin Rapp **4-5** DW **6-7** DW **8t** LOC
8b LOC **8-9b**g LOC **9t** LOC **9b** LOC **10-11**
BIA **12-13** DW

The Northeast

18-19 IO/ photolibrary.com pty. ltd. **20t** WI
20b UST **21** SS/Don Blais **22** BSP/Steve
Estvanik **22b** BSP/Roberta Gildart **23** DW
24 SS/Chee-Onn Leong **25t**r LOC **25b**
SS/Chee-Onn Leong **26t** WI **26b** UST **27**
SS/ShutterVision **28** WI **29** DW **30t** WI/LOC
30b LOC **31t**l LOC **31t**r WI **31b** WI **32t** WI
32b UST **33** SS/Stephen Mulcahey **34t**r SS/
Robert Manley **34b**l SS/Christy Thompson
34br WI **35** SS/Robert Manley **36t**r LOC
36bl SS/stephen mulcahey **37** LOC **38t** WI
38b UST **39** JI **40** SS/Daniel Padavona **40-
41** DW **41** LOC **43t**r LOC **43b**r WI **44t**r WI
44br SS/Joy Brown **45** WI/Jared C. Benedict
46t WI **46b** UST **47** SS/Mary Terriberry **48b**l
SS/Tom Oliveira **48t**r SS/Linda A. Lund **49t**
DW **49b** SS/Mary Terriberry **50t**r JI **50b** LOC
51tr BSP/Dan Logan **51b**l SS/Travel Bug **52t**

WI **52b** UST **53** BSP/David Biagi **54b**l WI
54br SS/Charley Socci **55t** DW **55b** IO/Bud
Freund **56t** WI **56b** LOC **57b**l WI/Iracaz
57br SS/Laura Stone **58t** WI **58b** UST **59**
SS/Joshua Haviv **60** SS/Vlad Ghiea **61t** DW
61b SS/Michael Coddington **62** LOC **63t**l WI
63tr WI/Chensiyuan **63c** LOC **64** LOC **65l**
SS/iofoto **65r** SS/Harris Shiffman **66t** WI **66b**
UST **67** SS/Jeremy Beeler **68** SS/Photos by
ryasick **69t** DW **70l** SS/Victorian Traditions
70r LOC **71t** LOC **71b**l SS/gary718 **72t**
WI **72b** UST **73** SS/Racheal Grazias **74-75**
DW **75b**l SS/Sigen Photography **75b**r SS/
Alex Neauville **76** LOC **77t**l SS/Michael J
Thompson **77t**r SS/Tony Spuria **77c** WI **78**
SS/Alex Neauville **79** LOC **80t** WI **80b** UST
81 BSP/David Biagi **82t**r BSP/Teresa Levite
82bl BSP/Teresa Levite **83** DW **84t** WI **84b**
LOC **85t**r WI **85b**l SS/Teresa Levite

The South

86-87 SS/Carolina K. Smith, M.D. **88t** WI
88b UST **89** SS/Henry E Stamm IV **90b**l
WI **90-91** DW **91b** WI **92c**r LOC **92b** LOC
93t LOC **93b**c LOC **94t** WI **94b** UST **95**
SS/2265524729 **96b**l LOC **96-97** DW **97b**
WI/Ken Thomas **98c** JI **98b**l SS/Travel Bug
98br JI **99t** LOC **99b** WI/NARA **100t**r JI
100b JI **101t** JI **101b** U.S. Department of
Defense **102t** WI **102b** UST **103** SS/Robert
Pernell **104** SS/Henryk Sadura **105** DW **106**
LOC **107t** WI/David G. Simpson **107b**r JI
108t WI **108b** UST **109** SS/catnap **110t**l WI
110bl SS/Jon Michael Weidman **110-111**
DW **111** SS/KennStilger47 **112t** LOC **112b**
LOC **113c** SS/Chad Palmer **113b** SS/Anne
Kitzman **114t** WI **114b** UST **115** JI **116l**
SS/MARKABOND **116r** BSP/Tim Markley
116-117 DW **117b** SS/Jill Lang **118** LOC
119tl Jonas N. Jordan, U.S. Army Corps of
Engineers **119t**r LOC **119b** SS/Jill Lang **120t**
WI **120b** UST **121** SS/Mary Terriberry **122b**l
SS/Danny E Hooks **122-123** DW **123b**l BSP/
Bryan Busovicki **123b**r SS/KennStilger47
124t LOC **124b** LOC **125c** LOC **125b**l LOC
125br SS/Cristi Bastian **126t** WI **126b** UST
127 SS/iofoto **128b**l SS/Sebastien Windal
128br SS/Jill Lang **128-129** DW **129b** JI **130**
LOC **131l** LOC **131t**r SS/Beth Whitcomb
131br LOC **132t** WI **132b** UST **133** SS/
Haessly Photography **134b**l SS/Sebastien
Windal **134t**r SS/ChrisIofoto **135** DW **136t**l

WI/Sir Mildred Pierce **136b**l LOC **136b**r
ISP/lillis photography/Lillis Werder **137t**
LOC **137b** LOC **138t** WI **138b** UST **139**
ISP/jondesign **140** SS/Robert Kyllo **141** DW
142t SS/Robert A. Mansker **142b** LOC **143l**
LOC **143r** LOC **144t** WI **144b** UST **145**
SS/viZualStudio **146** SS/Gregor Kervina
147 DW **148t**r JI **148b**c ISP/Hulton Archive
149t LOC **149c** LOC **149b**r WI/RMHerman
150t WI **150b** UST **151** IO/Richard Stockton
152bl IO/Charles Cangialosi **152b**r SS/Jeff
Kinsey **152-153** DW **153b**l SS/FloridaStock
154c JI/Clipart **154b** LOC **155b**r LOC **156t**r
SS/Mircea Bezergheanu **156b**l JI **157t**r SS/
MARKABOND **157b** SS/Carsten Reisinger
158t WI **158b** UST **159** SS/George Burba
160bl John James Audubon **160c**r SS/
Kathleen Struckle **161** DW **162c** LOC **162b**
LOC **163b**l LOC **163b**r WI **164t** WI **164b**
UST **165** SS/Larry Powell **166b**l SS/David
Huntley **166t**r NOAA Photo Library **166b**r
Shutterstock **167** DW **168b**l WI **168b**r JI **169**
LOC **170b**l SS/Rick Lord **170b**r SS/Leon
Ritter **171c** JI **171b**l JI **172t** WI **172b** UST
173 SS/Phil Anthony **174b**l SS/Darlene
Tompkins **175b**r SS/Patrick E Mitchell **176t**r
JI **176b** LOC **177t**r LOC **177b**r IO/FogStock
LLC **178t** WI **178b** UST **179** IO/James Denk
180bl LOC **180-181** DW **182** SS/Steve Maehl
183 LOC **184c** JI/Clipart **184b** SS/Christa
DeRidder **185c**r JI **185b**r SS/3032322252s

The Midwest

186-187 SS/Weldon Schloneger **188t** WI
188b UST **189** SS/Kevin Tavares **190b**l
SS/SNEHIT **190-191** DW **191** SS/Alexey
Stiop **192** LOC **193t**l SS/Julio Yeste **193b**r
LOC **194t** WI **194b** UST **195** SS/Bryan
Busovicki **196b**l SS/Robert J. Daveant **196b**r
SS/KennStilger47 **196-197** DW **198t** SS/
Bryan Busovicki **198b** LOC **199t** LOC **199b**r
SS/Robert J. Daveant **200t** WI **200b** UST **201**
SS/Wendy Kaveney Photography **202b**l SS/
LSqrd42 **202b**r FEMA/Leif Skoogfors **203**
DW **204** LOC **205t** SS/Winthrop Brookhouse
205b SS/W Shane Dougherty **206t** WI
206b UST **207** SS/iofoto **208** SS/Chas **209**
DW **210b**l LOC **210b**r WI/skubasteve834
211 LOC **212t**r LOC **212b** LOC **213b**l SS/
pasphotography **213t**r LOC **214t** WI **214b**
UST **215** SS/Suzanne Tucker **216** WI **216-
217** DW **218b**l LOC **218t**r LOC **219t** LOC

219b WI 220t WI 220b UST 221 IO/Wallace Garrison 222-223 DW 223bl SS/Near and Far Photography 223br Shutterstock 224 LOC 225tl SS/Glenda M. Powers 225tr SS/Pete Hoffman 226t WI 226b UST 227 SS/iofoto 228bl JI 229 DW 229b SS/Rusty Dodson 230c SS/Mario Bruno 230b LOC 231 LOC 232t WI 232b UST 233 IO/John Luke 234bl SS/blewisphotography 234-235 DW 235br NPS 236 LOC 237tl WI 237br WI 238t WI 238b UST 239 SS/Henryk Sadura 240-241 DW 241b WI 242c WI 242b LOC 243tr JI 243bl SS/Bartosz Wardzinski 243br SS/Rosemarie Colombraro 244t WI 244b UST 245 WI 246-247 DW 247bl SS/Chad Bontrager 247br SS/Chad Bontrager 248tr SS/Thoma 248br LOC 249t LOC 249br SS/MaxFX 250t WI 250b UST 251 SS/Philip Eppard 252 DW 253bl SS/Rusty Dodson 253br SS/Jothi Pallikkathayil 254c LOC 254br LOC 255t LOC 255c LOC 256t WI 256b UST 257 SS/Mary Lane 258bl SS/ Ravshan Mirzaitov 258-259 DW 259br SS/ Rusty Dodson 260bl NOAA 260br WI 261t LOC 261br SS/Wendy Kaveney Photography

The Mountain States

262-263 SS/1559209 264t WI 264b UST 265 IO/Mark Windom 266bl SS/Sharon Hay 266-267 DW 267br Marcel Brousseau 268tr SS/Jason Maehl 268br LOC 269t LOC 269br LOC 270t LOC 270cb LOC 271tc LOC 271b LOC 272t WI 272b UST 273 SS/Henry E. Stamm IV 274bl SS/Lee O'Dell 274c SS/Richard Thornton 275 DW 276tc LOC 276b LOC 277b SS/Katherine Welles 278t WI 278b UST 279 SS/Sascha Burkard 280bl JI 281t DW 281br LOC 282c JI 282br WI 283tr LOC 283b LOC 284t WI 284b UST 285 SS/Todd Pierson 286bl SS/Linda Armstrong 287t DW 287br SS/Debra James 288tr SS/Videowokart 288c LOC 289 LOC 290t WI 290b UST 291 IO/FogStock LLC 292 IO/FogStock LLC 293 DW 294t WI/ Scott Catron 294c LOC 295 LOC 296t WI 296b UST 297 SS/George Burba 298bl SS/ George Michael Warnock 298br SS/Jonathan Larsen 299 DW 300tr NPS 300b LOC 301c LOC 301br LOC 302t WI 302b UST 303 IO/Charlie Borland 304tl WI 304bl SS/Joao Virissimo 304br SS/Jo Ann Snover 305 DW

306 LOC 307tl JI 307bl LOC 308t WI 308b UST 309 IO/Cut and Deal Ltd. 310 WI/Stan Shebs 311 DW 312c WI 312b LOC 313 WI

The Pacific States

314-315 IO/Mark Windom 316t WI 316b UST 317 SS/Steffen Foerester Photography 318bl IO/FogStock LLC 318-319 DW 319bl WI/Brian Prechtel 320 LOC 321tl LOC 321bl LOC 321br USGS 322t WI 322b UST 323 IO/FogStock LLC 324-325 DW 325bl SS/Mike Norton 326tr LOC 326-327 LOC 327t LOC 327b LOC 328t WI 328b UST 329 IO/AbleStock 330 SS/Mike Brake 330-331 DW 331tr IO/FogStock LLC 332 LOC 333tl LOC 333br LOC 334 LOC 335 LOC 336t WI 336b UST 337 SS/Larry Brandt 338 SS/TTphoto 338-339 DW 340 LOC 341t LOC 341tr BSP/Lark Carlson Brown 342t WI 342b UST 343 SS/Keith Levit 344bl IO/ FogStock LLC 344br SS/Robert Spriggs 344-345 DW 346c WI 346bl WI/Bishop Musem, Honolulu 347t LOC 347br WI